Adaptive Co-Management

The Sustainability and the Environment series provides a comprehensive, independent, and critical evaluation of environmental and sustainability issues affecting Canada and the world today. Other volumes in the series are:

Anthony Scott, John Robinson, and David Cohen, eds., *Managing Natural Resources in British Columbia: Markets, Regulations, and Sustainable Development*

John B. Robinson, *Life in 2030: Exploring a Sustainable Future for Canada*

Ann Dale and John B. Robinson, eds., *Achieving Sustainable Development*

John T. Pierce and Ann Dale, eds., *Communities, Development, and Sustainability across Canada*

Robert F. Woollard and Aleck Ostry, eds., *Fatal Consumption: Rethinking Sustainable Development*

Ann Dale, *At the Edge: Sustainable Development in the 21st Century*

Mark Jaccard, John Nyboer, and Bryn Sadownik, *The Cost of Climate Policy*

Glen Filson, ed., *Intensive Agriculture and Sustainability: A Farming Systems Analysis*

Mike Carr, *Bioregionalism and Civil Society: Democratic Challenges to Corporate Globalism*

Ann Dale and Jenny Onyx, eds., *A Dynamic Balance: Social Capital and Sustainable Community Development*

Ray Côté, James Tansey, and Ann Dale, eds., *Linking Industry and Ecology: A Question of Design*

Glen Toner, ed., *Sustainable Production: Building Canadian Capacity*

Ellen Wall, Barry Smit, and Johanna Wandel, eds., *Farming in a Changing Climate: Agricultural Adaptation in Canada*

SUSTAINABILITY
AND THE
ENVIRONMENT

Edited by Derek Armitage, Fikret Berkes,
and Nancy Doubleday

Adaptive Co-Management: Collaboration, Learning, and Multi-Level Governance

UBCPress · Vancouver · Toronto

25 24 23 22 21 20 19 18   5 4 3 2

Printed in Canada on ancient-forest-free paper (100% post-consumer recycled) that is processed chlorine- and acid-free, with vegetable-based inks.

Library and Archives Canada Cataloguing in Publication

Adaptive co-management: collaboration, learning, and multi-level governance / edited by Derek Armitage, Fikret Berkes, and Nancy Doubleday.

(Sustainability and the environment)
Includes bibliographical references and index.
ISBN 978-0-7748-1383-9 (bound); ISBN 978-0-7748-1390-7 (pbk.)

1. Adaptive natural resource management. 2. Cultural property – Protection. I. Armitage, Derek R. (Derek Russel), 1967- II. Berkes, Fikret III. Doubleday, Nancy, 1951- IV. Series.

S944.A33 2007   333.7   C2007-905173-1

Canadä

UBC Press gratefully acknowledges the financial support for our publishing program of the Government of Canada through the Book Publishing Industry Development Program (BPIDP), and of the Canada Council for the Arts, and the British Columbia Arts Council.

Printed and bound in Canada by Friesens
Set in Stone by Artegraphica Design Co. Ltd.
Copy editor: Francis Chow
Proofreader: Dianne Tiefensee
Cartographer: Eric Leinberger
Indexer: Adrian Mather

UBC Press
The University of British Columbia
2029 West Mall
Vancouver, BC V6T 1Z2
604-822-5959 / Fax: 604-822-6083
www.ubcpress.ca

Contents

Figures, Tables, and Boxes

Boxes

Acronyms

AMB	Aquatic Management Board (West Coast Vancouver Island)
BARNUFO	Barbados National Union of Fisherfolk Organisations
CCA	Caribbean Conservation Association
CJC	Community Justice Committee
CJP	Community Justice Program
CMA	Coastal Management Area
CPUE	catch per unit effort
DFO	Department of Fisheries and Oceans
FAC	Fisheries Advisory Committee
FJMC	Fisheries Joint Management Committee
HTC	Hunters and Trappers Committee(s)
HTO	Hunters' and Trappers' Organization(s)
IFA	Inuvialuit Final Agreement
IQ	*Inuit Quajimaqatuqangit* (= Inuit traditional knowledge)
ISR	Inuvialuit Settlement Region
ITQ	Individual Transferable Quotas
LOMA	Large Ocean Management Area
MPA	Marine Protected Area
MSY	Maximum Sustainable Yield
NHLD	Northern Highlands Lake District
NLCA	Nunavut Land Claim Agreement
NWT	Northwest Territories
PC	Parks Canada
PCMB	Porcupine Caribou Management Board
PHTC	Paulatuk Hunters and Trappers Committee
RPP	Report on Plans and Priorities, DFO, 2004-05
RRCs	Renewable Resource Councils
RRSSC	Ruby Range Sheep Steering Committee
TEK	Traditional Ecological Knowledge
WCVI	West Coast Vancouver Island

Preface and Acknowledgments

Co-management is of growing interest among researchers, government, and non-government and community-based actors involved in natural resource management, conservation, and development activities. Co-management may be at a crossroads, however.

Nearly twenty years have passed since Evelyn Pinkerton's influential volume on co-management, *Co-operative Management of Local Fisheries: New Directions for Improved Management and Community Development,* was published by UBC Press. Co-management has since entered the adaptive age. New concerns with adaptive processes, feedback learning, and flexible partnership arrangements are reshaping the co-management landscape. Increasingly, ideas about collaboration and learning are converging in the literature. There is a tremendous opportunity to examine co-management through additional perspectives, explore alternative directions and concepts, and critically examine the emergence of adaptive co-management as an innovative governance approach to social-ecological complexity.

The chapters in this volume evolved over three meetings. They were selected from a commissioned set of papers presented at a two-day symposium, "Moving Beyond the Critiques of Co-Management: Theory and Practice of Adaptive Co-Management," held at Wilfrid Laurier University, Waterloo, Ontario, in February 2005. Researchers and practitioners from Canada, the United States, the Caribbean, and Europe were invited to explore the co-management of natural resources from multiple perspectives. Symposium activities were guided by the following objectives: (1) to bring together researchers and practitioners to discuss the evolution of co-management; (2) to create an opportunity for the sharing of ideas and strategies for innovative governance approaches in the context of social, institutional, and ecological uncertainty; and (3) to explore new avenues and directions that may serve to advance the theory and practice of adaptive co-management. Two follow-up meetings provided an opportunity to share and reflect further upon co-management ideas as they had evolved since the initial symposium: an authors' workshop held in Ottawa in May 2005, and a set of three panel sessions on adaptive co-management during the Ocean Management Research Network Conference, also in Ottawa, in September 2005.

The symposium and follow-up activities have resulted in a rich and complementary set of papers focusing on adaptive co-management. In particular, this collection highlights a number of emerging ideas and challenges in co-management, and charts potentially fruitful directions for the evolution of co-management in an adaptive age. In this regard, the promises and pitfalls of adaptive co-management explored by the different authors in this volume are grounded in social science, economic, and ecological theory. A diverse set of case studies reveal the challenges and implications of adaptive co-management thinking, and synthesize lessons for natural resource management in a wide range of contexts. The chapters are informed by collective experiences of researchers and practitioners, acquired over the past two decades, and by the work of a growing and diverse community of individuals with new case studies and new questions. The contributions thus offer insights into adaptive co-management as a context for exploring alternative management strategies and evolving forms of government and citizenship.

This book would not have been possible without the contributions of many individuals and organizations. The original symposium was made possible by a Strategic Grant from the Social Sciences and Humanities Research Council of Canada (SSHRC) and the Department of Fisheries and Oceans (DFO) to the Integrated Management Node of the Ocean Management Research Network (OMRN). We are grateful for the support provided by the National Secretariat of the OMRN under the leadership of Tony Charles at Saint Mary's University and, later, Dan Lane at the University of Ottawa. Special thanks as well to Megan Sikaneta, former Coordinator at the National Secretariat, for her assistance in hosting and managing links on the OMRN website (http://www.omrn-rrgo.ca), which greatly facilitated the sharing of materials. Supplementary funding for the symposium was provided by the Canada Research Chair in Community Based Resource Management at the University of Manitoba, and the Cold Regions Research Centre at Wilfrid Laurier University.

Each chapter in this volume was reviewed by an average of three referees. We are grateful to the following individuals, who participated in the peer review of chapters: Burton Ayles, Nigel Bankes, Grazia Borrini-Feyerabend, Hugh Beach, Lisa Campbell, Doug Clark, Johan Colding, Fay Cohen, William Crumplin, Ann Dale, Iain Davidson-Hunt, Alan Diduck, Milton Freeman, Lance Gunderson, Kevin Hanna, Derek Johnson, John Kearney, Anne Kendrick, Gary Kofinas, Al Kristofferson, Robin Mahon, Patrick McConney, Bruce Mitchell, Monica Mulrennan, Heather Myers, Garry Peterson, Ryan Plummer, Robert Pomeroy, Maureen Reed, Henry Regier, Yves Renard, Scott Slocombe, Derek Smith, Sonia Wesche, Melanie Wiber, Doug Wilson, Susan

Wismer, and Monika Zurek. The constructive comments and suggestions of two anonymous reviewers for UBC Press are also greatly appreciated.

We also wish to thank many people who contributed to the development of the ideas in this volume through their participation in various meetings, including: Lawrence Baschak (Saskatchewan Environment), Nancy J. Turner, Carla Burton, André Vallillee (University of Victoria), and Prateep Nayak (University of Manitoba). At Wilfrid Laurier University, special thanks to Sonia Wesche, who helped ensure that the original symposium ran smoothly, and Pam Schaus, who prepared several figures for this volume. Cover photography was generously provided by Kevin Hanna and Tony Charles. The editorial assistance provided by Nathan Deutsch and Jacqueline Rittberg of the Natural Resources Institute, University of Manitoba, has been instrumental to the production of this book, and their contribution is greatly appreciated. Finally, we would like to thank the editorial team at UBC Press for their assistance with the publication of this volume, including Randy Schmidt, Holly Keller, and Megan Brand.

Adaptive Co-Management

1

Introduction: Moving beyond Co-Management

Derek Armitage, Fikret Berkes, and Nancy Doubleday

Out of the crooked timber of humanity,
No straight thing was ever made.
— Immanuel Kant

No road is too long with good company.
— Turkish Proverb

This book attempts to bridge two separate but increasingly overlapping narratives, those on co-management and adaptive management. The co-management narrative has been primarily concerned with user participation in decision making and with linking communities and government managers. The adaptive management narrative has been primarily about learning-by-doing in a scientific way to deal with uncertainty. The bridging of these two narratives is, in many ways, a logical development in the evolution of both of these overarching approaches.

Centralized, top-down resource management is ill-suited to user participation, and it is often blamed for the increased vulnerability of resource-dependent communities worldwide (Zerner 2000; Colfer 2005). In response, co-management arrangements have emerged to secure an expanded role for stakeholder and community participation in decision making. Recognition that ecological systems are dynamic and non-linear (Levin 1999) has similarly highlighted the inadequacy of yield-oriented "command-and-control" resource management. Centralized bureaucracies are limited in their ability to respond to changing conditions, an anachronism in a world increasingly characterized by rapid transformations (Gunderson and Holling 2002; Berkes et al. 2003).

Changing ideas about the nature of resource management, ecosystems, and social-ecological systems (integrated systems of people and environment) have been catalyzed by insights from complex adaptive systems thinking

(Capra 1996; Levin 1999). Non-linearity, feedback processes, and system self-organization challenge established assumptions of scientific certainty, stability paradigms in both the ecological and social sciences, and the primacy of expert-driven solutions. In the resource management of the twenty-first century, these assumptions are yielding to new developments and trends, including: (1) the imperative of broad-based participation when devising management strategies that respond to change; (2) the need to emphasize knowledge, learning, and the social sources of adaptability, renewal, and transformation; and (3) an understanding of change and uncertainty as inherent in social-ecological systems. Such changes in direction represent an alternative narrative about how to approach the theory and practice of natural resource management and environmental governance.

This alternative narrative is taking shape through a number of recent interdisciplinary international efforts, such as the sustainability science program (Clark and Dixon 2003), the Millennium Ecosystem Assessment (2005), the Equator Initiative of the United Nations Development Programme (UNDP 2005), and *World Resources 2005* (UNDP/UNEP/World Bank/WRI 2005). These efforts share an explicit concern with the complexity of social-ecological systems, and an emphasis on learning from experience. They deal with multiple objectives, multiple knowledge systems, scale issues, stakeholder participation, and balancing top-down with community-based approaches. None of these efforts, however, systematically examines how the two narratives, co-management and adaptive management, can be combined. This volume aims to fill that gap.

Establishing the Foundations: Co-Management, Adaptive Management, and Adaptive Co-Management

Regarding the first narrative, trends towards *collaborative management* approaches are an outcome of the limitations of a "command-and-control" bureaucracy (Holling and Meffe 1996) and the privileging of formal science (Allen et al. 2001). Collaborative or cooperative management are generic terms "conveying the sharing of rights and responsibilities by the government and civil society" (Plummer and FitzGibbon 2004, 63). There are multiple strands of collaborative management, including integrated conservation and development, participatory natural resource management, participatory appraisal and participatory action research, decentralization and devolution, and community-based natural resource management and co-management (Berkes 2002). Co-management in particular has evolved as a more formalized management strategy with which to link local communities and governments. Some of these arrangements are codified in law, as in the various indigenous land and resource rights cases in the United States, Canada, Australia, and New Zealand.

Box 1.1
Definitions of co-management

- "A political claim [by users or community] to share management power and responsibility with the state" (McCay and Acheson 1987, 32)
- "The sharing of power and responsibility between the government and local resource users" (Berkes et al. 1991, 12)
- "Power-sharing in the exercise of resource management between a government agency and a community organization of stakeholders" (Pinkerton 1992, 331)
- "A partnership in which government agencies, local communities and resource users, NGOs and other stakeholders share ... the authority and responsibility for the management of a specific territory or a set of resources" (IUCN 1996).

There is no single appropriate definition of co-management (Box 1.1) because there is a continuum of possible co-management arrangements in the degree of power sharing (Borrini-Feyerabend et al. 2004). However, potential benefits of co-management include more appropriate, more efficient, and more equitable governance, and the improvement of a number of processes and functions of management (Box 1.2). In responding to demands for a greater role for resource users and communities in environmental management, co-management arrangements serve to democratize decision making, foster conflict resolution, and encourage stakeholder participation.

Box 1.2
Benefits of co-management

Benefits can be considered through processes and goals such as (1) co-management for community-based economic and social development, (2) co-management to decentralize resource management decisions, and (3) co-management as a mechanism for reducing conflict through participatory democracy.

Co-management may enhance the functions of (1) data gathering, (2) logistical decisions such as who can harvest and when, (3) allocation decisions, (4) protection of resources from environmental damage, (5) enforcement of regulations, (6) enhancement of long-term planning, and (7) more inclusive decision making (Pinkerton 1989, ch. 1).

Collaborative forms of management have also gained strength as policy makers and decision makers recognize that systematic learning and innovation under conditions of uncertainty are more likely to emerge through meaningful interaction of multiple stakeholders. In a collaborative management context, local knowledge and experience have equal status with experts and expert knowledge (Cardinal and Day 1999). Collaborative institutional arrangements, flexible policy conditions, and social organization are central to the stimulus of social learning, innovation, and adaptive capacity (Woodhill and Röling 1998; Armitage 2005). Policy decisions regarding natural resources are increasingly less a matter of appropriate expertise or the domain of specialist institutions, and more a question of negotiation and agreement among stakeholders (Brunner et al. 2005). These considerations bring co-management into the sphere of the second narrative.

A learning approach focusing on improving policy and practice in the face of uncertainty, *adaptive management* is often presented as a tool to frame the philosophical, methodological, and practical challenges associated with the management of natural resources (Holling 1978; Walters 1986; Lee 1993; Gunderson et al. 1995). Management strategies and policies are considered experiments (Lee 1993), and learning is encouraged through both structured experimentation and management flexibility. Hilborn and Walters (1992) have outlined a number of defining features of adaptive management: (1) identification of alternative hypotheses; (2) assessment of whether further steps are required to estimate the expected value of additional information; (3) development of models for future learning and hypotheses; (4) identification of policy options; (5) development of performance criteria for comparing options; and (6) formal comparison of options. The political, institutional, and individual risks of adaptive management are well documented (Lee 1993). In response, emerging hybrids of adaptive management involve integrated approaches to science and policy in which multiple actors are actively engaged in risk sharing around problem definition, analysis, and resolution of social-ecological challenges for the common good (Brunner et al. 2005).

Goals and objectives in hybrid adaptive management contexts are redirected from a traditional focus on economic productivity and maximum sustainable yield towards an integrative understanding of the system dynamics, feedbacks, and thresholds that may undermine social-ecological resilience. Increasingly, the concept of resilience is inimical to the application of adaptive management, and it refers to the capacity of a system to absorb disturbance without flipping into a qualitatively different state (Gunderson and Holling 2002). As a locus for adaptive management, resilience encourages a reconsideration of conventional science as an unambiguous source of information required to deal with contested social-ecological challenges. Resilience thinking helps to direct learning around key variables that enable linked social-ecological systems to renew and reorganize along sustainable trajectories in the face of perturbation. Resilience is a normative concept, however, and efforts to define it must be situated in the context of contested and evolving human interests and the uncertainties of human interaction.

An emergent outcome of the co-management and adaptive management narratives, *adaptive co-management* may represent an important innovation in natural resource governance under conditions of change, uncertainty, and complexity. Working definitions of adaptive co-management are provided by a number of authors (Box 1.3). As Olsson and colleagues (2004) note, a key feature of adaptive co-management is the combination of the iterative learning dimension of adaptive management and the linkage dimension of collaborative management in which rights and responsibilities are jointly shared.

Although much focus is on the local scale, where issues of management performance are felt most directly, adaptive co-management is a flexible system for environment and resource management that operates across multiple levels and with a range of local and non-local organizations. Key features of adaptive co-management include a focus on learning-by-doing, integration of different knowledge systems, collaboration and power sharing among community, regional, and national levels, and management flexibility (Olsson et al. 2004). In this regard, adaptive co-management provides an evolving and place-specific governance approach that supports strategies that help respond to feedback (both social and ecological) and orient social-ecological systems towards sustainable trajectories. Such strategies include dialogue among interested groups and actors (local/national); the development of complex, redundant, and layered institutions; and a combination of institutional types, designs, and strategies that facilitate experimentation

---

Box 1.3
Definitions of adaptive co-management

- "A long-term management structure that permits stakeholders to share management responsibility within a specific system of natural resources, and to learn from their actions" (Ruitenbeek and Cartier 2001, 8)
- "A process by which institutional arrangements and ecological knowledge are tested and revised in a dynamic, on-going, self-organized process of learning-by-doing" (Folke et al. 2002, 20)
- "Flexible, community-based systems of resource management tailored to specific places and situations, and supported by and working with, various organizations at different scales" (Olsson et al. 2004, 75).

Box 1.4
Selected features of adaptive co-management

- Shared vision, goal, and/or problem definition to provide a common focus among actors and interests
- A high degree of dialogue, interaction, and collaboration among multi-scaled actors
- Distributed or joint control across multiple levels, with shared responsibility for action and decision making
- A degree of autonomy for different actors at multiple levels
- Commitment to the pluralistic generation and sharing of knowledge
- A flexible and negotiated learning orientation with an inherent recognition of uncertainty.

and learning through change (Dietz et al. 2003). Box 1.4 captures some of these features.

As a conceptual and operational bridge, adaptive co-management is an interdisciplinary endeavour. Two relatively well-developed literatures provide a foundation upon which to extend the theory and practice of adaptive co-management. Many of the ideas shaping this volume emerge in large measure from the first, the field of common property (McCay and Acheson 1987; Ostrom et al. 2002; Ostrom 2005), over the past fifteen to twenty years, and its implications for collaborative management. There are a number of key works upon which this volume builds, including those that have critically engaged the concepts of co-management (Pinkerton 1989; Singleton 1998; Borrini-Feyerabend et al. 2000; Wilson et al. 2003; Nadasdy 2003; McConney et al. 2003; Borrini-Feyerabend et al. 2004).

The second literature upon which this volume builds concerns adaptive management and other approaches that address uncertainty and complexity, including the consideration of humans and ecosystems as an inseparably linked social-ecological system. Key contributions in these areas include those by Holling (1978), Walters (1986), Lee (1993), Gunderson and colleagues (1995), Berkes and Folke (1998), Levin (1999), Gunderson and Holling (2002), and Berkes and colleagues (2003).

Emerging Themes in Adaptive Co-Management
This volume builds upon the works cited above and poses the critical question: How can we move beyond the limits of co-management? Complex systems insights suggest the importance of adaptation and learning. Attributes associated with co-management, including flexibility and social learning, resonate with complex systems thinking. This volume highlights,

therefore, the salient dimensions of adaptive co-management that move co-management theory and practice towards issues not systematically addressed in the current literature. These issues include:

- the importance of the evolutionary dimension of co-management, and the recognition that institution building, trust building, and social learning all require time and repeated rounds of learning-by-doing
- the consideration of adaptive aspects, which takes co-management into the realm of complex adaptive systems, addressing issues of scale, multiple perspectives and epistemologies, uncertainty and non-linearity, self-organization, and emergence
- the development of a framework to study the linkages of different levels of political organization, such as the community level with the regional and/or national levels of government
- the expansion of the study of partnerships, recognizing that in many real-life co-management situations, one finds a rich web of network connections involving private actors and public actors
- the recognition of a diversity of government agencies with different roles and relationships and a diversity of interests within "communities"; rarely is "the state" or "the community" a monolithic actor.

In considering these dimensions of adaptive co-management, there is no single or "correct" locus of attention. Rather, as the chapters in this volume reveal, a number of emerging and overlapping themes provide a touchstone for analysis, synthesis, and policy development (Figure 1.1). A brief summary of each theme follows.

Complex systems thinking. Complex systems thinking offers a way of examining, describing, interpreting, and cognitively structuring not only ecological systems but also increasingly linked social-ecological systems. Specifically, complex systems thinking highlights the dynamic, non-linear relationships among coupled social and ecological phenomena that result in discontinuities, surprises, system flips, and the potential for multiple equilibrium states. Complex systems thinking provides valuable heuristics for understanding natural resource management, and emphasizes relationships, networks, and feedback processes. Complex systems thinking thus indicates the importance of institutional diversity and flexibility in improving the fit between ecological and social systems.

Adaptive capacity and resilience. Representing a shift in the way managers intervene in complex social-ecological systems, resilience management focuses on maintaining the ability of systems to absorb or buffer disturbance, maintain core attributes, continue to self-organize, and build capacity for learning, experimentation, and adaptation. Adaptive co-management is an institutional and organizational response to complex adaptive systems and

Figure 1.1

Key themes in adaptive co-management

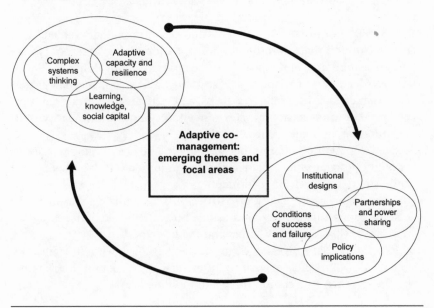

the challenge of resilience management. The institutional and social determinants of resilience management are not yet established, however. Developing adaptive capacity to deal with perturbation and stresses at the scale of institutions and societies provides a further area of examination. Building adaptive capacity is a priority, given the connection to learning and the need for social actors to experiment and foster innovative solutions in complex social and ecological circumstances.

Institutional design for adaptive co-management. A central theme in adaptive co-management inquiry is the institutional designs and frameworks required for effective decision making. The paths of this inquiry may go in many directions, but key features being explored include the importance of cross-scale linkages (horizontal and vertical) that build adaptive capacity and institutional resilience. Related to this are ongoing trends towards decentralization and devolution as a governance strategy, the drivers of which may be as much about political expediency as about broader concerns for institutional performance (e.g., efficiency, sustainability).

Partnerships and power sharing. Interrogating adaptive co-management involves a critical examination of the extent to which alternative governance approaches result in, or develop, decision-making processes that reflect true partnerships, and that devolve power to local resource users and communities. In this regard, cultural difference, unequal knowledge valuation, the historical role of government bureaucracies in management, and eco-logical/economic forces of globalization are identified as key influences on the reworking of stakeholder relationships required for the emergence of adaptive co-management.

Conditions of adaptive co-management success and failure. Adaptive co-management can be applied in a wide range of resource (e.g., coasts, fisher-ies, forests) and geographical contexts. Although context is of critical importance, emphasis is increasingly placed on measuring and monitoring the conditions from which adaptive co-management may emerge, and the success and failure of adaptive co-management in diverse situations. Identi-fication of a common set of structural and procedural prerequisites for suc-cess, or common reasons for failure, is helping to build theory and identify key propositions. Studies based on large number of cases and hypothesis testing are important areas requiring further examination.

Learning, knowledge use, and social capital. A key feature of adaptive co-management as an innovative governance approach is the explicit focus on linking collaborative efforts with systematic learning. Learning involves the collaborative or mutual development and sharing of knowledge by multi-ple stakeholders. Much learning is directed at modifying management strat-egies or actions (e.g., harvest rates, techniques) without challenging the assumptions upon which those strategies are based. This type of learning is sometimes referred to as "single-loop" learning. In contrast, "double-loop" or transformative learning involves resolving fundamental conflict over val-ues and norms, and promoting change in the face of significant uncer-tainty, and is identified as a particularly important component of adaptive co-management. The effort to foster double-loop learning requires a com-mitment to valuing different knowledge sources and epistemologies, how-ever. Double-loop learning is also linked to social capital or the social norms, networks of reciprocity and exchange, and relationships of trust that en-able people to act collectively.

Policy implications. Assessments of adaptive co-management must be rel-evant to policy makers. If adaptive co-management is to be a possible govern-ance approach, its economic and legal requirements should be identifiable and actionable. Thus, identification of opportunities and constraints sur-rounding the emergence of adaptive co-management involves the examin-ation of the adequacy of existing policy instruments (e.g., legislation, fiscal incentives) and the development of recommendations aimed at creating an enabling policy environment.

Most of the contributions to this volume address at least several of these emerging themes (see Chapter 16). These themes give substance to the al-ternative narrative of resource management and environmental govern-ance in the twenty-first century, and provide a reference point for different authors' explorations of key concepts and theoretical insights; lessons from on-the-ground experiences with adaptive co-management; the limitations, critiques, and assumptions embedded within the approach; and the evolving concepts and tools influencing adaptive co-management outcomes.

A Roadmap to This Volume

This volume is based on a two-day symposium and two follow-up meetings that took place in 2005. It aims to provide a synthesis of adaptive co-management, drawing on the insights of researchers and practitioners from diverse disciplines, using multiple analytical approaches and engaging with disparate geographies, both in Canada and internationally (Figure 1.2).

The book is divided into four parts to highlight features of adaptive co-management and to focus attention on the emerging themes in this area: (1) theory, (2) case studies, (3) challenges, and (4) tools.

In Part 1, "Theory," four chapters provide an introduction to many of the key concepts and ideas associated with adaptive co-management. Fikret Berkes (Chapter 2) begins by arguing that co-management is more varied,

Figure 1.2

Case study sites

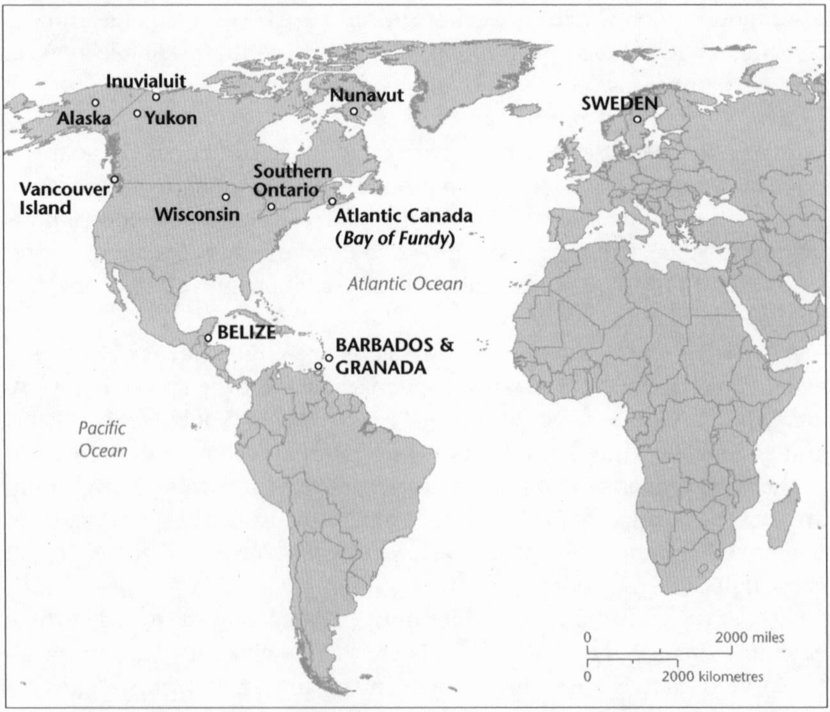

complex, and dynamic than described in a literature that often treats it as a "fixed" or simple category of arrangements. In contrast, Berkes provides an overview of the different "faces" of co-management as power sharing, as institution building, as trust building, as process, as social learning, as problem solving, and as governance. In doing so, he draws attention to the complexity inherent in adaptive co-management and many of the features of the alternative resource management narrative.

In Chapter 3, Ryan Plummer and John FitzGibbon extend this overview and further map the relationships among adaptive management, social learning, and social capital. They thus place much-needed emphasis on the social nature of adaptive co-management, and illustrate the importance of learning and social capital in the context of a multi-level, multi-actor collaborative efforts in three cases of river management in Ontario.

In Chapter 4, Derek Armitage examines the proposition that the livelihoods of people in resource-dependent communities are best characterized as exhibiting multiple dynamic equilibria, and that adaptive, multi-level co-management arrangements are likely to be best suited to respond to the dynamic, self-organizing feedbacks that shape livelihood outcomes. He emphasizes the need for multi-level development of adaptive capacity to facilitate the emergence of adaptive co-management, and proposes an expanded capabilities approach to provide direction in this respect.

Drawing on experiences from the Atlantic fishery for cod and other groundfish, Anthony Charles (Chapter 5) synthesizes much extant theory to identify four "ingredients" of adaptive co-management. As he illustrates, key ingredients for the sustainability and resilience of natural resource systems include: (1) maintaining diverse options for inclusion in a portfolio of resource management measures; (2) pursuing *robust management,* or management that results in a reasonable level of performance even when there is a high degree of uncertainty; (3) ensuring the full utilization of diverse knowledge sources; and (4) supporting institutional reform through new governance arrangements.

In Part 2, "Case Studies," the focus shifts to four chapters that emphasize on-the-ground experiences with building and sustaining conditions for learning and adaptation in a co-management context. In Chapter 6, Patrick McConney, Robin Mahon, and Robert Pomeroy synthesize a number of lessons learned and key challenges to coastal resource co-management from three Caribbean case studies: sea urchin harvesting in Barbados, a beach seine fishery in Grenada, and marine protected areas management in Belize. Co-management is a relatively new concept in the English-speaking Caribbean, and the recent experiences with co-management provide new opportunities for learning in the distinct socio-political, economic, and resource conditions that the authors examine.

In Chapter 7, Burton Ayles, Robert Bell, and Andrea Hoyt move the geographical focus from the South to the North, with case studies of three initiatives in the western Canadian Arctic. They examine how fisheries co-management, within the context of a comprehensive land settlement agreement, has led to adaptive management practices, and, in turn, how these adaptive management activities have fed back to strengthen the co-management process. This chapter offers an interesting counterpoint to Chapter 6 because co-management in the western Arctic involves a more formalized, legislatively driven sharing of management responsibilities between beneficiaries and the responsible government agency, in this case, the Fisheries Joint Management Committee.

In Chapter 8, Evelyn Pinkerton analyzes the West Coast Vancouver Island Aquatic Management Board. She poses a question that cuts to the core of the linkage feature of adaptive co-management: How does a local body based on holistic principles co-manage with a senior governing body based on segmental principles? Her analysis of this particular case exemplifies the difficulties in coordinating, and systematically learning through, the different perspectives of government bureaucracies and community-based actors in an adaptive co-management context.

In the final chapter of Part 2, Robert Pomeroy applies a broad analytical lens to present and discuss key conditions for the successful implementation of fisheries and coastal co-management as identified in Southeast Asia, Africa, and the Wider Caribbean. He notes that key conditions emerging at the regional scale are proving central to the development and sustainability of successful co-management arrangements. Many of the conditions synthesized in his review embrace a wide range of aspects and activities, from resources and fisheries to cultural and institutional dimensions.

In Part 3, "Challenges," three chapters integrate critical perspectives about adaptive co-management in concept and practice. These chapters, in particular, encourage researchers and policy makers to consider the embedded relationships among social actors that influence collaboration, learning, and adaptation, and they bring to the surface issues of power, cultural interplay in both formal and informal contexts, and the complexities of community. With an emphasis on the "local," John Kearney and Fikret Berkes (Chapter 10) question the assumptions about community that frame adaptive co-management. They expand on the concept of interdependence as a way to explore the importance and relevance of community and the local, while moving beyond monolithic conceptions of community driven by both populist and neoliberal narratives.

In Chapter 11, Paul Nadasdy adopts a critical stance in his analysis of Ruby Range sheep co-management in the Yukon Territory, Canada. He considers how adaptive co-management fares against the critique that co-management, despite claims about local empowerment, serves to perpetuate colonial-style relations by concentrating power in administrative centres rather than in the hands of local/Aboriginal people. In the process, he critiques the linking and learning rhetoric of adaptive co-management and some of its underlying concepts.

In Chapter 12, Nancy Doubleday investigates an apparent case of "dysfunctional intercultural co-management experience" at the community level, specifically the case of community justice in Cape Dorset, Nunavut. While recognizing that the inequalities rooted in power relations and cultural difference are an impediment to adaptive co-management, she explores the role of culture in resilience and adaptive capacity, and the subsequent potential for individuals and groups to engage and lead adaptation under difficult conditions. Doubleday suggests that culture and culture-derived identity may serve as *extra-formal* power-bases and that their implications for adaptive co-management should be differentiated from the role of negotiated formal powers. Chapters 11 and 12, in particular, both examine the political and cultural assumptions implicit in the project of adaptive management, yet each yields different perspectives and insights.

The foundations of adaptive co-management are still emerging. In Part 4, "Tools," three chapters highlight concepts and tools that may facilitate the development of adaptive co-management. In Chapter 13, Gary Kofinas, Susan Herman, and Chanda Meek examine the role of innovation in co-management and propose eight conditions that facilitate innovation. The authors view innovation as an outcome of co-management, and use this lens to link the scholarship of those who focus on power imbalances in formal co-management contexts with that of those who focus on the functional contributions of power-sharing institutions.

In Chapter 14, Per Olsson examines the case of adaptive co-management of the Kristianstads Vattenrike, a wetland complex south of Stockholm, Sweden. Olsson highlights the role of visioning as a tool to frame and direct adaptive co-management efforts. He explores how visioning in this region has played a key role in transforming and changing the social features of the governance system at multiple levels, helping to sustain the system and provide social sources of resilience that are important to adaptive co-management.

Drawing attention to another important tool, Garry Peterson describes in Chapter 15 how scenario planning has been used to build connections among separate groups and start a dialogue about the functioning of an intensively managed and human-dominated social-ecological system, the Northern Highland Lake District of Wisconsin. Peterson illustrates how scenario planning helped to build capacity for adaptive co-management, stimulating shared understanding and cooperation among a range of stakeholder groups.

This volume ends with a synthesis chapter (Chapter 16) on the lessons learned and the implications for adaptive co-management theory development, practice, and policy. Attention is directed towards the key themes previously described, and the manner in which authors touch on these themes to emphasize theory, lessons from the field, challenges, and evolving concepts and tools.

From the outset, the aim of this volume has been to contribute to the evolution of adaptive co-management and to respond to the needs and interests of community-based actors, policy makers, resource managers and other practitioners, and researchers. Most chapters link theory and practice, providing unique insights from case studies and examples representing diverse geographical settings and resource systems. Combined, the chapters in this book provide a perspective on a natural resource management approach that is evolving to meet the increasing challenges of a tightly connected world and the expectations for governance innovation in an adaptive age.

References

Allen, T.F.H., J.A. Tainter, J.C. Pires, and T.W. Hoekstra. 2001. Dragnet ecology – "Just the facts, Ma'am": The privilege of science in a postmodern world. *BioScience* 51 (6): 475-85.

Armitage, D. 2005. Adaptive capacity and community-based natural resource management. *Environmental Management* 35 (6): 703-15.

Berkes, F. 2002. Cross-scale institutional linkages: Perspectives from the bottom up. In *The drama of the commons*, ed. E. Ostrom, T. Dietz, N. Dolsak, P.C. Stern, S. Stonich, and E.U. Weber, 293-321. Washington, DC: National Academy Press.

Berkes, F., and C. Folke, eds. 1998. *Linking social and ecological systems: Management practices and social mechanisms for building resilience.* Cambridge: Cambridge University Press.

Berkes, F., P. George, and R. Preston. 1991. Co-management. *Alternatives* 18 (2): 12-18.

Berkes, F., J. Colding, and C. Folke, eds. 2003. *Navigating social-ecological systems: Building resilience for complexity and change.* Cambridge: Cambridge University Press.

Borrini-Feyerabend, G., M.T. Farvar, J.C. Nguinguiri, and V. Ndangang. 2000. *Co-Management of natural resources: Organizing negotiation and learning by doing.* Heidelberg: Kasparek Zverlag.

Borrini-Feyerabend, G., M. Pimbert, M.T. Farvar, A. Kothari, and Y. Renard. 2004. *Sharing power: Learning-by-doing in co-management of natural resources throughout the world.* Teheran: IIED, IUCN/CEESP, Cenesta.

Brunner, R., T. Steelman, L. Coe-Juell, C. Cromley, C. Edwards, and D. Tucker. 2005. *Adaptive governance: Integrating science, policy and decision making.* New York: Columbia University Press.

Capra, F. 1996. *The web of life: A new scientific understanding of living systems.* New York: Doubleday.

Cardinal, D., and J.C. Day. 1998. Embracing value and uncertainty in environmental management and planning: A heuristic model. *Environments* 25 (2 & 3): 110-25.

Clark, W.C., and N.M. Dickson. 2003. Sustainability science: The emerging research paradigm. *Proceedings of the National Academy of Sciences* 100: 8059-61.

Colfer, C.J.P. 2005. *The equitable forest: Diversity, community, and resource management.* Washington, DC: Resources for the Future.

Dietz, T., E. Ostrom, and P. Stern. 2003. The struggle to govern the commons. *Science* 302 (5652): 1907-12.

Folke, C., S. Carpenter, T. Elmqvist, L. Gunderson, C.S. Holling, B. Walker, J. Bengtsson, et al. 2002. *Resilience and sustainable development: Building adaptive capacity in a world of transformations.* International Council for Science, ICSU Series on Science for Sustainable Development, no. 3. http://www.sou.gov.se/mvb/pdf/resiliens.pdf.

Gunderson, L.H., and C.S. Holling, eds. 2002. *Panarchy: Understanding transformations in human and natural systems.* Washington, DC: Island Press.

Gunderson, L.H., C.S. Holling, and S.S. Light. 1995. *Barriers and bridges to the renewal of ecosystems and institutions.* New York: Columbia University Press.

Hilborn, R., and C. Walters. 1992. *Quantitative fisheries stock assessment: Choice, dynamics and uncertainty.* New York: Chapman and Hall.

Holling, C.S., ed. 1978. *Adaptive environmental assessment and management.* New York: John Wiley and Sons.

Holling, C.S., and G.K. Meffe. 1996. Command and control and the pathology of natural resource management. *Conservation Biology* 10 (2): 328-37.

IUCN (International Union for the Conservation of Nature and Natural Resources). 1996. World conservation congress, October 1996, Montreal.

Lee, K.N. 1993. *Compass and gyroscope: Integrating science and politics for the environment.* Washington, DC: Island Press.

Levin, S.A. 1999. *Fragile dominion: Complexity and the commons.* Reading, MA: Perseus Books.

McCay, B.J., and J.M Acheson, eds. 1987. *The question of the commons: The culture and ecology of communal resources.* Tucson: University of Arizona Press.

McConney, P., R. Pomeroy, and R. Mahon. 2003a. *Guidelines for coastal resource co-management in the Caribbean: Communicating the concepts and conditions that favour success.* Caribbean Coastal Co-management Guidelines Project. Barbados: Caribbean Conservation Association.

Millennium Ecosystem Assessment. 2005. *Ecosystems and human well-being: Synthesis.* Washington, DC: Island Press.

Nadasdy, P. 2003. *Hunters and bureaucrats: Power, knowledge, and Aboriginal-state relations in the southwest Yukon.* Vancouver: UBC Press.

Olsson, P., C. Folke, and F. Berkes. 2004. Adaptive co-management for building resilience in social-ecological systems. *Environmental Management* 34 (1): 75-90.

Ostrom, E. 2005. *Understanding institutional diversity.* Princeton, NJ: Princeton University Press.

Ostrom, E., T. Dietz, N. Dolsak, P.C. Stern, S. Stonich, and E.U. Weber, eds. 2002. *The drama of the commons.* Washington, DC: National Academy Press.

Pinkerton, E., ed. 1989. *Co-operative management of local fisheries: New directions for improved management and community development.* Vancouver: UBC Press.

–. 1992. Translating legal rights into management practice: Overcoming barriers to the exercise of co-management. *Human Organization* 51: 330-41.

Plummer, R., and J. FitzGibbon. 2004. Some observations on the terminology in co-operative environmental management. *Journal of Environmental Management* 70: 63-72.

Ruitenbeek, J., and C. Cartier. 2001. *The invisible wand: Adaptive co-management as an emergent strategy in complex bio-economic systems.* Occasional paper no. 34. Bogor, Indonesia: Center for International Forestry Research. http://www.cifor.cgiar.org.

Singleton, S. 1998. *Constructing cooperation: The evolution of institutions of co-management.* Ann Arbor: University of Michigan Press.

UNDP (United Nations Development Programme). 2005. The Equator Initiative. http://www.undp.org/equatorinitiative.

UNDP/UNEP/World Bank/WRI. 2005. *World resources 2005. The wealth of the poor: Managing ecosystems to fight poverty.* Washington, DC: United Nations Development Programme/United Nations Environment Programme/World Bank/World Resources Institute.

Walters, C.J. 1986. *Adaptive management of renewable resources.* New York: Macmillan.

Wilson, D.C., J. Nielsen, and P. Degnbol, eds. 2003. *The fisheries co-management experience: Accomplishments, challenges, and prospects.* Dordrecht, Netherlands: Kluwer Academic Publishers.

Woodhill, J., and N. Röling. 1998. The second wing of the eagle: The human dimension in learning our way to more sustainable futures. In *Facilitating sustainable agriculture: Participatory learning and adaptive management in times of environmental uncertainty,* ed. N.G. Röling and M.A.E. Wagemakers, 46-72. Cambridge: Cambridge University Press.

Zerner, C., ed. 2000. *People, plants, and justice: The politics of nature conservation.* New York: Columbia University Press.

Part 1: Theory

2
Adaptive Co-Management and Complexity: Exploring the Many Faces of Co-Management
Fikret Berkes

Complexities of co-management have emerged gradually, unfolding over the last two decades. Co-management has been approached in diverse ways, for example, as a problem in power sharing (Pinkerton 1989); a challenge in capacity building for both community and government (Pomeroy and Berkes 1997); a mechanism to implement Aboriginal rights, as in Australia, New Zealand, and Canada (Berkes et al. 1991; Taiepa et al. 1997); and an arena in which different systems of knowledge can be brought together (Kendrick 2000; Moller et al. 2004). "Co-management" has been used as a catch-all term for the various responses to growing demands for a role for users and communities in environmental management and conflict resolution.

These many aspects of co-management are reflected in some of the recent literature. For example, Pinkerton (2003) refers to "complete co-management," which includes the exercising of rights at multiple levels and the development of various linkages among stakeholders, potentially leading to greater democratization of civil society. Similarly, McConney and colleagues (2003) regard co-management broadly as an analysis of relationships, a combination of negotiation and action, and an approach to integrated resource management. Borrini-Feyerabend and colleagues (2004) point out in their review of co-management practice from around the world that they use the term in a broader, multidimensional sense (Table 2.1).

The history of the notion of "sharing of power and responsibility between the government and local resource users" (Berkes et al. 1991) goes back to earlier times, however. In the area of fisheries, for example, the earliest documented legal arrangement for what we would today call co-management seems to be in the Lofoten Islands cod fishery in Norway in the 1890s. This arrangement, codified as the Lofoten Act, started as a conflict management measure of last resort in a lucrative fishery involving a diversity of gear groups, and an allocation problem that the government was not able to cope with (Jentoft 1989; Jentoft and McCay 1995). In Japan, the origins of fisheries co-management may be found in the 1901 Fisheries

Table 2.1

The various ways in which collaboration, including co-management, is understood

Collaboration as a form of self-defence	In a changing world, indigenous peoples and local communities need more than ever strong internal and external forms of cooperation to be able to withstand various threats and dangers.
Collaboration as a response to complexity	The natural resource base of livelihoods cuts across a variety of political, administrative, cultural, and social boundaries, and there exist a multiplicity of concerned social actors.
Collaboration for effectiveness and efficiency	Different social actors possess complementary capacities and comparative advantages in management, which can be profitably harnessed together.
Collaboration for respect and equity	A fair sharing of the costs and benefits of managing natural resources and ecosystems is essential for initiatives aiming at human development and conservation with equity.
Collaboration through negotiation	At the core of most co-management arrangements are formal and/or informal plans and agreements. Such arrangements need to be negotiated through a fair and flexible process of learning-by-doing.
Collaboration as social institution	The harnessing of complementary capacities and the fair distribution of costs and benefits are the foundation of many institutional arrangements for co-management.

Source: Borrini-Feyerabend et al. (2004).

Act, updated in 1949. Under this act, village sea territories established during the feudal era were mapped, codified, and registered, and the management of the resources was devolved to local fisheries cooperative associations (Lim et al. 1995).

In the area of forest management, Agrawal (2005, 83) notes that in the Kumaon Himalayas in the 1920s and 1930s, measures were taken "for creating community forests that would be managed under a broad set of rules framed by the government but for which villagers themselves would craft specific rules for everyday use." This is, in effect, forest co-management. Better known in the co-management literature is the arrangement in India's more recent Joint Forest Management (Agarwal 2001), which started in 1972 as an innovative project in a district of West Bengal to share forestry revenues with villagers to provide them with incentives to replant degraded areas and to look after their trees.

The term "co-management" was not used until much later. For example, the earliest of the legal co-management arrangements in Canada, the James Bay and Northern Quebec Agreement of 1975, predates the term "co-management."

Chapter 24 of the agreement establishes the *comite conjoint,* tasked with "coordinating" resource management. The *comite conjoint* is clearly the co-management body in the agreement but it is not called that, either in French or English. Similarly, fisheries co-management undertaken under the Boldt Decision of 1974 was not called that initially. Pinkerton (2003) traces the earliest use of the term "co-management" to the late 1970s, by the US treaty tribes in Washington state, who were managing salmon under the Boldt Decision. Initially, the issue was simply the sharing of salmon harvests among the treaty tribes and commercial fishers, as determined by the court decision.

Pinkerton shows how co-management evolved through a series of stages. By 1984, protocols for salmon harvest had been agreed to, and this led to the emergence of the next set of issues. These included habitat protection, regional planning, policy setting, and international allocation. Thus, the initial co-management arrangement, which was about allocation, set the stage for a complex multi-stakeholder exercise and later led to complex multi-jurisdictional integrated resource management in the Pacific Northwest (Pinkerton 1992, 2003).

One can similarly examine the evolution of co-management in the context of Native land claim agreements in the Canadian North. In addition to legislated co-management regarding land and resources, as set up by the agreements, other kinds of joint management arrangements emerged under a favourable policy and legislative framework. One is struck by the diversity of incipient partnerships in such disparate areas as coastal zone management, protected areas, persistent organic pollutants (POPs), and climate change (Berkes et al. 2001; Berkes et al. 2005).

These experiences and many others elsewhere (e.g., McCay 2002) indicate that co-management is more varied, more complex, and more dynamic than might be concluded from the earlier literature, which appears to treat co-management as a fixed and simple category of arrangements. Two observations emerge from these findings. The first is that the evolutionary nature of collaborative management in such areas as the Pacific Northwest and the Canadian Arctic suggest that a theory of co-management should account for the evolutionary nature of co-management and should deal with adaptive processes and feedback learning. The second is that co-management is perhaps not very distinct from other collaborative and participatory arrangements.

A diversity of participatory relationships may be found in a wide range of areas of resource and environmental management. Co-management shares many features with other classes of partnerships and cooperative environmental governance arrangements (Plummer and FitzGibbon 2004). Co-management is perhaps not a unique category but one kind of partnership that bridges scales (Reid et al. 2006). There are other kinds of partnerships and participatory arrangements that share the characteristic of linking two or more levels of governance (Berkes 2002). They include multi-stakeholder bodies (McCay and Jentoft 1996; Kalikoski and Satterfield 2004), encompassing organizations (McCay 2002), policy networks (Carlsson 2000), institutional networks (Tompkins et al. 2002), boundary organizations (Cash and Moser 2000), polycentric systems (McGinnis 2000), and epistemic communities (Haas 1992).

Some of these areas have their own technical literature and somewhat different kinds of participants and linkages than does co-management. For example, boundary organizations and epistemic communities do not need to involve governments, and polycentric systems do not need to involve communities, but co-management in most definitions involves both. For example, according to the National Round Table on the Environment and the Economy (NRTEE), co-management implies a formal agreement between at least one government agency and another group, specifying government as a partner. "When community-based management does not include government as a partner in the decision making process, it is not co-management" (NRTEE 1998, 13).

Young's notion (2002) of institutional interplay provides one way to analyze partnerships and to sort between different kinds of co-management–like arrangements. The institutional interplay idea draws attention to the nature of linkages among institutions, both at the same level of social and political organization and across levels. It includes the linkage of institutions *horizontally* (across geographical space) and *vertically* (across levels of organization). Using this terminology, broader conceptualizations of co-management may focus on the dynamics or development of linkages and scale issues in governance (Berkes 2002). The former moves the discussion into the realm of adaptive co-management, and the latter moves it into complex systems thinking.

The objective of this chapter is to examine co-management as complexity, leading to broader conceptualizations of adaptive co-management. This is done by examining the different faces of co-management: as power sharing, as institution building, as trust building, as process, as social learning, as problem solving, and as governance (Table 2.2). The choice of these seven faces of co-management is of course subjective; they can be divided up or combined in various ways. This particular set and its order reflects my own experience with co-management. The first three items reflect earlier work (Berkes et al. 1991; Berkes 1998); the last four reflect more recent thinking, moving into multi-level management, learning, and complexity (Berkes 2002; Olsson et al. 2004; Carlsson and Berkes 2005). I deal with each in turn.

Co-Management as Power Sharing
The management of resources usually falls under the jurisdiction of the state. Historically, this has not always been so, and in many parts of the

Table 2.2

The many faces of co-management, moving towards an expanded notion of adaptive co-management that deals with complexity

Faces of co-management	Elements emphasized	Reference
Co-management as power sharing	Sharing power and responsibility for management; the degree of authority held by the community, ranging from mere consultation to effective control over the resource	Borrini-Feyerabend et al. (2004)
Co-management as institution building	Institution building for the local level, which rarely has a background of working with the government, and for government agencies, which are rarely ready for local or cross-scale partnerships	Pomeroy and Berkes (1997)
Co-management as trust building	Building trust, as a prelude to a working relationship; learning to respect differences in worldview, moving towards integration of different knowledge systems	Kendrick (2003); Singleton (1998)
Co-management as process	Focus on co-management as a continuous process rather than a fixed state or an endpoint; power sharing as the *result,* not the starting point, of co-management	Carlsson and Berkes (2005)
Co-management as social learning	Co-management with iterative feedback and learning from experience; learning-by-doing responds to social and ecological feedback and provides management flexibility	Pahl-Wostl and Hare (2004)
Co-management as problem solving	Networks of partners may transfer learning from one situation to another and may develop the confidence and skills to tackle increasingly more complex problems through time	Olsson et al. (2004)
Co-management as governance	Sharing management rights and responsibilities is consistent with the principles of good governance – legitimacy and authority based on a democratic mandate, transparency, and accountability	McCay and Jentoft (1996); Folke et al. (2005)

world, there are many kinds of resources that continue to be managed by communities (Ostrom et al. 1999). Even with resources managed by the government, however, resource users and resource-dependent communities have been demanding a role in making those decisions that affect their livelihoods. This is true in diverse parts of the world, such as Zimbabwe

(Hasler 1995), the Caribbean (Pomeroy et al. 2004), Chile (Castilla and Fernandez 1998), Brazil (Pinto da Silva 2004), Sri Lanka (Amarasinghe and De Silva 1999), and Cambodia (Marschke and Kim 2003). Sharing decision making can take many forms, from various kinds of partnerships to decentralization, deconcentration, delegated powers, and devolution (Pomeroy and Berkes 1997). The degree of power held by the community can vary widely, from merely being consulted to having effective control over the resource, along the lines of an "Arnstein ladder" for citizen participation, as initially conceived for city planning (Arnstein 1969).

Co-management requires some degree of power and responsibility sharing. Most definitions of co-management are based on this characteristic. For example, Berkes and colleagues (1991, 12) define co-management as "the sharing of power and responsibility between the government and local resource users," and Pinkerton (1992) defines it as "power-sharing in the exercise of resource management between a government agency and a community or organization of stakeholders." Hence, measures of equity and power sharing may be (and have been) used as criteria in assessing co-management success (Kruse et al. 1998).

It is the nature of power sharing, however, that often makes partnerships problematic. Typically, the less powerful sectors of the community are left out of shared decision making. For example, Agarwal (2001) found that women were selectively excluded from participation in India's Joint Forest Management as the process became more bureaucratized. In the Manali area of northwestern India, many women whose names appeared on state-mandated Joint Forest Management committees were not even aware that they were on those committees (Bingeman et al. 2004).

Power sharing can be made more equitable through state legitimization and formalized arrangements, institution building, capacity building, and knowledge sharing (Berkes 2002; Borrini-Feyerabend et al. 2004). The literature contains many suggestions on how to deal with power imbalances to achieve equity, but there are larger barriers to overcome, barriers that are embedded in broader social relationships. "In a nutshell, 'participatory management needs participatory roots,' i.e., some measure of effective dialogue, discussion of issues and participatory democracy *internal* to all relevant social actors" (Borrini-Feyerabend et al. 2004, 175).

A case in point is Dall sheep co-management in the Yukon. There was a formalized wildlife co-management arrangement between the government and indigenous groups, but no tradition of participatory democracy involving these Aboriginal groups. Nadasdy (2003a, 2003b) found that the co-management regime was merely inserted into existing structures of bureaucratic wildlife management, the very structures that disempowered the local First Nation in the first place. In such cases, co-management can not only perpetuate but also exacerbate existing power imbalances, rather than providing communities a measure of control over local resources. How common are such situations? Nadasdy (2003b, 368) argues that one should "cultivate a healthy skepticism of the 'co-management success story' and call for more critical and nuanced analyses of particular co-management processes."

Co-Management as Institution Building

Many of the co-management institutions in various parts of the world are very new, with the few exceptions noted earlier. Local institutions rarely have experience working with the government, and government agencies are rarely ready for partnerships (Pomeroy 1995; Ahmed et al. 1997). In developing countries in particular, preparation for co-management often involves institution building at the local level, although it is clear that the government side needs institution building as well (Pomeroy and Berkes 1997).

Can co-management develop in the absence of deliberate institution building? Ruitenbeek and Cartier (2001) advance the interesting notion that adaptive co-management may be an emergent property of complex systems of management. That is, it can evolve spontaneously from simple systems of management through feedback learning over time, and this can happen with little or no external intervention. Conversely, the authors suggest, policy intervention to introduce co-management could lead to failure. By contrast, other researchers have concentrated on the importance of institution building and institutional capital in general (Ostrom 1990). The idea is that successful co-management or community-based management depends on traditions of self-organization and problem solving. In a given society, it is easier to adapt existing institutions from one purpose to another than to develop them anew (Barrett et al. 2001; Folke et al. 2005).

Both arguments may be partially correct. Community-level institutions do spontaneously emerge through self-organization in various parts of the world, and management systems do evolve over time when appropriately nurtured and facilitated (Singleton 1998; Kendrick 2003). Although adaptive co-management cannot be imposed from the top down, its emergence can be assisted by creating a favourable policy environment and through such measures as enabling legislation that recognizes local rights over land and resources.

For example, in Tanzania, enabling legislation for decentralization was passed in the 1970s and the 1980s to foster self-reliance and local democracy (*ujamaa*). Although the *ujamaa* policy itself was generally considered a failure, the legislation enabled communities to manage their own affairs and later served as the basis of new legislation for protected area co-management (Anderson and Ngazi 1995). The general lesson from such cases is that there is an interplay between government policy and self-organized local institutions. Both local institutions and enabling policies (at least, non-interference from senior levels of government) are necessary for the evolution of co-management and commons institutions in general (Ostrom 1990; Agrawal 2001, 2005).

Co-Management as Trust Building

Constructing an effective co-management arrangement is not only a matter of building institutions; it is also a matter of building trust between the parties as a prelude to developing a working relationship (Singleton 1998). Kruse and colleagues (1998) studied the relationship between user involvement and caribou management effectiveness in Alaska and northern Canada. Contrary to expectations, they found that direct user involvement in joint management boards did not increase the likelihood of cooperation. Rather, frequent and continued presence of government biologists in Native communities and the establishment of trust were the key (Kruse et al. 1998). Trust appears to be a determinant of success in many cases of co-management; it is possibly a universal determinant. Trust is an essential part of the social capital that needs to develop among a group of people trying to solve a problem; trust lubricates collaboration (Pretty and Ward 2001).

Related to trust building is learning to respect differences in worldviews. This is not an issue if the co-managers share much the same values and knowledge systems, as in the co-management of crayfish in Swedish lakes, which involves local people and biologists (Olsson and Folke 2001). It can be particularly important, however, when the co-managers are coming from different epistemological backgrounds, or have different cosmologies or worldviews. Such cross-cultural co-management cases include those with indigenous groups (Kendrick 2000; Manseau et al. 2005).

For example, it is not easy to forge a working relationship between a group of wildlife biologists (who tend to hold strong views about "managing" caribou) and a group of northern Aboriginal hunters (who do not believe that animals can be "managed" and strongly dislike intrusive measures such as the use of radio collars). Assessments by Kofinas (1998), Kendrick (2000), and others of caribou co-management in northern Canada and Alaska indicate that co-management initially leads to an exchange of ideas between the parties and then to mutual education. There is an "emerging dialectic of conceptual diversity" (Kendrick 2003, 263), a process of learning to respect differences without which co-management can never work. The structure of the relationship is a two-way feedback.

Trust and respect make effective partnerships possible, in part because they are important for communication among the parties. Steins (1999) studied the efforts to build co-management arrangements in three European countries, and noted the importance of the images that the actors have of each other's activities. She found that these images posed barriers to partnership building by clouding the relationships among stakeholders. The key may be the ability of co-management arrangements to facilitate a process of communication to overcome these barriers.

In cross-cultural situations, negotiation of meaning itself is necessary for communication leading to mutual understanding (Lakoff and Johnson 1980). This entails a form of communication that enables participants to reconsider their worldviews and adjust the ways that they categorize experience, thus building new, shared metaphors. This is different from the "conduit" model of communication, in which messages are transmitted in a common language and knowledge is also held in common. Agreeing on the facts alone is not sufficient; co-managers also need to agree (or at least agree to disagree) on values and goals. Developing a common vision of the desired future is an important element of co-management success; there is an argument not only for developing such a common vision but also for "ritualizing" it (Borrini-Feyerabend et al. 2004).

Co-Management as Process

Co-management presupposes that parties have, in a formal or semi-formal way, agreed on a process for sharing management rights and responsibilities. But co-management involves institution building, the development of trust, and, in some cases, the negotiation of meaning itself and the reframing of images of one another among the parties. Hence, co-management is often the result of extensive deliberation and negotiation – a process rather than a fixed state. The actual arrangement evolves over time. Long-term studies characterize co-management not as an endpoint but as a process in which relationships among the parties are constantly changing.

The length of time needed for this evolution or development process may be quite substantial, perhaps as long as a decade, in regard to salmon of the Pacific Northwest (Singleton 1998) and caribou of the Canadian North (Kendrick 2003). Napier and colleagues (2005) conducted a statistical study of the conditions for co-management success in eleven subsistence fisheries in KwaZulu-Natal, South Africa. The oldest of these arrangements was nine years old and the youngest was two. They asked the co-managers (both government authorities and communities) about their perceptions of the success of the arrangement. The perceived success and the attainment of conditions assumed important for success were both strongly correlated with the length of time that co-management had been operating ($r = 0.85$ and 0.97, respectively).

The implication of such findings is that the time dimension of co-management is extremely important. Co-management should be regarded as a long and continuous process rather than an endpoint. In contrast to the ideal image of formal organizational hierarchy, co-management is not a one-shot arrangement. It should be understood as a process in which parties constantly negotiate and renegotiate their positions and change their activities (Carlsson and Berkes 2005). Hence, overemphasis on formal aspects of power sharing (e.g., legal details of co-management in land claim agreements) may put the parties at risk of overlooking the dynamics of the process and its temporal requirements.

Co-Management as Social Learning

The notion of social learning has been used in several different ways. In the learning literature, the classic model refers to the process of individual learning based on observation and imitation of others and their social interactions within the group. There is iterative feedback between the learner and the environment, the learner changing the environment and these changes, in turn, affecting the learner. Pahl-Wostl and Hare (2004) consider this approach to be too narrow to embrace the various learning processes that operate in resource management. They point out the relevance of the concept of "communities of practice" developed by Wenger (1998), who emphasized learning as participation. The co-management experience in diverse parts of the world is consistent with Wenger's learning-as-participation (e.g., Kendrick 2003; Napier et al. 2005; Wilson et al. 2003).

In adaptive management, learning-by-doing involves building social memory to respond to feedback from the environment, both human and natural. The adaptive management scholar K.N. Lee (1993, 136) uses "learning" in the sense of John Dewey: "reconstruction or reorganization of experience which adds to the meaning of experience, and which increases ability to direct the course of subsequent experience." In the context of adaptive management, he refers to learning by groups, relational learning, policy-oriented learning, and institutional learning at various points in his book.

This kind of learning, at the level of social groups and institutions, is particularly important with respect to uncertainty in complex and constantly changing environments. Adaptive management as an approach acknowledges uncertainty and assumes that management knowledge is not, and will never be, perfect. It therefore proceeds iteratively, learning from mistakes and responding to feedback. Many co-management cases seem to show this feature (Armitage 2003, 2005b; Marschke and Kim 2003; Berkes et al. 2003).

A collective learning process that builds experience with ecosystem change evolves as a part of the social memory. Such a process of social learning is linked to the flexibility of management in responding to feedback and in directing the coupled social-ecological system into sustainable trajectories (Folke et al. 2003). Management processes can be improved by making them adaptable and flexible through the use of multiple kinds of knowledge and diverse perspectives. The use of a broad range of ecological knowledge and understanding, including those of resource user communities, helps create management systems that are resilient, that is, those that have the capacity to adapt to change and that can better deal with uncertainty and surprise (Folke et al. 2002, 2005).

Social or organizational learning theory (Argyris 1993) talks about double-loop learning and transformative learning; these appear to be applicable to the investigation of how resource-dependent communities make adjustments over time (Diduck et al. 2005). Some place-based, resource-dependent groups may have the adaptive capacity to develop ways to solve exogenous and endogenous variables that impact upon collective action and effective problem solving (Armitage 2005a). There is evidence that community decision making helps transform those who participate in governance (Agrawal 2005), indicating that social learning may be operating at multiple scales.

Co-Management as Problem Solving

Management decision making implies choices between different alternatives, while problem solving has to do with the process of generating these alternatives. Co-management evolves over time and is very much a result of deliberate problem solving (Carlsson and Berkes 2005). Adaptive management is a way of learning, a method for iterative, collaborative, feedback-based problem solving (Lee 1993). It was born as a technocratic approach, however, and still carries an aura of "expert-knows-best" management. Hence, Lee (1999) emphasizes the necessity in adaptive management of collaborative processes to establish consensus among the parties before problem solving can proceed.

Adaptive co-management may be characterized as the collaboration of a diverse set of stakeholders operating at different levels, from local users to municipalities, regional and national organizations, and international agencies. In well-developed management systems, these parties often come together as flexible networks that "pulsate," forming and re-forming in accordance with the problems to be solved. This is governance in self-organized networks (Olsson et al. 2004; Folke et al. 2005).

The ability to solve problems collectively evolves through time. Using this evolutionary view, for example, the Native land claim agreement in the James Bay area can be seen not as an end in itself but rather as a means to create the political space within which communities and other groups can develop the knowledge and skills to solve their own problems. Cases from Canada and Sweden, traced over time spans of two to three decades, indicate that co-management as problem solving may be quite powerful, enabling parties to transfer learning from one situation to another, and to develop the confidence and skills to tackle increasingly more complex problems (Olsson et al. 2004).

If co-management is a matter of collaborative problem solving, analyzing co-management should preferably be task-oriented, concentrating on the *function* rather than on the formal structure of the arrangement. Such an

Box 2.1

Steps in researching a co-management process in which power sharing is the result rather than the starting point of the process

Feedbacks in this six-step process or iterative problem solving introduce a learning-by-doing element and turn the process into adaptive co-management (adapted from Carlsson and Berkes 2005).

1 Define the social-ecological system under focus. Define the unit of analysis – the resource system, the people, and the action arena and how it is structured.
2 Map the essential management tasks to be performed and the problems to be solved. What types of short-term, medium-term, and long-term management decisions must be made, and who is entitled to make these decisions?
3 Clarify the participants in co-management activities and related problem-solving processes. Who participates in the activities, and how is management organized? What is the web of relationships, and how is power shared?
4 Analyze linkages. How and to what extent do the identified relationships connect central levels of decision making to those of the local level? What is the historical and political context of the system?
5 Evaluate capacity-building needs. What efforts are needed to nurture, enhance, and utilize the skills and capabilities of people and institutions at all levels?
6 Prescribe remedies. What can be done better? The analyst can communicate the results of research to relevant groups in order to contribute knowledge for the general process of policy making and problem solving.

approach highlights the idea that power sharing may best be seen as the *result,* and not the starting point, of the co-management process (Carlsson and Berkes 2005). Box 2.1 shows the steps of such a co-management process.

Co-Management as Governance

Conventional governance involves top-down decision making, leaving little room for user participation and management flexibility. Evolving notions of governance include people-centred approaches in which the focus shifts to coordination and self-governance, manifested in different types of networks and partnerships. These alternative forms of governance may incorporate state, private, and civil society actors, and a form of governance in which management responsibility is shared (Pierre and Peters 2000). There are no ready-made formulas for such governance, however; management systems must be tailor-made to fit the contexts of particular cases (Kooiman 2003).

Co-management in which there is a diversity of players, including public and private actors, linked to one another through a variety of relationships, might as well be characterized as governance (see Chapter 1). This broader notion of "co-management as governance" is consistent with the principles of good governance – legitimacy and authority based on a democratic mandate, transparency (openness), and accountability (Rhodes 1997). The direct involvement of people in resource management decisions that affect their livelihoods is good governance. As Pinkerton (2003) points out, the tendency to apply co-management to merely the day-to-day operational rights is not sufficient. Co-management should also apply at the collective choice level, providing higher-level decision-making rights that inform the operational level.

Good governance involves effective user participation and problem solving at the lowest possible level of organization. The relevant principle, sometimes called the subsidiarity principle, prescribes that there be as much local solution as possible and only as much government regulation as necessary (Berkes et al. 1991). Article A of the Maastricht Treaty establishing the European Community uses the subsidiarity principle to indicate that "decisions [be] taken as closely as possible to the citizen" (McCay and Jentoft 1996). There are complications in implementation, however.

Implementing subsidiarity may require institutional reform, creating new organizations at a lower level and/or new legislation. Jentoft (2000) questions the determination of "the lowest possible level of organization" and raises the possibility that, in some instances, the subsidiarity principle may require centralization rather than decentralization. Achieving a fit between the scale of ecological systems and that of governance systems is never easy, and institutional misfit is often a major reason that management systems fail (Folke et al. 2002; Brown 2003).

The polycentric approach recognizes that effective governance often requires multiple links across levels and domains, and seeks overlapping centres of authority. Such a decision-making structure allows for testing of rules at different scales, and contributes to the creation of an institutional dynamic appropriate for adaptive co-management and, more broadly, for adaptive governance (Folke et al. 2005). Polycentric institutional arrangements do not fit the ideal of organizational efficiency; they are deliberately redundant. They are a good fit, however, for dealing with intersecting domains, as many areas of public policy do not fall neatly into one jurisdiction or one authority (McGinnis 2000).

Conclusions

Adaptive co-management is about power sharing, institution building, trust building, social learning, problem solving, and (good) governance. These many faces of co-management reflect the "unpacking" of the notion of co-management over the last two decades. The seven faces of adaptive co-management presented in this chapter no doubt overlap, and there may well be others – co-management as experiment and co-management as innovation (Chapter 13) are possibilities. Even though there is overlap, these faces help highlight the different elements of co-management that deserve attention.

The consideration of adaptive aspects takes co-management into the realm of complex adaptive systems. There are several lines of evidence for this: the cross-scale nature of co-management; adaptive co-management being possibly an emergent property of complex systems; the double feedback of trust building; learning from mistakes and learning-by-doing; use of multiple perspectives; use of different epistemologies and a wide range of information; and self-organizing networks for governance. Each of these features, addressing issues of scale, multiple perspectives and epistemologies, uncertainty and non-linearity, and self-organization and emergence, is a characteristic of complex adaptive systems (Berkes et al. 2003).

By definition, co-management links different levels of political organization, such as the community level with the regional and/or national levels of government. These relationships are anything but simple. The expanded notion of co-management suggests that there may be three ways to describe the complexity of these linkages. First, there are often various levels of vertical connections. The multiplicity of vertical connections is very real if, for example, one considers the number of linkages from the local to the international involved in the management of narwhals, polar bears, and persistent organic pollutants (POPs) in the Canadian Arctic (Berkes et al. 2005; Armitage 2005b).

Second, attention needs to be paid to horizontal linkages, such as the connections among the various communities in the Inuvialuit or the Nunavut land claims regions (Berkes et al. 2005) or those among the members of US Regional Fishery Management Councils (McCay and Jentoft 1996), as an important part of adaptive co-management.

Third, the expanded notion of co-management recognizes that, in many real-life co-management situations, one finds a rich web of relationships between a set of private actors and a set of public actors. These networks are found both in the West and in developing country settings (Mahanty 2002; Marschke and Kim 2003). The networks and links are easier to recognize once the simplistic notion of a unitary state is replaced by the recognition of a diversity of government agencies with different roles and relationships. Rarely is "the state" or "the community" a monolithic actor (Carlsson and Berkes 2005).

Adding to complexity, McCay and Jentoft (1998) point out that these various kinds of actors are embedded within discrete and changing histories, social and political relationships, and environmental conditions. This allows for an ethnographically rich, layered, or complex analysis, a "thick" as opposed to "thin" analysis. Using the embeddedness perspective of Karl Polanyi, McCay and Jentoft (1998) consider economic relationships such as resource use to be enmeshed in social relationships. Hence, processes of "disembeddedness" (Giddens 1994), whereby local communities lose critical control over resources and governance, open possibilities of community failure. Similarly, one can postulate mechanisms for state and market failure (McCay and Jentoft 1998).

What is the significance of adaptive co-management in counteracting forces of disembeddedness? Governance involving state, private, and civil society actors, and co-management that results in building institutions, capacity, trust, and problem-solving networks – in short, building social capital (Pretty and Ward 2001; Chapter 3) – has important implications. One practical significance of adaptive co-management is related to the call for governance "at all levels" at the 2002 World Summit on Sustainable Development, Johannesburg. The call acknowledges that the most difficult challenges of sustainable development involve problems and solutions that span multiple levels (United Nations 2002; Sachs 2002).

A second practical significance concerns the building of adaptive capacities (Armitage 2005a) of resource-user communities in a world in which problems are complex, uncertainties high, and controls limited. Hence, management is not a search for the optimal solution to one resource problem but an ongoing learning and negotiation process with a high priority for collaborative problem solving (Folke et al. 2002; Berkes et al. 2003; Pahl-Wostl and Hare 2004). Flexible, multi-level institutions and learning networks may be important for building adaptive capacity in a world characterized by rapid rates of change and abrupt transformations.

References

Agarwal, B. 2001. Participatory exclusions, community forestry, and gender: An analysis for South Asia and a conceptual framework. *World Development* 29: 1623-48.

Agrawal, A. 2001. Common property institutions and sustainable governance of resources. *World Development* 29: 1649-72.

–. 2005. *Environmentality: Technologies of government and the making of subjects*. Durham, NC, and London: Duke University Press.

Ahmed, M., A.D. Capistrano, and M. Hossain. 1997. Experience of partnership models for the co-management of Bangladesh fisheries. *Fisheries Management and Ecology* 4: 233-48.

Amarasinghe, U.S., and S.S. De Silva 1999. Sri Lankan reservoir fishery: A case for introduction of a co-management strategy. *Fisheries Management and Ecology* 6: 387-99.

Anderson, J.E.C., and Z. Ngazi. 1995. Marine resource use and the establishment of a marine park: Mafia Island, Tanzania. *Ambio* 24: 475-81.

Argyris, C. 1993. *On organizational learning*. Cambridge, MA: Blackwell Business.

Armitage, D.R. 2003. Traditional agroecological knowledge, adaptive management, and the socio-politics of conservation in central Sulawesi, Indonesia. *Environmental Conservation* 30: 79-90.

–. 2005a. Adaptive capacity and community-based natural resource management. *Environmental Management* 35: 703-15.

–. 2005b. Community-based narwhal management in Nunavut, Canada: Change, uncertainty and adaptation. *Society and Natural Resources* 18: 715-31.

Arnstein, S. 1969. A ladder of citizen participation. *American Institute of Planners Journal* 35: 216-24.

Barrett, C.B., K. Brandon, C. Gibson, and H. Gjertsen. 2001. Conserving tropical biodiversity amid weak institutions. *BioScience* 51: 497-502.

Berkes, F. 1998. New and not-so-new directions in the use of the commons: Co-management. IUCN *Collaborative Management News* (2).

–. 2002. Cross-scale institutional linkages for commons management: Perspectives from the bottom up. In *The drama of the commons*, ed. E. Ostrom, T. Dietz, N. Dolsak, P.C. Stern, S. Stonich, and E.U. Weber, 293-321. Washington, DC: National Academy Press.

Berkes, F., P. George, and R. Preston. 1991. Co-management. *Alternatives* 18 (2): 12-18.

Berkes, F., J. Mathias, M. Kislalioglu, and H. Fast. 2001. The Canadian Arctic and the Oceans Act: The development of participatory environmental research and management. *Ocean and Coastal Management* 44: 451-69.

Berkes, F., J. Colding, and C. Folke, eds. 2003. *Navigating social-ecological systems: Building resilience for complexity and change.* Cambridge: Cambridge University Press.

Berkes, F., N. Bankes, M. Marschke, D. Armitage, and D. Clark. 2005. Cross-scale institutions and building resilience in the Canadian North. In *Breaking ice: Renewable resource and ocean management in the Canadian North,* ed. F. Berkes, R. Huebert, H. Fast, M. Manseau, and A. Diduck, 225-47. Calgary: University of Calgary Press.

Bingeman, K., F. Berkes, and J.S. Gardner. 2004. Institutional responses to development pressures: Resilience of social-ecological systems in Himachal Pradesh, India. *International Journal of Sustainable Development and World Ecology* 11: 99-115.

Borrini-Feyerabend, G., M. Pimbert, M.T. Farvar, A. Kothari, and Y. Renard. 2004. *Sharing power: Learning-by-doing in co-management of natural resources throughout the world.* Teheran: IIED, IUCN/CEESP, Cenesta.

Brown, K. 2003. Integrating conservation and development: A case of institutional misfit. *Frontiers in Ecology and Environment* 1: 479-87.

Carlsson, L. 2000. Policy networks as collective action. *Policy Studies Journal* 28: 502-20.

Carlsson, L., and F. Berkes. 2005. Co-management: Concepts and methodological implications. *Journal of Environmental Management* 75: 65-76.

Cash, D.W., and S.C. Moser. 2000. Linking global and local scales: Designing dynamic assessment and management processes. *Global Environmental Change* 10: 109-20.

Castilla, J.C., and M. Fernandez. 1998. Small-scale benthic fisheries in Chile: On co-management and sustainable use of benthic invertebrates. *Ecological Applications* 8 (1) Supplement: S124-S132.

Diduck, A., N. Bankes, D. Clark, and D. Armitage. 2005. Unpacking social learning in social-ecological systems. In *Breaking ice: Renewable resource and ocean management in the Canadian North,* ed. F. Berkes, R. Huebert, H. Fast, M. Manseau, and A. Diduck, 271-92. Calgary: University of Calgary Press.

Folke, C., S. Carpenter, T. Elmqvist, et al. 2002. Resilience for sustainable development: Building adaptive capacity in a world of transformations. Rainbow Series 3. Paris: International Council for Scientific Unions (ICSU). http://www.sou.gov.se/mvb/pdf/resiliens.pdf.

Folke C., J. Colding, and F. Berkes. 2003. Synthesis: Building resilience and adaptive capacity in socio-ecological systems. In *Navigating social-ecological systems: Building resilience for complexity and change,* ed. F. Berkes, J. Colding, and C. Folke, 352-87. Cambridge: Cambridge University Press.

Folke, C., T. Hahn, P. Olsson, and J. Norberg. 2005. Adaptive governance of social-ecological systems. *Annual Review of Environment and Resources* 30: 441-73.

Giddens, A. 1994. *The consequences of modernity.* Stanford, CA: Polity Press.

Haas, P.M. 1992. Introduction: Epistemic communities and international policy coordination. *International Organization* 46: 1-35.

Hasler, R. 1995. Political ecologies of scale: The multi-tiered co-management of Zimbabwean wildlife resources. Wildlife and Development Series, no. 7. London: International Institute for Environment and Development.

Jentoft, S. 1989. Fisheries co-management. *Marine Policy* 13: 137-54.

–. 2000. Co-managing the coastal zone: Is the task too complex? *Ocean and Coastal Management* 43: 527-35.

Jentoft, S., and B.J. McCay. 1995. User participation in fisheries management: Lessons drawn from international experiences. *Marine Policy* 19: 227-46.

Kalikoski, D.C., and T. Satterfield. 2004. On crafting a fisheries co-management arrangement in the estuary of Patos Lagoon, Brazil. *Marine Policy* 28: 503-22.

Kendrick, A. 2000. Community perceptions of the Beverly-Qamanirjuaq Caribou Management Board. *Canadian Journal of Native Studies* 20: 1-33.

–. 2003. Caribou co-management in northern Canada: Fostering multiple ways of knowing. In *Navigating social-ecological systems: Building resilience for complexity and change*, ed. F. Berkes, J. Colding, and C. Folke, 241-67. Cambridge: Cambridge University Press.

Kofinas, G. 1998. The costs of power-sharing: Communities in Porcupine Caribou Herd co-management. PhD dissertation, University of British Columbia, Vancouver.

Kooiman, J. 2003. *Governing as governance*. London: Sage.

Kruse, J., D. Klein, S. Braund, L. Moorehead, and B. Simeone. 1998. Co-management of natural resources: A comparison of two caribou management systems. *Human Organization* 57: 447-58.

Lakoff, G., and M. Johnson. 1980. *Metaphors we live by*. Chicago: University of Chicago Press.

Lee, K.N. 1993. *Compass and gyroscope*. Washington, DC: Island Press.

–. 1999. Appraising adaptive management. *Conservation Ecology* 3 (2): 3. http://www.consecol.org/vol3/iss2/art3/.

Lim, C.P., Y. Matsuda, and Y. Shigemi. 1995. Co-management in marine fisheries: The Japanese experience. *Coastal Management* 23: 195-221.

Mahanty, S. 2002. Conservation and development interventions as networks: The case of the India ecodevelopment project. *World Development* 30: 1369-86.

Manseau, M., B. Parlee, and G.B. Ayles. 2005. A place for traditional ecological knowledge in resource management. In *Breaking ice: Renewable resource and ocean management in the Canadian North*, ed. F. Berkes, R. Huebert, H. Fast, M. Manseau, and A. Diduck, 141-64. Calgary: University of Calgary Press.

Marschke, M., and Kim Nong. 2003. Adaptive co-management: Lessons from coastal Cambodia. *Canadian Journal of Development Studies* 24: 369-83.

McCay, B.J. 2002. Emergence of institutions for the commons: Contexts, situations and events. In *The drama of the commons*, ed. E. Ostrom, T. Dietz, N. Dolsak, P.C. Stern, S. Stonich, and E.U. Weber, 361-402. Washington, DC: National Academy Press.

McCay, B.J., and S. Jentoft. 1996. From the bottom up: Issues in fisheries management. *Society and Natural Resources* 9: 237-50.

–. 1998. Market or community failure? Critical perspectives on common property research. *Human Organization* 57: 21-29.

McConney, P., R. Pomeroy, and R. Mahon. 2003. *Guidelines for coastal resource co-management in the Caribbean: Communicating the concepts and conditions that favour success*. Caribbean Coastal Co-management Guidelines Project. Barbados: Caribbean Conservation Association.

McGinnis, M.D., ed. 2000. *Polycentric games and institutions*. Ann Arbor: University of Michigan Press.

Moller, H., F. Berkes, P.O. Lyver, and M. Kislalioglu. 2004. Combining science and traditional ecological knowledge: Monitoring populations for co-management. *Ecology and Society* 9 (3): 2. http://www.ecologyandsociety.org/vol9/iss3/art2.

Nadasdy, P. 2003a. *Hunters and bureaucrats: Power, knowledge, and Aboriginal-state relations in the southwest Yukon*. Vancouver: UBC Press.

–. 2003b. Reevaluating the co-management success story. *Arctic* 56: 367-80.

Napier, V.R., G.M. Branch, and J.M. Harris. 2005. Evaluating conditions for successful co-management of subsistence fisheries in KwaZulu-Natal, South Africa. *Environmental Conservation* 32: 165-77.

NRTEE. 1998. *Sustainable strategies for oceans: A co-management guide*. Ottawa: National Round Table on the Environment and the Economy.

Olsson, P., and C. Folke. 2001. Local ecological knowledge and institutional dynamics for ecosystem management: A study of Lake Racken watershed, Sweden. *Ecosystems* 4: 85-104.

Olsson, O., C. Folke, and F. Berkes. 2004. Adaptive co-management for building resilience in social-ecological systems. *Environmental Management* 34 (1): 75-90.

Ostrom, E. 1990. *Governing the commons: The evolution of institutions for collective action*. Cambridge: Cambridge University Press.

Ostrom, E., J. Burger, C.B. Field, R.B. Norgaard, and D. Policansky. 1999. Revisiting the commons: Local lessons, global challenges. *Science* 284: 278-82.

Pahl-Wostl, C., and M. Hare. 2004. Processes of social learning in integrated resources management. *Journal of Community and Applied Social Psychology* 14: 193-206.

Pierre, J.B., and G. Peters, eds. 2000. *Governance, politics and the state*. Basingstoke, UK: Macmillan.

Pinkerton, E., ed. 1989. *Co-operative management of local fisheries: New directions for improved management and community development*. Vancouver: UBC Press.

–. 1992. Translating legal rights into management practice: Overcoming barriers to the exercise of co-management. *Human Organization* 51: 330-41.

–. 2003. Toward specificity in complexity: Understanding co-management from a social science perspective. In *The fisheries co-management experience: Accomplishments, challenges, and prospects*, ed. D.C. Wilson, J.R. Nielson, and P. Degnbol, 61-77. Dordrecht, Netherlands: Kluwer Academic Publishers.

Pinto da Silva, P. 2004. From common property to co-management: Lessons from Brazil's first marine extractive reserve. *Marine Policy* 28: 419-28.

Plummer, R., and J. FitzGibbon. 2004. Some observations on the terminology in co-operative environmental management. *Journal of Environmental Management* 70: 63-72.

Pomeroy, R.S. 1995. Community-based and co-management institutions for sustainable coastal fisheries management in Southeast Asia. *Ocean and Coastal Management* 27: 143-62.

Pomeroy, R.S., and F. Berkes. 1997. Two to tango: The role of government in fisheries co-management. *Marine Policy* 21: 465-80.

Pomeroy, R.S., P. McConney, and R. Mahon. 2004. Comparative analysis of coastal resource management in the Caribbean. *Ocean and Coastal Management* 47: 429-47.

Pretty, J., and H. Ward. 2001. Social capital and the environment. *World Development* 29: 209-27.

Reid, W.V., F. Berkes, T. Wilbanks, and D. Capistrano, eds. 2006. *Bridging scales and knowledge systems: Linking global science and local knowledge in assessments*. Washington, DC: Millennium Ecosystem Assessment and Island Press.

Rhodes, R.A.W. 1997. *Understanding governance: Policy networks, governance, reflexivity and accountability*. Buckingham, UK: Open University Press.

Ruitenbeek, J., and C. Cartier. 2001. *The invisible wand: Adaptive co-management as an emergent strategy in complex bio-economic systems*. Occasional paper no. 34. Bogor, Indonesia: Center for International Forestry Research. http://www.cifor.cgiar.org.

Sachs, W. 2002. Fairness in a fragile world: The Johannesburg agenda. *Development* 45 (3): 12-17.

Singleton, S. 1998. *Constructing cooperation: The evolution of institutions of comanagement*. Ann Arbor: University of Michigan Press.

Steins, N.A. 1999. All hands on deck: An interactive perspective on complex common-pool resources management based on case studies in the coastal waters of the Isle of Wight (UK), Connemara (Ireland), and the Dutch Wadden Sea. PhD dissertation, Wageningen University, Netherlands.

Taiepa, T., P. Lyver, P. Horsley, J. Davis, M. Bragg, and H. Moller. 1997. Co-management of New Zealand's conservation estate by Mâori and Pakeha: A review. *Environmental Conservation* 24: 236-50.

Tompkins, E., W.N. Adger, and K. Brown. 2002. Institutional networks for inclusive coastal management in Trinidad and Tobago. *Environment and Planning A* 34: 1095-1111.

United Nations. 2002. World summit on sustainable development plan of implementation. Johannesburg. http://www.johannesburgsummit.org/html/documents.

Wenger, E. 1998. *Communities of practice: Learning, meaning and identity.* Cambridge: Cambridge University Press.

Wilson, D.C., J. Nielsen, and P. Degnbol, eds. 2003. *The fisheries co-management experience: Accomplishments, challenges, and prospects.* Dordrecht, Netherlands: Kluwer Academic Publishers.

Young, O. 2002. *The institutional dimensions of environmental change: Fit, interplay and scale.* Cambridge, MA: MIT Press.

3
Connecting Adaptive Co-Management, Social Learning, and Social Capital through Theory and Practice

Ryan Plummer and John FitzGibbon

The practice of resource management, once reserved for technically trained specialists, has broadened considerably to involve a consortium of potential partners, including resource users, Aboriginal persons, private businesses, and citizens. Decentralization and/or devolution have become norms in the domain of resource management in Canada (Pinkerton 1999) and around the world (Ribot 2002).

These changes should not be surprising to resource theorists, given the recent proclivity to regard social-ecological systems as both dynamic and coupled. Berkes and Folke (1998, 2) observe that "tools and approaches for such people management are poorly developed, and the importance of social science of resource management has not generally been recognized." Acknowledging the significance of social relationships is emerging in common property (e.g., Ostrom 2001), environmental governance (e.g., Jiggins and Röling 2000), and sustainable development (e.g., Robinson 2004).

Co-management emerged in the early 1990s as a concept that reflected increasing interest in sharing the rights and responsibilities associated with managing natural resources (Pinkerton 1989; Berkes et al. 1991). Co-management has been the topic of a rich tapestry of dialogue. As signalled by the title of this volume, the time has come to move beyond the critiques of co-management to examine the core constructs of adaptive co-management.

Conceptual development in co-management is an appropriate place to start this chapter because it clearly establishes the importance of social considerations. Plummer and FitzGibbon (2004) have proposed a conceptual framework of co-management. In this framework, co-management is contextualized by particular resources, property rights regimes, and claims to those property rights. It is also viewed as involving three components – antecedent or preconditions, characteristics, and outcomes (Plummer and FitzGibbon 2004). These authors' work reinforces "the holistic and process qualities of co-management by acknowledging the social context and the nature of the resources concerned. It also raises the profile of co-management as a social process" (Plummer and FitzGibbon 2004, 883).

Adaptive management (Holling 1978; Walters 1986) further underscores the social nature of co-management and makes apparent its potential as an effective governance regime for social-ecological systems. Three working definitions of adaptive co-management are presented in the first chapter of this book. Adaptive co-management is therefore understood to include learning-by-doing, integrating multiple knowledge systems, emphasizing flexibility of management structures, and advancing collaboration through power sharing at multiple scales. As set out in Chapter 1, the potential ability of these governance regimes to reorient social-ecological systems towards sustainable trajectories and to robustly function under complex and uncertain circumstances necessitates further inquiry.

In this chapter, we aim to develop an understanding of how adaptive management, social learning, and social capital are connected and to discern why this association is important. The first section introduces and explores the central concepts. The second investigates how these concepts are reflected in three case studies of river management in Ontario. Relationships among the concepts are probed in the third section. The chapter closes with reflections upon future research needs and the implications for practice.

Central Concepts

Social Learning
Parson and Clark (1995) assert that theories of social dynamics are required to complement those of ecosystems if environment and development interactions are to be understood. They, like many others in this burgeoning area of the literature, turn to the process of social learning only to find that the term "conceals great diversity" (Parson and Clark 1995, 429). Diversity is evident in the very roots of social learning traced to John Dewey and his pragmatism philosophy (Friedmann 1987; Paquet 1999). Fundamental tensions between the roles of the individual and society in terms of knowledge creation and validation as well as the normative relationship between a learning public and expert decision makers have endured (Parson and Clark 1995). Theories of learning are diverse and have focused on the individual (neurological and psychological theories) (e.g., Skinner 1974; Bandura 1977), co-determination involving the individual and his or her environment (e.g., Giddens 1984), social aggregates or collectives such as formal organizations (e.g., Levitt and March 1988), and evolutionary thinking (e.g., Parson and Clark 1995). Where is social learning situated in environmental management in relation to this broad array of learning theories?

Social learning in environmental management takes an integrative perspective in which learning is viewed as a meaningful concept that is applicable to the full range of scales (Parson and Clark 1995; Diduck et al. 2005). It is defined as "the collective action and reflection that occurs among different individuals and groups as they work to improve the management of human and environment interrelations" (Keen et al. 2005, 4). Wenger's (1998) social theory of learning further develops the "synthetic perspective." He positions the social theory of learning at the intersection of four intellectual traditions. The central vertical axis represents the tension between theories of social structure, which stress cultural systems and institutions, and theories of situated experience, which emphasize the dynamic interactions among people and their environments. He places theories of practice and theories of identity at the poles of the horizontal axis to mediate the extremes of the vertical axis. Consequently, he views the social theory of learning as occurring though engagement (actions and interactions) that is embedded in social structures and that is also a mechanism for developing practice and transforming identities.

Conceptualizing social learning in environmental management has recently received considerable attention and is regarded by Diduck (2004) as an emerging perspective. Colleagues of Niels Röling employ the metaphor of a "wheelbarrow full of frogs" to capture the image of multiple actors coming together and interrelating in a new environment that is dynamic and unpredictable but that also offers an "elevated platform" from which different situation appraisals are possible (see Leeuwis and Pyburn 2002). Maarleveld and Dangbégnon (2002) conceptualize that social learning incorporates multiple perspectives, is concerned about people and the environment, involves "sense making" through action and reflection, and is oriented towards systems thinking. Particularly interesting is the parallel they draw between Holling's ecosystem renewal cycle and the social learning perspective as a dynamic process. King and Jiggins (2002) start from the premise that purposeful and systematic means are required to manage change processes in complex environments. They offer a systematic model to guide the facilitation of social learning based on five theories of the process of cognition. Their work connects to the efforts of Argyris and Schön (1974), who assert that single-loop (correcting errors from routines) and double-loop (correcting errors through examination of values and policies) learning are required in all organizations. They add to this the idea of triple-loop learning, which involves the design of norms and protocols that govern the two types of learning above (King and Jiggins 2002). Diduck (2004) builds on the theory of action perspective (outlined above; see also Argyris and Schön 1978) to include the civics approach. Social learning in the civics approach is interactive and integrative, with an emphasis on participatory dialogue, validity of multiple knowledge systems, and adaptive requirements of decision-making processes (Diduck 2004). Most recently, Keen and colleagues (2005, 7-18) weave together five braided strands (reflection, system orientation, integration, negotiation, participation) that interact, overlap, and have individual importance. They make the important connection between participation typologies in environmental management and multiple-loop learning (Keen et al. 2005, 15-16; see also Diduck 2004).

Social learning has also been specifically associated with co-management. Pinkerton (2003) connects the idea of social learning to the involvement of multiple horizontal negotiations, which are a key aspect of complete co-management. Schusler and colleagues (2003) specifically investigated social learning at the Lake Ontario Islands Search Conference and found that deliberation that enables social learning contributed to the development of a common purpose and fostered collaborative relationships, which are two requisites for co-management. Diduck and colleagues (2005) unpack the concept of social learning and expand upon the theory of action framework (see Argyris and Schön 1978) of social learning to investigate case studies of polar bear and narwhal management. They make the important observation that "learning occurs at both individual and social levels, but individuals are the agents for social collectives. Therefore, social learning does not occur until individuals encode what they have learned in social memory" (Diduck et al. 2005, 271). Their analysis of these cases found that learning was shaped by enabling political and institutional frameworks, willingness to experiment and openness to risk, and changing worldview and knowledge integration. Attributes of the social learning frameworks presented in the environmental management and co-management literature are summarized in Table 3.1.

Although social learning has been identified as a way to move forward in environmental management, the concept is also criticized. Parson and Clark (1995) observe that the term "social learning" often means very different things to different people. Situating social learning within the broader learning and environmental management contexts clarifies our employment but also makes clear theoretical tensions surrounding the concepts. Wenger (1998) positions the social theory of learning at the intersection of eight intellectual traditions. Keen and colleagues (2005) caution that the effectiveness of the approach somewhat hinges on the responsiveness of social organizations and structures in order to avoid administrative, competency, bureaucratic, and legitimacy traps. This observation was confirmed in the cases studied by Diduck and colleagues (2005). Others (Friedmann 1987; Paquet 1999) argue that the rationalistic basis of the approach is idealistic and that the consensual basis of knowledge as a social product to which access and competence are equal is unrealistic and utopian.

Table 3.1

Attributes associated with social learning in environmental management

Attribute	Description
Interaction, inclusion, and negotiations	Social learning occurs through interactions. Deliberative or face-to-face interactions are highlighted. All interested entities and those with a stake in the results need to be involved in the process of negotiation.
Systems orientation	The process of social learning involves making connections between people and the environment.
Integration	Innovation stems from diverse perspectives, approaches, and sources of information and knowledge.
Reflection and reflexivity	Action orientation involves diagnosis, designing, doing (undertaking shared collective action), and evaluating.
Learning	Mechanisms of reflection (critical thinking) facilitate different types of learning from action. Multiple-loop learning enables questioning of underlying values and fosters transformation.

Sources: Attributes are synthesized from Friedmann (1987); Woodhill and Röling (1998); Leeuwis and Pyburn (2002); Maarleveld and Dangbégnon (2002); King and Jiggins (2002); Diduck (2004); Diduck et al. (2005); Keen et al. (2005).

Social Capital

Bourdieu (1986), Coleman (1990), and Putnam (1993, 1995) are largely credited with developing and using the concept of social capital, although they did so in very different ways (King and Waldegrave 2003; St. Clair 2005). Although all three focused on social structure, Bourdieu (1986) utilized the term to explain the manner in which social forces reinforce hierarchical positions within the capitalist system; Coleman (1990) largely concentrated on functional aspects of social capital and its ability to increase human capital; and Putnam (1995) employed the concept to argue that the quality of democracy was threatened by declining civic participation. Despite the fact that social capital has been diversely developed and employed, the popularity of this notion is evidenced by its rapid adoption into the academic lexicon; Ostrom and Ahn (2003) identify an increase from 2 citations on the Web of Science index in 1991 to 220 in 2001.

So what is social capital? The Organisation for Economic Cooperation and Development (OECD) defines social capital as "networks together with shared norms, values and understanding that facilitate co-operation within or among groups" (2001, 41). Social capital consists of structural (objective) elements of networks that are necessary for transformation, as well as experiential (subjective) components (such as norms, values, and shared understanding) that shape social relationships (Wall et al. 2000; OECD 2001). Ostrom and Ahn (2003) highlight enhancement of trust as a critical link between the forms of social capital and successful collective action.

Social capital is also observed to have multiple dimensions or forms, including bridging, bonding, and linkages. The bonding form occurs among family, friends, and very close acquaintances, where a considerable relationship already exists; bridging extends from this close group outward to friends, colleagues, and other individuals or groups in the community; and linkages, which often focus on issues of power, pertain to the ability of an individual and/or group to leverage resources (Onyx and Bullen 2000; OECD 2001; Woolcock 2001; Leonard and Onyx 2003; Newman and Dale 2005; Dale and Onyx 2005). Newman and Dale (2005) observe that these types of connections are not equal. Onyx and her colleagues have examined bonding and bridging ties in actor networks to illustrate the complexities of these connections and the importance of discriminating among them as they ultimately influence successful problem engagement abilities (Leonard and Onyx 2003; Newman and Dale 2005; Dale and Onyx 2005).

While social capital has immense intuitive appeal, adaptation as an analytical device is complicated by diverse conceptualizations, varied empirical employment, and the fact that it is recognized as a positive and a negative good in human societies. Rudd (2000, 136) observes that "many of the academic debates over social capital result from issues of (1) the narrow definition of social capital constructed by a number of political scientists (e.g., Putnam 1993; Fukuyama 1995) and (2) the nature of endogeneity between social interactions, trust and economic and political performance." Brown (2001) describes the endogenous/exogenous debate as a "chicken or egg" argument and simply advocates acknowledgment of it as problematic and requiring examination.

Approaches for measuring social capital are not uniform (Van Der Gaag and Snijders 2005) and are criticized in the social capital literature (see Ostrom and Ahn 2003). Survey information and census data on volunteer participation or civic engagement is one avenue pursued (see Putnam 2001; OECD 2001; Onyx and Bullen 2000; Keele 2005) and has led to the adoption of social capital scales and instruments by international organizations (such as the World Bank) and governments (such as the Government of Canada). Others have employed qualitative inquiries (see Wall et al. 2000; Woolcock 2001; Plummer and FitzGibbon 2006). Still others have attempted to combine quantitative and qualitative measures through the use of indicators (see Wall et al. 2000; Woolcock 2001). The combined approach is supported by the OECD, which has suggested that "measures of social capital should be as comprehensive as possible in their coverage of key dimensions (networks, values and norms); and ii) balanced between attitudinal or subjective elements on the one hand (e.g., reported levels of trust) and behavioral aspects on the other (e.g., membership of associations and extent of social ties)" (2001, 43). Indicators that reflect social capital are synthesized in Table 3.2.

Table 3.2

Indicators of social capital

Nature of indicator	Indicator	Operational definition
Objective or structural	Networks	Membership, participation, and/or contributions to informal or formal organizations. Composite measures may include stability, homogeneity, and/or volunteer associations. Bonding, bridging, and linking ties are particularly important. *Example:* Belonging to a local conservation organization.
Subjective or experiential	Shared values and shared understanding	Elements (psychological) that facilitate social transactions. Shared feelings as to what is important or valuable and why it holds prominence. *Example:* Importance of protecting groundwater for drinking.
	Social norms	Elements (behavioural) of acceptable, expected, or desirable behaviours that are generally understood. May involve sanctions if violated. *Examples:* Trustworthiness and reciprocity.

Sources: Indicators are synthesized from Putnam (1995, 2001); Onyx and Bullen (2000); Wall et al. (2000); Woolcock and Narayan (2000); OECD (2001); Pretty and Ward (2001); Ostrom and Ahn (2003); Keele (2005); Van Der Gaag and Snijders (2005).

The novelty of and interest in social capital is largely due to the overwhelmingly positive outcomes (e.g., source of social control, family support, benefits via extrafamilial networks) almost exclusively associated with the concept (Portes 1998). Most pertinent to this chapter is the incorporation of social capital into the domain of natural resources. Newman and Dale (2005, 479) observe that, "despite a lack of detail on how it does so, there is a general intuitive sense that social capital strengthens communities and specifically that it is a necessary ingredient for sustainable community development." The connection between social capital and natural resource management is becoming increasingly well established (see Rudd 2000; Pretty and Ward 2001). Central to this is Ostrom's work that clearly connects social capital as well as, more narrowly, trust and reciprocity and second-generation collective action theories (see Ostrom and Ahn 2003; Ostrom and Walker 2003). Ostrom and Ahn (2003, xvi) explain that "in real-world collective-action situations, the success and failure of collective action is determined not by any single factor but by a complex configuration of various factors that we categorize as forms of social capital."

The applicability of social capital to co-management is incorporated by Pinkerton (2003) in her discussion of horizontal negotiations in complete co-management. The notion of social capital was used by Plummer and Arai (2005) to explore opportunities and barriers for working with citizen volunteers in co-management. Work by Plummer and FitzGibbon (2006) is most directly related to this chapter, as they specifically examine the contributions, forms, and functions of social capital relative to the emergence of co-management. In synthesizing their findings, they advance a theoretical model of social capital in the co-management process that consists of three stages. In the first, "unarticulated" stage, each actor type (e.g., landowners, stakeholders, government agency representatives) has an amount of inherent social capital with similar actors and with other types of actors. Through interactions, social capital develops in the "formulation" stage; it is duly recognized that this process is cyclical and that the level of social capital as well as affinity for bonding and bridging is influenced by past experiences. After a critical amount of social capital develops, the actors enter the "conjoint" stage, in which they are willing to undertake shared actions. According to Plummer and FitzGibbon (2006), it is in this final stage that co-management emerges and social capital continues to increase.

An important counter-current is emerging that calls attention to the negative consequences of social capital. Portes (1998) holds that it is important to acknowledge these negative consequences to avoid presenting such networks as unmixed blessings and to avoid moralizing statements. He accordingly recognizes that negative consequences may include "exclusion of outsiders, excessive claims on group members, restrictions on individual freedoms, and downward leveling norms" (15). Newman and Dale (2005, 2007) assert that the amount of social capital itself is a weak indicator, and they focus on the ability of a community to convert social capital into action (called agency). Central to their critique is the need to discriminate between bonding and bridging connections. Bonding connections may hinder innovation if they restrict needed information, foster social norms that depress improvement, and limit the acceptance of outsiders. Newman and Dale (2005, 2007) connect homophily (the tendency of similar actors to group together and for groups to increase in similarity over time) to the reduction of bridging ties, which may ultimately result in the loss of agency.

Moreover, caution is required when generalizations are made from success stories in which social capital is the only independent causal factor (Foley and Edwards 1999; Portes and Landolt 2000). Portes and Landolt (2000) observe that a common fallacy in much social capital research is the failure to distinguish correlation from causation.

Exploring a Multiple Case Study of Three River Corridors

This portion of the chapter is analytical and stems from our experiences with developing co-management schemes in three river corridors in Southern Ontario, Canada. It extends our line of research associated with these three cases (see Plummer and Arai 2005; Plummer and FitzGibbon 2006; Plummer 2006). Exploration here is aimed at uncovering how the cases reflect the characteristics of co-management, attributes of social learning, and indicators of social capital.

Box 3.1 outlines the particular nature of the resource and procedures undertaken in conducting the research, and gives a succinct summary of what

---

Box 3.1

Co-management of three Ontario river corridors

Rivers are an important part of Canada's heritage and are a complex resource to manage. Property adjacent to the river (sometimes including the river bottom) is under fee simple ownership. The water and organisms therein are publicly held and resemble attributes of common property (extractability and exclusion). Society in general maintains a keen interest in these resources, and demands being placed upon these river systems are increasingly coming under pressure and are often in conflict. The multi-jurisdictional nature of managing river resources further compounds these complexities. Especially apparent in southern Ontario is tension between demands from the general population and the owners of property adjacent to the resource, who can limit access.

Given the increasing demands being placed on river corridors, there is a need to find innovative solutions for their management. A multiple case study design was employed and interventions consistent with co-management theory were initiated by the researchers in three different river corridors. The researchers sought to foster co-management agreements in similar socio-political contexts. To do this, they selected three cases in relative geographical proximity that were entirely voluntary in nature, focused on discernible river reaches (about 15 kilometres in length), and addressed issues on rivers that were ecologically healthy. All actors (landowners, stakeholders, and government agencies) were contacted, interviewed (264 interviews in total), and invited to participate in the process (39 formal meetings). The researchers then facilitated an initial meeting of the actors to discuss the important qualities of the river and the pressing issues that the interviews identified. If the actors expressed an interest in meeting again, the researchers facilitated additional meetings. A very succinct overview of each case is provided. Pseudonyms (Little River, Main River, Eaden River) are used to refer to the cases, in compliance with the University of Guelph's research ethics procedures.

In the Little River case, relatively few people who originally expressed interest in participation did so; some even expressed opposition to the initiatives. Although participants generally expressed similar positive attitudes towards the integrity of the natural resource, they had different understandings of associated rights and responsibilities. Dialogue pertaining to these different perspectives was a major preoccupation during the first two meetings, particularly between landowners and government agencies. At the request of the group, the researchers developed and implemented a water quality workshop. The group also extended invitations to meet through the local paper, and requested guest speakers to make presentations so group members could better understand what was possible for the group.

Commitment to environmental integrity and heritage of the river were strongly shared values in the Main River case. Although participants shared similar values, landowners and some stakeholders clearly articulated skepticism about such initiatives due to previous experiences of working with government agencies and angling groups. Despite this skepticism, a diverse group formed out of a common concern for the river and repeatedly met to discuss both values and issues related to the river. A local resident and avid angler stepped forward to take a leadership role and facilitated subsequent meetings. The group eventually identified pertinent actions to be undertaken, although these actions were carried out by the resident volunteer and the researchers. Government agencies subsequently secured funding for a coordinator to continue the project.

Participants in the Eaden River case held the river resource in high regard due to robust ecological integrity, considerable recreational opportunities, and the sense of place it provided. Individuals were exuberant at the opportunity to exchange information regarding the river and keen to gather additional information about unique ecological features. Members of the group voluntarily took turns at chairing meetings and acting as the recorder. The group formed an identity and generated terms of reference that set forth their purpose. The already diverse group identified the need to increase the breadth of participants (especially landowners) and hosted a "community" information evening. The group continued to meet monthly and together undertook a number of actions, including generation and delivery of a summary of information about the river to landowners, hosting a series of "community barbeques" to generate interest in the resource, and completing a watershed plan.

occurred in the three case studies. As conveyed in Box 3.1, the same planned intervention in each of the cases resulted in very distinct experiences. A summary of how each case reflected adaptive co-management, social learning, and social capital is provided in Table 3.3.

Similarities and differences among the cases are evident when we compare the extent to which the cases exhibited characteristics of adaptive co-management. All the cases moderately to strongly exhibited the characteristics of pluralism/linkage, communication and negotiation, and transactive decision making. Greater variation is evident in the extent to which they reflected shared commitment and actions and dynamic learning. Shared action undertaken in the Little River and Main River cases was restricted to dialogue. Although some actors took action, knowledge was primarily gained from group meetings in which information was exchanged and values were discussed. The Eaden River case extensively exhibited both of these characteristics. The group collectively undertook many actions (such as contacting landowners and hosting community forums) and shared the consequences of those actions. Dynamic learning was apparent as the actors reflected upon the experience of taking actions and subsequently modified their approach (e.g., having landowners contact other landowners).

Attributes of social learning were also reflected in each of the cases. Interpersonal dialogue among interested actors in the Little River case focused on exchanging perspectives. These participants also expressed a desire to improve their understanding of systems by attending a water quality workshop and inviting guest speakers. To some degree, attributes of integration and learning were also exhibited; for example, citizens and the administrator of the local watershed agency engaged in dialogue regarding the "authority" for the resource, which led to an enhanced understanding of a different perspective on the issue (perspective taking). While such exchanges certainly demonstrate some degree of reflection and learning, the actors in the Little River case did not undertake shared action or critical reflection. Single- and double-loop learning was evident at an individual scale.

The Main River case similarly exhibited the attributes of social learning. The inclusive nature of the group and interactions among the actors permitted considerable dialogue around shared values. Multiple perspectives were clearly evident, as First Nations representatives, landowners, government agency representatives, and stakeholders acknowledged their shared interest in betterment of the riparian system. Many different actions were undertaken in Main River, but implementation was limited to the researchers and one fisheries representative. Nor were these actions reflected upon. Single- and double-loop learning were evident, again at an individual scale.

The Eaden River case exhibited all of the attributes associated with social learning in abundance. The group was inclusive early on and continued to encourage others to join. Recognizing the benefits and the need for multiple

Table 3.3

Analysis summary

	Core concepts		Case studies		
Characteristics	Description	Little River	Main River	Eaden River
Adaptive co-management					
Pluralism/linkage	Inclusion of diverse interests and representation of multiple scales in the process.	A few main types of interests were represented (e.g., fisheries, tourism, ecosystem health). Local and provincial scale were represented.	Initial interest from fisheries. Interests diversified with time. Multiple scales were represented.	Considerable diversity of interests, which became broader. Multiple scales were represented.
Communication and negotiation	Information exchange that leads to shared understanding or agreement.	Information was reciprocally exchanged. Shared understanding was limited.	Information was reciprocally exchanged. Shared understanding developed around fisheries, landowner, and management issues.	Information was reciprocally exchanged. Shared understanding was quickly reached regarding issues of river health.
Transactive decision making	Decisions achieved through dialogue involving diverse inputs or knowledge systems.	Decisions were made through dialogue. Diversity was limited.	Input from non-fisheries actors was initially limited. Consensus process developed with time.	Resource agencies initially influenced process. All transactive elements emerged.

▲

▼ Table 3.3

	Core concepts		Case studies		
	Characteristics	Description	Little River	Main River	Eaden River
Adaptive co-management	Shared commitment/action	Actors jointly committed to undertake and share the consequences of actions.	Shared actions were not undertaken or committed to.	Shared actions were limited to advising and meeting.	Group repeatedly undertook shared actions and jointly accepted the consequences.
	Dynamic learning	Knowledge gained by learning from actions and making modifications (experimenting).	Limited to gaining knowledge from meetings.	Limited to gaining knowledge from meetings.	Reflecting upon actions was evident and modifications were made to the approach (e.g., letter writing).

	Core concepts		Case studies		
	Attributes	Description	Little River	Main River	Eaden River
	Interaction, inclusion, and negotiation	Inclusive interpersonal dialogue exchanging perspectives.	Deliberative interactions were undertaken.	Deliberative interactions were undertaken.	Deliberative interactions were undertaken.
			All interested entities were involved.	All interested entities were involved.	Other potential actors were actively encouraged to attend.

System orientation	Connecting people and the environment.	Human interests were acknowledged and relationship to the natural environment was recognized.	Human interests were acknowledged and relationship to the natural environment was recognized.	Human interests were acknowledged and strong relationship to the natural environment was emphasized.
Integration	Innovation comes from diverse sources of information and knowledge.	Diverse sources of information were acknowledged but not pursued.	Multiple sources of information were recognized. Efforts to gain new knowledge were made, but largely from technical perspective.	Multiple sources of knowledge were recognized. Information acquisition and dissemination were initiated. Some attempt to incorporate multiple knowledge systems (e.g., local knowledge) was made.
Reflection and reflexivity	Action orientation to modifying procedures.	Some reflection was evident. No procedure modification based on actions.	Some reflection was evident. No procedure modification based on actions.	Clear and repeated evidence of reflection and reflexivity (e.g., approaching landowners).
Learning	Different types of learning fostered through action (multiple-loop learning).	Single-loop and double-loop learning were evident at an individual scale.	Single-loop and double-loop learning were evident at an individual scale.	Multiple-loop learning was evident at individual and collective scales.

▲ Table 3.3

	Core concepts		Case studies		
Indicator	Description	Little River	Main River	Eaden River
Social capital — Networks	Participation and/or con-tributions to informal and formal groups. Bonding, bridging, and linking ties are important forms.	Limited evidence of networks beyond net-works of landowners and anglers.	Some extensive networks were apparent (fisheries, landowners) with strong bonds.	A myriad of existing networks (formal and informal).
		Strong bonds among landowners discouraged participation (bridging).	Bridging ties appeared to slowly develop.	Strong bonding ties, which increased in strength.
		Concerns were expressed about authority.	Fisheries group was successful at leveraging resources, while other actors expressed con-cern about power.	Cognizant attempt to foster bridging ties.
				Successful linkages were formed and resources leveraged.
Shared values and shared understanding	Elements (psychological) that facilitate social transactions.	Some shared values were expressed.	Diversity of values was evident initially.	Common values of ecological integrity were immediately evident and subsequently codified in group mission.
	Shared appreciation for what is coveted and why.	Shared understanding developed over time.	Shared understanding developed around river corridor health and recreation.	Shared understanding deepened with time.

| Social norms | Elements (behavioural) of desirable actions that are generally understood. May involve sanctions if violated. | Clear tension evident among actors (stakeholders and landowners versus government) due to violation of trustworthiness. | The norm of cooperation was clearly evident between anglers and fisheries managers.

Landowners and other stakeholders expressed violation of trustworthiness towards others. | Collaborative action was a behavioural norm.

Group behaviours developed and strengthened with time. |

Sources: Evidence of adaptive co-management and social capital from these cases is adapted from Plummer and FitzGibbon (2006). Characteristics of adaptive co-management are synthesized from Plummer and FitzGibbon (2004); Ruitenbeek and Cartier (2001); Berkes (2004); Olsson et al. (2004); and Chapter 1 of this book.

perspectives and multiple knowledge sources, the group purposefully undertook activities such as community barbeques to encourage landowners to participate and share information with those having technical expertise pertaining to the river, such as aquatic ecologists. Although, during the first few meetings, the group extensively discussed values and shared information, they eventually coalesced around concerns for the river corridor system and moved towards undertaking action together and often used subgroups to do so. The initial action of writing a letter of introduction to landowners presented many challenges (e.g., different perspectives on what should be included, who should sign the letter, and so on); it also provided an opportunity for group reflection in which those in the subgroup expressed a need for the members to trust each other as they were working towards the same goal. Undertaking subsequent actions appeared easier as the group learned how to work together.

Social capital was also found in all three cases; however, notable variations were observed in both the presence of social capital as well as the forms it took among the three cases. Participants in the Little River case shared similar values but had different understandings of rights and responsibilities associated with the resource. Failure by government agencies to follow through violated normative standards and resulted in landowners' sharply questioning the authenticity of commitments by government representatives. The bonding form of social capital appeared to both encourage and discourage participation; relatively little bridging occurred and resources were not leveraged. This is consistent with research by Newman and Dale (2005, 2007), who recognize that the presence of strong bonding social capital often precludes bridging. Considerable networks of individuals were evident who shared similar values in the Main River. Previous experiences of participants with government agencies and other stakeholders who violated trustworthiness and reciprocity norms discouraged participation of some actors. Bonding was particularly strong in the networks of anglers, bridging was extended to include landowners and citizens at large, and resources were extensively leveraged by government agencies. In the Eaden River case, values were strongly shared among all participants, an abundance of well-established networks were immediately evident, and norms were developed through extensive face-to-face interactions that guided the functioning of the group. Bonds were observed to increase in strength as the group undertook shared actions; bridging connections were actively explored on an ongoing basis; and contributions of time, knowledge, and money were leveraged by the group.

Connecting Adaptive Co-Management, Social Learning, and Social Capital

So why are social learning and social capital important to adaptive co-management? Attention here shifts to connecting the major concepts in this paper. Literature reviewed in the first section and insights gained from the case studies in the second section form the basis on which we develop an initial understating of this relationship.

An appropriate starting point is to recognize that considerable overlap exists among the concepts. This is easily accounted for as all three concepts are situated within an environmental management framework that is "integrative, participatory, and adaptive" (see Diduck 2004; Keen et al. 2005, 6). The overarching goals of pursuing sustainable trajectories and fostering collective action are also associated with adaptive co-management (see Chapter 1), social learning (Diduck 2004; Keen et al. 2005), and social capital (Pretty and Ward 2001; Ostrom and Ahn 2003; Newman and Dale 2005; Dale and Onyx 2005). As a consequence of this shared orientation, four elements (interaction, dialogue, pluralism, and linkages) appear to cut across the core concepts presented in Table 3.3. This orientation is confirmed by Diduck's connection (2004) between social learning and the civics approach to environmental management. Another substantial area of overlap is between the dynamic learning characteristic of adaptive co-management and the core component of social learning.

The second portion of this chapter documented how three cases (Little River, Main River, and Eaden River) reflected the characteristics of adaptive co-management, attributes of social learning, and indicators of social capital. As summarized in Table 3.3, each case exhibited the core concepts in a correlated fashion. The Little River case reflected each of the concepts minimally, the Main River case exhibited each moderately, and the Eaden River case reflected all the core concepts strongly. The common orientation and overlap described above makes the correlated expression of the core concepts unsurprising. This does not explain why the cases reflected the core concepts to varying degrees.

To answer the question posed at the start of this section, we examine more closely the functional relationship among the core concepts. According to Schusler and colleagues (2003), deliberation that enables social learning can ultimately contribute to collaborative relationships. Falk and Harrison (1998) assert that learning consists of process and outcome components. The process component of learning permits interaction among individuals, which is a prerequisite for the development of social capital; it also develops understanding (through exchange of values and information) and embeds social learning in the larger structure (Kilpatrick et al. 2001; Kilpatrick 2002, 2003). The link to social capital is also made explicit as a product of the learning process and as a contributor to it (Kilpatrick et al. 1999). This leads Eames (2005, 87) to observe that "making ideas of social capital part of social learning process is a critical part of environmental management." Pinkerton connects this line of thinking to co-management. She instructs that "in the best circumstances, this social capital continues to contribute to evolving improvements in joint problem solving in the watershed, which is likely to be the place where 'social learning' occurs and is maintained because the processes are embedded in communities of place" (2003, 70). Where there is evidence of ongoing or continuous social learning, then, social capital may be produced and/or increased, and a group or network may be open to new ideas and become adaptive.

In each of the case studies, a space for deliberation was created by the researchers. As the actors came together, they began to identify issues, discuss values, and exchange information. The process of developing shared understanding was iterative, reflects many of the attributes of social learning (Table 3.1), and appears to also be connected to the development of social capital, which also intensified with subsequent iterations (see Box 3.1 and Table 3.3). This reinforces Newman and Dale's important observation (2005, 2007) that interactions may increase the density of network formation. It is also consistent with research by Plummer and FitzGibbon (2006), which found that iterative interactions among actors lead to the development of social capital. The bonding form of social capital was exhibited in each of the cases. In the case of Little River, strong bonds among landowners led to the active discouragement of bridging with other actors. Social capital is observed to be easily destroyed (fungible), in this case due to several landowners' negative experiences in the past. In the case of Eaden River, it is bridging social capital in particular that fostered the making of connections, forging of linkages, and leveraging of resources. This disjunction between bridging and bonding has been observed to be critical to movement from "getting by" to "getting ahead" (see Woolcock and Narayan 2000; Leonard and Onyx 2003).

While the Little River and Main River cases reflect some of the characteristics of adaptive co-management, the Eaden River case moved the furthest, as it clearly displays all the characteristics of adaptive co-management (see Table 3.3.). In this case, social learning (specifically, reflection and reflexivity, and multiple-loop learning; see Table 3.1) became embedded in the very structure of the group. This confirms that learning may occur at both individual and social levels, but that individuals must encode what they have learned into the memory of the group before learning occurs at a collective level (Diduck 2004; Diduck et al. 2005). As an outcome of this process, the strength of social capital also continued to grow and function extensively (bonding, bridging, and leveraging).

Extending the logic presented by Schusler and colleagues (2003), we contend that deliberation that enables social learning may produce social capital, both of which are requisite for adaptive co-management. Plummer and FitzGibbon's explanation (2006) of co-management achievement using social capital is therefore enriched and extended through the incorporation of social learning. Social learning is inextricably linked to social capital through process and product outcomes (see Kilpatrick et al. 2001; Kilpatrick 2002, 2003). There is also an important connection between the ability of a group to engage in social learning and the diversity of contacts critical to social capital (Dale and Onyx 2005).

Research Needs and Potential Pragmatic Implications

The novelty of this chapter lies in its breadth. Adaptive co-management, social learning, and social capital are three complicated and overlapping areas of environmental management literature. The case studies presented demonstrate that they may be even more intertwined in practice. In answering the central question posed in this chapter, we assert that deliberation that enables social learning may produce social capital, both of which are requisites for adaptive co-management.

We prefaced our understanding of these connections with the term "initial" to convey that exploration of social learning and social capital in this specific context is in its infancy. Parson and Clark (1995) contend that we should expect neither simple nor unambiguous answers when exploring this territory. Keen and colleagues (2005, 264) employ the analogy of a spider's web to convey the "many different components all interacting and affecting movements towards social action and change." While Parson and Clark's call (1995) for more case studies of social learning in environmental management has been answered somewhat, there is a need to document specific experiences with adaptive co-management.

We concur with Berkes and Folke's assertion (1998) that it is fundamentally important to recognize and pursue social science inquiry in natural resources management. This is a vast and fertile soil worthy of careful cultivation. Social learning and social capital highlight the need to study the interpersonal and constructed nature of the making of resource decisions. The need to examine the structure and connection of networks has been identified by Brown (2001) and Dale and Onyx (2005). While we demonstrate connections among adaptive co-management, social learning, and social capital, we avoid claiming causation due to the litany of other potential factors. Diduck and colleagues (2005, 285-86), for example, recognize other mechanisms/conditions that shape the learning process, including a political and institutional framework that enables conflict to be addressed, an inclination to experiment and an openness towards risk, and the incorporation (integration) of multiple knowledge sources and frameworks. Investigations may also consider how a particular network "is embedded in a system of political economy, and embedded in greater cultural or normative systems" (Brown 2001, 2).

Connecting adaptive co-management, social learning, and social capital also has implications for practice. Pinkerton (1989, 29) observes that "the successful operation of co-management ultimately rests on the relationships among human actors." Facilitating such interactions presents a formidable challenge as stakeholders have considerably diverse interests and values. If adaptive co-management is viewed as a process, and much evidence suggests that it should be (e.g., Olsson et al. 2004), then resource managers need to understand that they may well need to facilitate social interactions that, on the surface, appear to only superficially address resource issues. Models for facilitating social learning (e.g., King and Jiggins 2002) may have tremendous implications for adaptive co-management. Resource managers must also recognize that most participants enter the co-management process with previous experiences and values that may be either positive or negative and that will shape the process (Schusler et al. 2003; Plummer and Arai 2005; Plummer and FitzGibbon 2006). Connections among the core concepts highlight the potential for societal transformation to occur, as the values upon which governance systems are predicated are critically questioned through the process of multiple-loop learning. We end by echoing Pinkerton's observation (2003, 70-71) of the "potential of co-management to stimulate broader reforms toward more participatory democracy in civil society."

References

Argyris, C., and D. Schön. 1974. *Theory in practice: Increasing professional effectiveness*. San Francisco: Jossey-Bass.

–. 1978. *Organizational learning: A theory of action perspective*. Reading, MA: Addison-Wesley.

Bandura, A. 1977. *Social learning theory*. Englewood Cliffs, NJ: Prentice Hall.

Berkes, F. 2004. Rethinking community-based conservation. *Conservation Biology* 18 (3): 621-30.

Berkes, F., and C. Folke, eds. 1998. *Linking social and ecological systems: Management practices and social mechanisms for building resilience*. Cambridge: Cambridge University Press.

Berkes, F., P.J. George, and R.J. Preston. 1991. The evolution of theory and practice of the joint administration of living resources. *Alternatives* 18 (2): 12-18.

Bourdieu, P. 1986. The forms of capital. In *Handbook of theory and research for the sociology of education*, ed. J. Richardson, 241-58. New York: Greenwood Press.

Brown, T.F. 2001. *Theoretical perspectives on social capital*. http://jhunix.hcf.jhu.edu/~tombrown/Econsoc/soccap.html.

Coleman, J.S. 1990. *Foundations of social theory*. Cambridge, MA: Belknap Press.

Dale, A., and J. Onyx. 2005. *A dynamic balance: Social capital and sustainable community development*. Vancouver: UBC Press.

Diduck, A. 2004. Incorporating participatory approaches and social learning. In *Resource and environmental management in Canada*, 3rd ed., ed. B. Mitchell, 497-527. Don Mills, ON: Oxford University Press.

Diduck, A., N. Bankes, D. Clark, and D. Armitage. 2005. Unpacking social learning in social-ecological systems: Case studies of polar bears and narwhal management in northern Canada. In *Breaking ice: Renewable resource and ocean management*, ed. F. Berkes, R. Huebert, H. Fast, M. Manseau, and A. Diduck, 269-91. Calgary: University of Calgary Press.

Eames, R. 2005. Partnerships in civil society: Linking bridging and bonding social capital. In *Social learning in environmental management*, ed. M. Keen, V.A. Brown, and R. Dyball, 78-91. London: Earthscan.

Falk, I., and L. Harrison. 1998. Community learning and social capital: "Just having a little chat." *Journal of Vocational Education and Training* 50: 609-27.

Foley, M.W., and B. Edwards. 1999. Is it time to divest in social capital? *Journal of Public Policy* 19 (2): 141-73.

Friedmann, J. 1987. *Planning in the public domain: From knowledge to action*. Princeton, NJ: Princeton University Press.

Fukuyama, F. 1995. *Trust: The social virtues and the creation of prosperity*. Toronto: Penguin Books.

Giddens, A. 1984. *The constitution of society*. Berkeley, CA: University of California Press.

Holling, C.S., ed. 1978. *Adaptive environmental assessment and management*. New York: John Wiley and Sons.

Jiggins, J., and N. Röling. 2000. Adaptive management: Potential and limitations for ecological governance. *International Journal of Agricultural Resources: Governance and Ecology* 1 (1): 28-42.

Keele, L. 2005. Macro measures and mechanisms of social capital. *Political Analysis* 13: 139-56.

Keen, M., V.A. Brown, and R. Dyball. 2005. Social learning: A new approach to environmental management. In *Social learning in environmental management*, ed. M. Keen, V.A. Brown, and R. Dyball, 3-21. London: Earthscan.

Kilpatrick, S. 2002. *Learning and building social capital in a community of family farm businesses*. CRLRA Discussion Paper Series ISSN 1440-480X. Launceston, Tasmania: Centre for Research and Learning in Regional Australia.

–. 2003. *Facilitating sustainable resource management: Review of the literature*. CRLRA Discussion Paper Series ISSN 1440-480X. Launceston, Tasmania: Centre for Research and Learning in Regional Australia.

Kilpatrick, S., R. Bell, and I. Falk. 1999. The role of group learning in building social capital. *Journal of Vocational Education and Training* 51 (1): 129-44.

Kilpatrick, S., J. Field, and I. Falk. 2001. Social capital: An analytical tool for exploring lifelong learning and community development. CRLRA Discussion Paper Series ISSN 1440-480X. Launceston, Tasmania: Centre for Research and Learning in Regional Australia.

King, C., and J. Jiggins. 2002. A systematic model and theory for facilitating social learning. In *Wheelbarrows full of frogs*, ed. C. Leeuwis and R. Pyburn, 85-105. Assen, Netherlands: Koninklijke Van Gorcum.

King, P., and C. Waldegrave. 2003. Social capital, social networks, and access to employment. *Horizons* 6 (3): 13-19.

Leeuwis, C., and R. Pyburn. 2002. Social learning in rural resource management. In *Wheelbarrows full of frogs*, ed. C. Leeuwis and R. Pyburn, 11-25. Assen, Netherlands: Koninklijke Van Gorcum.

Leonard, R., and J. Onyx. 2003. Networking through loose and strong ties: An Australian qualitative study. *Voluntas: International Journal of Voluntary and Nonprofit Organizations* 14 (2): 189-203.

Levitt, B., and J.M. March. 1988. Organizational learning. *Annual Review of Sociology* 14: 319-40.

Maarleveld, M., and C. Dangbégnon. 2002. Social learning: Major concepts and issues. In *Wheelbarrows full of frogs*, ed. C. Leeuwis and R. Pyburn, 67-85. Assen, Netherlands: Koninklijke Van Gorcum.

Newman, L., and A. Dale. 2005. The role of agency in sustainable local community development. *Local Environment* 10 (5): 477-86.

–. 2007. Homophily and agency: Creating effective sustainable development networks. *Environment, Development, and Sustainability*, 9: 79-90.

OECD. 2001. *The well-being of nations: The role of human and social capital*. Paris: Organisation for Economic Cooperation and Development.

Olsson, P., C. Folke, and F. Berkes. 2004. Adaptive comanagement for building resilience in social-ecological systems. *Environmental Management* 34 (1): 75-90.

Onyx, J., and P. Bullen. 2000. Measuring social capital in five communities. *Journal of Applied Behavioral Science* 36 (1): 23-42.

Ostrom, E. 2001. Reformulating the commons. In *Protecting the commons,* ed. J. Burger, E. Ostrom, R.B. Norgaard, D. Policansky, and B.D. Goldstein, 17-44. Washington, DC: Island Press.

Ostrom, E., and T.K. Ahn. 2003. Introduction. In *Foundations of social capital,* ed. E. Ostrom and T.K. Ahn, xi-xxxix. Cheltenham, UK: Edward Elgar.

Ostrom, E., and J. Walker. 2003. Introduction. In *Trust and reciprocity,* ed. E. Ostrom and J. Walker, 1-18. New York: Russell Sage Foundation.

Paquet, G. 1999. *Governance through social learning.* Ottawa: University of Ottawa Press.

Parson, E.A., and W.C. Clark. 1995. Sustainable development as social learning: Theoretical perspectives and practical challenges for the design of a research program. In *Barriers and bridges to the renewal of ecosystems and institutions,* ed. L.H. Gunderson, C.S. Holling, and S.S. Light, 428-61. New York: Columbia University Press.

Pinkerton, E. 1989. Attaining better fisheries management through co-management prospects, problems and propositions. In *Co-operative management of local fisheries: New directions for improved management and community development,* ed. E. Pinkerton, 3-33. Vancouver: UBC Press.

–. 1999. Factors in overcoming barriers to implementing co-management in British Columbia salmon fisheries. *Conservation Ecology* 3. http://www.consecol.org/vol3/iss2/art2.

–. 2003. Towards specificity in complexity: Understanding co-management from a social science perspective. In *The fisheries co-management experience: Accomplishments, challenges, and prospects,* ed. D.C. Wilson, J.R. Nielsen, and P. Degnbol, 61-77. Dordrecht, Netherlands: Kluwer Academic Publishers.

Plummer, R. 2006. Sharing the management of a river corridor: A case study of the co-management process. *Society and Natural Resources.* 19: 1-13.

Plummer, R., and S. Arai. 2005. Co-management of natural resources: Opportunities and barriers to working with citizen volunteers. *Environmental Practice* 7 (4): 221-34.

Plummer, R., and J. FitzGibbon. 2004. Co-management of natural resources: A proposed framework. *Environmental Management* 33 (6): 876-85.

–. 2006. People matter: The importance of social capital in the co-management of natural resources. *Natural Resources Forum* 30: 51-62.

Portes, A. 1998. Social capital: Its origins and applications in modern sociology. *Annual Reviews Sociology* 24: 1-24.

Portes, A., and P. Landolt. 2000. Social capital: Promise and pitfalls of its role in development. *Journal of Latin American Studies* 32: 529-47.

Pretty, J., and H. Ward. 2001. Social capital and the environment. *World Development* 29 (2): 209-27.

Putnam, R.D. 1993. *Making democracy work: Civic traditions in modern Italy.* Princeton, NJ: Princeton University Press.

–. 1995. Tuning in, tuning out: The strange disappearance of social capital in America. *Political Science and Politics* 28: 665-83.

Putnam, R. 2001. Social capital measurement and consequences. *ISUMA* 2 (1): 41-51.

Ribot, J.C. 2002. *Democratic decentralization of natural resources.* Washington, DC: World Resources Institute.

Robinson, J. 2004. Squaring the circle? Some thoughts on the idea of sustainable development. *Ecological Economics* 48: 369-84.

Rudd, M.A. 2000. Live long and prosper: Collective action, social capital and social vision. *Ecological Economics* 34: 131-44.

Ruitenbeek, J., and C. Cartier. 2001. *The invisible wand: Adaptive co-management as an emergent strategy in complex bio-economic systems.* Occasional paper no. 34. Bogor, Indonesia: Center for International Forestry Research. http://www.cifor.cgiar.org.

Schusler, T.M., D.J. Decker, and M.J. Pfeffer. 2003. Social learning for collaborative natural resource management. *Society and Natural Resources* 15: 309-26.

Skinner, B.F. 1974. *About behaviorism.* New York: Knopf.

St. Clair, R. 2005. *Introduction to social capital.* Working paper 1. Glasgow: Centre for Research and Development in Adult and Lifelong Learning.

Van Der Gaag, M., and T.A.B. Snijders. 2005. The resource generator: Social capital quantification with concrete items. *Social Networks* 27: 1-29.

Wall, E., D.J. Connell, and T. Fuller. 2000. *Profitable associations: The role of social capital in rural economic development.* Paper presented at the Canadian Employment Research Forum conference, Laurentian University, Sudbury, ON.

Walters, C. 1986. *Adaptive management of renewable resources.* New York: Macmillan.

Wenger, E. 1998. *Communities of practice.* Cambridge: Cambridge University Press.

Woodhill, J., and N.G. Röling. 1998. The second wing of the eagle: The human dimension in learning our way to more sustainable futures. In *Facilitating sustainable agriculture,* ed. N.G. Röling and M.A.E. Wagemakers, 46-72. New York: Cambridge University Press.

Woolcock, M. 2001. Microenterprise and social capital: A framework for theory, research, and policy. *Journal of Socio-Economics* 30 (2): 193-98.

Woolcock, M., and D. Narayan. 2000. Social capital: Implications for development theory, research, and policy. *World Bank Observer* 15 (2): 225-49.

4
Building Resilient Livelihoods through Adaptive Co-Management: The Role of Adaptive Capacity
Derek Armitage

Novel management approaches under conditions of uncertainty are required to achieve dual outcomes of ecosystem protection and livelihood sustainability. Multi-level institutional arrangements characterized by collaboration and iterative learning, or adaptive co-management, may constitute one such approach (Buck et al. 2001; Ruitenbeek and Cartier 2001; Olsson et al. 2004). Circumspection is warranted, however, about the goals and assumptions of adaptive co-management and the socio-institutional and political relations that frame the approach (Chapters 10 and 11). Key features of adaptive co-management, including trust, social networks, and leadership, interact at multiple levels of decision making (see Folke et al. 2005) and require explicit consideration. The diverse "faces" of co-management (Chapter 2), moreover, highlight difficult issues with respect to power sharing, institutional development, and the capacity for learning and adaptation.

The purpose of this chapter is to highlight the role of adaptive capacity in supporting adaptive co-management and resilient livelihoods. Adaptive capacity serves as a useful entrée into the challenging social and institutional terrain of novel management strategies and the manner in which those strategies help to sustain the livelihoods of people in resource-dependent regions (Armitage 2005a). Several propositions guide this chapter. First, I suggest that livelihoods are best characterized as exhibiting multiple dynamic equilibria, not as a stable construct around which individuals and social groups converge. Second, I argue that adaptive, multi-level co-management arrangements are likely best suited to respond to the dynamic, self-organizing feedbacks that shape livelihood outcomes. Third, and finally, I posit that attention to the multi-level development of adaptive capacity can facilitate the emergence of adaptive co-management, and I propose an expanded capabilities approach to provide direction in this respect. Concepts from development studies, complex adaptive systems, and community-based natural resource management are thus linked to examine the relationship among livelihoods, adaptive capacity, and adaptive co-management. Using a case study of narwhal management from Nunavut, Canada, I offer some empirical evidence consistent with the propositions highlighted above. I do not offer a formal test of these propositions, but rather seek to illustrate the potential applicability of a contextually rich understanding of adaptive capacity to the challenge of adaptive co-management and livelihoods.

Resilient Livelihoods and Adaptive Co-Management

A livelihood refers to the strategies employed by individuals and communities to make or gain a living, including capabilities and tangible (e.g., natural resource, human, physical) and intangible (e.g., claims and access relationships) assets (Chambers and Conway 1992). Resilient livelihoods are those strategies, adopted by households or communities, that: (1) cope with and are able to recover from shocks and stresses, (2) maintain or enhance existing capabilities and assets despite uncertainty, and (3) ensure the provision of sustainable livelihood opportunities for future generations (Chambers and Conway 1992; DFID 1999; Ellis 2000). Livelihood analyses expend much effort on the identification of when, where, and how individuals, families, and communities can absorb the shocks and stresses that determine livelihood outcomes (see Chambers and Conway 1992; de Haan and Zoomers 2005). The sustainable livelihoods framework (DFID 1999; Ellis 2000) adopted by a wide range of bilateral, multilateral, and non-governmental development organizations (Table 4.1), moreover, encourages a recognition of the impact of policies, institutions, culture, and market forces on the assets (e.g., natural, social, physical, and financial) of individuals and communities, along with the vulnerabilities created by economic, market, and biophysical uncertainty. As revealed by this framework, livelihood decisions involve difficult trade-offs among social, economic, and ecological values. Fostering resilient livelihoods that balance competing values is an ongoing struggle, which is complicated by change and uncertainty in a globalizing world (Armitage and Johnson 2006).

The incidence of persistent poverty, inadequate living standards in many resource-dependent regions, and few alternatives suggests that most livelihood systems are not resilient to change. Gains made in one time period are often short-lived (de Haan and Zoomers 2005; Barrett and Swallow 2006). For a given set of actors in a given time period, livelihood outcomes may be sustainable and lead to lower levels of economic hardship. Episodic events (small or large) and chronic economic, social, and/or ecological challenges at multiple scales can, however, often trigger a return to unsustainable livelihoods and increased poverty. Recognition of change, uncertainty, and complexity in livelihood systems thus highlights their dynamic nature and the subsequent responses by different social actors to varying types of disturbances. As Scoones and Wolmer (in de Hann and Zoomers 2005, 43) noted, "pathways of change are non-linear and appear non-deterministic

Table 4.1

Components of the sustainable livelihoods approach

Livelihood assets	Vulnerability context	Policies, institutions, and processes	Livelihood strategies	Livelihood outcomes
Human capital • Skills, knowledge, health, etc. *Social capital* • Networks, groups, rules, norms, sanctions • Relationships of trust, reciprocity, exchange *Natural capital* • Stocks (fish) and key ecological services (nutrient cycling) *Physical capital* • Infrastructure and producer goods *Financial capital* • Financial resources (e.g., cash, bank deposits, livestock, jewels, and regular inflows of money)	External environment in which people exist Livelihoods, availability of assets affected by: • Trends (e.g., market change) • Shocks (economic, biophysical) • Seasonality	Institutions, organizations, policies (macro, sectoral, etc.), and decision-making context (social processes, culture, gender, age, class, caste, etc.) that influence assets and vulnerability context Often referred to as "transformative structures"	Livelihood options: • Expansion of subsistence-based activities • Intensification of subsistence-based activity • Modernization, commercialization of traditional non-farm activities • Engaging in new non-farm activities Multiple livelihood strategies typically practised (diversification): • Distress diversification • Progressive diversification	• Increased well-being and reduced incidence of poverty • More income • Reduced vulnerability • Improved food security • Sustainable use of natural resource endowments

Sources: Adapted from DFID (1999); Bouahom et al. (2004).

inasmuch as various actors starting from different positions of power and resource endowments may have arrived at similar configurations by very different intermediate steps." This instability indicates that livelihood systems, as mutually reinforcing bundles of strategies, capabilities, and assets, are more appropriately analyzed as multiple dynamic equilibria operating concurrently, with self-organizing feedbacks functioning at micro-, meso-, and macro-level scales (Barrett and Swallow 2006). A multiple dynamic equilibria construction of livelihoods extends the conventional sustainable livelihoods framework to highlight the difficulty in predicting outcomes and, more importantly, the limits of scale-specific and techno-bureaucratic policy interventions.

Although cross-scale effects are recognized in the sustainable livelihoods framework (Table 4.1), the conventional model is premised on a single dynamic livelihood equilibrium, and assumes that investments and interventions directed at building sustainable livelihoods will converge upon a stable, idealized state (de Haan and Zoomers 2005). Multiple livelihood equilibria are possible, however, with each exhibiting higher or lower levels of livelihood resilience, vulnerability, and sustainability. Livelihood systems (at a household or community scale) can gravitate towards or away from a number of potential dynamic equilibria, depending on the livelihood bundles available in a given time period and the manner in which they are utilized.

Different dynamic equilibria possess "attractors" that serve to maintain the structure and function of a particular system configuration (Kay et al. 1999; Gunderson and Holling 2002). A household or community with limited capability and asset bundles (acting as attractors) may gravitate towards dynamic equilibria characterized by low livelihood resilience, greater vulnerability, and persistent poverty. The basin of attraction of such dynamic equilibria can be overcome, but only through significant investments and the creation of enabling conditions that can radically change the capabilities and asset bundles of the household or community. Such changes can place the system on a positive growth trajectory, and propel it into dynamic equilibria characterized by a greater degree of livelihood resilience and sustainability.

Alternative trajectories (de Haan and Zoomers 2005) in response to system perturbations (such as significant investments in livelihoods over a short time period) point to the importance of critical thresholds, or periods in time when the attraction of one equilibrium is superseded by the attraction of another. Without the appropriate livelihood capabilities or assets, individuals, households, and resource-dependent communities may find it difficult to cross those critical thresholds that lead to higher-level dynamic equilibria. On the other hand, the often limited resilience of many livelihood systems indicates that even small perturbations (such as a poor harvest, failed hunt, or unexpected event) can cause the system to cross back through a critical threshold and flip into dynamic equilibria characterized by poverty and vulnerability. A multiple dynamic equilibria perspective on livelihood resilience thus highlights a governance challenge.

In the livelihoods literature, considerable attention is devoted to an examination of the transformative structures and processes (e.g., policies, institutions) that influence livelihoods. Such analyses, however, are not typically connected to an examination of the collaborative and adaptive governance regimes required to mitigate the dynamic, cross-scale effects of livelihood change differentially experienced by multiple social actors. Multi-level co-management approaches are required to address the cross-scale feedbacks that determine when and how the spatio-temporally diverse livelihood strategies of households and communities cross threshold points that lead to different dynamic equilibria – that is, gravitating from dynamic equilibria exhibiting low livelihood resilience, significant vulnerability, and poverty to equilibria characterized by greater livelihood resilience and sustainability. Scale-dependent or scale-insensitive management and decision-making frameworks are likely to prove insufficient to buffer the cross-scale feedbacks that determine when, if, and how livelihood systems will cross key thresholds and in which direction. As Pritchard and Sanderson (2002, 152) noted, a key governance challenge emerges in response to "systems that are not only cross-scale but dynamic, where the nature of cross-scale influences in the linked ecological/economic/social system changes over time, creating fundamental problems for division of responsibility between centralized and decentralized agents."

Prospects for achieving resilient livelihoods are thus linked to decision-making arrangements that encourage social actors at multiple scales to collaboratively define problems (Adams et al. 2003), interact in ways that support learning (Pretty 2003), respond to changing patterns of resource use (e.g., intensification, commodification) and ecological complexity, and design institutional responses that encourage adaptation in the context of change (Dietz et al. 2003). In short, prospects for resilient livelihoods are closely linked to the formation of adaptive capacity in a multi-level co-management context.

Understanding Adaptive Capacity: Endowments, Entitlements, and Capabilities

Institutional design principles for collective action are well developed (Pinkerton 1989; Ostrom et al. 2002). Such principles have been identified as being instrumental in the development of community-based management and in creating the conditions for successful co-management. Less explicit in these design principles are the challenges of adaptation and collaborative learning in cross-scale (vertical, horizontal) institutional contexts, especially where livelihood outcomes are closely connected to common pool resources under intense access and harvest pressure. Thus, institutional design principles should also emphasize how communities, organizations, and institutions linked vertically and horizontally reorganize or evolve in the context of significant perturbations (whether ecological or social in nature) (see Stern et al. 2002; Dietz et al. 2003) while maintaining the conditions for positive collective action. This requires an examination of the composition and functioning of social actors (local, regional), the capacity of those social actors to adapt to social-ecological change (Folke et al. 2005), and the development of adaptive governance arrangements that support resilient livelihoods.

Adaptive capacity can be defined as an attribute of resource management that creates opportunities for learning and the ability to experiment, adapt, and foster resilient livelihood strategies in complex social-ecological circumstances (adapted from Walker et al. 2002; Folke et al. 2003). Thus, adaptive capacity refers to the *capability* of a system to adapt to change and respond to disturbance yet still retain essential self-organizing structure, function, and feedback mechanisms (Berkes et al. 2003). A number of authors have expanded on the attributes of adaptive capacity, although the definitions utilized are similar (see Box 4.1). Folke and colleagues (2003), for example, describe four dimensions of adaptive capacity: (1) learning to live with uncertainty and change by allowing and/or encouraging small-scale disturbance events before there is a build-up of pressure leading, inevitably, to some sort of collapse; (2) supporting and promoting diversity, and highlighting the positive connection between diversity and redundancy, both biological and institutional, as a risk-diffusion mechanism; (3) combining different types of knowledge, including western scientific knowledge and local and/or traditional knowledge across multiple scales; and (4) maintaining opportunities for self-organization of social, institutional/organizational, and ecological systems in the direction of sustainability. These attributes provide a useful starting point for understanding adaptive capacity. The social and institutional foundations of adaptive capacity as described by Folke and colleagues (2003) and others (see Box 4.1) can be further deconstructed, however.

In the climate change literature, adaptive capacity is often discussed in tandem with vulnerability reduction and the development of coping strategies in response to climatic variability and extreme weather events (Smith et al. 2003). According to Smit and Pilifosova (2003), for example, reducing vulnerability to climate change necessitates greater adaptive capacity, a process that is less about the implementation of specific measures (e.g., resettlement or development controls, as has been the traditional focus of hazards research) and more about examining and defining the *capabilities* of system actors that determine their propensity to respond positively to change. The determinants of adaptive capacity are complex and varied, but include the

Box 4.1
Selected descriptions of adaptive capacity

- An "aspect of resilience that reflects learning, flexibility to experiment and adopt novel solutions, and development of generalized responses to broad classes of challenges" (Walker et al. 2002)
- An attribute of socio-ecological systems that permits coping with disturbance and change while retaining critical functions, structures, and feedback mechanisms (Olsson et al. 2004)
- The "ability of a system to evolve in order to accommodate perturbations or to expand the range of variability within which it can cope" (Adger 2003, 32).

state of, and access to, economic resources, the type of technology available in a given context, levels of knowledge, information and skill sets, existing infrastructure, and the capacity and resilience of institutions and organizations.

More recently, emphasis on identifying key features of adaptive capacity has led to the application of social capital (Pretty and Ward 2001) as a way to explore the co-evolution of social networks and norms that produce adaptive capacity within and among communities and organizations (Pelling and High 2005), and to examine the influence of institutions and cultural and political change required to facilitate adaptation (Adger 2003; Smith et al. 2003). As Folke and colleagues (2005) suggest, successful social transformations involving adaptive capacity are often preceded by the emergence of informal social networks that facilitate information flows, highlight knowledge gaps, and create nodes of expertise essential in the management process. Key individuals or leaders can play a catalytic role in supporting the emergence of these networks. This expanded emphasis on the social and institutional relationships that determine adaptive capacity has begun to resonate more closely with the holistic "capabilities" framework (Sen 1992, 1999; Leach et al. 1999) firmly entrenched in the development studies literature, particularly as applied to analyses of famine, food security, and, more recently, livelihoods.

Sen's articulation (1992, 1999) of "capabilities" focuses a political/economic lens on the attributes of adaptive capacity as derived by endowments (e.g., land, resources, labour) and the socio-institutional relationships of exchange that determine access to, and command over, endowments.[1] For example, a number of endowments are required to support the learning and adaptation required to shift livelihood systems into socially and ecologically more productive equilibria. These endowments may include adequate financial resources, technical skills, institutional support, clear organizational mandates, stated rights to participate in decision making, equitable property rights, and so on. Developing and maintaining these endowments is clearly important and has been the focus of mainstream capacity development and institution-building efforts. A capabilities perspective, however, encourages greater emphasis on the variety of ways in which adaptive capacity can be enriched or impoverished by exploring self-organizing, socio-institutional relationships of exchange involved in knowledge sharing, development of a collective vision, social networks, and trust building (Folke et al. 2005).

Capabilities are scale-dependent, however. Certain capabilities are possessed more readily at one scale than at another. Focusing on scale-specific assets or endowment requirements necessary for adaptive capacity (e.g., technical skills, financial resources) to the neglect of the multi-layered relationships that constrain access to those endowments will undermine efforts to build adaptive, multi-level co-management arrangements and livelihood resilience. Figure 4.1 highlights selected attributes that can determine how, when, and for what length of time different social groups obtain, maintain, and/or protect their command over endowments. This cross-scale interplay among endowments and relationships of exchange is a powerful influence on adaptive capacity and creates a self-organizing subtext to collaboration and learning. Ultimately, this subtext will also shape the emergence of multi-level governance approaches required to address livelihood systems that are both cross-scale and dynamic. An explicitly layered capability approach can highlight how social actors can be positioned to mediate spatio-temporally diverse and contested livelihood trajectories, thus enabling livelihood systems to cross key thresholds and to flip into and remain in dynamic equilibria characterized by greater resilience and sustainability.

Adaptive capacity is an emergent outcome of the social and institutional relationships that facilitate collaboration and cooperation for mutual benefit, and that determine whether social groups are able to craft a "common framework of understanding" (see Schusler et al. 2003, 311). While specific endowments are important, fostering adaptive capacity requires an understanding of: (1) the cross-scale relationships, interconnections, and networks among formal institutions and organizations that provide context for social processes of renewal and transformation; (2) existing and evolving power relationships among different groups with scale-specific (a community-based organization) or multi-scale responsibilities (a government agency); (3) the informal, and often more intangible, socio-political relationships of trust and influence that shape collaboration and learning; (4) control over knowledge and the valuation of different types of knowledge by different social actors; and (5) the degree to which evolving cultural norms and values remain consistent with collective action and collaborative learning.

Figure 4.1

Selected attributes of adaptive capacity

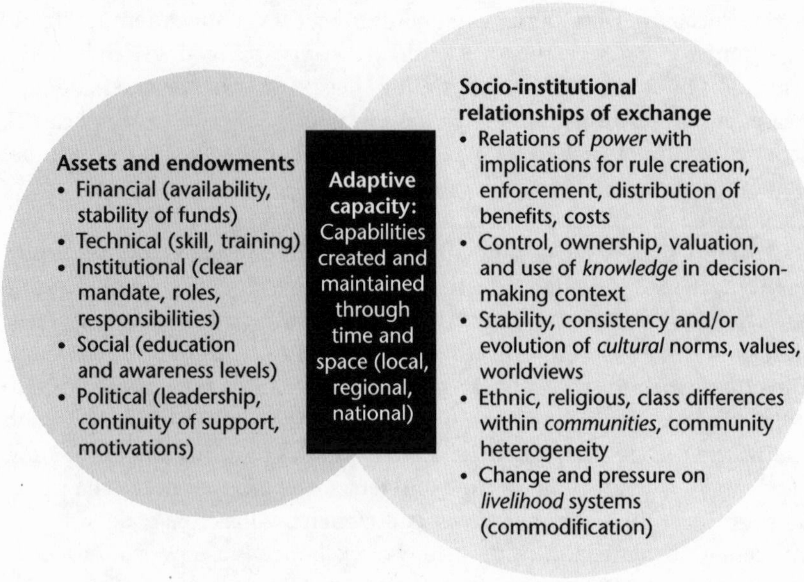

Assets and endowments
- Financial (availability, stability of funds)
- Technical (skill, training)
- Institutional (clear mandate, roles, responsibilities)
- Social (education and awareness levels)
- Political (leadership, continuity of support, motivations)

Adaptive capacity: Capabilities created and maintained through time and space (local, regional, national)

Socio-institutional relationships of exchange
- Relations of *power* with implications for rule creation, enforcement, distribution of benefits, costs
- Control, ownership, valuation, and use of *knowledge* in decision-making context
- Stability, consistency and/or evolution of *cultural* norms, values, worldviews
- Ethnic, religious, class differences within *communities*, community heterogeneity
- Change and pressure on *livelihood* systems (commodification)

In heterogeneous, resource-dependent communities, issues of power and the flows or distribution of resources and information between formal and informal social actors are particularly crucial. Much analysis of power is directed at the cross-scale relationships (local versus extra-local) that often result in relative winners and losers (Adger et al. 2005). There are also, however, deeply rooted relationships of power in even the most seemingly homogeneous community, played out through differential levels of capacity, representation, and status (Colfer 2005). Casting the local-scale dimension of adaptive co-management as apolitical will risk overlooking critical points of conflict or inequity and, therefore, windows of opportunity to foster collaboration and learning around contested livelihood trajectories.

In social-ecological contexts where multiple dynamic equilibria are possible, and the attractors towards unsustainable livelihood systems and resource degradation are strong (see Armitage and Johnson 2006), there are many potential roadblocks to the development of adaptive capacity. Building the capacity of individuals and social groups to adapt, or "learn to learn," such that critical thresholds, feedbacks, and possible livelihood trajectories are identified is an intrinsically social exercise. As illustrated in the narwhal management case below, there is no optimal approach that will build the capability of institutions and actors required to respond to the dynamics of livelihood systems. Progress will be made, however, by highlighting rather than obscuring the social, institutional, and political foundations of adaptive capacity.

Livelihoods, Adaptive Capacity, and Narwhal Management in Nunavut, Canada

Using a case study of narwhal management from Nunavut, Canada, I offer evidence consistent with the propositions explored above and examine the relationship among livelihood resilience, adaptive capacity, and adaptive co-management. The narwhal management case represents a unique governance innovation in a resource-dependent region in northern Canada, and is consistent with definitions and attributes of adaptive co-management (see Chapter 1).

The case study is based on reviews of literature and documents from the key organizations participating in community-based narwhal management, field visits and two meetings with 8 members of the Hunters' and Trappers' Organization in the community of Qikiqtarjuaq, 15 semi-structured interviews with hunters and representatives of resource management boards and government departments in Nunavut, and the outcomes of a two-day multi-stakeholder workshop attended by approximately 45 local and regional resource management representatives and government officials (Terriplan/IER 2002). Highlighted here are the linkages and relationships among key actors at different levels; the capabilities required to support adaptive, multi-level co-management; and the implications for livelihood resilience.

The 1993 Nunavut Final Agreement (NFA) negotiated between the Inuit of the eastern Arctic and the federal government created a unique policy environment in which to experiment with resource management approaches. Consistent with provisions in the NFA for decentralized management, and in an effort to respond to Inuit concerns about federal government control of narwhal management in a consistent manner, a three-year pilot community-based narwhal management process was initiated in 1999. The Nunavut Wildlife Management Board describes the community-based narwhal management process as follows:

A system of wildlife management characterized to date by the formal removal of annual [community] quotas and a transfer of the initial management responsibility away from the NWMB [Nunavut Wildlife Management Board] and Government, directly to a community. Under this system, which is supervised by the NWMB and Government, the community Hunters and Trappers Organization (HTO) must establish and enforce appropriate by-laws and hunting rules to control harvesting by members. The HTO must also develop – in collaboration with Government – a reporting system to accurately record harvesting information, such as the number of animals struck, landed and lost.

Key changes associated with the community-based narwhal management regime include a shift from a rigid community quota system to a more flexible "limits" approach, greater local management control exercised through locally developed harvest bylaws, and the intention to incorporate local knowledge of resource stocks into the management process. In creating opportunities for local decision making, the community-based narwhal management framework is also intended to create a more collaborative and partnership-based management approach. A review of the initial management experiment was completed in 2003, and the program was extended for a further five years. Currently, the process is being implemented in five communities across Nunavut: Arctic Bay, Qikiqtarjuaq (Broughton Island), Pond Inlet, Repulse Bay, and Kugaaruk (Pelly Bay).

Narwhal management in Nunavut is a multi-level co-management effort involving a number of different stakeholder groups. At the local scale, community-based Hunters' and Trappers' Organizations (HTOs) in each of the five participating communities reflect local goals and values and are a source of local knowledge that can be transmitted to higher-level management authorities. At the next level up, three regional wildlife organizations (RWOs) responsible for distinct territories in Nunavut mediate concerns among HTOs in each region. As the main wildlife co-management body in Nunavut, the Nunavut Wildlife Management Board (NWMB) balances local, regional, and national priorities. Fisheries and Oceans Canada (Department of Fisheries and Oceans, or DFO), whose minister has ultimate authority over all management decisions pertaining to narwhal, is linked to the NWMB as well as to international actors. At the territorial level, the claims implementation organization, Nunavut Tunngavik Inc. (NTI), provides a political voice for Inuit concerns but has a limited management function. Collaboration and learning are a challenge in this context because the different actors within and among levels may not necessarily share a consistent perspective or goal with regard to narwhal management (Table 4.2).

Narwhal play an important historical and current role in the livelihoods of many communities in Nunavut, providing a source of food and income (through the sale of tusks) as well as cultural benefits. Because of the livelihood connection and different perspectives about narwhal populations (Table 4.2), narwhal management has long been a point of contention between the federal government and Inuit stakeholders, who argued that quotas were set too low, premised as they were on aerial surveys undertaken in the late 1970s. In 2002/2003, however, population estimates of the Baffin Bay narwhal population were revised upward from an estimated 35,000 to approximately 50,000 (see Armitage 2005b). These recent survey data indicate that the Baffin Bay stock is larger than originally assumed and also more wide-ranging. Conflicts have also emerged in the current community-based management process because of uncertainty about harvest levels, high struck

Table 4.2

Multi-level actors and interests in narwhal management in Nunavut

Actor or group	Primary mandate	Key interests/concerns
Hunters' and Trappers' Organizations	HTOs represent principally the resource access interests and rights of hunters in each community.	Main concern has been the perceived inadequacy of narwhal quotas available to Inuit harvesters Concerns compounded by the lack of integration of local knowledge of narwhal stocks into the formal management process Key interests also centre on the regulation of harvesting practices and management of harvesting among members
Regional wildlife organizations	Subregional organizations (three in Nunavut) represent local and regional harvest interests and concerns.	Focus on coordination and creation of horizontal linkages among individual HTOs in each region Responsible for harvesting at regional level
Nunavut Wildlife Management Board	The NWMB has key responsibility for marine mammal management in the Nunavut Settlement Area.	Primary concern is balancing Inuit harvest and wildlife co-management rights established under the Nunavut Final Agreement (1993) with the principles of stock conservation and sustainability
Fisheries and Oceans Canada (DFO)	The Minister of Fisheries and Oceans has ultimate authority over the management of narwhal.	Within the new narwhal co-management framework, stock conservation is a key priority Concerns about commercialization of the narwhal harvest Interests also centre on reducing scientific uncertainty about narwhal with further research (surveys and stock assessments)

and loss rates in several communities,[2] and the subsequent wastage of the animals. Such conflict even led to the temporary closure of the hunt by the DFO in one community. Management complexity is compounded by scientific uncertainty with regard to narwhal ecology, including stock identity, distribution, reproduction, and natural mortality. In this challenging context, a number of connections emerge among livelihoods, adaptive capacity, and multi-level co-management.

Livelihood practices associated with narwhal and other wildlife are increasingly influenced by competing demands to retain a subsistence orientation while providing potentially new sources of income and formal economic activity. In northern mixed economies (subsistence and wage-based), multiple livelihood trajectories and basins of attraction are possible, especially given the boom/bust nature of northern economic systems. In the case of narwhal, for example, pressure to support a collective, subsistence-oriented hunt competes with incentives to commercialize the hunt consistent with trends towards a wage-based economy. Yet, determination of which basin of attraction fosters greater livelihood resilience – a wage-based system, a subsistence system, or some combination of the two – is actor- and scale-dependent. Resilience is, after all, a normative concept that requires negotiation among contested alternatives (Carpenter et al. 2001; Armitage and Johnson 2006), and it will inevitably confront many social and institutional obstacles.

In Nunavut, emerging economic pressures (e.g., large-scale resource extraction) and livelihood change (Myers et al. 2005) create further uncertainties that have the potential to undermine adaptive capacity and the social sources of renewal (e.g., values, worldviews, leadership). As noted, a particular challenge to joint learning and collective action is created by the potential commodification of commons resources – specifically, the private incentives to harvest narwhal tusks, which can fetch several thousands of dollars (a major benefit in an increasingly cash-based society). Related to this are changing norms, values, and worldviews about property rights within formerly subsistence-based communities, and the potential for conflict that can result. Traditional Inuit practices associated with sharing of the harvest, for example, are evolving (Dahl 2000). Changes of this nature influence collaborative rule creation, levels of trust, community-driven enforcement, and the equitable distribution of access rights in the narwhal management context.

Attention to adaptive capabilities as previously defined also serves to highlight the strain on local and regional organizations with mandates to mediate ecological and livelihood objectives in the community-based narwhal management context. Hunters' and Trappers' Organizations are intended to be full partners in the management process, yet their relationships with regional management organizations (i.e., the NWMB) and the federal government remains at times hierarchical – an issue of power sharing compounded by very tangible asset constraints, including financial, technical, and human resource limitations (see Figure 4.1). For instance, despite their significant responsibilities, HTOs have a limited operational budget (around $45,000) and a paid staff of one (usually a secretary-manager). Partly as a result, the historical role of the DFO as the principal source of information and authority has staying power in the current multi-level co-management regime, a situation that may not lend itself to collaboration and learning (Armitage 2005b).

Levels of trust and challenges associated with the integration of different knowledge systems in the narwhal management system also constrain learning. As noted, harvesters have previously argued that the historical quota system was unresponsive to their needs and, more specifically, did not take into account their views that narwhal stocks were healthy and growing. According to Inuit participants on a Joint Commission on the Conservation and Management of Narwhal and Beluga and North Atlantic Marine Mammal Commission consultation, biologists simply do not use hunters' understanding of the stocks. While partner groups participating in the multi-level narwhal management process are supposed to be equals, the lack of trust associated with traditional knowledge and the privileging of formal science can compromise effective partnership formation. Ironically, recent revisions to stock estimates based on new surveys by the federal government may support claims by Inuit hunters that narwhal populations in the Baffin Bay region are healthy (Armitage 2005b).

The community-based narwhal management process reveals linkages among collaboration and learning, the development of adaptive capabilities, and difficult livelihood decisions in a multi-equilibria universe. Community-based, regional, and national resource management organizations face key capacity challenges to learning, adaptation, and collaboration, including very real technical and financial limitations and other endowment-related constraints. Efforts to foster adaptive capabilities are further framed by power, knowledge integration, community heterogeneity, cultural change, and evolving livelihood incentives. Although the particular instances that shape the prospects for adaptive capacity in Nunavut are unique, such experiences are consistent with those of other resource-dependent communities where endogenous and exogenous forces intersect with efforts to craft adaptive governance arrangements.

Connecting Livelihoods, Adaptive Capacity, and Adaptive Co-Management

Building adaptive capacity in a multi-level co-management context is a key component of efforts to mediate among contested livelihood alternatives. Explicit recognition of these relationships highlights opportunities for adaptive policy intervention, and can help extend the institutional design principles for collective action. A number of lessons emerge from this analysis.

Linking Resilient Livelihoods and Adaptive Co-Management

Adaptive co-management represents a governance approach to support livelihoods, particularly in resource-dependent communities experiencing rapid socio-economic and ecological change. In linking livelihoods and adaptive co-management, however, two cautionary notes are required. First, processes of globalization, including market penetration and technological change, call into question the feasibility of certain livelihood systems and the pretence of shared community livelihood aspirations. Many communities previously engaged in subsistence activities are increasingly characterized by dualistic livelihood strategies in which individuals and the organizations or associations (e.g., resource user groups, cooperatives) with which they are related are interested in both diversifying and protecting traditional livelihood portfolios. This may be accomplished by engaging in market-based economic opportunities where feasible, while also challenging the direct and indirect causes of livelihood stress through political mobilization for control over natural resources and property rights. Multiple livelihood trajectories and states are thus possible and are determined by many, often competing variables and feedbacks. As illustrated in the Nunavut example, increasing heterogeneity catalyzed in part by ongoing market integration in relatively remote communities leads to increased requirements for cash to purchase goods and services (such as hunting equipment or store-bought food) (Myers et al. 2005). Transitions of this type can alter the livelihood motivations that drive natural resource management decision making, such that individual harvest incentives may increasingly conflict with collective decision-making processes, as appears to be the case in the narwhal management context. Multi-level governance is likely required to encourage sustainable responses to these situations, but only if efforts are directed at building adaptive capacity at all levels in response to a commonly defined problem. An expanded capabilities orientation highlights the role of value change, the transformation of formal and informal relationships, and variable levels of trust that make collaboration and learning difficult.

Second, there is a built-in paradox when adaptive co-management is proposed as an approach to fostering resilient livelihoods that are threatened in many instances by the economic and institutional forces of globalization. Adaptive co-management is itself an outcome of a particular approach and globalized discourse on participatory resource management. Thus, the potential of adaptive co-management to contribute to resilient livelihoods should be approached critically (as many of the chapters in this volume suggest). Where livelihoods are at stake, or where local livelihood claims threaten extra-local interests, entrenched political and economic incentives necessitate the careful examination of conditions under which adaptive co-management may emerge. Adaptive co-management is no panacea for deeply rooted resource and livelihood conflicts, but where the impediments to building adaptive capacity are recognized and addressed, adaptive co-management may provide openings for interaction among disparate groups that might not otherwise engage one another.

Fostering Adaptive Capabilities: A Holistic Perspective

As indicated in the Nunavut example, change and uncertainty come in many forms, including increased community heterogeneity, economic transformation and livelihood pressures, and the management problems created by ecological uncertainty (such as those associated with mobile resource stocks). An effort by co-management participants to adapt to change and learn through uncertainty is central to the performance of novel governance arrangements. The creation of multi-level governance arrangements may in fact foster the political space for the emergence of adaptive capacity. As the Nunavut case reveals, however, even in a multi-level co-management context, significant structural and process barriers will need to be resolved (see also Chapter 8).

In the first instance, development of adaptive capacity can focus on the capacity assets and endowments that will improve coordination across institutional scales and address a number of stumbling blocks to effective partnerships among local and regional actors. In Nunavut, these stumbling blocks are, in part, related to technical, financial, and human resource capacity limitations confronting local participants and key resource management organizations. Such stumbling blocks are particularly acute in the case of Hunters' and Trappers' Organizations, but extend as well to actors and organizations at the regional and national levels. Limited capacity, whether it involves financial resources, technical skills, or an openness to experiment, is by no means only a local-level challenge.

An expanded capabilities approach demonstrates the value in moving beyond a focus on technical, financial, and other resource endowments that shape day-to-day rules and procedures of management. Rather, the socio-institutional relationships of exchange that determine actual command over these endowments (or entitlements) provide the essential subtext to the formation of adaptive capacity and will influence whether individuals, community-based organizations, and extra-local actors collaborate, adapt, and learn through change. Thus, differential levels of power in a participatory management process, the extent to which local knowledge and expertise are valued, and the stability of norms, values, and worldviews must also be carefully examined. Opportunities to jointly adapt and refine management strategies while overcoming historically hierarchical relationships among key actors (local, regional, national) will involve significant effort. Place-specific examinations of social and institutional windows of opportunity are necessary to identify critical points when relationships of exchange among social actors can be modified to foster learning and collaboration under conditions of uncertainty.

Examination of socio-political relationships must be done in light of the perturbations created by socio-economic and ecological change, and the implications for equity and true power sharing arrangements required for adaptive co-management (Colfer 2005). It is naïve to expect actors with entrenched interests to voluntarily create windows of opportunity. Yet, the emergence of indigenous rights movements and the existence of Nunavut itself (see Chapter 12) suggest that within formal *and* informal actor relations, key pressure points exist to shift political and institutional trajectories. Critiques of the socio-political relationships that frame co-management (Nadasdy 2003; Stevenson 2004) are helpful in specifying the nature of these relationships, and thus are important in formulating recommendations for institutional change and policy intervention. Overly structuralist, political economy interpretations of co-management, however, risk diminishing the role of individual leaders, informal relationships, and actor agency in creating positive opportunities for change (see Chapter 12).

Adaptive capacity is more likely to emerge in contexts in which participating actors can meaningfully interact and communicate. In the narwhal management experiment, communication issues have been a source of tension among the different actors, highlighted in particular by the temporary closure of the narwhal harvest in one participating community. Substantive procedural issues as well as structural impediments are at the root of the communication challenges. Despite the formalized co-management context required by the Nunavut Final Agreement (1993), and an operational interest in developing effective partnerships among key actors, principles of collaborative management are not always followed. Access to information, the exchange of the information (e.g., the form it takes), and the valuation of information vary among the main participants involved. Such differences, moreover, are also experienced within communities because of economic, class, and other heterogeneities, creating processes of unequal communication at different scales in the management process. The structural impediments of language, distance between key stakeholder groups, and the lack of technical capacity among all the actors involved in narwhal management to communicate in ways that are effective further constrain the development of adaptive capacity. Careful attention to the policy environment in which adaptive co-management may emerge can help to address these issues.

Cultivating a Supportive Policy Environment

Learning under uncertainty may be a matter of survival, as those in vulnerable, resource-dependent communities are aware. There is also, however, a strongly normative dimension to the process of learning that requires a committed policy environment. In the case of narwhal management, there is an implicit policy to support learning, as evidenced by the experimental nature of the community-based narwhal management process. However, the experience with the valuation of traditional knowledge by higher-level agencies, and different perspectives regarding how best to interact with the resource, temporarily, at least, foreclosed some opportunities for collaboration and learning. Critical reflection cuts both ways. Different experiences with narwhal management in different communities have revealed that some communities (i.e., Hunters' and Trappers' Organizations and their members) have been more open to the requirements of the new management regime, such as developing the harvest bylaws and reporting systems. In other words, actors at multiple levels must reflect critically on their role in the management of resources and habitats, the implications for livelihood resilience and sustainability, and the internal constraints placed on building adaptive capacity.

Other policy-related constraints exist. Policy makers whose ideologies and interests will support or undermine governance change (see Chapters 5 and 8) face scarce resources and are under pressure to manage resources efficiently. If bureaucracies are to support something more than "instrumental" forms of co-management (see Neilson et al. 2004), or co-management characterized by the involvement of communities only during implementation stages of externally driven, top-down programs and policies, the benefits of greater attention to adaptive capacity must outweigh the fiscal and political costs. The tendency towards standardization as a cost reduction strategy may pose a problem in the long term, however. Generalized institutional models are unlikely to be appropriate, given the speed and intensity of social-ecological change and multiple livelihood trajectories experienced in resource-dependent regions where adaptive co-management may be most appropriate. The details of a particular institutional design that works for narwhal management in one community, moreover, may not work in an adjacent community, let alone be appropriate in other nearby communities with a different resource system and livelihood focus (e.g., polar bear; see Diduck et al. 2005). This is a drawback from a policy perspective. In the long term, however, recognizing the context-specific attributes of adaptive capacity can highlight the costs and benefits of policy interventions aimed at supporting system trajectories that gravitate towards dynamic equilibria with greater livelihood resilience and sustainability.

Conclusions

Under conditions of social-ecological uncertainty, strategies for developing capacity to adapt to change and for identifying management directions that build resilience to deal with change are critical (Berkes et al. 2005). The complexity of management in complex social-ecological systems is well documented (Carpenter et al. 2001; Ludwig 2001; Gunderson and Holling 2002), and no single institutional approach or management design will prove sufficient in all contexts. Adaptive capacity has been presented here as a potentially valuable entrée to this challenge. It is rare, however, for the capacity for learning, adaptation, and collaboration to emerge spontaneously. An expanded emphasis on identifying the drivers of adaptive capacity in a multi-level co-management context is required to reconcile entrenched socio-political and institutional interests with the windows of opportunity for change, and to mediate spatio-temporally diverse and contested livelihood trajectories. Amid the fragmentation, indeterminacy, and paucity of enduring patterns of social-ecological behaviour, a decidedly post-modern approach to management seems unavoidable. The emergence of adaptive co-management may offer one such approach. As Pritchard and Sanderson (2002, 168) acknowledge: "For such a profoundly *dis*organized and multiscale approach to thrive, government, market, and citizen must share a common vision – that all must address these puzzles in order that they might be engaged and worked on – not solved forever; that 'expertise,' popular voice, and power are separable, and none holds the dice for more than a pass."

Acknowledgments

I wish to thank two anonymous reviewers and Paul Nadasdy for constructive comments on this chapter. Research in Nunavut was supported by the Social Sciences and Humanities Research Council of Canada and a Petro-Canada Young Innovators Award.

Notes

1 Endowments are resources (e.g., assets) and rights that, in principle, social actors possess. Entitlements are the resources and rights that individuals can actually obtain or achieve and are an outcome of social and institutional relationships that are neither consistent nor necessarily harmonious. Capabilities are an outcome of the endowments/entitlements interplay and represent what social actors can do or be (see Leach et al. 1999).
2 "Struck and loss" refers to a narwhal that has been shot (and likely mortally wounded) but not actually captured before it sank.

References

Adams, W., D. Brockington, J. Dyson, and B. Vira. 2003. Managing tragedies: Understanding conflict over common pool resources. *Science* 302 (5652): 1915-16.
Adger, N. 2003. Social aspects of adaptive capacity. In *Climate Change, Adaptive Capacity and Development*, ed. J. Smith, J. Klein, and S. Huq, 29-49. London: Imperial College Press.
Adger, N., K. Brown, and E. Tompkins. 2005. The political economy of cross-scale networks in resource co-management. *Ecology and Society* 10 (2): 9. http://www.ecologyandsociety.org/vol10/iss2/art9/.
Armitage, D. 2005a. Adaptive capacity and community-based natural resource management. *Environmental Management* 35 (6): 703-15.

–. 2005b. Community-based narwhal management in Nunavut, Canada: Uncertainty, change and adaptation. *Society and Natural Resources* 18: 715-31.

Armitage, D.R., and D. Johnson. 2006. Can resilience be reconciled with globalization and the increasingly complex conditions of resource degradation in Asian coastal regions? *Ecology and Society* 11 (1): 2. http://www.ecologyandsociety.org/vol11/iss1/art2/.

Barrett, C., and B. Swallow. 2006. Fractal poverty traps. *World Development* 34 (1): 1-15.

Berkes, F., J. Colding, and C. Folke, eds. 2003. *Navigating social-ecological systems: Building resilience for complexity and change.* Cambridge: Cambridge University Press.

Berkes, F., N. Bankes, M. Marschke, D. Armitage, and D. Clark. 2005. Cross-scale institutions and building resilience in the Canadian North. In *Breaking ice: Renewable resource and ocean management in the Canadian North,* ed. F. Berkes, R. Huebert, H. Fast, M. Manseau, and A. Diduck, 225-48. Calgary: Arctic Institute of North America and University of Calgary Press.

Bouahom, B., L. Douangsavanh, and J. Rigg. 2004. Building sustainable livelihoods in Laos: Untangling farm from non-farm, progress from distress. *Geoforum* 35: 607-19.

Buck, L., C. Geisler, J. Schelhas, and E. Wollenberg. 2001. *Biological diversity: Balancing interests through adaptive collaborative management.* Boca Raton, FL: CRC Press.

Carpenter, S., B. Walker, J. Anderies, and N. Abel. 2001. From metaphor to measurement: Resilience of what to what? *Ecosystems* 4: 765-81.

Chambers, R., and G.R. Conway. 1992. Sustainable rural livelihoods: Practical concepts for the 21st century. IDS discussion paper 296. Institute for Development Studies. Brighton, UK.

Colfer, C.J.P. 2005. *The equitable forest: Diversity, community, and resource management.* Washington, DC: Resources for the Future.

Dahl, J. 2000. *Saqqaq: An Inuit hunting community in the modern world.* Toronto: University of Toronto Press.

de Haan, L., and A. Zoomers. 2005. Exploring the frontier of livelihoods research. *Development and Change* 36 (1): 27-47.

DFID (Department for International Development). 1999. Sustainable livelihoods guidance sheets. London: DFID.

Diduck, A., N. Bankes, D. Clark, and D. Armitage. 2005. Unpacking social learning in social-ecological systems: Case studies of polar bear and narwhal management in northern Canada. In *Breaking ice: Renewable resource and ocean management in the Canadian North,* ed. F. Berkes, R. Huebert, H. Fast, M. Manseau, and A. Diduck, 269-90. Calgary: Arctic Institute of North America and University of Calgary Press.

Dietz, T., E. Ostrom, and P. Stern. 2003. The struggle to govern the commons. *Science* 302 (5652): 1907-12.

Ellis, F. 2000. *Rural livelihoods and diversity in developing countries.* Oxford: Oxford University Press.

Folke C., J. Colding, and F. Berkes. 2003. Synthesis: Building resilience and adaptive capacity in socio-ecological systems. In *Navigating social-ecological systems: Building resilience for complexity and change,* ed. F. Berkes, J. Colding, and C. Folke, 352-87. Cambridge: Cambridge University Press.

Folke, C., T. Hahn, P. Olsson, and J. Norberg. 2005. Adaptive governance of social-ecological systems. *Annual Review of Environment and Resources* 30: 8.1-8.33.

Gunderson, L.H., and C.S. Holling, eds. 2002. *Panarchy: Understanding transformations in human and natural systems.* Washington, DC: Island Press.

Kay, J.J., H.A. Regier, M. Boyle, and G. Francis. 1999. An ecosystem approach for sustainability: Addressing the challenge of complexity. *Futures* 31: 721-42.

Leach, M., R. Mearns, and I. Scoones. 1999. Environmental entitlements: Dynamics and institutions in community-based natural resource management. *World Development* 27 (2): 225-47.

Ludwig, D. 2001. The era of management is over. *Ecosystems* 4: 758-64.

Myers, H., H. Fast, M. Kislalioglu Berkes, and F. Berkes. 2005. Feeding the family in times of change. In *Breaking ice: Renewable resource and ocean management in the Canadian North,* ed. F. Berkes, R. Huebert, H. Fast, M. Manseau, and A. Diduck, 23-45. Calgary: Arctic Institute of North America and University of Calgary Press.

Nadasdy, P. 2003. *Hunters and bureaucrats: Power, knowledge, and Aboriginal-state relations in the southwest Yukon.* Vancouver: UBC Press.

Nielsen, J., P. Degnbol, K.K. Viswanathan, M. Ahmed, M. Hara, and N.M.R Abdullah. 2004. Fisheries co-management – an institutional innovation? Lessons from South East Asia and southern Africa. *Marine Policy* 28: 151-60.

Olsson, P., C. Folke, and T. Hahn. 2004. Socio-ecological transformation for ecosystem management: The development of adaptive co-management of a wetland landscape in southern Sweden. *Ecology and Society* 9 (4): 2. http://www.ecologyandsociety.org/vol9/iss4/art2.

Ostrom, E., T. Dietz, N. Dolšak, P.C. Stern, S. Stovich, and E.U. Weber, eds. 2002. *The drama of the commons.* Washington, DC: National Academy Press.

Pelling, M., and C. High. 2005. Understanding adaptation: What can social capital offer assessments of adaptive capacity? *Global Environmental Change* 15 (4): 308-19.

Pinkerton, E., ed. 1989. *Co-operative management of local fisheries: New directions for improved management and community development.* Vancouver: UBC Press.

Pretty, J. 2003. Social capital and the collective management of resources. *Science* 302 (5652): 1912-14.

Pretty, J., and H. Ward. 2001. Social capital and the environment. *World Development* 29: 209-27.

Pritchard, L., and S. Sanderson. 2002. The dynamics of political discourse in seeking sustainability. In *Panarchy: Understanding transformations in human and natural systems,* ed. L.H. Gunderson and C.S. Holling, 147-69. Washington, DC: Island Press.

Ruitenbeek, J., and C. Cartier. 2001. *The invisible wand: Adaptive co-management as an emergent strategy in complex bio-economic systems.* Occasional paper no. 34. Bogor, Indonesia: Center for International Forestry Research. http://www.cifor.cgiar.org.

Schusler, T.M., D.J. Decker, and M.J. Pfeffer. 2003. Social learning for collaborative natural resource management. *Society and Natural Resources* 15: 309-26.

Sen, A. 1992. *Inequality reexamined.* Oxford: Oxford University Press.

–. 1999. *Poverty and famine.* New York: Clarendon Press.

Smit, B., and O. Pilifosova. 2003. Adaptive capacity and vulnerability reduction. In *Climate change, adaptive capacity and development,* ed. J. Smith, J. Klein, and S. Huq, 9-28. London: Imperial College Press.

Smith, J., J. Klein, and S. Huq, eds. 2003. *Climate change, adaptive capacity and development.* London: Imperial College Press.

Stern, P., T. Dietz, N. Dolsak, E. Ostrom, and S. Stonich. 2002. Knowledge and questions after 15 years of research. In *The drama of the commons,* ed. E. Ostrom, T. Dietz, N. Dolšak, P.C. Stern, S. Stovich, and E.U. Weber, 445-89. Washington, DC: National Academy Press.

Stevenson, M. 2004. Decolonizing co-management in northern Canada. *Cultural Survival Quarterly* (Spring): 68-71.

Terriplan/IER. 2002. *Integrated ocean management in Baffin Island and Canada's Oceans Strategy.* Workshop report prepared for Fisheries and Oceans Canada, Winnipeg and Iqaluit.

Walker, B., S. Carpenter, J. Anderies, N. Abel, G. Cumming, M. Janssen, L. Lebel, J. Norberg, G. Peterson, and R. Pritchard. 2002. Resilience management in socio-ecological systems: A working hypothesis for a participatory approach. *Conservation Ecology* 6 (1): 14. http://www.consecol.org/vol16/iss1/art14.

5

Adaptive Co-Management for Resilient Resource Systems: Some Ingredients and the Implications of Their Absence

Anthony Charles

Adaptive co-management is an approach to environmental and resource management that brings together two key aspects – adaptive management and co-management. The former refers to a capability to learn and adapt under uncertain conditions and in the face of changing circumstances, while the latter refers to the sharing of management power and responsibilities between governments, resource users, and resource-based communities. While each of these has been the subject of considerable research, and a reasonable understanding is evolving of the combination "adaptive co-management," there is still much uncertainty over what is required to achieve these goals. This chapter seeks to provide some insights into this challenge by (1) focusing attention on a set of four potential ingredients of adaptive co-management, and (2) motivating the need for these ingredients by examining the implications of their absence, using a specific case study – the historic collapse of the fishery for cod and other groundfish on Canada's Atlantic coast.

The premise here is that desirable resource management policies and practices – in this case, those relating to adaptive co-management – are those that enhance the sustainability and resilience needed in any "healthy" resource system. In particular, for a resource system to be resilient, the relevant ecosystem and the corresponding human and management systems must all be able to absorb or "bounce back" from unexpected shocks and perturbations, so that the system as a whole retains its integrity (Holling 1973; Berkes and Folke 1998). Both sustainability and resilience may be seen as being composed of ecological, socio-economic, community, and institutional components, all of which must be approached simultaneously (Charles 2001). Thus, a well-functioning resource system requires sustainability and resilience in its ecosystems, its management institutions, its economic structure, and its communities.

The rationale for exploring adaptive co-management might therefore be stated as a claim that such an approach can enhance the sustainability and resilience of natural resource systems. This chapter examines that claim by assessing the extent to which a set of four ingredients of adaptive co-management were present (or absent) in a specific case study and examining the implications of that for success (or failure) in resource management.

It is important to emphasize, however, that adaptive co-management, and indeed adaptive management and co-management individually, are relative concepts rather than all-or-nothing phenomena. Management in a certain situation may rate highly in its adaptive nature but low on the scale of co-management, or vice versa. Further, some aspects of management may be adaptive, but not others, and some may operate in a context of co-management, but not others. For example, a governmental resource management agency may choose to involve the resource users in co-management for *operational* management decisions (such as annual harvesting plans) but not *strategic (policy)* decisions (such as allocations of use rights and access between groups of resource users). Given this diversity, it would be unwise to attempt to judge whether adaptive co-management is, on balance, present or absent in a resource system. Instead, this chapter will focus on a limited number of key aspects of resource management at a scale compatible with an assessment of the specific ingredients of adaptive co-management.

This chapter first describes the set of proposed ingredients of adaptive co-management that form the core of the discussion, then turns to the specific case study – the fishery for cod and other groundfish in Atlantic Canada – to examine the extent to which these ingredients were or were not present in that fishery.

Four Ingredients of Adaptive Co-Management

The adaptive co-management ingredients considered here are as follows: (1) the availability of a diverse "toolkit" of possible management measures, and adoption of an appropriate "portfolio" of such measures; (2) the pursuit of *robust management;* (3) full utilization of the knowledge base in the resource system; and (4) appropriate institutional reform (Charles 2001, 2004). The following discussion will make a case for the importance of these ingredients, although space limitations prevent a full exploration of all their complexities. Furthermore, no claim is made that other possible ingredients are any less relevant in contributing to the sustainability and resilience of resource systems.

A Management Portfolio

Any natural resource management system utilizes a particular set of management measures, which in turn has been chosen from a toolkit of possibilities – ranging from input controls (such as limited entry licensing or restrictions on harvesting activity) to output controls (over total and/or individual harvests), and from technical measures (such as regulations on the technology used and characteristics of the harvested resource, e.g., individual trees, fish, or wildlife) to ecosystem-oriented tools (such as protected areas). The choices made from this overall toolkit are critical to the success of the resulting management system. This is because each resource management instrument has its advantages and disadvantages, so a key objective is for the management portfolio – the set of management measures actually chosen – to be *mutually reinforcing* in that the gaps in any one measure are filled by other measures.

Thus, it is important that (1) a suitably broad, diverse set of "tools" be available within the management toolkit, and that (2) the right portfolio is ultimately selected from among these tools. With respect to the diversity of tools for management, one might draw an analogy with biological diversity – whether at the genetic, species, or landscape level – and how its presence builds resilience into the system and provides greater options in an uncertain world.

The opportunity to select a more diverse *portfolio* of management measures can reduce the risk of a failure in resource management (Charles 2001), just as a more diverse investment portfolio can reduce risk in financial terms. Of course, the availability of many management tools from which to choose does not imply that the management system should utilize them all, or that it should be a particularly complex system. Sometimes, the right management portfolio may be a simple one; there are examples of successful resource management based on a small set of straightforward, well-accepted tools (see, for example, Berkes 1989). This reinforces the second point above, namely, that making the right choices among management measures is equally crucial.

Consider, for example, a management system that places quantitative limits on resource extraction (for example, output controls such as harvest limits on the catch of fish or the cutting of trees). This is a common method in resource management, but there are also examples of failure, and consequent resource collapse, in part, as a result of overreliance on such a management approach (an example is provided later in this chapter). This negative experience may lead to a conclusion that harvest controls are unsuitable in those situations, and alternatives (drawn from the toolkit) should be tried. For example, protected areas could be added to the mix, to restrict resource use in specified areas (e.g., Roberts and Hawkins 2000), or harvest limits could be supplemented with input controls, to limit how, when, and where resource use takes place or how much equipment or time is allowed (e.g., Pope 2002). The idea is that adaptively replacing or supplementing management measures may improve the chances of achieving sustainability and resilience.

As noted above, however, it is important not to add excessively to the set of management measures, as the use of too large a number of instruments will lead to unwieldy and overly costly management. Instead, one must continually seek the best package on a case-by-case basis, taking into account (1) society's objectives, (2) physical and/or biological aspects of the natural resource, (3) human aspects such as tradition and experience, (4) the level of uncertainty and complexity in the resource sector, and (5) the predicted consequences of the various instruments, as well as availability of financial and organizational resources for management. This approach, i.e., seeking the best management portfolio, lies at the heart of adaptive management – to adapt and learn from experience, with the aim of improving future management (e.g., Walters 1986).

Robust Management
Adaptive management can be as basic as adjusting the rate at which a resource is exploited as new information becomes available on the state of the resource. The challenge may be greater, however, reflecting the reality that many uncertainties in resource systems are of a *structural* nature, with *structural uncertainty* reflecting basic ignorance about the nature of the resource system, its components, structure, and dynamics. Structural uncertainty can have a major impact on the outcome of management, manifesting itself, for example, in poorly understood resource/environment interactions, spatial complexity, technological change, and societal/management objectives.

How can we implement an adaptive approach in the face of structural uncertainty? This requires not just quantitative adjustments (e.g., in exploitation rates) but rather substantial change (redesign) in the practice of resource management, so that its structure and methods are *robust*. Specifically, we define "robust management" as follows: "*Robust Management* of a resource system is management designed to be able to achieve a reasonable level of performance (i.e., acceptable level of success) even under conditions in which (i) the current understanding of the system (e.g., the status of the resources), its environment and the processes of change over time turns out to be faulty, and/or (ii) there is a highly imperfect capability to control resource exploitation" (Charles 1998a, 1998b, 2001).

As an ingredient of adaptive co-management, robust management is meant to minimize the potential negative impact of decision making in a context of structural uncertainty, by reducing the reliance of resource management on methods that are sensitive to highly uncertain variables or that depend on high levels of controllability. To this end, a policy move towards robust management must overcome two counter-tendencies found in many resource management systems (Charles 1998a, 2001, 2004):

- *The illusion of certainty.* Resource systems are among the most complex and uncertain, yet many resource management institutions exhibit a perverse tendency to ignore major elements of uncertainty; these institutions suffer from an "illusion of certainty," in which policy, management, and/or operating practices take place as though major elements of uncertainty could be ignored, or even as though the world were somehow certain and predictable. Far from recognizing and working within the bounds of the uncertainty, the illusion of certainty leads to the opposite result.
- *The fallacy of controllability.* Natural resource management is intrinsically an imperfect endeavour, with resource systems at best partially and imperfectly controlled. Unfortunately, this is by no means universally recognized. A "fallacy of controllability" is often in place, reflecting a perception that more can be known, and more controlled, than can be realistically expected in the real world.

The move to robust management requires a rethinking of these tendencies and of the very philosophy of management. There is a need to focus on utilizing management measures that optimize the overall sustainability of inherently uncontrollable resource systems, including such crucial structural and decision-making tools as the "precautionary approach" and the "ecosystem approach" (e.g., FAO 1996, 2003). Furthermore, no matter how successful a management system is in lessening its sensitivity to uncertainty, such uncertainties will not disappear, so it remains important to *institutionalize* adaptation within robust management. This involves: (1) accounting systematically for uncertainty by proper use of available information, and adaptively seeking out new information; (2) maintaining a capability and willingness to make appropriate adjustments, over both short and long time scales, adapting in a timely manner to unexpected circumstances, so that management goals are not compromised.

This has implications for the structural nature of resource management, since resource use plans, and individual business plans for resource industries, must be flexible if they are to allow for the uncertain nature of the natural resource. While this does not imply responding drastically to the smallest apparent change in the resource, there must be the *capability* to adapt to change – both short-term and long-term (Charles 2001). In particular, while it may well be desirable from a resource user's perspective to adopt fixed annual production plans, the apparent *stability* so obtained may be at the expense of ecological (and long-term economic) well-being.

Full Use of the Knowledge Base
Building and/or maintaining sustainability and resilience in resource systems requires a suitable knowledge base for decision making. It is important,

then, that resource management (1) implement suitable means to monitor the resource system, acquire knowledge accordingly, and report on its status to all concerned, and (2) make full use of all *available* sources of information, and properly assess knowledge requirements and gaps.

With respect to monitoring, the knowledge base is used to assess the state of the resource system, including ecological, human, and management aspects, and monitor its dynamics. A key approach to such monitoring lies in developing sets of quantitative indicators that can track the system's evolution. Such indicators might include levels of resource use, resource abundance, socio-economic impact, and institutional management performance. Development of indicators for resource systems has been substantial, especially in agricultural systems, forests, rangelands, and wildlife. There is particular interest in using indicators to monitor progress towards sustainability and resilience – through *sustainability assessment* and sustainability indicators (for fisheries, see, for example, Charles 1997, 2001; FAO 1999) – but properly determining what constitutes an indicator of sustainability remains an active subject of research.

With respect to utilization of knowledge, it is clear in the literature (e.g., Berkes 1999; Johannes et al. 2000) that resource use and resource management involve a variety of forms of knowledge and that, in particular, traditional ecological knowledge (TEK) and local knowledge tend to have been underutilized as tools for resource management. These forms of knowledge reflect the accumulated information and wisdom about the natural world, built up over time through the experience of resource users and communities in their regular interaction with their environment and natural resources. This could include information on resource-related aspects, such as spatial distribution of the resource and timing of migrations, and may also include management-related knowledge of what arrangements work best within local cultural systems, what measures help improve compliance among resource users, or what harvesting techniques are locally most effective or most conservation-oriented (Berkes 1999).

This knowledge base may have been developed over long time periods, but it may also have been acquired in recent years, notably through resource use. The nature of this knowledge can vary from place to place, from one user group to another, and even between individual resource users, so it cannot be viewed as homogeneous, but rather as a rich, diverse body that, through careful analysis, can provide useful guidance in resource assessment and management. While traditional or local knowledge often lies beyond the purview of the standard scientific apparatus, and the inertia in modern resource science can be an obstacle to its use, it has proven important to link together such knowledge with "scientific knowledge" (e.g., Neis et al. 1999).

It is notable that full utilization and continuous updating of the knowledge base, a key element of *adaptive management,* is closely linked with the collaborative nature of *co-management,* the other fundamental component of adaptive co-management. In particular, to ensure not only that local and traditional knowledge is utilized but that it is maintained and regenerated implies a need for policies supporting (1) secure access by local resource-based communities and their residents to adjacent resources (to maintain the close connection of local people and resources), and (2) participation by these communities in resource management and associated research, thereby reinforcing the buy-in and interaction of those most familiar with, and most attached to, the local resources and their environment.

Institutional Reform
What kinds of resource management institutions are needed to build sustainability and resilience in resource systems? It has been noted that institutional effectiveness interacts with the achievement of sustainability and resilience. Folke and Berkes (1998) highlight situations in which "adaptiveness and resilience have been built into institutions so they are capable of responding to and managing processes, functions, dynamics and changes in a fashion that contributes to ecosystem resilience." In other words, institutions that are themselves resilient can help to maintain and promote resilient ecosystems in the face of intensive resource exploitation. Folke and Berkes suggest that resilience can be enhanced when management institutions draw on traditional ecological approaches such as (1) embracing of small-scale disturbances to avoid major catastrophes, (2) use of reserves and habitat protection measures, and (3) avoiding reliance on exploitation of a single species in the ecosystem, by encouraging multiple occupations and sources of livelihood. There is clearly also an important place for better utilization of the various sources of knowledge, as described above.

Building such measures into natural resource management institutions likely requires real reform, shifting them towards being *self-regulatory institutions,* ones that reinforce desirable behavioural incentives and thereby reinforce management goals, helping to enhance resilience in the resource system. Specifically, increasing the involvement of resource users in management can help to "get the incentives right," by providing a tighter feedback loop between harvesting and management – that is, linking success in harvesting more closely to success in management. Indeed, many real-world examples have been compiled of self-regulatory institutions producing conservation actions supporting sustainability and resilience, perhaps beyond what a central authority could have achieved alone (e.g., Hanna and Munasinghe 1995; Ostrom 1990).

Figure 5.1

Co-management triangle

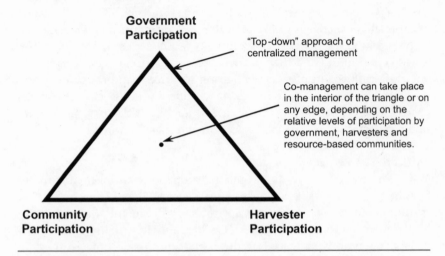

**Government
Participation**

"Top-down" approach of
centralized management

Co-management can take place
in the interior of the triangle or on
any edge, depending on the
relative levels of participation by
government, harvesters and
resource-based communities.

**Community
Participation**

**Harvester
Participation**

A major illustration of self-regulatory institutions is that of "co-management," in which the management of resources is shared between the government and the resource users (e.g., Wilson et al. 2003). Particularly helpful is *community-based co-management,* in which local resource-based communities are also involved (Charles 2001; Pinkerton and Weinstein 1995) (see Figure 5.1). As noted above, this can provide a mechanism to make use of local resource knowledge and indigenous methods of management. Equally important, it can make resource management more efficient and effective by bringing community pressure to bear on the actions of resource users – that is, by using social mechanisms and moral suasion at the community level to overcome incentives acting against conservation, inducing the resource users to comply with regulations.

Case Study: The Atlantic Canadian Groundfishery

This section explores the extent to which the four ingredients of adaptive co-management proposed above (appropriate management portfolios, robust management, knowledge utilization, and institutional reform) were evident in the management of a particular natural resource system – the fishery for cod, haddock, and other groundfish on the Atlantic coast of Canada. This fishery has a history of over 500 years of ongoing exploitation (Kurlansky 1997), but in the early 1990s, a broad collapse occurred in many elements of the fishery, especially those targeting cod stocks. Specifically, the "northern cod" off Newfoundland, which previously supported one of the largest fisheries in the world, had its biomass of adult (spawning) fish reduced to less than 1 percent of former levels (Myers et al. 1997). This collapse led to the closure of many fisheries and severe reductions in others, with large-scale negative human impacts. Ecologically, an accompanying phenomenon has also been observed, known as "fishing down the marine food chain" – the reduction over time in the average trophic level of species exploited in the northwest Atlantic fishery as a whole (Pauly and Maclean 2003).

The collapse itself has been examined from a range of perspectives (e.g., Finlayson and McCay 1998; Hutchings and Myers 1994). The discussion here builds on this author's previous contributions (e.g., Charles 1995, 1998b, 2001) to assess the collapse through the lens of adaptive co-management. The focus in particular is on past shortcomings with respect to four adaptive co-management ingredients, the role that these shortcomings played in the collapse of the fishery, and an examination of whether current trends in the fishery are improving the situation.

Missing: An Appropriate Management Portfolio
Since the 1970s, the cornerstone of management for the Atlantic Canadian groundfishery has been quota management (Parsons 1993). This method, which is widespread and increasing in the world's fisheries (at least in developed countries), involves two steps: (1) for each fish stock of interest, setting a limit on what is allowed to be caught – the total allowable catch (TAC) – and then (2) subdividing the TAC into *quotas* (fractions of the TAC) that are then allocated to specific nations, fishing gear types, vessel categories (e.g., by boat size), and possibly individual fishery participants. Quota management has two key components, each with its own appeal: its first step (the TAC-setting process) aspires to limit human impact on the resource, and the second step (setting quotas) is meant to provide a simple mechanism to allocate fish among competing users. It also has its flaws, however, and overreliance on this one management tool appears to have adversely affected sustainability and resilience in the fishery.

First, the root of the problem lies in the fact that setting a TAC requires knowledge of the current fish biomass, but such knowledge is highly uncertain and even biased, due largely to the challenges of assessing the size of fish populations. Surveys of those populations carried out by government research vessels provided only temporal snapshots of abundance, and often were limited in spatial extent (for example, since large survey vessels cannot travel close to shore), covering only a fraction of the spatial diversity of the stocks. This had two consequences: estimates of the stock were biased, and fishers could easily question the validity of the scientific process, which thus tended to be disputed.

Second, it was often assumed that higher catches of fish per boat per unit time implied a greater abundance of fish in the sea. Hence these "commercial fishery catch rates" were used as direct indicators of the state of the fish stocks. In fact, this is a dangerous assumption: the rate at which fish are caught may have little connection to fish abundance, since even as stocks decline, fish-finding technology enables catching of much of the remaining fish. Yet high catch rates created the faulty illusion of a healthy stock, leading to the setting of excessive TACs.

These problems meant that uncertainty and biases in the estimates of biomass led to serious errors in setting excessive quotas (and, as will be discussed below, it proved difficult to reduce quotas even when they were recognized as being too high). This, along with other factors discussed below, contributed to overexploitation of groundfish stocks, a loss of ecological sustainability, reduced resilience, and the subsequent collapse (Charles 1995; Walters and Pearse 1996).

While various biologically oriented "technical measures" – such as fishing gear restrictions and closed areas – supplemented quota management, there was a reluctance to broaden the toolkit of options for management to allow for significant alternatives, such as input controls (as used in Canada's lobster fishery) or ecosystem-level measures like protected areas. To what extent might a collapse have been avoided, or its impact lessened, if management had drawn on a broader toolkit? This would seem to be a relevant question to address, yet it is one that has received little attention. Even a review of groundfish management experience (Angel et al. 1994) did not incorporate a critical assessment of the reliance on quota management.

Missing: Robust Management

It was argued earlier that a key ingredient of adaptive co-management involves making the management system more *robust,* that is, designing the system to make it less sensitive to structural uncertainty. This in turn includes a need for adaptive management and a precautionary approach. There are, however, various illustrations of how management of Canada's Atlantic groundfish fishery lacked this robust, adaptive approach (e.g., Charles 1995).

First, the strong reliance, noted earlier, on a single management tool (quota setting) in groundfish management was not conducive to robust management, given the very high levels of uncertainty in the stocks (and thus the challenges in setting TACs) and the limited capability to control the fishing behaviour of vessels out at sea.

Second, even within the TAC system, robust management implies that greater attention be paid to dealing with the uncertainties in fish stock abundance that affect quotas. Although scientists knew that the TAC calculations were highly uncertain, quota management demanded a single number for the TAC so that it could be easily divided up and allocated into quotas.

While providing a range of numbers would more realistically reflect the underlying uncertainty, that would not have been as convenient for quota setting. This system therefore provides little incentive for properly high-lighting the fishery's inherent uncertainty. Furthermore, since an allocation approach based on "dividing up the pie" can be carried out regardless of the quality of underlying biomass estimates, the system will *appear* to work, even with poor data and correspondingly incorrect TACs. While better esti-mates of the biomass would likely have produced more accurate TACs, the above reality may have led to reduced incentives for dealing with the inher-ent uncertainty and biases in fish stock estimates.

Third, institutionalized barriers were in place within the management process itself that limited adaptive adjustments to TACs as new information became available over time. Notably, the "50% rule" (DFO 1991, 5) stated that when scientific evidence called for a reduction in the harvest of a groundfish stock, government would reduce the TAC by only 50 percent of the required amount, unless scientists could "prove" a conservation crisis. This gradualism did not apply in the opposite direction; if scientific analy-sis suggested that an increase was possible in the TAC, the full increase could be made immediately. This rule was used to reduce the socio-economic im-pacts of stock declines, but it also had the effect of preventing conservation targets from being met.

Fourth, within the fishing season, when the scientific process resulted in adjustments to the understanding of fish stock levels, the TACs that had been set prior to the start of the season were rarely adjusted based on this new information. An allowance was made for in-season revisions "as a con-sequence of major changes in the scientific advice" (DFO 1991), but this rarely occurred. Instead, in the face of declining stocks, any changes to the TAC proposed within the course of a given fishing season as a result of the scientific process were typically delayed at least until the following year's fishing plan.

This lack of adaptive management likely contributed to the collapse of the groundfishery. But why was groundfish management in Atlantic Can-ada non-adaptive? Two reasons might be noted. First, the methodologies and assumptions used in the stock assessment process led government sci-entists to conclude (unfortunately, in retrospect) that such a rapid response was unnecessary from a conservation perspective. Second, once quota allo-cations were made for a given fishing season, changes within the course of the season were inconvenient to the fishing industry and so were rarely contemplated.

The latter reason is linked to the "illusion of certainty" described above. As each TAC is subdivided into allocations for distribution to fishery sec-tors, these were seen as unchangeable "pieces of the pie." This attitude was particularly apparent when quotas were further subdivided to individual companies or fishers, which were then encouraged to make market commitments, literally banking on these shares. This led to a situation in which, even if scientific evidence arose during a fishing season indicating potential conservation problems, TAC reductions were delayed, at least to the following year. Such non-adaptive management and within-season rigidity contributed to poor conservation practices (Angel et al. 1994).

Missing: Full Use of the Knowledge Base
The Atlantic Canadian groundfishery involves a multiplicity of species (such as cod, haddock, and pollock) and an equal variety of fleets and gears. Given this complexity, the knowledge base in the fishery may never be entirely adequate, yet a case can be made that even the range of knowledge available prior to the groundfish collapse was not well utilized.

First, the northwest Atlantic region has been the subject of abundant oceanographic and ecological research, but the fishery management process, at least prior to the groundfish collapse and the popularization of "ecosystem approach" ideas, was not developed to use this knowledge. Indeed, the appeal of quota management lies in its apparent simplicity – for each fish stock, the TAC is calculated as a fraction of the estimated biomass, and then the resulting TAC is divided into pieces. This "simple" process can proceed without considering ecosystem or oceanographic aspects (changes in ocean temperature, salinity, predator abundance, etc.), even though it may produce neither a reasonable assessment of biological productivity nor a reasonable TAC value, in the absence of knowledge of this sort (e.g., Drinkwater and Mountain 1997).

Also crucial in fishery management, but underutilized in the past, are the various forms of knowledge referred to earlier – fisher knowledge, local knowledge, and traditional ecological knowledge (TEK). These are particularly important in providing a complement to scientifically determined knowledge (e.g., Johannes et al. 2000; Neis et al. 1999; Neis and Felt 2000). Indeed, prior to the groundfish collapse off the coast of Newfoundland, many fishers expressed concern about the state of the cod stock and the need for conservation (e.g., Finlayson 1994). This may have reflected the fundamental idea in adaptive co-management of "learning by doing," to the extent that some inshore small-boat fishery participants learned of fish stock declines through declines in their own fishing success (diminished "catch rates"). On the other hand, such an assessment was not uniform; there were also more positive, and mixed, views on the state of the fish stocks from others in the fishery (Finlayson and McCay 1998). The range of commentaries that occurred may have reflected natural variations in the knowledge base, as noted above, or the variations may have been designed to influence management responses (for example, implying that fishing should be reduced or that it should be continued). In any case, it is clear that fishery managers at the time had no systematic means of analyzing this fisher knowledge base, and thus missed out on significant information that could have been utilized in parallel with scientific analyses to better maintain the fishery's sustainability.

Missing: Institutional Reform

At the time of the collapse, the Atlantic Canadian groundfishery, like many other fisheries, was managed in a relatively top-down manner by the federal government. Although some fishery participants were invited into processes of "consultation," overall an us-versus-them situation emerged, in which many fishers had little respect for the regulations that were imposed on them without their participation. As a result, efforts to thwart the regulations were commonplace, yet management seems to have overestimated how closely its measures would be adhered to by fishers. This may have been due in part to a lack of attention within governmental research to understanding the people side of the fishery (for example, the behavioural response of fishers to the regulations).

This problem was compounded by the incentives created by the quota management system for fishers to catch more fish, and more valuable fish, than allowed in the established quotas. Such incentives led not only to overfishing beyond the TAC but, more insidiously, to the dumping of lower-valued fish overboard, out at sea, by fishing enterprises seeking to maximize the value of their quotas (Angel et al. 1994; Charles 1995). While such behaviour could be anticipated, given the incentives in place, what went on at sea received little attention in the groundfish management process, which focused instead on whether the amounts of fish actually brought to shore matched the annual TAC. Little attention was paid to assessing the total amount of fish killed – not only the fish brought to shore but also the lower-valued or over-quota fish dumped overboard at sea, out of sight of the monitoring, by those thwarting the regulations.

This all contributed to a *fallacy of controllability*, as described earlier – a perception on the part of fishery management that more can be controlled through management than is realistically the case. Indeed, the results were clearly opposite to those sought by the governmental managers trying to control the fishery – illegal fishing and wasteful practices led to severe negative impacts on conservation (Charles 1995, 1998a; Walters and Pearse 1996).

The lack of buy-in from the fishers meant that efforts to achieve better enforcement of fishery regulations proved insufficient (Angel et al. 1994). As elsewhere, enforcement has not proven particularly successful where regulations were imposed on fishers. Instead, it is clear that successful resource management requires compliance measures that alter the inherent incentives to overharvest. This requires institutional reform to change the basic nature of management (e.g., de Young et al. 1999; Pitcher et al. 1998). As

noted earlier, a crucial aspect of this is co-management – increased participation of harvesters in setting the rules and encouraging compliance with
them, which leads to a more inclusive and often a more local-level approach
to management. Some moves in this direction since the groundfish collapse are described below.

Moving to Adaptive Co-Management

The foregoing has painted the Atlantic Canadian groundfishery, in the time
leading up to the collapse of the early 1990s, as a resource system lacking in
robustness, a precautionary approach, adaptive decision making, and co-
operative management arrangements. These shortcomings manifested themselves through an "illusion of certainty," a "fallacy of controllability," and
overall management rigidity, resulting in a notable lack of resilience and
sustainability, and ultimately in a major fishery collapse. It would be difficult to argue that the groundfishery in Atlantic Canada was an example of
successful resource management.

The argument has been made here that a lack of four key ingredients of
adaptive co-management may have contributed to the collapse of that fishery. This is not to suggest that there was a total absence of adaptive co-
management. As noted at the outset, it is not an all-or-nothing proposition,
and such ingredients are unlikely to be either entirely present or entirely
absent. Instead, there can be implications arising from the degree to which
adaptive co-management is present or absent, and the point here is that a
lack of certain elements of adaptive co-management seems to have led to
specific, damaging impacts on the achievement of a sustainable, resilient
resource system.

This section shifts from a focus on the period of the groundfishery collapse to briefly explore whether, since that time, the ingredients of adaptive
co-management are becoming better incorporated in the fishery. At the
outset, it is worth noting that the early 1990s – the time of the collapse – was
also a time of transition in the overall thinking on fishery management.
Concepts of robust and adaptive management were still being developed.
The value of scientific, local, and fisher knowledge was just becoming more
widely understood. And the institutional reform involving a shift from
top-down management to co-management had not yet been fully implemented. In some senses, then, the collapse came at an unlucky time, before
the importance of these ingredients of adaptive co-management were fully
comprehended. Since then, there has been a mixed bag of progress, discussed briefly here as it relates to this chapter's four ingredients of adaptive
co-management.

(1) There have been some positive moves towards a more diversified
management portfolio and greater robustness in management. For example, there is greater attention, at least at the policy level, to implementing a

precautionary approach and an ecosystem approach. There has been a clear addition to the management portfolio of marine protected areas (MPAs), areas of the ocean designated for particular protection and management attention. Although few MPAs have been put in place to date, so the impact on fishery conservation is limited, the option to create MPAs has the potential to increase fishery resilience by providing additional insurance if other management measures should fail (e.g., Gell and Roberts 2003).

On the other hand, the reliance on quota management in the groundfishery remains intact, meaning that successful fishery conservation continues to depend largely on properly setting and enforcing total allowable catches, while the allocation structure continues to revolve around dividing the TAC pie into quota pieces. Canada is similar to many countries in using quotas, and it must be noted that this approach provides various political and administrative benefits. For example, within the federal management agency, moves to implement allocation schemes such as individual transferable quotas rely on the mechanisms inherent in quota management, and within the fishing industry, those who receive the largest quota allocations are naturally keen to preserve them. These realities limit the motivation for change among many in the fishery. Yet if there is value in moving towards adaptive co-management to enable better adaptation to natural variability and change, it may be necessary to rely less on this single approach and more on the creation of local-level management portfolios, based on choices of management tools more suited to local situations.

A compromise may be to combine current output-based quotas with input-based controls on fishing effort (Pope 2002). From the perspective of adaptive co-management, such effort controls have the advantage of being less sensitive to uncertainty, since the key variables tend to be more easily observed and since harvests adapt naturally to the state of the resource. This form of management has already benefited the lobster fishery in Atlantic Canada. While "perverse incentives" are created by both effort and quota controls, when used separately (the former leading to increasing fishing capacity and the latter to dumping and discarding of fish), a combination of quota and effort management could provide greater assurance that conservation measures are not thwarted. This diversification of the management portfolio was proposed for the groundfishery by fishers (e.g., in the Bay of Fundy) and conservation bodies (e.g., FRCC 1996), but has yet to be adopted.

(2) With respect to sources of knowledge, there appears to be progress in developing indicator systems to monitor the fishery and its surroundings more systematically (e.g., Charles et al. 2002; Halliday et al. 2001). There have also been positive moves towards greater incorporation of fisher knowledge into fishery and fish stock assessments, and towards a participatory approach to research (King et al. 1994; Neis and Felt 2000; Wiber et al. 2004).

On the other hand, where local and/or fisher knowledge does not mesh with the dominant approach of governmental fishery management, there may be resistance to the application of such knowledge. For example, fishers in the Bay of Fundy area have long sought to have their fishery managed separately from others, in keeping with local knowledge of fishing methods that are utilized in a fundamentally different way due to the bay's strong tides. The validity of this proposal has been reinforced by biological research demonstrating that the local cod stock is genetically distinct from those elsewhere. This combined base of fisher and scientific knowledge points logically to the desirability of a local management system in the Bay of Fundy. Such a move, however, while apparently compatible with adaptive co-management and an ecosystem approach to fisheries, has not been implemented, perhaps because the management adjustments it would require (possible changes to fishing zones and quota allocations) make it unpalatable to some, and thus politically undesirable to put into place.

(3) With respect to institutional reform, considerable change has taken place since the fishery collapse. There have been major moves by government to entrench a permanent set of quota allocations in the groundfishery and to engage in greater co-management with the various fishery sectors. These moves have been underway for over a decade, and are reflected in writing in the government's new *Policy Framework for the Management of Fisheries on Canada's Atlantic Coast* (DFO 2004). The analysis in this chapter suggests that such moves may have mixed results in terms of adaptive co-management.

On the one hand, this could lead to management being less adaptive, with allocations becoming more rigid and with a narrower concentration of quota holdings. On the other hand, there is clearly more co-management. A significant example is the inshore small-boat groundfish sector of the Scotia-Fundy administrative region (Bay of Fundy and Scotian Shelf), which has developed innovative local-level management through community fishery management boards (Charles et al. 2007). This fisher-initiated system has operated since 1995 and is widely considered to have been successful in devolving operational management decisions to the community level (Bigney 2005). It also has a notably adaptive nature in allowing for diverse models of local management. Other examples of grassroots initiatives include local approaches to crab and lobster management in the eastern Gulf of St. Lawrence (Loucks 2005) and community-based approaches by fishers' associations for managing allocations and harvesting in snow crab fisheries in the Scotia-Fundy administrative region (Wiber et al. 2004).

If the new policy framework (DFO 2004) leads to a greater commitment to local-level ("place-based") management, it would support the institutional reform needed for adaptive co-management. A complicating factor in any institutional reform, however, is the reality of the power structure in the groundfishery, which limits the flexibility of management to make changes. While more significant change may be preferable for adaptive co-management, change may be feasible only within the constraints of existing structures, allocations, and management processes.

Conclusions

This chapter has explored the role of four possible ingredients of adaptive co-management: (1) diverse options for a portfolio of management measures, (2) adoption of robust management approaches, (3) full utilization of knowledge, and (4) appropriate institutional reform. It examined the implications of an absence of adaptive co-management, or, more precisely, an absence of the above ingredients, in a particular case study – Atlantic Canada's groundfishery and its historic collapse in the 1990s. The analysis showed how an absence of each ingredient contributed to a loss of sustainability (e.g., through declining stocks) and resilience (e.g., through "fishing down the food chain" and a lack of self-regulatory institutions).

Of course, to argue that certain policy directions are ingredients of adaptive co-management is not to claim that they are the only ingredients. This chapter has not attempted to define what might constitute a sufficient set of ingredients, or to describe the appearance of a fishery with "complete" adaptive co-management. Indeed, it is questionable whether this would be possible at all, and whether, as with related concepts such as sustainable development and resilient systems, there can really be a complete recipe for adaptive co-management. This is a topic worthy of further research, and adaptive co-management, as a direction in which to take natural resource policy, is a ripe field for research.

The groundfishery case study, for example, noted that since the fishery collapse, there has been some increased awareness of the risks to sustainability and resilience posed by current practices, and some progress in adopting adaptive co-management. It was also clear, however, that much more could be done to incorporate the ingredients of adaptive co-management into fishery management. Why, following one of the most dramatic resource collapses globally, has there not been more complete adoption of these ingredients? A full examination of this question is beyond the scope of the present discussion but is certainly worthy of further study. Possible reasons might range from a lack of suitable mechanisms for effective learning over time (a core aspect of adaptive co-management) to the diversity of conflicting interests and centres of power that create resistance to new policy directions.

Whatever the reason, the broad conclusion from this discussion provides a sobering counterpoint to the sense that many may have that the logic of adaptive co-management is persuasive and unstoppable. The reality is that, at least in some cases, the changes that may be needed in order to implement adaptive co-management may not fit well within the existing management system, which was likely developed and structured to meet very different priorities. As a result, adaptive co-management may face significant barriers. On the other hand, this chapter has emphasized the point that adaptive co-management is not an all-or-nothing proposition. It may be possible for suitable approaches – aspects of adaptive management and co-management – to be implemented to varying degrees and over varying time frames. In this incremental way, there may well be scope for progress towards adaptive co-management in any natural resource system.

Acknowledgments
The author is grateful to Derek Armitage, Fikret Berkes, and Nancy Doubleday for their initiative in producing this volume, and to participants in the adaptive co-management workshops on which it is based, for their constructive comments on this chapter. The support provided by a Pew Fellowship in Marine Conservation and by the Natural Sciences and Engineering Research Council of Canada, operating grant 6745, is gratefully acknowledged.

References
Angel, J.R., D.L. Burke, R.N. O'Boyle, F.G. Peacock, M. Sinclair, and K.C.T. Zwanenburg. 1994. *Report of the workshop on Scotia-Fundy groundfish management from 1977 to 1993.* Canadian Technical Report of Fisheries and Aquatic Sciences no. 1979. Ottawa: Department of Fisheries and Oceans.

Berkes, F., ed. 1989. *Common property resources: Ecology and community-based sustainable development.* London: Bellhaven Press.

–. 1999. *Sacred ecology: Traditional ecological knowledge and resource management.* Philadelphia: Taylor and Francis.

Berkes, F., and C. Folke, eds. 1998. *Linking social and ecological systems: Management practices and social mechanisms for building resilience.* Cambridge: Cambridge University Press.

Bigney, K. 2005. *Co-managing troubled waters: Community-based co-management in the Scotia Fundy groundfishery.* Master of Environmental Studies thesis, Dalhousie University, Halifax.

Charles, A.T. 1995. The Atlantic Canadian groundfishery: Roots of a collapse. *Dalhousie Law Journal* 18: 65-83.

–. 1997. *Sustainability indicators: An annotated bibliography with emphasis on fishery systems, coastal zones and watersheds.* Ottawa: Strategy for International Fisheries Research, International Development Research Centre.

–. 1998a. Fisheries in transition. In *Ocean yearbook 13,* ed. E.M. Borgese, A. Chircop, M. McConnell, and J.R. Morgan, 15-37. Chicago: University of Chicago Press.

–. 1998b. Living with uncertainty in fisheries: Analytical methods, management priorities and the Canadian groundfishery experience. *Fisheries Research* 37: 37-50.

–. 2001. *Sustainable fishery systems.* Oxford: Blackwell Science.

–. 2004. Sustainability and resilience in natural resource systems: Policy directions and management institutions. In *Encyclopaedia of Life Support Systems (EOLSS),* ed. Y-K. Ng and I. Wills. Oxford: EOLSS Publishers.

Charles, A.T., H. Boyd, A. Lavers, and C. Benjamin. 2002. *The Nova Scotia GPI fisheries and marine environment accounts: A preliminary set of ecological, socioeconomic and institutional indicators for Nova Scotia's fisheries and marine environment.* Tantallon, NS: GPI Atlantic.

Charles, A.T., A. Bull, J. Kearney, and C. Milley. 2007. Community-based fisheries in the Canadian Maritimes. In *Fisheries management: Progress towards sustainability,* ed. T. McClanahan and J.C. Castilla, 274-301. Oxford: Blackwell Publishing.

de Young, B., R.M. Peterman, A.R. Dobell, E. Pinkerton, Y. Breton, A.T. Charles, M.J. Fogarty, G.R. Munro, and C. Taggart. 1999. *Canadian marine fisheries in a changing and uncertain world.* Canadian Special Publication of Fisheries and Aquatic Sciences, no. 129. Ottawa: NRC Research Press.

DFO (Department of Fisheries and Oceans). 1991. *1992 Atlantic groundfish management plan.* Ottawa: Minister of Supply and Services.

–. 2004. *A policy framework for the management of fisheries on Canada's Atlantic coast.* DFO 2004-64. Ottawa: Communications Branch, Department of Fisheries and Oceans.

Drinkwater, K.F., and D.G. Mountain. 1997. Climate and oceanography. In *Northwest Atlantic groundfish: Perspectives on a fishery collapse,* ed. J.G. Boreman, B.S. Nakashima, J.A. Wilson, and R.L. Kendall, 3-25. Bethesda, MD: American Fisheries Society.

FAO (Food and Agriculture Organization of the United Nations). 1996. *Precautionary approach to capture fisheries and species introductions.* FAO Technical Guidelines for Responsible Fisheries, no. 2. Rome: FAO.

–. 1999. *Indicators for sustainable development of marine capture fisheries.* FAO Technical Guidelines for Responsible Fisheries, no. 8. Rome: FAO.

–. 2003. *The ecosystem approach to fisheries.* FAO Technical Guidelines for Responsible Fisheries, no. 4, suppl. 2. Rome: FAO.

Finlayson, C. 1994. *Fishing for truth: A sociological analysis of the northern cod stock assessments from 1977-1990.* St. John's, NL: ISER Books.

Finlayson, A.C., and B.J. McCay. 1998. Crossing the threshold of ecosystem resilience: The commercial extinction of northern cod. In *Linking social and ecological systems: Management practices and social mechanisms for building resilience,* ed. F. Berkes and C. Folke, 311-37. Cambridge: Cambridge University Press.

Folke, C., and F. Berkes. 1998. *Understanding dynamics of ecosystem-institution linkages for building resilience.* Beijer Discussion Paper Series, no. 112. Stockholm: Beijer International Institute of Ecological Economics, Royal Swedish Academy of Sciences.

FRCC (Fisheries Resource Conservation Council). 1996. *Quota controls and effort controls: Conservation considerations.* Discussion paper FRCC.96.TD.3. Ottawa: Fisheries Resource Conservation Council.

Gell, F.R., and C.M. Roberts. 2003. Benefits beyond boundaries: The fishery effects of marine reserves. *Trends in Ecology and Evolution* 18: 448-55.

Halliday, R.G., L.P. Fanning, and R.K. Mohn. 2001. *Use of the traffic light method in fishery management planning.* Canadian Science Advisory Secretariat research document 2001/108. Ottawa: Department of Fisheries and Oceans.

Hanna, S., and M. Munasinghe, eds. 1995. *Property rights in a social and ecological context: Case studies and design applications.* Stockholm: Beijer Institute of Ecological Economics; Washington, DC: World Bank.

Holling C.S. 1973. Resilience and stability of ecological systems. *Annual Review of Ecology and Systematics* 4: 1-23.

Hutchings, J.A., and R.A. Myers. 1994. What can be learned from the collapse of a renewable resource? Atlantic cod, *Gadus morhua,* of Newfoundland and Labrador. *Canadian Journal of Fisheries and Aquatic Sciences* 51: 2126-46.

Johannes, R.E., M.M.R. Freeman, and R.J. Hamilton. 2000. Ignore fishers' knowledge and miss the boat. *Fish and Fisheries* 1: 257-71.

King, P.A., S.G. Elsworth, and R.F. Baker. 1994. Partnerships – the route to better communication. In *Coastal Zone Canada '94, cooperation in the coastal zone: Conference proceedings,* ed. P.G. Wells and P.J. Ricketts, 596-611. Dartmouth, NS: Coastal Zone Canada Association.

Kurlansky, M. 1997. *Cod: A biography of the fish that changed the world.* New York: Walker Publishing.

Loucks, L.A. 2005. *The evolution of the Area 19 Snow Crab Co-Management Agreement: Understanding the inter-relationship between transaction costs, credible commitment and collective action.* PhD dissertation, Simon Fraser University, Burnaby, BC.

Myers, R.A., J.A. Hutchings, and N.J. Barrowman. 1997. Why do fish stocks collapse? The example of cod in Atlantic Canada. *Ecological Applications* 7: 91-106.

Neis, B., and L. Felt, eds. 2000. *Finding our sea legs: Linking fishery people and their knowledge with science and management.* St. John's, NL: ISER Books.

Neis, B., D.C. Schneider, L. Felt, R.L. Haedrich, J. Fischer, and J.A. Hutchings. 1999. Fisheries assessment: What can be learned from interviewing resource users? *Canadian Journal of Fisheries and Aquatic Sciences* 56: 1949-63.

Ostrom, E. 1990. *Governing the commons.* Cambridge: Cambridge University Press.

Parsons, L.S. 1993. *Management of marine fisheries in Canada.* Canadian Bulletin of Fisheries and Aquatic Sciences, no. 225. Ottawa: National Research Council of Canada.

Pauly, D., and J. Maclean. 2003. *In a perfect ocean: The state of the fisheries and ecosystems in the North Atlantic Ocean.* Washington, DC: Island Press.

Pinkerton, E., and M. Weinstein. 1995. *Fisheries that work: Sustainability through community-based management.* Vancouver: The David Suzuki Foundation.

Pitcher, T.J., P.J.B. Hart, and D. Pauly, eds. 1998. *Re-inventing fisheries management.* Dordrecht, Netherlands: Kluwer Academic Publishers.

Pope, J. 2002. Input and output controls: The practice of fishing effort and catch management in responsible fisheries. In *A fishery manager's guidebook: Management measures and their application,* ed. K. Cochrane, 75-93. FAO fisheries technical paper no. 424. Rome: FAO.

Roberts, C.M., and J.P. Hawkins. 2000. *Fully-protected marine reserves: A guide.* Washington, DC: WWF Endangered Seas Campaign; York, UK: Environment Department, University of York.

Walters, C.J. 1986. *Adaptive management of renewable resources.* New York: Macmillan.

Walters, C.J., and P.H. Pearse. 1996. Stock information requirements for quota management systems in commercial fisheries. *Review of Fish Biology and Fisheries* 6: 21-42.

Wiber, M., F. Berkes, A.T. Charles, and J. Kearney. 2004. Participatory research supporting community-based fishery management. *Marine Policy* 28: 459-68.

Wilson, D.C., J.P. Nielsen, and P. Degnbol, eds. 2003. *The fisheries co-management experience: Accomplishments, challenges, and prospects.* Dordrecht, Netherlands: Kluwer Academic Publishers.

Part 2: Case Studies

6

Challenges Facing Coastal Resource Co-Management in the Caribbean

Patrick McConney, Robin Mahon, and Robert Pomeroy

Only since the 1980s has coastal and fisheries management become a major concern for governments in the English-speaking countries of the Caribbean. Often their concerns come from trying to satisfy obligations under international agreements, and they seek solutions through a range of stakeholders (McConney and Mahon 1998). Attempts to co-manage fisheries and coastal resources have increased as new and more participative approaches to governance have been sought. To resource managers, users, and other stakeholders in these countries, however, the term "co-management" has different meanings, even when qualified by explanatory words such as "consultative," "collaborative," and "delegative" (McConney et al. 2003c). These different meanings, elicit different responses to co-management. Understanding the ways in which people perceive and cope within ecological and social systems at various scales is critical to determining what types of co-management arrangements and processes are likely to succeed. Recent applied research projects in Barbados, Grenada, and Belize have added to the information available on co-management as a component of sustainable development, identified challenges, and raised questions about success (e.g., McConney et al. 2003c).

In Barbados, the national Fisheries Advisory Committee developed a strategic plan to strengthen its role and effectiveness as a policy advice mechanism, seeking to renegotiate its position in the legal/institutional structure of fisheries management. The sea urchin harvesters in Barbados have determined what arrangements will enable them to participate in management with least exposure to the risks of resource fluctuations and the uncertainties of management decision making. In Grenada, beach seine fishers have devised means of establishing formal co-management arrangements in response to the declining effectiveness of their system of community-based territorial use rights. In Belize, co-management agreements for marine protected areas (MPAs) are struggling to perform under competing agencies whose jurisdictions operate at different scales with different purposes.

These four cases contribute to learning about the co-management of coastal resources in the Caribbean and highlight some of the challenges involved. This chapter presents an evaluation of the conditions for success-ful co-management in these cases, and recommends further research on some key aspects of co-management in the Caribbean in order to overcome these challenges.

Concepts

Concepts that give context to the cases include complexity, uncertainty, cross-scale linkages, adaptation, and co-management. The treatment here will be brief, since each of these terms has associated with it a large body of literature (e.g., McCay and Acheson 1987; Pinkerton 1989; Hilborn and Walters 1992; Berkes and Folke 1998; Gunderson and Holling 2002; Ostrom et al. 2002; Ostrom 2005). (See also Chapter 1 and other chapters in this volume.)

Simply put, complexity is a feature of systems consisting of diverse com-ponents among which there are many interactions, such as social and eco-logical systems (Gunderson and Holling 2002). Institutional complexity (with redundancy, feedback loops, nested systems, and so on) may be beneficial and may facilitate resilience and robustness (Ostrom 2005). Complex pro-cesses and organizational structures may also contribute to chaos, however (Eoyang 1997). Uncertainty reflects the probability that a particular quanti-tative or qualitative estimate, piece of advice, or management action may be incorrect, and researchers distinguish several types (Berkes et al. 2001). Ostrom (2005) also makes the important distinction between the situational and cognitive aspects of uncertainty. Charles (2001, 311) refers to the "illu-sion of certainty" and the "fallacy of controllability" as perceptual and con-ceptual problems of complexity and uncertainty that require rethinking in fisheries management. He and others (e.g., Wilson 2001) provide additional examples of types and sources of complexity and uncertainty that illustrate the multi-dimensional nature of these features of ecological and human systems and their consequences for resource management.

The point is that complexity and uncertainty challenge our ability to fully understand social and ecological systems. Participants in action are-nas (Ostrom 2005) such as pre-implementation stages of co-management may view complexity and uncertainty as quite overwhelming and problem-atic. This may be dealt with partly through processes of systematic learning and flexible management based upon lessons learned. Some approaches to management that combine knowledge of ecological and social systems can accommodate complexity and uncertainty better than approaches that more rigidly seek to categorize, compartmentalize, and control. One of the more promising responsive systems is co-management, which is often simply defined as the sharing of power and responsibility between the state and

Figure 6.1

Types of co-management

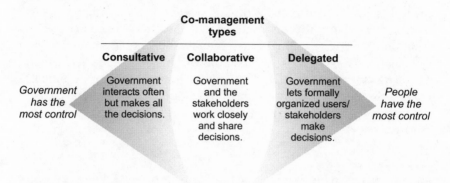

Source: Adapted from ICLARM and IFM (1998).

resource user groups in the management of natural resources (Pinkerton 1989). The degree and type of sharing among the stakeholders can be illustrated as a spectrum of co-management arrangements, with consultative, collaborative, and delegated being the types used in researching the cases described later (Figure 6.1).

Community-based co-management has its locus of responsibility and authority at the local level. It is most relevant where local-level resource use and governance systems are evident, particularly for delegated co-management, but delegated co-management may also be at district or national scales. There are also different phases of co-management: pre-implementation, implementation, and post-implementation. It may take several years for even the most successful co-management initiative to progress from one phase to the next. Many make no progress, others regress, and some fail completely. Each phase has different characteristics (Figure 6.2).

Figure 6.2

Phases of co-management

Pre-implementation	→	Implementation	→	Post-implementation
• Realize need for change. • Meet and discuss change. • Develop new management.		• Try out new management. • Educate people in new ways. • Adjust and decide what is best.		• Maintain best arrangements. • Resolve conflicts and enforce. • Accept as standard practice.

Source: Based on Pomeroy (1998)

Co-management (any type or phase) is adaptive where ecological knowledge and institutional arrangements are tested and revised in a dynamic, ongoing, self-organized process of learning-by-doing (Folke et al. 2002). These processes involve cross-scale linkages (Berkes 2001) among diverse stakeholders, often at the level of the ecosystem in cases of resource management on a large scale, and may help to build resilience in social-ecological systems (Olsson et al. 2004). Adaptation with horizontal and vertical linkages across various scales (e.g., local, national, transboundary) is desirable but is currently not a strong feature of these cases. This point is taken up in the discussion that follows the presentation of methods, cases, and other research results.

Methods

Cases to be researched were selected to illustrate two different examples of co-management initiatives in each of the three project countries. Four of the six cases are reported on here. Participatory research was undertaken by the authors and local collaborators between 2002 and 2004 through a project implemented by the Caribbean Conservation Association (CCA). Participatory research involved the case study stakeholders in the research design, data collection, analysis, interpretation, and validation of results. This collaboration serves to enlighten both stakeholders and investigators through information exchange (Berkes et al. 2001). The research framework used in the cases (Figure 6.3) illustrates how local contexts and exogenous factors may shape patterns of interaction with outcomes that feed back into the system through consequences and learning (ICLARM and IFM 1998).

Figure 6.3

Modified ICLARM/IFM institutional analysis and design research framework

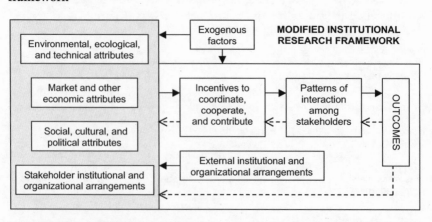

Data collection methods included structured, semi-structured, and informal interviews; focus groups; document content analysis; and workshops of various types. Stakeholder workshops were held in each country to evaluate the extent to which participants thought that conditions favouring successful co-management were met. Some of the conditions concern problem identification, management area, stakeholder participation, power sharing, conflict, trust, respect, communication, coordination, compliance, capacity, enforcement, external agents, leadership, legislation, decentralization, adaptation, socio-cultural fit, and more. The list of conditions used in this research (see Table 6.2) was drawn from international and Caribbean literature on co-management (Pomeroy et al. 2001, 2003). Each condition was ranked by the participants according to its perceived presence using the following scale: 0 = absent; 1 = present but weak; 2 = present to a fair extent; 3 = strong feature.

Despite the fact that criteria for success were somewhat situation-specific, certain conditions have emerged as favouring co-management (Berkes et al. 2001) and a range of common-pool resource institutions (Agrawal 2001). Evaluation results for Barbados, Grenada, and Belize are presented after summaries of the cases.

Cases

Co-management within different social-ecological systems was examined through participatory research that contributed to the development of guidelines for coastal resource co-management in the Caribbean (McConney et al. 2003c). Four cases (two in Barbados and one each in Grenada and Belize; see Figure 6.4) are outlined below to illustrate the ways in which stakeholders have attempted to establish institutional arrangements for co-management. These are still evolving as participants try to cope with numerous challenges.

Barbados Fisheries Advisory Committee

This case concerns the struggle of a national-level, legally established co-management body to empower and position itself to effect change across the entire fisheries sector. Barbados is the most eastern of the Caribbean islands, being entirely surrounded by the Atlantic Ocean (Figure 6.4). The island shelf is only 320 square kilometres, and deep water is found close to shore. Eight main fisheries take place in the waters of Barbados, categorized by target species, fishing gear, and location. Large pelagic fishes (e.g., dolphinfish, tunas, and billfish) are caught offshore with hand lines, troll lines, and longlines. Flyingfish are caught offshore with gillnets, hand lines, and dip nets. Shallow-shelf reef fish are caught with fish traps, set nets, and spearguns on and around coastal coral reefs. Deep-slope fishes (e.g., snappers and groupers) are caught mainly with fish traps and hand lines on the deep-reef slope, bank reefs, and deep shelf. Coastal pelagics (e.g., small jacks

Figure 6.4

Case study locations in the Caribbean

and tunas) are caught by many gear types on the island shelf. Sea urchins are harvested by hand from shallow waters. Small amounts of lobster and conch are taken in fish traps and by divers (by hand and with spears) in coastal waters on the island shelf. Some of the inshore fisheries are considered to be overexploited, and all fisheries are open-access.

All of the fisheries are small-scale, using motorized vessels ranging from 5 to 15 metres in length on trips lasting a couple of hours to a couple of weeks. The sector employs about 2,000 fishers, or triple this number when post-harvest and ancillary services are included. Although the annual catch is about 5,000 metric tonnes, a similar volume of seafood is imported to supply local residential and tourism demands. The few fish-processing plants mainly export fresh tunas and swordfish. The harvest sector is poorly organized in terms of producer groups. The annual contribution of fishing to gross domestic product (GDP) is less than 1 percent.

A feature of harmonized fisheries legislation in the eastern Caribbean is that national Fisheries Advisory Committees (FACs) are expected to advise fisheries ministers on management (both conservation and development). The FAC in Barbados, which has existed since 1995, is potentially a statutory national consultative co-management arrangement via a multi-stakeholder body (McConney and Mahon 1998). McConney and colleagues (2003a) examined the institutional relationships of the Barbados FAC in a case study that focused on what its members wanted to do to enhance its co-management capacity in addressing several unmanaged, open-access, small-scale fisheries.

In Barbados, the nine-member FAC has fairly low status, despite being mandatory under the Fisheries Act and being affiliated with the Ministry of Agriculture and Rural Development. It consists of four members from the fishing industry appointed on the basis of individual expertise (fish processor, vendor, boat owner, and fisher), and one organizational representative (Barbados National Union of Fisherfolk Organisations, or BARNUFO). The Chief Fisheries Officer of the government's Fisheries Division is an ex officio member. Other government members come from the Markets Division of the fisheries ministry, and from the environment ministry, which is responsible for coastal management. A fisheries biologist (to date from the private sector or university) is the ninth member.

The committee has had a difficult history in terms of gaining recognition and receiving feedback from fisheries ministers and senior administrators of the ministry. The FAC has achieved reasonable success, due mainly to support from the Fisheries Division in following up on its management and policy advice. For example, the FAC was instrumental in developing the first fisheries management plan and encouraging the state to become party to several important international fisheries instruments (McConney et al. 2003a). There is, however, little collaboration between the Fisheries Division, which manages the harvest sector, and the Markets Division, which is concerned with post harvest (and which often does not attend FAC meetings). This dysfunction affects the livelihoods of fisherfolk directly and concerns the industry members of the FAC, who seek indicators of success more at the operational (local) level of the industry than at the management-decision or policy (mainly national and international) levels (McConney et al. 2003a). Fisherfolk are interested mainly in ensuring functioning fisheries infrastructure for development, not in the status of resources or conservation-oriented management measures.

Recently, a newly appointed FAC undertook an institutional and performance self-analysis, and then developed a strategic plan for itself. The plan stressed the need to build its capacity and to empower itself through better fisheries information (e.g., economic valuation); to increase communication among members and with the ministry and industry; to strengthen shared interests; and to move from being a consultative body to being a collaborative co-management body by amending its legal mandate. The status of fisheries resources did not feature in the FAC's strategic planning. The focus was on the ministry's organizational and procedural constraints. At present, the FAC is without executive authority, a coordinating role, or an operational budget, and members do not trust the ministry to implement advice on local-level fishery matters, such as improvements to certain fish landing sites.

The case study revealed an uncomfortable fit between the conditions that appear to favour successful co-management and the prevailing situation in Barbados (McConney et al. 2003a). This raises questions about the scope for co-management to be institutionalized through the FAC. The FAC has demonstrated a willingness to learn and adapt but has limited power to effect change. It has made a positive difference in management at higher levels and large scales, but local-level advances that are also important to the industry are less apparent. Members of the FAC have concluded that stronger vertical linkages, upward to policy makers and downward to the people in the industry, are critical for effecting change and transforming the FAC into the type of body that exemplifies collaborative co-management (McConney et al. 2003a). There remain, however, questions for future research on other feasible options for fisheries co-management in Barbados, especially in terms of institutional arrangements, since weakly enforced and complied with government command-and-control systems have not succeeded.

Barbados Sea Urchin Fishery
The challenge in this case is for the policy makers, fisheries authority, and resource users to each demonstrate their commitment to co-management in order to improve trust and learn from collaboration. The open-access sea urchin (sea egg) fishery of Barbados has a long history of command-and-control regulations, primarily via closed seasons and gear restrictions, which have largely been ignored by all stakeholders (Mahon et al. 2003). It is a low-capital fishery for nearshore sedentary animals that are vulnerable to overfishing. The fishery is socially, economically, and culturally important to the fishing industry and consuming public. As an off-season livelihood strategy, it is a vital source of household income for fishing families. Exacerbated by overfishing, however, the fishery has gone through boom-and-bust cycles that have become particularly severe since the 1980s. The low periods have prompted national multi-season fishery closures, but persistent illegal fishing and high levels of effort during open periods have hindered sustainable recovery, despite sea urchin recruitment being good.

Little enforcement, low compliance, and the reluctance of the judiciary to treat contravention of fishery regulations as serious offences contribute to uncertainty and are among the challenges that demand adaptive and innovative solutions in this fishery. Challenges are compounded by the tendency of policy makers to regulate the fishing season based more on the wishes of vocal minorities in their coastal constituencies than on the management advice agreed upon and recommended by the fisheries authority and BARNUFO, which have tried to demonstrate collaborative co-management as a learning experience (Mahon et al. 2003).

In some ways, this case appears, superficially, to be a candidate for collaborative co-management that is community-based, and in St. Lucia, this has been tried with some success (Smith and Berkes 1991; George and Joseph 1999). Barbados is different from St. Lucia, however, in terms of attitudes towards property and access rights, community empowerment, and conservation. Open-access problems, little community-level governance, and fisher acceptance of resource depletion are more evident in Barbados (CCA et al. 2003). Recently, there have been efforts by governmental (fisheries and coastal management authorities) and non-governmental agencies (CCA and BARNUFO) to introduce co-management. The focus was initially upon collaboration with academic researchers in data collection, but recent initiatives have included participatory fisheries planning and policy recommendations. Most have met with limited success (Mahon et al. 2003). Fishers have said that they can cope with fluctuations in sea urchin abundance due to nature or fishing, but they cannot take co-management seriously when the government does little to protect the resource (and compliant fishers) from opportunistic illegal fishers (McConney et al. 2003b). A classic "tragedy of the commons" (Hardin 1968) is unfolding.

One of the key conditions for consultative or collaborative co-management to succeed is strengthening the capacities of the fisheries authority and fisherfolk organizations to manage the fishery. For fisherfolk organisations, this means gaining the trust and active participation of their members. Improving the enforcement of laws may encourage industry participants to view the state as a more serious and committed co-management partner. The state also needs to demonstrate faith in the fisherfolk organizations by building their capacity and devolving power so that it can enter into meaningful partnerships with them. Currently, the fisheries authority and sea urchin fishers have concluded that consultative co-management should be limited to forming an "advisory management council" based on community-level representation with a strong element of individual expertise. Future research on adaptive co-management will need to consider other options for reducing the challenges in this fishery and determine whether ineffective arrangements for joint decision making among stakeholders reduce the chances of co-management's being successful.

Grenada Beach Seine Fishery
This is a case of determining whether formalizing traditional rules is likely to be more successful than strengthening and empowering the fishing community to regain control of the fishery by improving compliance with informal rules and increasing capacity to adapt. Traditional fishery rules are

poorly documented in the eastern Caribbean. An outstanding exception is the work of Finlay (1995), whose research on the beach seine rules in Grenada has led to their being thoroughly documented and recommended for formal legalization. The rules dictate the ways in which boats take turns to harvest fish when several are competing for catch. This case is about how the fishery stakeholders want government to approach legalization (McConney 2003). Lessons learned here have national and regional significance. The study site was Gouyave, a west coast town known as the fishing capital of Grenada, where beach seining for coastal pelagics and small-scale longlining for tunas are very important and interactive fisheries.

A variety of conflicts have arisen out of interactions between the seine and longline fisheries, and within the seine fishery itself, because fewer fishers are following the traditional rules. Although the recommendation to reduce conflict by formally legislating the rules has been made by the government's fisheries manager (Finlay 1995), and the fishing industry appears to agree with it, judging from consultations (McConney 2003), it is not clear whether or how the process will proceed. A critical question concerns the extent to which local interpretation, adaptation, and development of traditional community rules can continue once the rules are legislated. Caribbean fisheries legislation is not known for flexibility and adaptation. Community-based ownership of the rules is likely to continue only if the seine fishers become empowered and steer the process of legalization with the full cooperation of the government.

Although Gouyave has a rich history of fishing organization formation, there has not been much success in sustaining these groups, despite external assistance. There is little economic motivation for the seine fishery to become organized. Collective action stops at the harvest level, seldom extending into post-harvest. The findings on these fisheries interactions and the legalization of the traditional rules show that the seine fishers have limited capacity for taking on the responsibility of managing the fishery without considerable support and direction from government. The fishers and net owners have concluded that there is no longer sufficient respect for the rules formulated long ago through community structures and processes. Older fishers do not trust younger fishers. Lack of respect for the rules followed by the older fishers and ineffectiveness of social sanctions for noncompliance are most obvious among the younger generation of fishers, who see fishing as providing quick money for immediate expenditure rather than as a livelihood (McConney 2003).

The lack of trust in community decision processes to solve problems has led to increasing dependence on government to manage conflicts and generally provide solutions. The fisheries authority does not have the capacity to be a conflict manager, however. Consequently, the fishers wish for a legal structure and process that is responsive to the particular needs of the fishery and that is also less cumbersome than the normal judicial process. They are intent on retaining control by participating actively in the legalization process and the implementation of the resulting legal arbitration arrangements. A major challenge is to convince the fisheries authority and political decision makers that this joint approach to legalization is likely to be successful. In the absence of effective leadership within the seine fishery to spearhead this approach, a policy decision to pursue legalization is unlikely. It is likely that the informal rules will persist but weaken further unless new leadership arises from within the fishery to strengthen the social basis of the rule system. Alternatively, if fishers can become politically empowered through collective action, authorities may be pressured into formalizing the rules with adequate provision for adaptation.

Belize Marine Protected Area

In an environment of diminishing government capacity, it is difficult for the state to support co-management functions delegated to the local level and to also address transboundary issues. Friends of Nature (FON) is a non-governmental organization based in Placencia, Belize, that has co-management responsibility (with the Forest Department and the Fisheries Department) for day-to-day management of Laughing Bird Caye National Park (LBCNP) and Gladden Spit Marine Reserve (GSMR). These two marine protected areas are located in the southern coastal zone and the Southern Reef Complex. Both lie within the Mesoamerican Barrier Reef Reserve System. FON has become active in the management of the Placencia Lagoon in addition to the two MPAs. Fishing and tourism dominate the economy of the area, which is based on the cayes. Threats to the marine and coastal resources include unsustainable fishing practices, the tourism industry, poorly planned land use, effluent discharges, policy and enforcement, and transboundary issues.

FON is responsible for public protected areas co-managed with government through a local advisory committee. This is a form of co-management in which management authority is delegated to local institutions (in this case FON). In return, the government is informed of, and reviews and endorses where it sees fit, decisions made by FON. The co-management arrangement with FON is in the implementation phase. FON has a strategic plan, a board of directors, an executive director, and staff. It has an office and equipment. A management plan exists for both MPAs. Financing has been secured for the immediate future. The MPAs are in operation and the resources are being conserved (Pomeroy and Goetze 2003).

Overall, the design and implementation of the concept of co-management for MPAs in Belize appears to be fundamentally one of devolving government management responsibilities to local NGOs. It is felt that the NGOs will improve the management of coastal resources, and that the government will reduce the burden on its already inadequate fiscal and human resources to effectively manage some of the country's most economically valuable natural resources by encouraging NGOs to seek donor funding for resource conservation and management (Pomeroy and Goetze 2003).

In general, the delegated co-management of MPAs in Belize does not involve broad-based community participation. Co-management arrangements in Belize have not been designed primarily as community-based systems with the attendant participatory decision-making structures and processes. The dominant understanding of "community participation" appears to involve appointing a representative from the community, regardless of whether that individual in fact represents the many interests of the community or, indeed, communicates the activities of the managing NGO to its members. Thus, communities impacted by the MPA often have very little real determinative impact on the MPA management design or on decisions that affect the local resources they depend upon for their personal and economic survival. There is a pressing need to develop mechanisms to more directly and actively involve local communities in management decision making for local resources in cooperation with the NGOs that have been granted this responsibility by the government.

A key problem with co-management for MPAs in Belize is jurisdiction – that is, competition, tension, and personality politics among and between managers and policy makers in various government departments and ministries. This has resulted in a lack of coordination, cooperation, and commitment among the agencies responsible for MPA management issues. These inconsistencies need to be resolved at a legislative level. Two possible routes for resolving these issues include: (1) the creation of overarching legislation governing and coordinating MPA management activities and co-management, and (2) the creation of national-level policies and related (clear) guidelines concerning MPA creation, management, and regulation. Cooperative implementation of these policies and guidelines is imperative, despite decreasing governmental capacity as a viable co-management partner. The state must remain a powerful actor in support of its delegated co-management functions and must address the numerous transboundary issues along the Mesoamerican Barrier Reef.

Types and Phases

The conceptual framework summarizes these main types of co-management as consultative, collaborative, and delegative, and identifies the three phases of co-management as pre-implementation, implementation, and post-implementation. Table 6.1 sets out how the four cases are located among these categories.

Table 6.1

Types and phases of co-management in the four case studies

Case study	Type of co-management	Phase of co-management
Barbados Fisheries Advisory Committee (FAC)	Consultative: movement towards collaborative	Implementation: adjusting, adapting
Barbados sea egg fishery	Consultative: elements of collaboration in projects	Pre-implementation: government and fishers still discussing how to proceed
Grenada Gouyave seine net fishery	Consultative: little mutual interest in collaboration	Pre-implementation: not likely to advance beyond current state in near future
Belize Friends of Nature (FON) marine protected areas (MPAs)	Delegated: maintained; national system under review	Implementation: adjusting, adapting

Three of the cases illustrate consultative co-management, but two of these show tendencies towards greater collaboration as the state begins to involve the other stakeholders more deeply. The fourth case (Belize) is of contractually delegated co-management that is being maintained, but the national legal/institutional framework for protected area co-management is under review in that country. The cases are evenly split among being at the pre-implementation and early implementation phases of establishment. None of the initiatives is mature, reflecting the recent introduction of coastal resource co-management to the Caribbean (McConney et al. 2003c; Pomeroy et al. 2003, 2004).

Co-Management Conditions

Table 6.2 presents the findings of the workshops, showing stakeholder perceptions of the extent to which various conditions for successful co-management were met in the three countries (McConney et al. 2003a, 2003b; McConney 2003; Pomeroy and Goetze 2003).

For the purpose of this discussion, the findings are divided into minor, medium, and major challenges based on ranked average scores. Since the initiatives are recent, the discussion and ranking by the stakeholders was necessarily based on limited experience with co-management. The scores cannot be used in a rigorously quantitative analysis, but the ranking and labelling provide a rough guide as to which conditions are generally more

Table 6.2

Stakeholders' perceptions of conditions for successful co-management in Barbados, Grenada, and Belize

Co-management condition	Barbados	Grenada	Belize
Minor challenges			
Clear objectives for management can be defined based on the problems and interests	3	3	3
Membership is clearly defined with regard to who really has a stake in the fishery (is a stakeholder)	3	3	2
There is shared recognition of a resource use problem that needs to be addressed	3	2	3
External agents provide support for management but do not encourage dependency	3	2	3
Management rules are enforceable by resource users and the management authority	3	2	2
There are clearly defined boundaries of the resource, of the management area, of the "community"	2	1	3
There is a good fit between the scale of the resource and feasible management arrangements	2	1-2	2
Medium challenges			
Management approaches and measures are flexible to suit changing circumstances	1	2	2
Communication among the stakeholders is effective, and there is adequate networking	2	2	1
Coordination between government, local community, and other stakeholders is effective	1	2	2
Benefits of participation must exceed costs from the levels of individuals up to larger groups	2	1	2
Individuals and groups affected by management arrangements are included in decision making	2	2	1
Legislation gives users authority to make management decisions, perhaps shared	1	2	2
Leadership exists, and is adequate, at the resource user level and in government, etc.	1-2	2	1
Major challenges			
Cooperation exists, and is adequate, at the resource user level and in government, etc.	1	2	1

▶

◄ *Table 6.2*

Co-management condition	Barbados	Grenada	Belize
There is group cohesion where fishers, managers, and others can act collectively within their groups	2	1	1
There are mechanisms for managing conflicts within and among stakeholder groups	1	1	2
Organizational capacity exists for all stake-holders to participate effectively in management	2	1	1
Adequate financial, and hence physical, resources are available for management tasks	2	1	1
Co-management has a good social and cultural fit to the circumstances of the situation	1	1	2
Trust and mutual respect characterize the relationships among the key stakeholders	0-1	2	1
Decentralization and delegation of authority is part of the policy of resource management	1	0	2
Legislation gives users some meaningful level of ownership or control over resource use	0	0	1

Note: 0 = absent; 1 = present but weak; 2 = present to a fair extent; 3 = strong feature

problematic across the cases. Based on the brief description of the cases and the evaluation, challenges are discussed in the next section, and some conclusions are drawn, mainly about where further research needs to be applied. The focus is on major challenges such as cooperation, collective action, conflict management, organizational capacity, financial resources, social and cultural fit, trust and respect, decentralization and devolution, and legislated user control or ownership. These are the conditions favouring success that are less evident than others in the four cases.

Discussion and Conclusions
These cases illustrate variation among some recent, mainly consultative co-management initiatives in the Caribbean. They range from a national fishery body (Barbados), to inshore fisheries (Barbados and Grenada), to a marine protected area (Belize). Many, usually interrelated, factors have to be taken into account by all parties in creating or sustaining conditions that favour successful co-management, regardless of how the stakeholders define success under their particular agreement or informal arrangement. For example, having clear boundaries can assist in reducing conflict, as can good communication and coordination. Deficiencies or strengths in one or two areas can have negative or positive impacts on other conditions. Some conditions are more challenging than others in particular places and at certain times.

The minor and medium challenges in Table 6.2 are those that Caribbean government authorities and their partners are more able to handle. Strategic management planning (e.g., McConney and Mahon 1998; Mahon et al. 2002, 2003) has assisted in elucidating problems, goals, boundaries of various types, and stakeholders, often through externally funded projects. Through participatory action research, these projects have tried to build capacity and leadership with improved communication and coordination. In Barbados, Belize, and Grenada, there is legislation and policy that encourages the decisions and plans of authorities to be based on stakeholder consultation or more meaningful involvement (e.g., the harmonized fisheries laws). The results also identify some major challenges that warrant devoting even more attention to applied research on coastal resource co-management in the Caribbean.

Inadequate cooperation is related to the prevalence of collective action's being primarily crisis-oriented, and the limited ability to manage conflict is often a feature of low organizational capacity. Low levels of cooperation were evident particularly in the Barbados and Grenada cases, and this was among stakeholders (seine and sea urchin fishers), among government agencies (Fisheries and Markets Divisions in Barbados), and between government and some key stakeholders. The need to manage conflict was urgent in the seine fishery case, particularly as the situation is weakening fishing rules developed at the community level and causing fishers and officials to consider legislation as the principal way to encourage fisher compliance. The co-management guidelines (McConney et al. 2003c) give simple advice on how collective action can be maintained, conflicts managed, and capacity built. Much research is still needed, however, on relationships between group size, heterogeneity, the power to exclude others, and a host of other dimensions that influence collective action and conflict management (Agrawal 2001).

Scarce financial resources to support co-management initiatives, especially over the medium term (five to ten years), reflect the short-term project funding of many co-management activities and the generally lower level of investment of Caribbean governments in the institutional or governance aspects of resource management compared with biophysical aspects and physical infrastructure. In all of the cases, there were short-term projects to support activities that enabled stakeholders to learn about co-management through experience. There is a need to develop means for the sustainable financing of co-management arrangements. Funds are required to support the institutions of co-management, which may differ from the tasks. For example, funds are allocated annually to hold meetings of the Barbados FAC, but there are no clearly identified funds through which the FAC can develop itself as an institution by improving its relationships with the resource users or policy makers. It is imperative for financing to be available in support of co-management initiatives progressing through all three phases, and funding and planning horizons should be longer-term. Government and stakeholder organizations' financial resources are scarce. Research is needed on innovative ways of making longer-term financing for the development of co-management more available.

The poor social and cultural fit of co-management is a multi-dimensional challenge. The full case study reports contend that, partly as a result of colonial rule by relatively autocratic public administration and by patronage politics following independence, some Caribbean citizens are not inclined to seek or accept leading roles in coastal resource co-management. Connected to this is the question of whether Caribbean state authorities genuinely support decentralization and devolution as part of the co-management process, and see legislated user control or ownership as means towards this end. Perhaps colonial history continues to shape institutional arrangements for governance in this post-independence era. The Barbados sea urchin fishers did not perceive the state as a viable partner because it did not exercise its power in enforcement or in providing them with a real say in decision making on season openings (McConney et al. 2003b). In the Grenada beach seine case, fishers saw government and the judicial system as instrumental in managing conflicts that arose at the community level, but in workshops they were skeptical about collaborative co-management being an approach that the authorities would support if fishers were to be empowered through legislation (McConney 2003). In Belize, having formal instruments of delegated co-management authority has not made co-management arrangements much more effective than they are in places without such agreements (Pomeroy and Goetze 2003). Politics, political processes, and power are important areas for further research in resource management (Gunderson and Holling 2002).

Insufficient trust and respect conclude the list of major challenges. In comparative analyses of coastal resource co-management in the Caribbean (Pomeroy et al. 2003, 2004) and internationally (see Chapter 9), and in guidelines for successful co-management (McConney et al. 2003c), the importance of sharing trust and respect among stakeholders has emerged. Trust and respect to support leadership have been identified as important components of building resilience in social-ecological systems (Olsson et al. 2004). In Barbados and Grenada, the resource users had low levels of trust in their governments and among themselves as partners in co-management. Of all the major challenges, these aspects of coastal resource governance have been least researched. Given that these are small countries in which relationships between government authorities and stakeholders can be more personal than in larger countries with massive agencies, it will be critical to pay attention to trust and respect in the Caribbean.

In general, these findings raise questions as to how co-management initiatives can most effectively be strengthened in the Caribbean, including questions about the roles of external agents. Aside from these cases, other action research, emphasizing stakeholder collaboration in learning-by-doing, is in progress (e.g., Mahon et al. 2002; Almerigi et al. 2003). Berkes (2004) has argued for a rethinking of community-based conservation. The need for more interdisciplinary investigation, especially socio-cultural and institutional, to guide co-management interventions and coastal resource governance in the Caribbean is shown by the social and institutional nature of the major challenges identified here and in recent governance literature (Mahon et al. 2005).

Emerging approaches towards effecting change in complex systems are oriented towards enabling self-organization in which participants can learn, adapt, and restructure to meet new challenges (Eoyang 1997). Enabling strategies include developing values and principles as a basis for self-organization, strengthening the capacity of organizations to take part in self-organization, and enhancing learning capability as a means of developing flexibility and adaptability (Mahon et al. 2005). There is much to learn about these approaches and their application to co-management in the Caribbean. Especially important are changing perspectives on how people structure governance across various scales to adapt and sustain themselves under conditions of uncertainty and complexity (Eoyang 1997; Gunderson and Holling 2002; Ostrom et al. 2002; Mahon et al. 2002; Almerigi et al. 2003; Mahon et al. 2005).

There are more questions than answers about how to overcome the major challenges facing coastal resource co-management in the Caribbean. This is not necessarily a bad thing, since it presents opportunities. The time is right for interdisciplinary research applied to the real and pressing issues affecting coastal resource co-management and the sustainable use of coastal resources in the region. Through innovative research, combined with learning and adaptation, improvements should be possible. Such improvements are urgently needed if management and development are to be sustainable.

References

Agrawal, A. 2001. Common resources and institutional sustainability. In *The drama of the commons,* ed. E. Ostrom, T. Dietz, N. Dolsak, P.C. Stern, S. Stonich, and E.U. Weber, 41-86. Washington, DC: National Academy Press.

Almerigi, S., R. Mahon, P. McConney, C. Ryan, and B. Whyte. 2003. Coastal resources and livelihoods in the Grenadine Islands. In *Voices from the field: An introduction to human systems dynamics,* ed. G. Eoyang, 145-57. Circle Pines, MN: Human Systems Dynamics Institute.

Berkes, F. 2001. Cross-scale institutional linkages: Perspectives from the bottom up. In *The drama of the commons,* ed. E. Ostrom, T. Dietz, N. Dolsak, P.C. Stern, S. Stonich, and E.U. Weber, 293-322. Washington, DC: National Academy Press.

–. 2004. Rethinking community-based conservation. *Conservation Biology* 18: 621-30.

Berkes, F., and C. Folke, eds. 1998. *Linking social and ecological systems: Management practices and social mechanisms for building resilience.* Cambridge: Cambridge University Press.

Berkes, F., R. Mahon, P. McConney, R. Pollnac, and R. Pomeroy. 2001. *Managing small-scale fisheries: Alternative directions and methods.* Ottawa: International Development Research Centre.

CCA (Caribbean Conservation Association), Canadian National Resources Institute, and Laborie Fishers and Consumers Cooperative. 2003. Learning from sharing and comparing experiences in sea urchin management in Barbados and St. Lucia. Report of the workshops held in Laborie, St. Lucia, 30-31 January. Barbados: Caribbean Conservation Association.

Charles, A.T. 2001. *Sustainable fishery systems.* Oxford: Blackwell Science.

Eoyang, G.H. 1997. *Coping with chaos.* Cheyenne, WY: Lagumo.

Finlay, J.A. 1995. Community-level sea use management in the Grenada Beach seine fishery: Current practices and management recommendations. MSc thesis, University of the West Indies, Cave Hill campus, Barbados.

Folke, C., S. Carpenter, T. Elmqvist, L. Gunderson, C.S. Holling, and B. Walker. 2002. Resilience and sustainable development: Building adaptive capacity in a world of transformations. *Ambio* 31: 437-40.

George, S., and W. Joseph. 1999. A new participatory approach toward sea urchin management in St. Lucia, West Indies. *Proceedings of the Gulf Caribbean Fisheries Institute* 46: 197-206.

Gunderson, L.H., and C.S. Holling, eds. 2002. *Panarchy: Understanding transformations in human and natural systems.* Washington, DC: Island Press.

Hardin, G. 1968. The tragedy of the commons. *Science* 162: 1243-48.

Hilborn, R., and C.J. Walters. 1992. *Quantitative fisheries stock assessment: Choice, dynamics and uncertainty.* New York: Chapman and Hall.

ICLARM (International Centre for Living Aquatic Resources Management) and IFM (Institute for Fisheries Management and Coastal Community Development). 1998. *Analysis of co-management arrangements in fisheries and related coastal resources: A research framework.* Report prepared by the Coastal Resources Co-Management Research Project core staff at ICLARM and IFM. Hirtshals, Denmark.

Mahon, R., S. Almerigi, P. McConney, C. Ryan, and B. Whyte. 2002. Coastal resources and livelihoods in the Grenadine Islands: Facilitating change in self-organising systems. *Proceedings of the Gulf and Caribbean Fisheries Institute* 55: 56-67.

Mahon, R., S. Almerigi, P. McConney, C. Parker, L. Brewster. 2003. Participatory methodology used for sea urchin co-management in Barbados. *Ocean and Coastal Management* 46: 1-25.

Mahon, R., M. Bavinck, and R. Roy. 2005. Governance in action. In *Fish for life: Interactive governance of fisheries,* ed. J. Kooimann, M. Bavinck, S. Jentoft, and R. Pullin, 351-74. MARE Publication Series, no. 3. Amsterdam: University of Amsterdam Press.

McCay, B.J., and J.M. Acheson, eds. 1987. *The question of the commons: The culture and ecology of communal resources.* Tucson: University of Arizona Press.

McConney, P. 2003. *Grenada case study: Legalisation of beach seine traditional rules at Gouyave.* Caribbean Coastal Co-management Guidelines Project. Barbados: Caribbean Conservation Association.

McConney, P.A., and R. Mahon. 1998. Introducing fishery management planning to Barbados. *Ocean and Coastal Management* 39: 189-95.

McConney, P., R. Mahon, and H. Oxenford. 2003a. *Barbados case study: The Fisheries Advisory Committee.* Caribbean Coastal Co-management Guidelines Project. Barbados: Caribbean Conservation Association.

McConney, P., R. Mahon, and C. Parker. 2003b. *Barbados case study: The sea egg fishery.* Caribbean Coastal Co-management Guidelines Project. Barbados: Caribbean Conservation Association.

McConney, P., R. Pomeroy, and R. Mahon. 2003c. *Guidelines for coastal resource co-management in the Caribbean: Communicating the concepts and conditions that favour success.* Caribbean Coastal Co-management Guidelines Project. Barbados: Caribbean Conservation Association.

Olsson, P., C. Folke, and F. Berkes. 2004. Adaptive co-management for building resilience in social-ecological systems. *Environmental Management* 34 (1): 75-90.

Ostrom, E. 2005. *Understanding institutional diversity.* Princeton, NJ: Princeton University Press.

Ostrom, E., T. Dietz, N. Dolsak, P.C. Stern, S. Stonich, and E.U. Weber, eds. 2002. *The drama of the commons.* Washington, DC: National Academy Press.

Pinkerton, E., ed. 1989. *Co-operative management of local fisheries: New directions for improved management and community development.* Vancouver: UBC Press.

Pomeroy, R.S. 1998. A process for community-based co-management. *AFSSRN News.* ICLARM Contribution no. 1448.

Pomeroy, R.S., and T. Goetze. 2003. *Belize case study: Marine protected areas co-managed by Friends of Nature.* Caribbean Coastal Co-management Guidelines Project. Barbados: Caribbean Conservation Association.

Pomeroy, R.S., B.M. Katon, and I. Harkes. 2001. Conditions affecting the success of fisheries co-management: Lessons from Asia. *Marine Policy* 25: 197-208.

Pomeroy, R., P. McConney, and R. Mahon. 2003. *Comparative analysis of coastal resource co-management in the Caribbean.* Caribbean Coastal Co-management Guidelines Project. Barbados: Caribbean Conservation Association.

Pomeroy, R., P. McConney, and R. Mahon. 2004. Comparative analysis of coastal resource co-management in the Caribbean. *Ocean and Coastal Management* 47: 429-47.

Smith, A.H., and F. Berkes. 1991. Solutions to the "tragedy of the commons": Sea urchin management in St. Lucia, West Indies. *Environmental Conservation* 18: 131-36.

Wilson, J. 2002. Scientific uncertainty, complex systems and the design of common-pool institutions. In *The drama of the commons,* ed. E. Ostrom, T. Dietz, N. Dolsak, P.C. Stern, S. Stonich, and E.U. Weber, 327-60. Washington, DC: National Academy Press.

7
Adaptive Fisheries Co-Management in the Western Canadian Arctic
Burton G. Ayles, Robert Bell, and Andrea Hoyt

For a thousand years, the Inuvialuit and their ancestors' people have occupied the lands in the western part of the Canadian Arctic bordering the Beaufort Sea (McGhee 1976; Taylor 1976; Alunik et al. 2003). Although significant economic, social, and political change has occurred in the last fifty years, and the majority of Inuvialuit are now part of the wage economy, hunting and fishing, particularly subsistence fishing, remain critical to the livelihoods of the Inuvialuit (Ayles and Snow 2002; Day 2002; Usher 2002; Alunik et al. 2003).

In 1984, the Inuvialuit and the government of Canada signed the first comprehensive land claim settlement for a region wholly within Arctic Canada, the Inuvialuit Final Agreement (IFA) (Canada 2005; McCann 2005). Established by the IFA, the Inuvialuit Settlement Region (ISR) has an area of approximately 1.09 million square kilometres of land, water, and ice (Bailey et al. 1995). (See Ayles and Snow [2002] for a description of the communities and streams discussed in this chapter.) The IFA also established a co-management system for all matters relating to the management of living resources and their habitats in the ISR (Bailey et al. 1995). Berkes and colleagues (2005) discuss various aspects of the evolution of renewable resource co-management in the ISR and elsewhere in the Canadian Arctic. Kristoffersson and Berkes (2005) make the argument that adaptive co-management has been a step in the evolution of resource management of Arctic char in the Cambridge Bay area of Nunavut. The concept of adaptive management, as developed by Holling (1978) and Walters (1986), emphasizes the notion of treating resource management actions as experiments from which managers could learn. Adaptive co-management, as defined in Chapter 1, combines the learning dimension of adaptive management with the sharing of rights and responsibilities of co-management.

This chapter examines how co-management of fisheries, within the context of a comprehensive Arctic land settlement agreement, has led to adaptive management practices and how adaptive management feeds back to strengthen the co-management process. The co-management context is described, as are adaptive management practices and their results. Three case studies of adaptive fisheries co-management initiatives are discussed. The initiatives vary in terms of complexity of the fisheries, relationships between agencies, and level of success or failure. Themes addressed in this chapter include: partnerships and power sharing; institutional designs for adaptive co-management; and conditions of adaptive co-management success and failure. Recommendations are made for the management of Western Arctic fisheries, and lessons learned for fisheries co-management in other parts of the world are presented.

Fisheries Co-Management in the Western Arctic

In the Western Arctic, co-management refers to the legislatively based sharing of management responsibilities between beneficiaries and the responsible government agency (Bailey et al. 1995; FJMC 2005). The Fisheries Joint Management Committee (FJMC) is the co-management board with responsibilities for fish and marine mammals in the ISR. Specific responsibilities of the FJMC are defined in the IFA, the Fisheries Act, and the Oceans Act. Some decisions are assigned to a single agency; for example, the FJMC is responsible for allocating subsistence quotas among communities, while local Hunters and Trappers Committees (HTCs)[1] are responsible for the sub-allocation of community shares and other quotas among individuals. Other decisions are shared; for example, the FJMC advises the Minister of Fisheries and Oceans on regulations and research, and funds research by the Department of Fisheries and Oceans (DFO), universities, and the communities.

The FJMC is a mature organization that has operated for over twenty years and has fully institutionalized procedures (FJMC 2005; Iwasaki-Goodman 2005). While post-IFA agreements are structured differently and have transferred some additional responsibilities to the co-management bodies (Ayles and Snow 2002), fisheries co-management in the ISR essentially meets Pinkerton's (2003) key aspects of "complete co-management."[2]

In the years since it was established, the FJMC, in cooperation with the DFO and the HTCs, has moved towards the development of integrated fisheries management plans for individual fish stocks or stock complexes as the process for establishing conservation, socio-economic, and ecosystem objectives; strategies to support those management objectives; and plans to implement those strategies. The evolving process (Figure 7.1) follows a general DFO model[3] and remains flexible enough to reflect the specifics of the resource and the needs of the communities. The development of each fisheries management plan is an ongoing, cyclical process driven by a multiagency working group. The group is responsible for assessing the problem, considering a range of management alternatives, monitoring the implementation of the consensus decisions, reviewing the results, and modifying the

Figure 7.1

A generalized cycle of adaptive fisheries co-management in the Inuvialuit Settlement Region

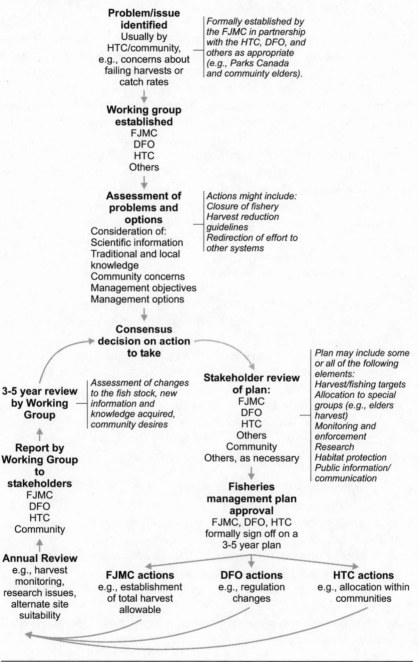

actions at the end of the planning cycle. The HTCs, the DFO, and the FJMC are responsible for the final decisions and implementation.

The development of the process has been driven by several institutional factors (see Chapter 4), primarily the goals of the IFA, the terms of reference for the FJMC, the terms of reference for the HTCs, and DFO policies related to integrated fisheries management planning. Table 7.1 summarizes these key institutional factors in relation to Walters' three cyclical phases (1986) in the adaptive management process (identifying a range of management alternatives, developing key management indicators, and designing and implementing an effective monitoring system) and Hilborn's three essential steps (1992) in institutional learning from trial and error (documenting decisions, evaluating results, and responding to evaluation).

The institutional factors identified in Table 7.1 are further developed through the FJMC's strategic plan (FJMC 2002). The vision of the FJMC is that fish and marine mammal resources will be managed and conserved for the wise use and benefit of present and future generations through the use of sound scientific and traditional knowledge, effective co-management, and support of Inuvialuit culture, beliefs, and practices with respect to fish and marine mammals. Fundamental principles particularly related to adaptive co-management are the following:

- Incorporate the "precautionary principle" in the FJMC's approach to the management of the renewable freshwater and marine resources of the ISR.
- Support the spirit and principles of co-management in the FJMC's approach to the management of the fish and marine mammals of the ISR.

Besides the institutional factors summarized above, the FJMC has established practices that, while not specifically directed towards adaptive management, have fostered cross-scale interactions and social learning within the HTCs, the FJMC, and the DFO. These practices include:

- frequent FJMC meetings (at least five annually) and teleconferences to discuss fisheries issues in the ISR
- meetings with the Minister of Fisheries and Oceans to discuss critical issues and provide advice and recommendations
- facilitation of numerous resource management workshops that involve both scientific and community members
- meetings in each community every eighteen months to discuss community issues
- active participation (non-voting) of the regional DFO representative in virtually all meetings

Table 7.1

Relationship between some of the key institutional factors in the development of the fisheries management planning process in the Inuvialuit Settlement Region (ISR) and their significance for adaptive fisheries management*

Key institutional factors	Significance for an adaptive management process
The goals of the Inuvialuit Final Agreement are (Section 1.[1]): (a) to preserve Inuvialuit cultural identity and values within a changing northern society; (b) to enable Inuvialuit to be equal and meaningful participants in the northern and national economy and society; and (c) to protect and preserve the Arctic wildlife, environment and biological productivity.	Inuvialuit need to be involved in management decision making, thereby ensuring input of local and traditional ecological knowledge, and the aspirations and needs of local people, as well as considering a range of alternatives for managing the fisheries resource(s).
The terms of reference for the Fisheries Joint Management Committee (FJMC) gave the Inuvialuit certain rights and priorities for fish harvests (Sections 14.[24]-[35]) and require the FJMC (Section 14.[61]-[72]) to review fisheries information, determine harvest levels, restrict and regulate aspects of fishing, allocate quotas among communities, recommend to the Minister of Fisheries and Oceans on a range of topics, and advise the minister on any issues related to fisheries in the ISR (14.[61]-[72]).	The FJMC as well as the Department of Fisheries and Oceans (DFO) has to be involved in the management of the fisheries of the ISR. The involvement of the different agencies ensures consideration of a range of alternatives for managing the stock(s). The requirement to review information and determine harvest levels necessitates the establishment of monitoring programs in order to provide the necessary information and make decisions. Because they involve different agencies, these requirements necessitate a formal decision-making process and documentation and evaluation of results on a regular (cyclical) basis. This also means that the FJMC should have funding to address the necessary tasks.

▶

◄   *Table 7.1*

Key institutional factors	Significance for an adaptive management process
The terms of reference for the Hunters and Trappers Committees (HTCs) (Section 14.[75]-[79]) give them responsibilities for sub-allocating quotas within their jurisdiction, making bylaws with respect to their own harvest, and assisting in providing harvest data.	Individual HTCs as well as the FJMC and DFO have to be involved in the management of local fisheries. It also requires the establishment of a system to monitor the results of decisions on harvests.
DFO policies for the development of integrated fisheries management plans provide a process for stan-dardized development of plans nationally but allow regional flexibility to address specific needs.	In the ISR, the framework has been modified to ensure that Inuvialuit traditional ecological and local know-ledge is publicly documented and considered in scientific stock evaluations and that Inuvialuit are fully involved in all aspects of the development of the plans. The process also requires formal performance reviews.

* As identified by Walters (1986) and Hilborn (1992).

- meetings with industry to discuss development issues of relevance to the committee
- direct involvement of individual members in working groups responsible for developing fish management plans
- leadership, training, and assessment of community-based projects by the FJMC resource biologists and DFO staff.

In her analysis of personal interactions during FJMC meetings, Iwasaki-Goodman (2005) noted consensus decision making, respect for differences of opinion of other members, personal friendships that had developed among members, and recognition by members of the important role that the FJMC plays in resolving conflicts.

It is our assessment that the overarching institutional factors, including legislation, federal policies for integrated fisheries management, the FJMC strategic plan and vision, and FJMC operating procedures, have been criti-cal for the development of an adaptive co-management process for fisheries in the ISR. These institutional factors have been supported by the strategic factors of social organization that have facilitated the necessary cooperation. In the following section, we discuss three fisheries co-management initia-tives that vary in terms of complexity of the fisheries, relationships between agencies, and level of success or failure but have all evolved towards a system of adaptive management (Figure 7.1). This system has strengthened co-management in the local community and the ISR. As we will see, however, not all fisheries management initiatives in the ISR have met with success.

Case Studies

Fish were probably the single most important element in the traditional diet of the Inuvialuit (Alunik et al. 2003), and two very similar species, Dolly Varden char (*Salvelinus malma*) in streams west of the Mackenzie River and Arctic char (*Salvelinus alpinus*) in streams east of the Mackenzie River, are the most highly valued culturally and nutritionally.

Char are anadromous. According to the simplest description of their life history, they spawn, the eggs incubate and hatch, and the young spend their first few years in fresh water. At four to five years of age, the char migrate to the sea in the summer to feed in the richer marine environment and then return, generally to the river in which they were hatched, to overwinter. The concentrations of char summering (feeding) in nearshore coastal waters and later returning to the rivers in the late summer are the focus for local harvests. In reality, both char species exhibit complex life histories and complex stock interrelationships that are not well understood, and fisheries management can be problematic. Kristofferson and Berkes (2005) have discussed some of the problems of conventional management of Arctic char and described have how Inuit traditional management practice and conventional scientific management practice can potentially complement each other in an effective adaptive management regime.

This section describes the management of char fisheries in three highly traditional communities – Paulatuk, Holman, and Aklavik (Table 7.2) – where one-half to three-quarters of the population are involved with hunting and fishing (compared with 36.7 percent for the Northwest Territories as a whole), and one-third to one-half of the households indicate that traditional foods comprise at least half of their daily intake (compared with 17.5 percent for the Northwest Territories as a whole). This reliance on country foods may be further encouraged by the fact that the food price index for the communities is almost twice that of Yellowknife (Yellowknife food price index = 100). These figures demonstrate the importance of the subsistence economy and the potential impact of the loss of one of its main constituents, in this case, Arctic char or Dolly Varden char.

All three systems were periodically harvested for subsistence use prehistorically and more heavily beginning in the last century as people moved off the land and communities became established (Table 7.2). In the 1960s and 1970s, governments encouraged the establishment of commercial fisheries in these systems, but all eventually closed (Corkum and McCart 1981). Present-day fisheries are primarily for subsistence use.

Table 7.2

Basic community information for the three Inuvialuit communities involved in the case studies

	Paulatuk	Holman	Aklavik
Community information			
Total population	312	421	631
% hunters and fishers	49.5	76.1	49.3
% of households that rely on traditional foods*	51.9	45.8	35.5
Food price index**	193	182	183
Number of HTC members	119	Not available	238
Working group membership	Chair (HTC), HTC (5), DFO (1), FJMC (1), PC (1)	Chair (HTC), HTC (varied), FJMC (2), DFO (2)	Chair (HTC), HTC (2), FJMC (3), DFO (1), PC (1), Elders Committee (2)
Key developments in the adaptive co-management of char fisheries			
Pre-1960s	Subsistence fishery.	Subsistence fishery.	Subsistence fishery.
1960s and 1970s	Commercial fishery established with support from INAC. Very small sport harvest established, then ended.	Small sport fishing outpost established on Kuujjua River, then closed.	At least two attempts made to initiate commercial fisheries. Large subsistence harvests in the late 1970s.
Early 1980s	Total harvests rose gradually, then declined.	Assessments of the potential for establishing commercial fisheries.	Harvesters reported concerns about decreasing harvests and observed numbers of fish.

1984-86	IFA was signed and new roles were determined for FJMC and HTCs.	IFA was signed and new roles were determined for FJMC and HTCs.	IFA was signed and new roles were determined for FJMC and HTCs.
Late 1980s	*1986:* Age and length of fish had decreased and CPUE was very low. *1986:* Commercial fishing ends. Subsistence harvests continued at a low level.	*1987:* Community members expressed concern over decline in size and abundance of char. Scientific assessment studies were carried out.	HTC asked for an investigation into decreasing harvests. Scientific assessment (weir counts and tagging) indicated that overfishing was the problem. *1987:* HTC asked that the fishery be closed.
1990s	Subsistence harvests rose. *1995-97:* Fishers expressed concerns as harvest, average size, age, and CPUE decreased. *1996:* Working group established. *1997:* Draft fishing plan in place. *1998-2002:* Formal plan approved by HTC, DFO, and FJMC, and implemented.	*1991:* Review of scientific and local knowledge and community issues. *1993-95:* First fishing plan developed by HTC, FJMC, and DFO. *1996:* Working group established.	Some fishers reported changes in water levels and water quality in river. *1992-97:* Fishery reopened to limited subsistence harvest but catches remained poor. Conflict between community members and DFO. *1998:* Preliminary habitat survey indicated low water flows and possible changes in water chemistry.

▼ *Table 7.2*

	Paulatuk	Holman	Aklavik
2000-4	2003-5: New plan of expanded scope implemented.	1996-2003: Series of fishing plans, usually with three-year life spans, and progressively more comprehensive.	2000: FJMC proposed new management regime. Minister of Fisheries and Oceans agreed, contingent upon completion of a satisfactory management plan. 2001: Working group formed. 2003: Scientists and fishers explicitly recognized that habitat change was likely limiting the size of the stock.
2005	Fishery has recovered from its low point and stock is healthy. Plan is being reviewed and modified for 2006 implementation. Working group is functioning very well.	Fishery remains stable and the stock remains healthy. 2004-6 plan is in place. Working groups are functioning very well.	No evidence of stock recovery. No formal plan yet in place. Decreasing interest by fishers. Working group now trying to shift focus to environmental monitoring by community youth and elders.

Note: CPUE = catch per unit effort; DFO = Department of Fisheries and Oceans; FJMC = Fisheries Joint Management Committee; HTC = Hunters and Trappers Committee; IFA = Inuvialuit Final Agreement; INAC = Indian and Northern Affairs Canada; PC = Parks Canada.
* NWT (2005).
** Yellowknife food price index = 100.

Paulatuk Arctic Char Management Plan

The Arctic char harvested by the community of Paulatuk come from what is believed to be a discrete stock, geographically isolated and confined to the Hornaday river system (DFO 1999). Although the char were undoubtedly harvested in past centuries, modern subsistence use dates back to the 1940s (PHTC 1999). Characteristics of the fisheries prior to 1986 are summarized in Table 7.2.

A decline in harvests and catch per unit effort (CPUE) in the early 1980s suggested to the community and to the DFO that the stock was being overexploited. As a consequence, no further commercial fishing licences were issued for this stock (DFO 1999). The subsistence fishery, monitored by the community through the Inuvialuit Harvest Study (Harwood 1999; Anonymous 2003) continued at a low level (1,800 to 3,200 char) from 1988 to 1994, then rose to 3,851 char in 1995. Harvests, average size and age, and CPUE decreased each year from 1995 to 1997 (Harwood 1999). Fishers became concerned about potential overharvesting, and a need for action to help the fishery recover was first identified formally at the Paulatuk HTC annual general meeting in the spring of 1996.

In the fall of 1996, with the support of the FJMC and the DFO, the Paulatuk HTC established a working group (Table 7.2) and charged it with assessing the problem and with developing options for a management plan for the fishery. The group met four times from 1996 to 1998; each meeting lasted two to three days so that there was ample time to discuss and review the details and the data and to discuss options. Eventually, the group developed a plan that was much broader than a more common western scientific approach. It was based on the blending of scientific and traditional knowledge and community aspirations for the fishery. It included not only harvest guideline recommendations but also seasonal and area closures, alternate fishing area strategies, community monitoring programs, community bylaws for fishing gear, identification of key habitat areas, and advice for research and monitoring programs (PHTC 1999). Reflecting the important role that elders play in Inuvialuit culture, the plan also contained special provisions for elders fishing. The goals of this co-management plan were:

- to ensure a healthy stock(s) of char in the Hornaday River and other char fishing locations in the Paulatuk area
- to preserve and protect char habitats in the Hornaday River and other char fishing locations in the Paulatuk area, to ensure that the char stocks continue to thrive
- to manage and conserve Hornaday River and other char in the Paulatuk area to ensure that subsistence needs of the residents of Paulatuk are met today and in the future.

Key elements to protect the stock and still maintain the fishery that was so critical to community members' culture and livelihoods were:

• limitation of the total annual harvest to 1,700 char per year, with a guaranteed portion of this set aside for elders
• continued endorsement of an ongoing fisher-based monitoring program to provide biological samples and catch and harvest data at the end of the fishing season
• limitation of maximum lengths for gillnets to 45.5 metres (50 yards) and minimum mesh size to 11.4 centimetres (4.5 inches)
• closure of fishing in areas of the Hornaday system that were critical for spawning and overwintering of char
• establishment of a financial support program enabling fishers to fish at alternate locations and for alternate species. The fishers who accepted support then agreed not to fish at all on the Hornaday.

Especially important was gaining support of the community fishers. The contents of the plan were presented to the public by the community working group members in three well-attended public workshops. The FJMC and DFO members of the working group provided technical support and background information and gave short presentations on the status of the stock, but most of the communication was from the community working group members to the fishing public. It took time and effort for the provisions of the plan to be accepted, digested, discussed in the community, and finally ratified.

The draft fishing plan was put into place for the 1997 fishing season, and a formal plan for the years 1998 to 2002 was approved by the HTC, the DFO, and FJMC in July 1998. The fishery operated for the next five years. Although there were no formal actions taken by the working group, it was critical to maintain the group momentum, so annual meetings were held. The DFO biologist on the committee provided the data analysis and reported annually to the HTC and FJMC on the state of the fishery and the plan. During the five-year period, fewer char were caught at the mouth of the Hornaday during the August upstream migration, closed areas were not fished, fish were provided to community elders, and the annual average harvest was 1,670 fish. The char stock responded in the way that the working group had anticipated. The DFO/community biological data showed an increase in CPUE and an increase in the average size of harvested char. The average age remained fairly stable through the first four years of the plan and then increased in 2002.

In 2002, the working group reconvened as usual but with a larger task at hand: to prepare the next version of the plan. The group's assessment was that the fish stock was recovering but that a recovery plan needed to remain in place for at least another three years. Major changes proposed for the new plan included the following (PHTC 2003):

- an increase in total harvest from 1,700 to 2,000 fish
- opening of the closed area for fishing for 300 char explicitly for elders
- recognition that fish harvested in coastal fisheries of Darnley Bay should be considered part of the total harvest
- formalization of the community monitoring
- assessment of char stocks in the nearby Brock River system and implementation of a tagging program to assess the relationship between Brock River and Hornaday River char.

The proposed 2003-05 Paulatuk Char Management Plan was presented to the public in Paulatuk at two public meetings and came into effect in June 2003. In December 2005, the current plan expired and the working group is assessing the latest data from DFO scientists, community-based monitoring results, harvest studies, and local knowledge on the Paulatuk fishery.

Although institutional factors (Table 7.1) helped guide the process, it is the assessment of some of the working group members that personal relationships and a common understanding of co-management were essential to the success of the plan. Group membership changed very little during the period, and this continuity was important for the development of personal relationships, social learning, and group dynamics. Members trusted each other and understood the role that each played within the overall process. Three members of the group – the original chair, the DFO biologist, and the FJMC member – had all worked together on the FJMC and had a similar understanding of how co-management should function in the ISR. The DFO and FJMC members provided technical, scientific, and management advice, but the leadership for plan development rested with the HTC members. In particular, their interests can be seen in the parts of the plan that relate to fairness, equity, and fish for elders. This made it a stronger plan and ensured community support. In the past, the DFO would establish the plan internally, based on biology, and then inform the community. The DFO plans were not even public documents.

The success of the plan, as exhibited not just by the recovery of the char stock but also by the community support it garnered, is a matter of pride for the working group and the Paulatuk HTC. It is viewed as a success for co-management in the wider ISR community, and in 2003, the working group members received the FJMC Co-Management Award for their contribution to co-management in the Arctic. A further result is that community members are ready to take greater personal responsibility for the management of their resources. A telling example occurred during the 2004 FJMC community meeting in Paulatuk, during which the working group reported on the continued recovery of the char stocks and their intention to renew the plan when it expired in December 2005. The current working group chair stated, "Some of the fellows in the HTC feel that, since the stock has recovered we don't need a Fishing Plan any more. But, don't worry. That is our problem. We will bring them around."

Holman Arctic Char Management Plan

The Arctic char harvested by the community of Holman on Victoria Island are from a mixed-stock complex. The primary fishery is based on char that spawn in the Kuujjua River, but char from the Kuuk, Kagloryuak, Naloagyok, and Kagluk rivers on Prince Albert Sound may also be harvested.

In 1987, at one of the first FJMC-sponsored community meetings, residents of Holman expressed concern over a decline in the size and abundance of char captured in the Kuujjua River system, the most intensely fished of the lake and river systems in the area. At that time, little biological information was available for any of the systems, so over the period from 1986 to 1992, a series of weir counts was carried out to estimate char populations in each of the four accessible river systems (Kuuk: Baker 1986; Stewart and Sparling 1987; Kagluk: Sparling and Stewart 1988; Naloagyok: Lemieux and Sparling 1989; Kagloryuak: Lemieux 1990). Each weir count was a collaborative operation involving individuals identified by the HTC, technicians and scientists from the DFO, and funding from the FJMC. Involvement of community members ensured that informal information from the projects was almost immediately available to the residents of the community.

In 1991, the FJMC, the DFO, and the HTC reviewed the scientific and local knowledge of the stock and addressed community issues. Results from weir counts and tagging and subsequent recapture of fish by Holman residents revealed not only that there was a significant harvest during the fall at Tatik Lake and elsewhere on the Kuujjua but also that 50 percent of the coastal char harvest that occurred every summer in the vicinity of the community was of Kuujjua River origin (Kristofferson et al. 1984). Thus, reducing harvests in one area (e.g., Tatik Lake) was not going to accomplish the objective of stock rebuilding if fish were merely harvested at another location. There was therefore agreement that a larger plan was needed to ensure that all stocks within the area were effectively managed and that no single stock was overharvested. The resulting series of fishing plans, described below, usually had three-year life spans and they were progressively comprehensive.

The Holman Area Charr Fishing Plan (Holman HTC et al. 1993), which covered the years 1993 to 1995, was approved by the officers and directors of the HTC, endorsed by the FJMC and the DFO, and had three main elements:

- reduction of the harvest at Tatik Lake to near zero from the previous year's 2,700

- targeted reduction of the summer coastal fishery in the vicinity of Holman, largely fish from the Kuujjua River system, from the previous year's 4,000 fish to 1,000
- increase in the number of char taken from the four major rivers of Prince Albert Sound from 2,000 to 6,200.

The plan gave the HTC the role of allocating the 200 Kuujjua fish within the community, as well as devising mechanisms for reducing the coastal fishery. The plan was given a life span of three years.

In 1996, a formal working group was established (Table 7.2). At its first multi-day meeting in July 1996, and as a result of its deliberations plus discussions at a well-attended public evening meeting, the group agreed to a limited reopening of Tatik Lake, recommending a harvest of 25 char per household (Holman Charr Working Group 1996). The plan also recommended safe harvest levels for the Kuuk, Kagluk, Kagloryuak, and Naloagyok rivers.

By 1998, there was growing concern that, given current scientific models, data on harvest levels from the Inuvialuit Harvest Study, and the estimated population size, the Kuujjua River char population was again being overharvested. To assess the situation, the FJMC convened a workshop that involved its members, scientists and managers from the DFO, and representatives of the HTC, including members of the working group (Ayles 1998). In the discussion, it was agreed that both community experience and the technical monitoring programs suggested that there was no significant decrease in the size of fish caught or in the CPUE. Thus it was concluded that the population size was probably being underestimated, that other populations were contributing to both the coastal fishery in Holman and to the Kuujjua overwintering population, and that fishing should continue as described in the fisheries management plans. Given that the harvests were high relative to the population estimate, however, the community-based monitoring program at Tatik Lake would be carried out each winter, and annual harvest levels would be determined. In addition, an assessment project for Tatik Lake and the Kuujjua River was recommended and was undertaken in 1998 and 1999 to examine the use of these areas by char during the summer months (Holman Charr Working Group 1998). Further, as a result of positive monitoring program results combined with pressure of community needs, the take of char from Tatik Lake was increased from 25 to 30 per household (Holman Charr Working Group 1999).

Working group meetings and the associated community open houses were held annually during this period. Following review of the data to 1999, a new three-year plan was adopted. The increase in the allowable harvest per household was reaffirmed (a total of approximately 1,000 fish), and a small commercial fishery of 500 char per year from the rivers of Prince Albert

Sound was initiated to enable the sale of char to the local restaurant and visiting cruise ships and to enable other small entrepreneurial opportunities (Holman Charr Working Group 2004).

The plan, for 2004-6, signed 9 June 2004 (Holman Charr Working Group 2004), has evolved from a one-page document that served for 1997-99 to a thirteen-page commercially printed booklet containing sections dealing with historical, current, and safe harvest levels; the allocation of harvests in the community; storage and processing of char; research and monitoring needs; and commercial fishing. Although most of the plan's provisions are similar to those of its predecessor, the commercial fishing section was adjusted to close the Kagloryuak River and to support the issuance of exploratory fishery licences[4] (500 char) to the HTC for the Kagluk and Kuuk River systems and for the Holman coast.

The record suggests that the Holman char fishery can be divided into two phases. The first phase occurred prior to 1998 and relied upon a river system's weir-generated population estimate combined with a comprehensive harvest study to determine whether current harvests were sustainable. The second phase, from 1999 to the present, relies heavily on community-based fishing plans, annual monitoring of CPUE, and a sample's size and physical characteristics, along with harvest monitoring. Annual working group and community meetings are held, where information is reviewed; decisions are made based on a combination of western science and community wisdom. To date, no element of the community-based plan has been challenged by any community or government organization.

There is little question that the HTC, the FJMC, and the DFO all consider the Holman process a success. One small measure is that DFO staff are greeted with hugs and handshakes when they arrive in the community, a rather different welcome from that which frequently occurs on Canada's other two coasts. Reasons for success may be related to the following:

- Importance of the resource. Char are central to the domestic economy of Holman. The thought of losing the fishery captures everyone's attention and makes bearable the need for short-term inconvenience.
- Trust and respect. As the HTC, the FJMC, and the DFO gained experience and trust in themselves and their partners, they developed the confidence to test non-conventional management approaches.
- Continuity. The DFO scientist in charge of developing the community-based monitoring program had been a Canada member of the FJMC, knew its goals, and took a special interest in the project. The DFO biologist was involved in all meetings up to 2004. The FJMC member of the working group was a retired DFO conservation officer who began working in the area in the 1960s and was well known and liked by the community.

- Community involvement. Community members and the HTC are responsible for most of the provisions of the plan, including harvest monitoring, allocation of the commercial catch, the field portions of research projects, and the setting of "safe" harvest levels. The role of the DFO and the FJMC at group meetings is to provide technical support and background information to assist the fishers, not to seek support for decisions that have already been made.
- Community ownership. The plan is viewed as a community document and it is now only witnessed by the FJMC and the DFO. In all, seventeen HTC members participated in working group meetings and many more were involved in the evening community meetings. In the past, the DFO would establish the plan internally, based on biology, and then inform the community. The DFO plans were not even public documents.

Aklavik Dolly Varden Char Management Plan

The Inuvialuit have harvested anadromous Dolly Varden from the rivers and along the coast of the Yukon North Slope for many generations (Papik et al. 2003). Dolly Varden were harvested along the coast in late summer, as part of a mixed-stock fishery, and at the mouth of the Big Fish River in early fall, before the fish went upstream to spawn. In the 1940s, as people moved off the land and into settlements, the Big Fish River became a preferred fishing area because of its proximity to Aklavik (Table 7.2).

In the 1980s, Aklavik fishers became concerned about decreasing harvests and numbers of fish at the Fish Hole, and the Aklavik HTC asked the DFO and the FJMC to investigate the decline. The two agencies commissioned a number of projects, including weir and mark-and-recapture studies, to estimate population size and harvest rate. The scientific consensus was that the decline in fish size and abundance was due to overfishing, and that the fishery should be closed to allow the stock to recover (DFO 2002). In 1987, at the request of Aklavik harvesters, the FJMC asked the DFO to close the Big Fish River char fishery for five years while the coastal mixed-stock fishery remained open. In 1992, the Big Fish River was reopened to limited subsistence harvests, but catches were poor, and harvests in the next five years never exceeded 300 fish in total (DFO 2002).

In the years following the 1992 limited reopening, tensions between the DFO and Aklavik fishers rose as it became clear that the stock had not recovered as had been anticipated. Harvesters were frustrated by what they felt was a "wait a while and see" attitude from the DFO. Some community members reported that changed environmental conditions in the Fish Hole were the problem; others disputed the DFO's estimates of the numbers of fish. DFO biologists, having become concerned when individual fishers proposed to "harvest the remaining char before they are gone completely," complained that they were not receiving timely reports of fish from the community and felt that the fishers were ignoring the primary cause of the problem: excess harvests. As early as 1990, Aklavik fishers reported that water levels and water quality were changing, but no habitat research was done until several years later (Stabler 1998; Sandstrom and Harwood 2002), suggesting that the decisions were being made based on incorrect scientific understanding.

In 2000, the FJMC moved to resolve the conflict by proposing to the Minister of Fisheries and Oceans that the community should become responsible for the management of the Big Fish River Dolly Varden and that all regulations governing the fishery be removed. The minister accepted that there must be a shift beyond the current management regime to community-based management, but was prepared to adopt such a regime only when a management plan had been completed and approved by the FJMC and the DFO.

In response to the minister, in February 2001, the FJMC, with the DFO and the HTC, formed a working group (Table 7.2) to coordinate the development of fisheries management plan(s) for the rivers and streams in the ISR west of the Mackenzie Delta to the Canada/Alaska border. The terms of reference for the group were broader than just Big Fish River char, in the hope that tensions would be defused by having community representatives, federal government staff, and FJMC members working together towards a less contentious common goal.

The first tasks of the working group focused on assembling traditional and local knowledge, while the DFO consolidated the scientific information (Figure 7.1). It was becoming increasingly clear by this time that there had been changes in the river, possibly as a result of earthquake activity (Clark et al. 2001; Sandstrom and Harwood 2002). Decreased water flows and significantly lower salinity potentially reduced spawning and over-wintering habitat (Stabler 1998; Sandstrom and Harwood 2002; Papik et al. 2003). These observations supported some fishers' long-held contention that overfishing was not the only, or even the primary, cause of the reduction in stock size. During the DFO Regional Advisory Process for North Slope Dolly Varden (DFO 2002), scientists and fishers explicitly recognized that habitat change was likely limiting the size of the stock.

In June 2003, the FJMC and the DFO organized a public meeting in Aklavik to discuss the status of the stock and future actions. The working group had addressed the conflicts, established an ongoing dialogue between agencies, and increased the understanding of the stock and the social and cultural needs of the community. There was no apparent solution to the reduced numbers of char and the underlying environmental problem of habitat loss, however. HTC members still considered the Big Fish River and the char to be important historically and culturally for the community, and it was decided that the working group would continue the dialogue. The group discussed the next step in the planning process (Figure 7.1) and drafted the following management goals:

- to ensure the maintenance of char, and other important fish stocks, in rivers and streams west of the Mackenzie Delta primarily for the purpose of subsistence food and as a mechanism for the support of traditional Inuvialuit culture
- to manage, to the extent possible, the char fisheries in a manner consistent with Inuvialuit cultural practices
- to manage the char and other important fisheries using adaptive management processes with full community participation.

The second goal was particularly important to the Inuvialuit even though the group could not specifically define what those "cultural practices" might mean in practice for Dolly Varden fisheries in the Babbage or Firth Rivers to the west. The uncertainty was discomforting for some DFO staff, who could not see how such a goal might be implemented under the present federal regulatory regime. Similarly, neither the DFO nor the working group had developed any specific hypotheses that might be evaluated using "adaptive management" practices. Nevertheless, the objectives were eventually accepted by DFO regional management, a clear indication of that agency's support for the co-management process.

By 2006, the fishery had still not recovered and the outlook remains uncertain, but it is possible that lessons have been learned that will ensure the long-term protection of other stocks on the North Slope. The working group is now shifting its focus to community involvement in the study and management of the Big Fish River. A program has been developed that involves students from the high school, HTC members, and elders in monitoring the river. A project to monitor the char harvest at Shingle Point was also initiated in 2005, and in future years, tagging projects and biochemical genetics projects will add to understanding of the movement of Big Fish River Dolly Varden and other char in rivers along the Yukon North Slope.

The successes and failures related to the management of the Big Fish River char were due to various factors. In the early years of concern over the declining char population, the emphasis of management efforts was on scientific research and western science–based solutions. When fishers brought their concerns to the DFO and later the FJMC, the response was to do population estimates and, based on those data, close the fishery, on the assumption that overfishing was the cause of the population declines. The preference for science was supported by a group of younger harvesters from Aklavik, who were educated and had faith in western scientific approaches. In later years, this division between the younger "radicals" and older "traditionalists" created some friction within the community of harvesters. Further, within the working group, personality conflicts between members slowed down the progress of the group as a whole, and a lack of consistent leadership meant that the group changed and adjusted as the goals and procedures were being developed. Finally, and most importantly, the ecosystem was not well understood, so when the system didn't respond in expected ways (i.e., stop fishing and the populations will increase), all the organizations involved were disillusioned and unhappy.

There have been successes, however. Despite the two decades of uncertainty, the almost complete loss of the fishery, and the probability that neither scientific knowledge nor traditional knowledge will be able to restore the environment, a dialogue continues among the agencies. Community monitoring of the river will result in greater understanding of the Big Fish River ecosystem, and the use of science and traditional knowledge will help increase capacity in the community, promote social and cultural values, and develop scientific research skills in the youth of Aklavik.

Discussion

These three char fisheries have several common elements and thus provide a special opportunity to examine the development of fisheries management processes in a co-management setting. The co-management body (the FJMC) and key partners (the DFO and the Inuvialuit), as well as the overarching institutional factors – including legislation, federal policies for integrated fisheries management, the FJMC strategic plan and vision, and FJMC operating procedures – are the same for all three fisheries. The fisheries are also generally very similar. They are single-species, subsistence fisheries that have had negative experiences with commercial operations. Although the fisheries are based on closely related fish species with similar life histories and biological productivity, there are significant scientific unknowns with respect to growth rates, reproductive rates, stock mixing, and safe harvest levels. Each fishery involves a single community with a small renewable resource base, and the community differences are small. All three communities are isolated and heavily dependent on governments for incomes. Paulatuk and Holman are exclusively Inuvialuit and, although Aklavik has First Nations (Gwich'in) and non-indigenous people as well as Inuvialuit, the fishery was prosecuted almost exclusively by Inuvialuit. The primary differences between the three fisheries are (1) differences in the nature of the crisis or problem with the stock at the beginning of the process (two of the stocks were probably being overfished and responded to the management action, while the third stock was declining, at least in part, because of changes in water flows and reduced spawning and rearing habitat), and (2) differences in leadership and personalities among fishers, HTCs, and the task groups.

As illustrated by these three fisheries, the evolving fisheries management planning systems in the ISR have led to incorporation of the key features of adaptive co-management:

- The processes developed meet the need for common policies, regulations, and procedures but are flexible enough to also meet specific biological and community needs.
- The processes are public, leading to greater involvement and collective accountability for decisions.
- Local community involvement in planning and decision making means that outcomes are based on cultural and social factors and not just economic or resource-protection factors.
- Community involvement means that local or traditional ecological knowledge, not just western science, is explicitly considered in the processes.
- The processes established are ongoing, with built-in review times for learning, feedback, and making changes in response to the outcomes of earlier decisions.

We have argued that the institutional factors – legislation and federal and FJMC policies and procedures – have supported the development of adaptive co-management, but we do not mean to imply that this was inevitable. Although the institutional factors may have been a prerequisite, our case studies illustrate the importance of the strategic factors of social organization discussed in Chapter 4 – the trust that developed with long associations, the common goals, the personal friendships and expressions of respect, the willingness of DFO staff to assume new supportive roles, and the willingness of HTC members to accept their responsibilities – which, though not measurable, are at least as important as the institutional factors. Both the institutional and strategic factors were necessary for success.

An additional element that cannot be ignored was the response of the fish stocks to the management actions, especially at the beginning of the process. In Paulatuk and Holman, the char stock responded positively to reduced fishing. This helped to build the confidence of fishers, scientists, and managers in the co-management process. On the other hand, the Big Fish River char stock did not respond to reduced harvests and continued to decline, most likely as a result of the changes in the river's water quantity and quality. One could certainly argue that this was the primary cause of any conflicts between individuals and agencies and that, if the fishery had responded as anticipated by most, then those conflicts would now be forgotten. One could also argue that if managers had paid more attention to the local knowledge of some of the fishers in the early years, the possibility that environmental changes were a major cause of the reductions would have been recognized sooner. Although the recognition of traditional knowledge was required under the IFA, imbalances with scientific knowledge remain (see Ellis 2005 for a general discussion for the Northwest Territories), and it was not until the stock status review in 2002 (DFO 2002) that this local knowledge was explicitly recognized. It is perhaps a mark of the overall strength of the co-management process that the community members remain willing to be engaged with programs on the Big Fish River, even though the probability of the stock recovering in the near term is minimal.

Recent syntheses have identified numerous conditions that facilitate the successful implementation of co-management (e.g., McConney et al. 2003; Pinkerton 2003; Berkes et al. 2005; Chapter 9). Our three case studies demonstrate that when the adaptive management techniques of acknowledging uncertainty, learning from experience, feedback, and new actions taken have been applied to the fisheries of the ISR, the outcome is an enhanced co-management system. Acknowledging scientific uncertainty of Arctic ecosystems and incorporating traditional and local knowledge improved decision making and increased the sense of empowerment and satisfaction of fishers in all three communities. Community involvement in monitoring and research on problems identified in common has helped to build links between fishers and scientists and to enhance the acquisition of knowledge and understanding. Local fishers are more trusting and supportive of scientific interpretations of data, and scientists have more respect for the local knowledge and experience of fishers. Management actions in Paulatuk and Holman, which led to expected changes/improvements in the resource, helped to build the confidence of fishers, scientists, and managers in the co-management process. Even actions that led to failure or that did not improve circumstances, such as on the Big Fish River, can be viewed positively because they were based on a consensus decision with unknown, but real, risks of failure rather than on decisions based on government fiat. The process has helped to build trust and willingness to take chances, and has built confidence among regulators and users that decisions have the support of all involved. A particular example of this trust was the willingness of the DFO to accept the proposed management objectives for fisheries west of the Mackenzie River, even though the working group could not explain what traditional Inuvialuit cultural practices might mean for fisheries management.

Our review of these three systems has also helped us identify some shortfalls in this developing adaptive management process as viewed from the perspective of Walters (1986) and Hilborn (1992). We need to document actions and rationale more carefully. Our assessment has relied heavily on the memory of specific individuals within the DFO and the FJMC, and this corporate memory needs to be supplanted with proper documentation. As well, if we are going to make full use of the techniques of "adaptive management," we need to make explicit hypotheses and develop management actions to test those hypotheses. Further, we may need to consider how to use different systems as "experiments" to be able to probe some of the many unknowns related to managing char in the Arctic. The necessary actions are all well within the mandates and capabilities of the FJMC, the DFO, and the HTCs.

Our review has also helped us identify some specific factors that we believe would help promote adaptive co-management of small artisanal fisheries in general:

- a strong co-management process (legislation, money, and a mandate accepted by communities as well as government)
- joint planning for research to develop innovative questions and proposed programs
- a willingness to accept the ideas, beliefs, and practices of others to reach a consensus for change
- plans with renewal times built in to allow feedback, learning, and modification
- regular biological monitoring and communication of results among all parties
- both new scientific and new community knowledge accepted as valid
- a willingness by all parties to trust and to share authority.

The DFO has never had the resources necessary for adequate research, management, or enforcement in the Arctic, and regional and area managers have long tried to work with the communities and fishers on a consensus basis (Kristofferson and Berkes 2005). Nevertheless, prior to 1984 and the signing of the IFA, fisheries management was formally the responsibility of the DFO. Now, clearly, power has been shifted to the FJMC and the Inuvialuit. They have been prepared to accept their responsibilities for these fisheries and to work cooperatively with the DFO, and, arguably, the resource and the fishers have benefited under the new management. The adaptive co-management model described here will not necessarily work under all circumstances (Nadasdy 2003; Chapter 11), but it is working for fisheries in the western Canadian Arctic.

Acknowledgments
We would like to acknowledge the members of the Paulatuk Char Working Group, the Holman Charr Working Group, and the West Side Working Group for their contributions. Their belief in the importance of the resource and in the importance of working together for the resource and for the people of the area are the foundations upon which co-management of char has been built in the Western Arctic. In particular, we would like to recognize the members of the HTCs who chaired and led the various groups, and the late Don Dowler of the FJMC and Lois Harwood of the DFO, who played critical roles in the Holman and Paulatuk groups during their early stages. Special thanks to Erin Hiebert for her contribution to the description of the Paulatuk char fisheries.

Notes

1 The IFA established local Hunters and Trappers Committees in each community in the ISR. HTCs are co-management partners – with the DFO and the FJMC – responsible for fish and marine mammals in their local areas.

2 Pinkerton (2003) has proposed that comparisons between co-management situations be made by distinguishing core aspects of co-management arrangements through a framework that considers the specific rights and powers of fishing communities.

3 Beginning in the 1990s, the DFO developed an "Integrated Fisheries Management Plan" process in order to standardize the fisheries management plan process, identify performance outputs, ensure greater integration within the DFO, and improve program delivery. In the early 2000s, the DFO introduced an objectives-based management approach to help with the application of a more precautionary approach and the use of ecosystem and fishery performance measures. (Many specific plans are available on the departmental website, http://www.dfo-mpo.gc.ca/communic/fsh_man/ifmp/index_e.htm.) A specific initiative emphasized that stakeholders should have a more direct role in developing the plan rather than commenting on a DFO proposal. The following steps are based on current and evolving practices within the Central and Arctic Region of the DFO: (1) Establish working group; (2) assemble background information on the stock(s); (3) set conservation limits for the stock; (4) set fisheries management objectives and fisheries management strategies for the stock; (5) develop the fisheries management operational plan; (6) plan implementation; and (7) review.

4 Exploratory fishing licences may be issued under Section 52 of the federal Fishery (General) Regulations when there is insufficient information to issue a formal commercial fishing licence and more scientific information is required.

References

Alunik, I., E.D. Kolausok, and D. Morrison. 2003. *Across time and tundra: The Inuvialuit of the Western Arctic.* Vancouver: Raincoast Books.

Anonymous. 2003. *Inuvialuit harvest study: Data and methods report 1988-1997.* Available from the Joint Secretariat, Inuvik, NT.

Ayles, G.B. 1998. The FJMC/DFO/Holman HTC Kuujjua River Charr Workshop. Unpublished report. Available from the Fisheries Joint Management Committee, Inuvik, NT.

Ayles, G.B., and N.B. Snow. 2002. Canadian Beaufort Sea 2000: The environmental and social setting. *Arctic* 55 (Supp.): 4-17.

Bailey, J.L, N.B. Snow, A. Carpenter, and L. Carpenter. 1995. Cooperative wildlife management under the Western Arctic Inuvialuit land claim. In *Integrating people and wildlife for a sustainable future. Proceedings of the First International Wildlife Management Congress* (19-25 September, San Jose, Costa Rica), ed. J.A. Bissonette and P.R. Krausman, 11-15. Bethesda, MD: Wildlife Society.

Baker, R.F. 1986. *Report on the test fishery of the Kuuk River, Prince Albert Sound, Northwest Territories, 1986.* Fisheries Joint Management Committee report no. 86-004.28p. Inuvik, NT: Fisheries Joint Management Committee.

Berkes, F., R. Huebert, H. Fast, M. Manseau, and A. Diduck, eds. 2005. *Breaking ice: Renewable resource and ocean management in the Canadian North.* Calgary: University of Calgary Press.

Canada. 2005. *The Western Arctic claim: The Inuvialuit Final Agreement as amended.* Ottawa: Department of Indian Affairs and Northern Development.

Clark, I.D., B. Lauriol, L. Harwood, and M. Marschner. 2001. Groundwater contributions to discharge in a permafrost setting, Big Fish River, NWT, Canada. *Arctic, Antarctic and Alpine Research* 33 (1): 62-69.

Corkum, L.D., and P.J. McCart. 1981. *A review of the fisheries of the Mackenzie Delta and nearshore Beaufort Sea.* Canadian Manuscript Report of Fisheries and Aquatic Sciences, No. 1613, November.

Day, B. 2002. Renewable Resources of the Beaufort Sea for our children: Perspectives from an Inuvialuit elder. *Arctic* 55 (Supp): 1-3.

DFO (Department of Fisheries and Oceans). 1999. *Hornaday River Arctic charr.* DFO Science Stock Status report D5-68. http://www.dfo-mpo.gc.ca/csas.

–. 2002. *Big Fish River Dolly Varden.* DFO Science Stock Status report D5-60. http://www.dfo-mpo.gc.ca/csas.

Ellis, S.C. 2005. Meaningful consideration? A review of traditional knowledge in environmental decision making. *Arctic* 58: 66-77.

FJMC. 2002. Fisheries Joint Management Committee vision: 2000-2010. http://www.fjmc.ca/about_fjmc/FJMC_docs.htm.

–. 2005. Fisheries Joint Management Committee info. http://www.fjmc.ca/about_fjmc/about_the_fjmc.htm.

Harwood, L.A. 1999. *Status of anadromous Arctic charr* (Salvelinus alpinus) *of the Hornaday River, Northwest Territories, as assessed through community-based sampling of the subsistence fishery, August-September 1990-1998.* Canadian Stock Assessment Secretariat research document 99/182. Ottawa: Department of Fisheries and Oceans.

Hilborn, R. 1992. Can fisheries agencies learn from experience? *Fisheries* 17 (4): 6-14.

Holling, C.S., ed. 1978. *Adaptive environmental assessment and management.* New York: John Wiley and Sons.

Holman Charr Working Group. 1996. *Holman Charr Newsletter,* vol. 1. http://www.fjmc.ca/publications/.htm.

–. 1998. *Holman Charr Newsletter,* vol. 3. http://www.fjmc.ca/publications/.htm.

–. 1999. *Holman Charr Newsletter,* vol. 4. http://www.fjmc.ca/publications/.htm.

–. 2004. Holman Charr fishing plan 2004-2006. http://www.fjmc.ca/publications/.htm.

Holman HTC (Hunters and Trappers Committee), FJMC (Fisheries Joint Management Committee), and DFO (Department of Fisheries and Oceans). 1993. Holman area charr fishing plan (draft). Unpublished report. http://www.fjmc.ca/publications/.htm.

Iwasaki-Goodman, M. 2005. Resource management for the next generation: Co-management of fishery resources in the western Canadian Arctic region. In *Indigenous use and management of marine resources,* ed. N. Kishigami and J.M. Savelle. National Museum of Ethnology, Osaka, Japan; and *Senri Ethnological Studies* 67: 101-20.

Kristofferson, A.H., and F. Berkes. 2005. Adaptive co-management of Arctic char in Nunavut territory. In *Breaking ice: Renewable resource and ocean management in the Canadian North,* ed. F. Berkes, R. Huebert, H. Fast, M. Manseau, and A. Diduck, 249-68. Calgary: Arctic Institute of North America and University of Calgary Press.

Kristofferson, A.H., G. Low, and D.K. McGowan. 1984. Test fishery for Arctic charr, Prince Albert Sound (Safety Channel), August-September 1983. Unpublished manuscript, Department of Fisheries and Oceans, Winnipeg.

Lemieux, P.J. 1990. A biological assessment of Arctic char in the Kagloryuak River, Victoria Island, NWT, 1990. Unpublished report. Available from the Fisheries Joint Management Committee, Inuvik, NT.

Lemieux, P.J., and P.D. Sparling. 1989. *A biological assessment of Arctic char in the Naloagyok River, Victoria Island, NWT, 1989.* Fisheries Joint Management Committee report no. 89-006. Inuvik, NT: Fisheries Joint Management Committee.

McCann, D. 2005. Inuvialuit Final Agreement. In *Encyclopedia of the Arctic,* ed. M. Nuttall, 1012-13. New York: Routledge.

McConney, P., R. Pomeroy, and R. Mahon. 2003. *Guidelines for coastal resource co-management in the Caribbean: Communicating the concepts and conditions that favour success.* Caribbean Coastal Co-Management Guidelines Project. Barbados: Caribbean Conservation Association.

McGhee, R. 1976. Mackenzie Eskimos in the 19th century. In *Inuit land use and occupancy project,* ed. M.M.R. Freeman, 141-51. Ottawa: Department of Indian and Northern Affairs.

Nadasdy, P. 2003. Reevaluating the co-management success story. *Arctic* 56: 367-80.

NWT (Northwest Territories). 2005. Northwest Territories Bureau of Statistics. http://www.stats.gov.nt.ca/profile/profile.html.

Papik R., M. Marschke, and G.B. Ayles. 2003. *Inuvialuit traditional ecological knowledge of fisheries in rivers west of the Mackenzie River in the Canadian Arctic.* Canada/Inuvialuit Fisheries Joint Management Committee technical report 2003-4. Inuvik, NT: Fisheries Joint Management Committee.

PHTC (Paulatuk Hunters and Trappers Committee). 1999. *Paulatuk charr management plan 1998-2002.* Paulatuk Charr Working Group. http://www.fjmc.ca/publications.htm.

–. 2003. *Paulatuk char management plan 2003-2005*. Paulatuk Char Working Group. http://www.fjmc.ca/publications.htm.

Pinkerton, E. 2003. Toward specificity in complexity: Understanding co-management from a social science perspective. In *The fisheries co-management experience: Accomplishments, challenges, and prospects,* ed. D.C. Wilson, J.R. Nielson, and P. Degnbol, 61-77. Dordrecht, Netherlands: Kluwer Academic Publishers.

Sandstrom, S.J., and L.A. Harwood. 2002. *Studies of anadromous Dolly Varden (*Salvelinus malma*) of the Big Fish River, NT, Canada 1972-1994*. Canadian Manuscript Report of Fisheries and Aquatic Sciences, No. 2603.

Sparling, P.D., and D.B. Stewart. 1988. A biological assessment of Arctic char in the Kagluk River, Victoria Island, NWT, 1988. Unpublished report prepared for the Holman Hunters and Trappers Association. Available from the Fisheries Joint Management Committee, Inuvik, NT.

Stabler, J.M. 1998. Big Fish River habitat inventory project. Unpublished report. Available from the Fisheries Joint Management Committee, Inuvik, NT.

Stewart, D.B., and P.D. Sparling. 1987. *A biological assessment of Arctic charr stocks in the Kuuk and Kagluk Rivers, Victoria Island, NWT*. A report prepared by Arctic Biological Consultants, Pinawa, MB. Available from the Department of Fisheries and Oceans, Central and Arctic Region, Winnipeg, MB.

Taylor, W.E. 1976. The fragments of Eskimo prehistory. In *Inuit land use and occupancy project,* ed. M.M.R. Freeman, 105-8. Ottawa: Department of Indian and Northern Affairs.

Usher, P. 2002. Inuvialuit use of the Beaufort Sea and its resources, 1960-2000. *Arctic* 55 (Supp): 18-28.

Walters, C.J. 1986. *Adaptive management of renewable resources*. New York: McGraw-Hill.

8

Integrating Holism and Segmentalism: Overcoming Barriers to Adaptive Co-Management between Management Agencies and Multi-Sector Bodies

Evelyn Pinkerton

In January 2005, I and another evaluation team member,[1] Anita Bedo, delivered an evaluation of a three-year pilot initiative in adaptive co-management to the co-managing body, the West Coast Vancouver Island Aquatic Management Board (AMB).[2] This body is attempting to move towards integrated ecosystem-based management of a coastal area covering some two-thirds of the west coast of Vancouver Island in British Columbia. The evaluation was intended to inform not only the co-management board itself but also the four levels of government that fund and sponsor it, as the pilot project was to end in March 2005 (and to be up for renewal). The sponsoring governments are the federal Department of Fisheries and Oceans (DFO), the Province of British Columbia, the Regional Districts of Alberni-Clayoquot and Comox-Strathcona, and the Nuu-chah-nulth Tribal Council. By far the most important funder (50 percent) and sponsor (because they have the legal mandate to manage most aquatic resources) was the DFO.[3]

The DFO eventually opted to continue supporting the AMB, at least for another two years beyond the three-year pilot, but their continued support and vision for the future of the AMB is uncertain. The nature of these differences exemplifies the difficulties in coordinating the perspectives of government bureaucracies and community-based (or regionally based) co-managers. This discussion explores key dimensions of these difficulties and options for overcoming them. After briefly noting how these difficulties surfaced in our evaluation and the discussion surrounding it, I review some aspects of what the literature on organizational behaviour contributes to the discussion. This review is not comprehensive but is meant to highlight key aspects relevant to adaptive co-management.

Local and Non-Local Differences in Perspective on Appropriate Scope and Scale of AMB Issues

Among the challenges facing the Aquatic Management Board that the evaluation team identified was the frequent insistence by DFO board members

Box 8.1.
Objectives of the WCVI Aquatic Management Board

- Protect, maintain, and rehabilitate aquatic resources
- Manage aquatic resources on an ecosystem basis
- Respect and protect First Nations' food, social, and ceremonial require-
  ments, and treaty obligations
- Support a precautionary approach to aquatic resource management
- Consolidate information relating to different aquatic resource uses and
  utilization to provide a holistic picture of the health of ecosystems within
  the management area
- Integrate expertise and knowledge from First Nations, local, scientific,
  and other sources
- Ensure opportunities for coastal communities and other persons and
  bodies affected by aquatic resource management to participate in all
  aspects of integrated management, protection, and restoration of
  aquatic resources
- Foster initiatives that maintain or enhance opportunities for coastal
  communities to access and benefit from local aquatic resources, while
  achieving sustainable social, cultural, and economic benefits from the
  integrated management and harvesting of aquatic resources for British
  Columbians and other Canadians.

that the AMB not involve itself in coast-wide issues or migratory species.
This prohibition was frustrating to most non-DFO board members, since
the principles guiding their vision were to take steps towards integrated
management and ecosystem-based management, meaning that they would
look broadly at connections among multiple species and their habitats. Box
8.1 summarizes the objectives of the AMB.

Board members were mostly local residents of the WCVI from Aboriginal,
commercial, recreational, environmental, and local government sectors (First
Nations, regional districts). A smaller number of non-local members were
from processing, aquaculture, labour, and senior governmental sectors, and
some of them agreed with the local members on this issue. Local members
who had worked for some seven years to create the AMB were certain that
migratory species such as salmon, many of which spawned in their watersheds, were part of the WCVI ecosystem. Furthermore, they felt that coast-
wide decisions made in non-local forums regulating access to migratory
and non-migratory species such as halibut in their adjacent oceans also had
an important effect on WCVI ecosystems. They repeatedly requested inclusion in advisory processes dealing with these issues, but were denied.[4] Our
evaluation reflected on this frustration and connected it to some of the

difficulties the board was experiencing in being able to significantly engage with an issue of appropriate scope and scale. The broader question being raised implicitly was: "How does a local body based on holistic principles co-manage with a senior governing body based on segmental principles?" Here, this question is considered in the context of a co-management arrangement at a formative stage (after the initial negotiation stage, but long before the mature institutionalized stage). The discussion is relevant to theory building because it involves an arrangement with an unusually broad vision and scope of objectives, operating at a regional scale and involving a complex mix of parties (see Day 2003 for a discussion of the developmental stages of the arrangement).

An Alternative Vision: Multi-Sector Involvement at the Coastal Management Area Scale

Reflections on segmentalism versus holism in our draft evaluation report to the AMB meeting (Pinkerton et al. 2005), and other comments by board members, elicited an open and helpful response from a new DFO representative on the AMB at one meeting. He drew a chart to illustrate the DFO's traditional consultative arrangements with stakeholder groups, and how the AMB differed from other stakeholders in the scope of issues considered, the geographic scale covered in planning, and the complexity of parties involved. Figure 8.1, adapted from his drawing, illustrates these contrasts. It is meant to represent the more than fifty traditional "stovepipe"[5] arrangements whereby the DFO attempts to solve problems with (usually) single-sector parties over single-species management for the entire coast. For example, the DFO works separately with the Herring Industry Advisory Board, the Commercial Salmon Advisory Board, and the Sportfish Advisory Board, each of which is a body representing fishers in that sector coast-wide.

These traditional consultative arrangements are like stovepipes in several ways. First, they separate one species from another, even though one species (herring) is the prey of another species (salmon), and their relationship could affect management considerations. Second, they separate one sector of fishers from another (commercial versus sport versus Aboriginal), although these sectors all fish many of the same species. Third, they make decisions on a coast-wide basis regarding situations that are complex and varied in different parts of the coast because of both societal and ecological variability. Advisors elected to these sectoral processes represent sector-wide economic interests but not communities or geographical regions. At the opposite end of the spectrum, occasional watershed-based pilot projects are not integrated into larger regional processes, and represent small, geographically isolated stovepipes. These stovepipe aspects of the consultations give the decisions a narrowness and a top-down configuration, even though stakeholders are involved, because of what the decisions have to ignore.

Figure 8.1

The "stovepipe" consultative processes of the Department of Fisheries and Oceans. There are approximately fifty stovepipe consultative processes of the DFO functioning at different geographical scales. This figure illustrates how the WCVI AMB includes sectors and species at the Coastal Management Area scale.

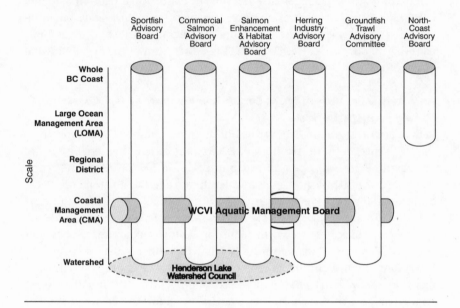

The DFO representative explained that the DFO found its stovepipe consultations frustrating, because they were costly (involving around fifty separate processes) and often unproductive. That is, even if they resolved conflict within one sector, the decisions of one sector were often in conflict with the decisions of another sector. For example, Aboriginal groups had considerable power to question decisions made by the commercial and sport sector (because of constitutionally protected Aboriginal rights), sometimes causing those sectors to have to rework their solutions to problems within their sectors (thus, making their first efforts a waste of time and resources).

As discussed above, some of the dilemmas with stovepipe consultation resulted from the *scope* at which a problem was defined – for example, how many species and how many sectors were really involved in and affected by a problem. Other stovepipe dilemmas resulted from the coast-wide geographical *scale* of the consultations. The DFO member reminded the meeting attendees that the DFO's Oceans Strategy called for management units at several geographical scales: (1) the watershed, (2) the Coastal Management

Area (CMA; six on the BC coast), and (3) the Large Ocean Management Area (LOMA; two on the BC coast). The DFO is already dealing with a BC North Coast LOMA, attempting to reach agreement on a few major policy issues at a large scale and to do coastal planning involving eight First Nations' tribal councils. The DFO member considered the AMB to be an example of the second-order scale of management, a CMA, and spoke to the importance of working on co-management at this scale.[6] The implication was that it might be possible to deal with more complex issues at the CMA scale, especially if only one tribal council were involved.

For the DFO to make management decisions with a co-managing partner at a CMA scale would be a significant departure from the stovepipe model in three ways. First, more decisions would be made at a much smaller geographical scale. A large co-management literature documents how a relatively small geographical and human scale of interactions enables more meaningful and manageable dialogue across many sectors/stakeholder groups (Pinkerton and Weinstein 1995). This possibility creates the second major difference from the stovepipe model: decisions at the CMA scale cut across and include sectors usually operating in separate stovepipes. Decisions would thus be integrated, *multi-sectoral* decisions (instead of single-sector), bringing together, in addition to the four levels of government, commercial, sport, Aboriginal, processor, aquaculture, environmental, and labour interests. Having these sectors reach agreement among themselves at one table and plan jointly would mean that this particular CMA could potentially have the sort of cross-sectoral management that is called for in Canada's Oceans Act and Oceans Strategy (in language that is general and vague, however). The DFO's 2004-05 Report on Plans and Priorities (RPP) to the Treasury Board of Canada clearly states the priority for the Aboriginal fishery: "Assisting Aboriginal people to build the capacity to participate more effectively in the *multi-stakeholder processes* used for aquatic resources and oceans management will help to *avoid separate management solitudes*" (10, emphasis added).

The AMB, then, is an example of a body at a second-order geographical scale (CMA) that cross-cuts many of the stakeholder sectors. It is an appropriate vehicle for coordinating non-Aboriginal stakeholders with Aboriginal governance processes in the same geographical area. It operates at a scale that is of great interest to government agencies because it is large enough that there would be only about six such areas on the whole west coast of Canada. If the DFO could find stakeholders able to make agreements in areas this large, it would have a relatively efficient means of consulting that would bypass a number of the stovepipe dilemmas and contribute to management solutions. Stovepipe processes that effectively solved other problems would remain, but a different model for addressing the types of complexity outlined above would emerge, including ways to link processes operating at different scales (e.g., integrating watershed-scale processes with CMA-scale processes).

Third, and finally, the CMA geographical scale would presumably be large enough to include significant aspects of ocean and freshwater ecosystem structure and function. The DFO would then be responding to the call in the Oceans Act to do "integrated management," moving beyond the single-species models in the stovepipe consultations to consider species interactions, habitat linkages, and broader questions of coastal planning such as cumulative effects.[7] Some natural scientists have built ecosystem-based models at the CMA scale, including a first-generation one for an area somewhat larger than the WCVI (Pauly et al. 1996; Christensen and Walters 2004). Others believe either that our knowledge of coastal ecosystems is not sufficient to know at what scale we should be studying them (de la Mare 2005) or that there are inherent difficulties in models at this scale but a better chance of modelling them at a smaller scale (Cox et al. 2002a, 2002b). We do know something about the scale at which multi-party boards can function, however, so a reasonable approach is to be guided by this scale. This scale could indicate what is politically and socially feasible, providing an opportunity to learn what we can about ecosystems in the process (de Young et al. 1999).

It should be noted that the level of power being exercised by all the aforementioned processes is officially only advisory, since the Minister of Fisheries and Oceans has the authority to make all decisions. Decision making that results from agreement across sectors is inherently powerful, however, because senior governments are relieved of the burden of resolving conflict among those sectors and can bless as well as help craft their agreements. While a senior government may, in order to further an agenda, make a different decision than the one recommended, doing so would weaken the power of both government and the consultative body, because trust will have been weakened and parties will become less willing to collaborate. A major policy role of government is always to broker agreements among conflicting users. As suggested by the discussion below, there can be more power for both stakeholders *and* government in such multi-party agreements.[8]

How Can Shifts in Governance towards This Vision Occur?

A number of questions arise from the project of co-managing at the CMA scale. Some of them on the "community" side concern matters such as how to have enough face-to-face encounters among stakeholders at the CMA geographical scale to make and implement agreements effectively on an ongoing basis. And what types of agreements? On the senior government side, different questions arise, ones posed sincerely by the DFO representative at the meeting. Can the agency actually shift to another way of working with stakeholders? What would be required to get beyond the stovepipe way of dealing with stakeholders? Would new models co-exist with or replace the stovepipe consultations (thus potentially altering long-standing power and client relationships)? Are third-order aggregations of coast such as Large Ocean Management Areas (LOMAs), which are twice as large as CMAs, too large for reaching and implementing more than very general agreements effectively? The North Coast LOMA appears to be driven mostly by government's desire to bring stakeholders to agreement on possible oil, gas, and aquaculture development, possibly the kinds of issues that *could* be dealt with fruitfully at a LOMA scale. More complex issues, such as dealing with species and habitat/species interactions, may be more effectively handled at a CMA scale. In the discussion below, I show how some actions undertaken by the AMB (or which the AMB aspired to undertake, but was prevented) either counteracted some of the problems in senior levels of governance or could have done so.

Identifying Types of Barriers to Achieving Adaptive Co-Management
Here I conceptualize the types of barriers that the senior governing agency, a large federal bureaucracy, would have to overcome in order to move in the direction of greater use of multi-stakeholder boards at the CMA scale. The key barriers are a feature of the behaviour of complex organizations, of which government bureaucracies and agencies are one class. Government agencies are predominantly hierarchical structures functioning according to instrumental values and technical considerations (Cyert and March 1963). In order to deal with the complexity and diversity of an ecosystem, the hierarchy would have to be able to delegate a great deal of control and initiative to various local arms of the bureaucracy. These would need to have the capacity to be adaptive, learning bodies with considerable autonomy, even while being coordinated in their operational objectives at a policy level from the top (de la Mare 2005). Wilson (1989) has shown that battles are won by armies that have the capacity for intelligent autonomous actions at the lowest level, informed by an overall strategic plan coordinated at the highest level. Clarke and McCool (1996) have noted that the most successful federal resource management agencies have adopted these key aspects of military structure. Yet, this optimal practice may be more honoured in the breach than in the observance, if we consider the usual modus operandi of government agencies. Wilson (1989) shows as many failures as successes of government bureaucracies in achieving this type of structure and coordination.

Some analysts focus on how government agencies have moved from failure to success in their attempt to cope with complexity in their policy environment. In his analysis of the US Forest Service's transition to ecosystem management, alternative dispute resolution planner and policy analyst Steven Yaffee (1997) identified five "behavioural biases" or tendencies (which a sociologist, following Max Weber, might call forms of "bureaucratic rationality") of government agencies: (1) preference for short-term rationality over long-term rationality; (2) preference for competition over cooperation; (3) fragmentation of interests and values; (4) fragmentation of responsibilities and authorities; and (5) fragmentation of information and knowledge. These behavioural biases inform the ways agencies tend to make decisions, ways that unfortunately lead to ineffective outcomes, and in this case make adaptive co-management impossible.

In the discussion below, I conceptualize these five tendencies as barriers to adaptive co-management, and include Yaffee's and others' ideas about which practices show promise for overcoming these tendencies. Yaffee's approach is supplemented especially by the complementary approach of political scientist William Ascher (2001), which examines policy failures through "perverse learning." It is instructive to review how these two scholars, who do not cite each other's work and draw on different aspects of the literature, have reached remarkably similar conclusions, based on their experience with natural resource management agencies. The similarities make their findings more convincing, especially because Yaffee's experience is mostly in North America while Ascher's is mostly in developing countries. Both authors have drawn upon at least some of the literature on the behaviour of complex organizations, a literature that appears most frequently in the fields of political science, sociology, and administrative science; relatively little of this literature has focused on how natural resource management agencies behave. Finally, I will note how various authors recommend dealing with these behavioural tendencies and how the AMB either responded or had the potential to do so.

Behavioural Bias 1: Preference for Short-Term Rationality over Long-Term Rationality

Management agencies seek to minimize the energy needed to respond to a situation while maximizing control and predictability. These are reasonable short-term responses but miss the long-term objective of solving the problem at hand or creating the conditions to do so. For example, agency leaders often try to force controversies into organizational procedures that are not effective at dealing with these particular controversies. They tend to stifle productive dissension and protect ongoing organizational processes from disruption, resulting in reduced creativity and effectiveness. They then rationalize past behaviour and become entrapped in bad decisions. These procedures reduce the agency's fitness over time by limiting innovation and adaptation. This bias towards short-term rationality parallels the prisoner's dilemma and the tragedy of the commons tendencies, in which individually rational choices lead to socially undesirable outcomes.

Ascher calls this tendency "complexity reduction" or "oversimplification," leading to "perverse learning." He attributes oversimplification especially to institutional convenience, because the lessons that the agency needs to learn in order to solve a problem run counter to established institutional modus operandi. The planning and reward structure of the agency is based on short-term considerations: rewards for immediate results are often enhanced at the expense of rewards for long-term performance. Likewise, natural resource management agency decision makers often do not face the consequences of poor decisions whose outcomes may not appear immediately, such as the decline of fish populations.

Behavioural Bias 2: Preference for Competition over Cooperation
Government agencies tend to protect their power preserves at all costs and to perceive the sharing of power and resources as always a zero-sum game: if some is shared with stakeholders, they believe they will enjoy exactly this much less (Clarke and McCool 1996; Yaffee 1997; Songorwa et al. 2000). This mode of thinking inhibits the sharing of information and resources, promotes biasing or misrepresentation of information that is shared, and perpetuates the protection of turf even within divisions of the agency, even when there is a clear mutual benefit to be derived from cooperation. Such competitive behaviour leads to stalemates, low morale, and low legitimacy in the eyes of the public. Turf protection can also determine the models that management agencies are willing to entertain. Insistence on the use of conventional agency models limits the way partners can think of co-management, disallowing traditional forms of access or scales of knowledge of community members. For example, many communities have traditionally used regulation of gear and allocation of fishing space to limit fishing effort. This approach is often based on detailed local knowledge of stocks and may be a highly effective regulatory approach in certain situations (Wilson et al. 1994). Agencies' conventional regulatory tools, such as limited entry and quantifiable stock models, provide predictability over large scales and are thus preferred (Degnbol 2003). Combinations of these approaches are seldom attempted because of a perceived competition between them.

Ascher points out that the "bias in favour of government control" causes all negative outcomes to be attributed to the lack of government control and consequently leads to a felt need to increase regulatory stringency: the possibility that poorly designed government policies could be the cause is not entertained. The feedback loop that would enable the agency to adapt its policies and practices is often missing or obscured by competitive behaviour.

Behavioural Bias 3: Fragmentation of Interests and Values
Interest groups lobby agencies for privileged access to the resource. The more energetic, powerful, or privileged these interest groups are, the more influence they tend to have. Agencies may respond by institutionalizing their response to the most powerful interest groups through formal consultative

mechanisms. In extreme cases, an agency may be "captured" by the most powerful interest group(s). In this case, the interests of the latter will have an influence on policy that is disproportionate to the public benefit of the latter's extraction activities (McFarland 1987). In cases where there are many conflicting interests, stakeholders will engage in turf battles as energetic as those within the agency: positions will be exaggerated, and non-productive conflict will predominate. Exaggerated positions make it impossible for government decision makers not to be attacked by all sides. This manner of dealing with management and allocation decisions is inherently competitive and allows no means of inter-sectoral communication or cooperation, especially not at the level of shared geographical territory. At this level, one would expect to find the greatest incentive to perceive a shared destiny and to recognize that the game may not be a zero-sum one – that there may be mutual benefits to joint problem solving. If fragmented interests are not brought together and forced to identify and integrate their common interests in sustainable management and ecosystem health, the decision-making process will reflect fragmented values rather than shared or program objectives, and conflict will be continually forced to higher and higher governmental levels. If conflicts are resolved for political reasons at higher levels, regional decision makers in the agency lose power, and decisions will be more informed by politics than by program objectives.

Behavioural Bias 4: Fragmentation of Responsibilities and Authorities
The structuring of agencies into divisions tends to divide up responsibilities but not to integrate them at a higher or lower level. Similarly, the legislation creating the mandates of an agency may be inherently contradictory or incompatible. The Oceans Act and the Fisheries Act, implemented by two different branches of the DFO, have not been reconciled. Turf battles among agency divisions and among different agencies with jurisdiction over different aspects of the resources and its habitat both create and reinforce stovepipe management structures within the agency. Decisions are focused on various statutorily defined questions that are much narrower than required for an effective problem-solving process. For example, commercial fisheries are regulated by the federal agency, the DFO, while freshwater and anadromous sport fisheries and aquaculture are mostly regulated by the province. In addition, forest management and coastal development planning, two of the largest threats to fish habitat, are provincial jurisdictions.

While some level of division of responsibility and authority is obviously necessary to develop expertise and accomplish specific tasks, it comes at a cost if not institutionally counterbalanced. Yaffee (1997) emphasizes the tendency for individuals in such situations to build niches for themselves as they seek turf. The goal of protecting their turf may then override the goal of cooperative promotion of conservation goals. In addition, uncoordinated decisions are likely to lead to piecemeal solutions that are not effective at addressing larger problems, and to diminished accountability in dealing with overall issues. This tendency can be exacerbated by stovepipe sectoral processes, as discussed above. Conservation objectives, moreover, are often neglected when other mandated objectives (such as exploitation) are more consistent with the organization's institutional interests or the individual ambitions of leaders and staff (Ascher 2001). As March and Simon's classic analysis (1958) showed, there is a tendency to favour those aspects of their objectives that are most consistent with the agency's resource base. Thus, exploitation interests are likely to have priority over conservation interests, and the sustainable extraction rules for one species will ignore the impact of that extraction on other species and their habitats.

Behavioural Bias 5: Fragmentation of Information and Knowledge
Information and analysis are fragmented among professional disciplines, economic sectors, levels of government, and divisions of agencies. Because information is collected in response to specific needs, it is generally biased towards past problems and reflects particular organizational contexts and interests. It may not even be useful to other interests in its current forms. Furthermore, information as a form of power is hoarded by divisions and agencies; it is seen as a possible weapon in conflicts and as property not to be shared until it can be claimed by an author through publication. Government information-gathering resources will never be sufficient to obtain the information needed to make fully scientifically informed harvesting decisions (Wilson et al. 1994). Although the literature shows many cases of sustainable community-based management or co-management based on allocation of geographical space or other indirect means of keeping harvest effort at sustainable levels (Schlager and Ostrom 1993; Wilson et al. 1994), it is very difficult for governments to trust these proxies or the knowledge on which they are based (Finlayson 1994; Holm 2003; Wilson 2003). Harvesters' knowledge may be tacit, eluding the discursive world of scientific experiment, and dismissed because of dissimilar cognitive cultures and the use of alien rules, norms, and languages in the negotiation of validity (Palsson 1995; Neis and Felt 2000). Thus, government agencies often reject forms of knowledge that could help close the information gap, especially when combined with agency knowledge.

Ascher emphasizes the complexity of the classic "principal-agent problem" that arises when agency officials have both superior information and some autonomy. How does the "principal" (supervisor, administrator) monitor the performance of the "agent" (a party who implements the directives of the principal)? In a situation in which competitive behaviour results in less flow of information on individual activities and resources, individuals within government have more opportunity to pursue their own individual or institutional interests rather than the public interest. The problem is complex, because "agents" have multiple motives that differ from one agent to the next, and the same incentives or monitoring strategy may not work for all. Ascher also notes that complexity, uncertainty, and limited resources will discourage analysis of new situations on their own terms, and promote their interpretation in terms of the most recent or familiar example at hand, often leading to inadequate analysis.

Dealing with the Behavioural Biases

Yaffee (1997) notes that visioning future undesirable states and binding oneself to alternative policies for achieving different outcomes is a large step towards long-term rationality (overcoming Behavioural Bias 1 towards short-term rationality). Table 8.1 demonstrates how the AMB has bound itself to alternative policies by spelling out its objectives. Ideally, board members are required to uphold the objectives as a condition of serving on the board, although in practice this has not always been the case with all non-local members. To monitor how much and how well such a step is made means implementing performance measures, with monitored results reported to remind agencies of their commitments. Although not focused on specific performance measures, the AMB has acted as a monitor of processes or commitments of government, and the action or inaction of the latter on a particular issue. It has monitored government's lack of response to requests for stakeholder input in various fisheries and planning processes, and has determined which elements are missing from planning processes that leave key concerns unaddressed.

Another step towards long-term rationality is to reward risk taking and experimentation with creative solutions, as is done routinely by successful companies such as 3M, which encourages all employees to allocate up to 15 percent of their time to innovation (3M policy on its website, http://www. 3M.com). Co-management arrangements themselves have often been documented to serve the function of designing what the future commitments should be and then holding agencies accountable for these commitments (Pinkerton and Weinstein 1995). Thus, they can be helpful in overcoming this dysfunctional tendency in management agencies and in steering management towards longer-term goals. Co-management could open the door to "double-loop learning" (Argyris and Schon 1978): bureaucratic outsiders such as the AMB may redefine the problem or how to approach it, helping insiders (the management agency) consider how they could rearrange their standard operating procedures so as to allow themselves to consider a broader range of options or "to learn how to learn." As a discussion and learning forum, and as a convenor of processes to explore options, the AMB exemplifies this process.

Ascher (2001) recommends tying government officials' long-term benefits (such as pensions and professional recognition) to the continued and sustainable operation of resource extraction activities. He believes that reducing the rotation of officials to different locations will increase their involvement in long-term projects oriented towards sustainability goals. Westley (2002) goes further by showing how a manager who "goes local" can work effectively to change conflict with stakeholders into collaboration. Long-term familiarity with the problem and the stakeholders enables a manager to discover a way to engage stakeholders in scientific experiments and to discover windows and moments of opportunity, as well as the appropriate scale at which to define and solve problems. Ascher's belief and Westley's conclusions are consistent with my own (as yet unpublished) findings on the successful strategies of the Alaska Department of Fish and Game, in which area managers may have twenty years' service in the same area. This finding is also consistent with the human resources strategy of firms that invest in hiring the right people, rewarding them well, training and educating them, and sharing the rewards through means such as gain sharing, stock options, employee ownership, and so on. Some firms go further and tie top managers' bonuses to successful performance measured on an index agreed to and rated by subordinates (Bolman and Deal 1997). In a similar use of visible sustainability indicators, agencies could explicitly plan for sustainability goals and evaluate for sustainability achievements, thus improving and rewarding performance oriented towards longer-term objectives. Many scholars have noted the influence of budgetary cycles on the time frame of government agency planning, and even the influence of annual budgetary spending requirements on division or departmental performance. Rewards to agencies and even departments for budgetary carry-over and allocation to long-term projects and planning would help combat short-term rationality as it appears in spending patterns at the end of the fiscal year, for example.

As a corrective for Behavioural Bias 2, preference for competition over cooperation, Yaffee (1997) recommends the use of alternative dispute resolution with professional facilitation. Such processes would be additionally helped by a focus on superordinate goals and shared objectives (such as the sustainable management of the resource, habitat protection, and increased understanding of species interactions that affect the health of the resource). With leadership from the agency concerning program objectives in the public interest, but flexibility about how to achieve these objectives and help from facilitators in principled negotiation, competition could be reduced significantly. The AMB has played a significant role in the WCVI region in a number of ways that have tended to counteract Behavioural Bias 2. In creating cooperation between government and local groups, it has played several roles. As a two-way communication funnel between governments and local bodies, it has provided information both ways to meet the needs of all parties; it has provided analysis of issues and options that consolidate opinion in the region and explain government perspectives to locals; and it has acted as a clearinghouse to which issues are referred for resolution.

In a more proactive role, the AMB has acted as a mediator of everyday interactions among the DFO, local fishers, and Nuu-chah-nulth Tribal Council biologists in developing a new fishery for gooseneck barnacles. The AMB has also facilitated formal meetings among the DFO, the province, and other actors by providing an educated balance through a neutral informed vision, conducting surveys in advance to identify the priority issues of attendees, and analyzing and framing issues in advance to promote problem solving at meetings. In its relations with non-governmental bodies, the AMB has also acted as a facilitator for groups inside and outside the region, as a convenor of processes for exploring options, as an umbrella under which groups in the region could come together, and as a culture broker promoting communication among parties with different values, perspectives, and worldviews.

My research on agency/tribal fisheries co-management in Washington State provides another surprising finding: leaders in the state fisheries agency believed that the agency was better off after co-management was established. One dimension of the perceived improvement was increased resources for management. Cooperation between the tribes and the agency enabled them to finally come together to negotiate a Pacific Salmon Treaty with Canada. The treaty produced new funds not previously available to the agency. In addition, the tribes were able to access funds from different sources and to hire their own professional biological and management experts. The tribes and agency then began to allocate tasks among themselves more effectively, spreading resources more efficiently. Finally, the entry into management of new colleagues who reported to different authorities stimulated debate and innovation (Pinkerton 2003). While a group such as the Aquatic Management Board is dependent on governmental support in the first few years, the charitable status it has obtained, the nature of its mission, and the record of other multi-party bodies suggests that it could eventually become self-supporting and a net contributor of management resources.

Possibilities for counteracting the last three behavioural biases, as variants of the bias towards competition over cooperation, are best discussed together, as these biases and their resulting behaviours overlap considerably (fragmentation of interests and values, fragmentation of responsibilities and authorities, fragmentation of information and knowledge).

Yaffee (1997) suggests the creation of coordinating mechanisms such as ecosystem-level multi-party policy councils, interagency management teams, revitalized regional planning bodies, and information clearinghouses to build a shared understanding of what is at stake. He emphasizes that such bodies would need some incentives, such as a substantive mandate and/or new resources. They would also require clear and shared measures of success and ways to monitor progress towards desired ends. They could overcome fragmentation of information through shared databases and interpretations that integrate information and different forms of knowledge.

The AMB provides an almost formulaic example of some of what Yaffee recommends. To the extent allowed by its limited funding, the AMB plays the role of a multi-party council, an interagency management team, a regional planning body, and an information clearinghouse. Because it did not receive the funding originally budgeted for project management, the AMB has acted mostly to coordinate with and provide perspectives on projects of other bodies. For example, it contributed to the Kyuquot Coastal Zone Plan, where it observed and reviewed the Provincial Coastal Use Plan, provided recommendations, and participated in follow-up activities. The AMB's participation in the plan was acknowledged as resulting in a more truly integrated plan than was initially envisioned.

One unique AMB contribution to counteracting these three fragmentation behavioural tendencies is its production of an Internet-accessible, integrated, geo-referenced database linked to a document database containing the principal key writings about any resource on the WCVI. Furthermore, a substantive mandate (to make progress towards ecosystem-based management) allowed comprehensive actions. For example, the AMB can coordinate habitat and stock status information in a comprehensive manner. It has recently been mapping the effects of activities in the uplands, such as agriculture and toxics; the effects of nearshore activities such as fish farms, sewage, and estuary drainage; and the effects of ocean conditions such as salinity and activities such as driftnetting to produce a map of the cumulative effects of upland, nearshore, and ocean conditions on salmon and other aquatic species. Two separate maps – salmon stock status and cumulative effects – are being produced and will eventually be integrated into one map.

Clarke and McCool (1996) found that the most successful agencies are those best able to mobilize and infuse their staff with a sense of the mission of the agency and to tie the programmatic goals closely to the mission. Such agencies were also able to deal with the principal-agent problem by identifying peer professional performance with the standing of the agency and with programmatic goals, which are seen also as consistent with those of the public. This finding is consistent with Westley's conclusions (2002) about the success of agencies that work closely with stakeholders and allow them to experiment and learn.

An AMB project exemplifying these findings is the creation of a new goose-neck barnacle experimental fishery. Previously a "lost" fishery under con-ventional management (closed because it could not be managed sustainably), the gooseneck barnacle fishery was opened in late January 2004 and, by April, showed substantial benefits in economic, ecological, and social terms. Economically, the fishery directly employs thirty-two harvesters and sup-ports one full-time and eleven part-time additional jobs in monitoring, management, purchasing, transportation, and processing. The development of the project involved extensive research integrating local knowledge and natural science (a major AMB objective). Since the first three months of operations, the AMB has been able to introduce new buyers for gooseneck barnacles and develop new protocols for the fishery, and is in the process of creating a product-tracking system for which the AMB has a five-year plan and fundraising proposal. The AMB predicts that this fishery will be self-sustaining by its fourth or fifth year.

Ecologically, the experimental fishery is being conducted in a sustain-able manner satisfactory to the DFO, the province, and the AMB, enabling effective monitoring of both the stock and its habitat. Detailed assessments on control and index sites, an adaptive management plan, and a decision framework to verify the sustainability of the fishery under a precautionary approach have been established, and all parties are satisfied that the AMB was able to revive a fishery that would otherwise be closed and probably poached.

Socially, the AMB worked closely with the DFO and the Nuu-chah-nulth Tribal Council and gained the confidence of the harvesters, who are now recommending a lower level of harvest on particular rocks that they feel are not growing back fast enough. This is a positive sign that the AMB has been able to develop a management regime that harvesters consider legitimate and effective, and thus a regime that will be able to elicit not only high levels of compliance but also intervention by harvesters to make the regime more precautionary in specific instances. This happened partially because the AMB staff worked closely with the harvesters to record and include their knowledge and gain their cooperation in the generation of harvest rules. The AMB has also developed an efficient method of recording stock and habitat conditions through scanned photographs and data, which are in-stantly recorded electronically and are easily viewed by managers, trigger-ing warning signals if precautionary thresholds are passed.[9]

This method of creating a new fishery blazes a path for innovative ways of rule making, monitoring, and enforcement, and demonstrates the poten-tial of bodies like the AMB to contribute to management in ways unique to their position as stakeholder representatives. It also demonstrates the use of performance measures, adaptive management, and transparency. At an AMB meeting, the DFO representative marvelled at the process surrounding the re-creation of the fishery and stated that he "would never have thought this possible" (since the DFO had closed the fishery as being impossible to manage). The DFO was, of course, a partner in the creation of the new fishery and still exercises oversight, but the innovations that made it possible were led by the AMB.

Conclusion

In considering selected literature on five behavioural biases of resource management agencies, this discussion has identified sixteen ways by which agencies can overcomes those biases. The first eleven of these relate directly to the creation of multi-party co-management bodies, particularly ones that could operate at a regional scale and that would have characteristics similar to those of the Aquatic Management Board. The biases may be overcome by the agency, in collaboration with a co-managing body, by:

- visioning future undesirable states and binding itself to alternative policies for achieving different outcomes
- designing what the future commitments should be, and then holding agencies responsible for these commitments
- monitoring how much and how well alternative activities are done by implementing performance measures, with monitored results reported to remind agencies of their commitments
- rewarding risk taking and experimentation with creative solutions
- practising "double-loop learning" (questioning standard operating procedures so as to consider a broader range of options)
- using alternative dispute resolution, with professional facilitation
- focusing on superordinate goals and shared objectives of multiple parties (such as the sustainable management of the resource, habitat protection, and increased understanding of species interactions that affect the health of the resource)
- leading by putting forth program objectives in the public interest, but being flexible about how to achieve these objectives
- reducing stereotypes and building concurrence across interest groups
- creating ecosystem-level multi-party policy councils, interagency management teams, and revitalized regional planning bodies to build a shared understanding of what is at stake
- creating information clearinghouses to build a shared understanding of what is at stake and interpretations that integrate information and different forms of knowledge.

In addition to these eleven classes of activities related to working with co-managers, there are five types of actions that management agencies could take internally to overcome the behavioural biases:

- creating incentives for agency staff to identify simultaneously with agency mission, program objectives, and professional peer expectations
- tying government officials' long-term benefits (such as pensions and professional recognition) to the continued and sustainable operation of resource extraction activities
- rewarding agencies and even departments for budgetary carry-over and allocation to long-term projects and planning
- reducing the rotation of officials to different locations to increase their involvement in long-term projects oriented towards sustainability goals; "going local" over the long term by building relationships that engage stakeholders in scientific experiments, discovering windows and moments of opportunity to create collaboration
- planning explicitly for sustainability goals and evaluation of sustainability achievements, through the use of visible sustainability indicators.

This discussion has identified the segmental tendencies of conventional resource management (as specified in the five behavioural biases) as a major barrier to achieving sustainable resource management and moving towards ecosystem-based management. I have considered how the conventional stovepipe consultative mechanisms of agencies tend to be produced by and to reinforce this segmentalism. I have also considered the capacity of multi-stakeholder boards such as the AMB to promote communication among the warring stakeholder sectors and to integrate stakeholder's concerns by discussing problems holistically. Although we may not know the scale at which we should be studying ecosystems, this discussion suggests that multi-party co-managing bodies such as the AMB operating at the Coastal Management Area (or what may be termed the "integrated management") scale are a workable human scale at which to take a productive first step in this direction. Such bodies can have the capacity to be managers themselves in innovative ways, as exemplified in the gooseneck barnacle fishery, and can also be effective co-managers, as exemplified in the many other roles they play both with government and within the region.

Acknowledgments

I warmly thank Tom Pater and Andrew Day for being willing to serve as the AMB reviewers of this chapter, and I am equally grateful to three DFO reviewers who prefer to remain anonymous. The internal workshops and review process organized by the editors were very provocative, stimulating, and helpful in herding us into a common corral. Everyone's comments have improved the chapter but only the author can be held responsible for any errors of judgment or fact.

Notes

1 The evaluation had three co-authors (Pinkerton, Bedo, and Hanson 2005) and is posted at http://www.westcoastaquatic.ca.

2   A detailed description of the AMB is beyond the scope of this paper, as it is meant here to serve as an example of the structural nature of problems with which government agencies have to cope, and potential solutions to these problems. Briefly, the AMB was formed following eight years of activism in the WCVI region by First Nations, commercial fishers, recreational fishers, and environmental interests, plus two regional districts. These parties had formed an organization to work together towards sustainable integrated aquatic management. The terms of reference that were finally negotiated with federal and provincial governments called for the inclusion on the AMB of members to broadly represent the interests of processors, salmon farmers, the province, and the federal Department of Fisheries and Oceans (DFO). All members agreed to support the principles and vision developed by the original WCVI members, consistent with the Nuu-chah-nulth First Nation's principle of *Hishukish Ts'awalk* ("Everything is one"), ecosystem management, and the Oceans Act principle of integrated management.

3   The Nuu-chah-nulth have been negotiating a treaty with Canada to clarify their own rights to co-manage and access aquatic resources, a process recently interrupted by their 2004 court proceedings against the DFO and the federal government for not allowing adequate commercial access to aquatic resources. Key Nuu-chah-nulth leaders consider the Aquatic Management Board an Interim Measures Agreement for their eventual treaty with Canada.

4   For example, the AMB requested inclusion in the three levels of salmon planning – the Area Harvest Committees, the Commercial Salmon Advisory Board, and the Integrated Harvest Planning Committees – but was denied. AMB members pointed out that Stephen Owen's Institute for Dispute Resolution, which had been commissioned to advise the DFO on their advisory processes, had identified the AMB as an important model for a new way to do policy work and had strongly recommended its connection to other advisory processes (and specifically salmon) (see Institute for Dispute Resolution 2001).

5   The term "stovepipe" is widespread in the organizational behaviour literature, and was also used by the DFO representative on the AMB.

6   Since this presentation, it has become evident that the WCVI region offers opportunities to conduct management activities far more complex and integrated that those envisaged in the CMA scale in the Oceans Strategy. The term for that scale that has come into DFO parlance is the "integrated management" scale. Management at this scale has elicited more interest from the province recently because of the opportunity it could offer the province to be involved as a partner with the federal government in integrated oceans planning, unlike the North Coast LOMA process, which does not include the province.

7   Although the DFO has gone through a second generation of strategies to achieve sustainable development, as required of all federal government agencies in Canada, there has been little implementation of these strategies so far.

8   The DFO was unwilling to abandon traditional stovepipe consultative processes, however, and, during summer and fall 2005, began exploring how to combine these processes with new Aboriginal co-managing bodies that were to receive significant funding under a new Aboriginal Aquatic Resource and Oceans Management (AAROM) Program (because of new court cases recognizing greater Aboriginal management rights). The West Coast of Vancouver Island was the first area in BC to pilot the AAROM program, partly because of its experience with the AMB and partly because of the proactive stance of the Nuu-chah-nulth. In this situation, the DFO saw the AMB in the limited role of an oceans planning body between the AAROM concept and the traditional stovepipe consultations, but with a project-specific versus a continuing mandate. At one point, the DFO decided to terminate all funding, but intense pressure from AMB supporters at federal and provincial levels restored it. AMB members did not agree with the proposed change to its mandate, and the nature of their role is under negotiation at this writing. The AMB currently cooperates with the Nuu-chah-nulth AAROM process on the operational level in projects such as stock status mapping, creating a stock assessment framework, and developing conservation units for the Wild Salmon Policy initiative.

9   The fishery was not pursued in 2006 because of competition from Chile in the Spanish market; the AMB hopes to identify other markets. The precautionary procedures adopted do not allow a fishery to occur at much lower prices for the product.

References

Argyris, C., and D. Schon. 1978. *Organizational learning: A theory of action perspective*. Reading, MA: Addison-Wesley.

Ascher, W. 2001. Coping with complexity and organizational interests in natural resource management. *Ecosystems* 4: 742-57.

Bolman, L.G., and T.E. Deal. 1997. *Reframing organizations: Artistry, choice, and leadership*, 2nd ed. San Francisco: Jossey-Bass.

Christensen, V., and C.J. Walters. 2004. Ecopath with ecosim: Methods, capabilities and limitations. *Ecological Modelling* 172: 109-39.

Clarke, J.N., and D. McCool. 1996. *Staking out the terrain: Power differentials among natural resource management agencies*. Albany, NY: SUNY Press.

Cox, S.P., S.J.D. Martell, C.J. Walters, T.E. Essington, J.F. Kitchell, C. Boggs, and I. Kaplan. 2002a. Reconstructing ecosystem dynamics in the central Pacific Ocean, 1952-1998. I. Estimating population biomass and recruitment of tunas and billfishes. *Canadian Journal of Fisheries and Aquatic Sciences* 59 (11): 1724-35.

–. 2002b. Reconstructing ecosystem dynamics in the central Pacific Ocean, 1952-1998. II. A preliminary assessment of the trophic impacts of fishing and effects on tuna dynamics. *Canadian Journal of Fisheries and Aquatic Sciences* 59 (11): 1736-47.

Cyert, R.M., and J.C. March. 1963. *A behavioral theory of the firm*. Englewood Cliffs, NJ: Prentice Hall.

Day, C.A. 2003. Building aquatic co-management on the West Coast of Vancouver Island, Canada: What does *hishukish ts'awalk* mean? PhD dissertation, School of Resource and Environmental Management, Simon Fraser University, Burnaby, BC.

Degnbol, P. 2003. Science and the user perspective: The gap co-management must address. In *The fisheries co-management experience: Accomplishments, challenges, and prospects*, ed. D.C. Wilson, J.R. Nielsen, and P. Dengbol, 31-49. Dordrecht, Netherlands: Kluwer Academic Publishers.

de la Mare, W.K. 2005. Marine ecosystem-based management as a hierarchical control system. *Marine Policy* 29: 57-68.

de Young, B., R.M. Peterman, A.R. Dobell, E. Pinkerton, Y. Breton, A.T. Charles, M.J. Fogarty, G.R. Munro, and C. Taggart. 1999. *Canadian marine fisheries in a changing and uncertain world*. Canadian Special Publication of Fisheries and Aquatic Sciences, no. 129. Ottawa: NRC Research Press.

Finlayson, C. 1994. *Fishing for truth: A sociological analysis of the northern cod stock assessments from 1977-1990*. St. John's, NL: ISER Books.

Holm, P. 2003. Crossing the border: On the relationship between science and fishermen's knowledge in a resource management context. *MAST/Maritime Studies* 2 (1): 5-34.

Institute for Dispute Resolution. 2001. *Independent review of improved decision-making in the Pacific salmon fishery: Final recommendations*. Victoria: University of Victoria.

March, J.G., and H.A. Simon. 1958. *Organizations*. New York: Wiley.

McFarland, A. 1987. Interest groups and theories of power in America. *British Journal of Political Science* 17: 129-47.

Neis, B., and L. Felt, eds. 2000. *Finding our sea legs: Linking fishery people and their knowledge with science and management*. St. John's, NL: ISER Books.

Palsson, G. 1995. Learning by fishing: Practical science and scientific practice. In *Property rights in a social and ecological context: Case studies and design applications*, ed. Susan Hanna and M. Munasinghe, 85-97. Stockholm: Beijer Institute of Ecological Economics; Washington, DC: World Bank.

Pauly, D., V. Christensen, and N. Haggen, eds. 1996. *Mass-balance models of northeastern Pacific ecosystems*. Fisheries Centre Research Reports, 4 (1). Vancouver: University of British Columbia. http://www.fisheries.ubc.ca/publications/reports.

Pinkerton, E. 2003. Toward specificity in complexity: Understanding co-management from a social science perspective. In *The fisheries co-management experience: Accomplishments, challenges, and prospects*, ed. D.C. Wilson, J.R. Nielsen, and P. Dengbol, 61-77. Dordrecht, Netherlands: Kluwer Academic Publishers.

Pinkerton, E., and M. Weinstein. 1995. *Fisheries that work: Sustainability through community-based management.* Vancouver: The David Suzuki Foundation.

Pinkerton, E., A. Bedo, and A. Hanson. 2005. *Final evaluation report: West Coast Vancouver Island Aquatic Management Board (AMB).* http://www.westcoastaquatic.ca.

Schlager, E., and E. Ostrom. 1993. Property rights regimes and coastal fisheries: An empirical analysis. In *The political economy of customs and culture: Informal solutions to the commons problem,* ed. Terry L. Anderson and Randy T. Simmons, 13-41. Lanham, MD: Rowman and Littlefield.

Songorwa, A., T. Buhrs, and K.F.D. Hughey. 2000. Community-based wildlife management in Africa: A critical assessment of the literature. *Natural Resources Journal* 40: 603-43.

Westley, F. 2002. The devil in the dynamics: Adaptive management on the front lines. In *Panarchy: Understanding transformations in human and natural systems,* ed. L.H. Gunderson and C.S. Holling, 333-59. Washington, DC: Island Press.

Wilson, D.C. 2003. Fisheries Co-Management and the Knowledge Base for Management Decisions. In *The fisheries co-management experience: Accomplishments, challenges, and prospects,* ed. D.C. Wilson, J.R. Nielsen, and P. Dengbol, 265-79. Dordrecht, Netherlands: Kluwer Academic Publishers.

Wilson, J.Q. 1989. *Bureaucracy: What government agencies do and why they do it.* New York: Basic Books.

Wilson, J., J. Acheson, M. Metcalfe, and P. Kleban. 1994. Chaos, complexity, and community management. *Marine Policy* 18 (4): 291-305.

Yaffee, S. 1997. Why environmental policy nightmares recur. *Conservation Biology* 11 (2): 328-37.

9

Conditions for Successful Fisheries and Coastal Resources Co-Management: Lessons Learned in Asia, Africa, and the Wider Caribbean

Robert Pomeroy

Fisheries and coastal resources offer a unique opportunity and challenge for the development of co-management due, in part, to the independent nature of the resource users, the dynamic nature of aquatic resources, and the open-access nature of aquatic resources. Co-management should be viewed not as a single strategy to solve all problems of fisheries and coastal resources management but, rather, as a process of resource management maturing, adjusting, and adapting to changing conditions over time. The co-management process is inherently adaptive, relying on systematic learning and the progressive accumulation of knowledge for improved resource management (Pomeroy and Rivera-Guieb 2006).

Over the last two decades, research and case studies undertaken at different locations around the world have documented many examples, both successful and unsuccessful, of co-management in fisheries and other coastal resources (White et al. 1994; Smith and Walters 1991; Hoefnagel and Smit 1996; Jentoft and Kristoffersen 1989; Berkes et al. 1996; DeCosse and Jayawickrama 1998; Normann et al. 1998). The results of this research point to key conditions that are central to developing and sustaining successful co-management arrangements (Pinkerton 1989, 1993, 1994). The list is long and varied, and is growing. Research and practical experience are continuing to reveal more about co-management arrangements and the factors affecting their successful implementation and performance. It should be noted that these conditions are not absolute or complete. There can be successful co-management even if all the conditions are not met. Consensus is growing, however, that the more conditions are satisfied in a particular situation, the greater the chances for successful implementation of co-management.

The purpose of this chapter is to present and discuss key conditions for the successful implementation of fisheries and coastal co-management identified in Southeast Asia, Africa, and the wider Caribbean. These three regions were selected because several recent research and development projects have produced outputs in which key conditions have been identified. The conditions are reported on a regional basis, not for a specific country, as this is how the authors have presented their results. It is expected that specific conditions would differ by country. These conditions will embrace the wide range of elements that can affect the implementation and performance of co-management. Adaptive management as a key condition in co-management will be discussed. The chapter will conclude with a discussion of policy implications for fisheries and coastal adaptive co-management.

Definitions and Concepts
The term "key conditions" is used in the sense of Ostrom (1990), as "an essential element or condition that helps to account for the success of these institutions in sustaining common property resources and gaining the compliance of generation after generation of appropriators to the rule of use." Berkes and colleagues (2001) regard key conditions as variables or attributes that emerge as being central to the chances that co-management can be developed and sustained. For the purposes of this chapter, the term "successful co-management" is defined as better overall institutional performance – in terms of efficiency (optimal rate of resource use; transaction costs), equity (equitable distribution of benefits; pattern of redistribution of benefits), and sustainability (stewardship of the resource; resilience of the management system; rule compliance) – as compared with other resource management arrangements, such as centralized management (ICLARM/IFM 1996). The term "co-management," as used in this chapter, includes various partnership arrangements and degrees of power sharing, ranging from instructive (where the community is informed about decisions that government has already made) to community control (where power is delegated to the community and they inform government of decisions) (Berkes 1994; Sen and Nielsen 1996).

It should be noted that these studies focused on co-management in general and not specifically on adaptive co-management, defined here as the linking of the iterative learning dimension of adaptive management with the shared management responsibility of co-management (Olsson et al. 2004; see Chapter 1).

Conditions for Sustainable Community-Governed Commons
The research work of Ostrom (1990, 1992, 1994) and others (e.g., Pinkerton 1989) has identified key conditions for sustainable community-governed commons, including the following:

- Clearly defined boundaries.
- Clearly defined membership. Those with rights to fish in the bounded fishing area and to participate in area management should be clearly defined.

- Group cohesion. The group permanently resides near the area to be managed; there is a high degree of homogeneity, a willingness to engage in collective action, and a common understanding of the problem and of alternative solutions.
- Existing organizations. There has been prior experience with traditional management and organizations.
- Benefits that exceed costs. Benefits to be derived from participation will exceed the cost of the investment. There is a proportional relationship between the amount of harvest allocated and rules requiring user input.
- Participation by those affected. Individuals affected by the management arrangements are included in the decision making.
- Management rules that are enforced. Rules are simple, and monitoring and enforcement can be effected and shared by, and accountable to those involved.
- Legal rights to organize and make management arrangements.
- Cooperation and leadership at the community level. There is an incentive and willingness on the part of fishers to actively participate in management.
- Decentralization and delegation of authority. Government has established formal policy and laws for decentralization and delegation for management.
- Coordination between government and community. There is a mechanism to coordinate local management arrangements, resolve conflict, and reinforce local rule enforcement.

With common property theory emerging as the basis of co-management (Berkes et al. 2001), these conditions have served as the foundation for much of the research and development project results discussed below.

Conditions Affecting Successful Co-Management
The conditions for successful co-management identified in studies from Asia (White et al. 1994; Pomeroy et al. 2001), Africa (Sverdrup-Jensen and Nielsen 1998; Hauck and Sowman 2003; Geheb and Sarch 2002; Khan et al. 2004), and the wider Caribbean (CANARI 1999; McConney et al. 2003; Pomeroy et al. 2004) will be grouped according to three categories of contextual variables identified by Pollnac (1998):

- Supra-community level – Supra-community conditions affecting the success of co-management are external to the community, including enabling legislation and supportive government administrative structures at the national level, and markets. They may also include demographic factors and technological change.

- Community level – Community-level conditions affecting the success of co-management are found within the community and include both the physical and the social environment in terms of potential relationships with fisheries and coastal resource management.
- Individual and household level – The individual is responsible for making the decision to carry out co-management. Individual and household decision making and behaviour are thus central to the success of co-management.

Adaptive management as a key condition will be discussed separately.

Supra-Community Level

Enabling Policies and Legislation

Pomeroy and colleagues (2001), presenting the results of a research project on co-management in Asia, stated that if co-management initiatives are to be successful, basic issues surrounding government action to establish supportive legislation, policies, rights, and authority structures must be addressed. Policies and legislation need to spell out jurisdiction and control; provide legitimacy to property rights and decision-making arrangements; define and clarify local responsibility and authority; clarify the rights and responsibilities of partners; support local enforcement and accountability mechanisms; and provide fisher groups or organizations the legal right to organize and make arrangements related to their needs. The legal process formalizes rights and rules and legitimizes local participation in co-management arrangements.

In South Africa, Hauck and Sowman (2003) found that government's reluctance to relinquish a large degree of power was one of the most difficult challenges facing co-management, especially if government is wary of the capacity of people to manage resources. Hauck and Sowman (2003) further state that while laws and policies exist to support co-management, there needs to be a fundamental shift in the attitude and behaviour of government. Geheb and Sarch (2002), summarizing management challenges facing Africa's inland fisheries, state that too many political agendas are being pursued, resulting in poor performance for co-management. There needs to be a fixed definition of co-management that is accepted by all stakeholders, and policies that support and direct implementation. In a review of co-management in nine African countries, Khan and colleagues (2004) state that an honest willingness on the part of governments to relinquish exclusive control of aquatic resources is needed in order to establish trust and confidence among the various partners.

In the Caribbean, Pomeroy and colleagues (2004) found that management approaches of governments for coastal resource management are not flexible and responsive to changing circumstances. They also state that limited trust between government and fishers restricts the development of co-management. Sverdrup-Jensen and Nielsen (1998), summarizing findings from eight co-management case studies in Africa, report that governments should not leave the local partners with management responsibilities that they are not capable of shouldering. They also report that a balance needs to be struck between the responsibilities given to communities and the means placed at their disposal.

External Agents

External change agents, such as non-governmental organizations, academic or research institutions, religious organizations, and others, can facilitate the co-management process (Pomeroy et al. 2001). Hauck and Sowman (2003) found that external agents provide impartiality, knowledge, training, logistical support, and financial aid, and often act as intermediaries between the resource users and government. McConney and colleagues (2003), presenting guidelines for establishing coastal resource co-management in the Caribbean, found that it is useful to have a trained facilitator guide the co-management process. Pomeroy and colleagues (2004) found that external agents provide support for co-management but must not encourage dependency upon them by the community.

Alliances and Networks

White and colleagues (1994) found that alliances and networks can help to solve larger issues. Mutually beneficial alliances and networks can be formed to counteract conflicting and often powerful interests outside the community. The alliances and networks can also be used to further policy agendas supported by many organizations from different sectors of society.

Community Level

Appropriate Scale and Defined Boundaries

Pomeroy and colleagues (2001) found that scale for co-management may vary a great deal but should be appropriate to the area's ecology, people, and level of management. This includes the size of the physical area to be managed and how many members should be included in a management organization so that it is representative but not so large as to be unworkable. The scale and boundaries of the area to be managed should be appropriate to human resources and the ecology of the area. Geheb and Sarch (2002) found that having international boundaries traversing a fishery significantly impedes its co-management. If the unit around which co-management occurs is the landing site, the community, or an access area, then the size of the fishery becomes largely irrelevant. McConney and colleagues

(2003) found that resources that are generally more easily co-managed are those that are sedentary, those whose distribution corresponds with human settlements, and those that fall under one political jurisdiction. These authors further state that boundaries and scale for co-management should match the abilities of the resource users to manage the area. Boundaries enable stakeholders to know where their responsibilities lie.

Membership Is Clearly Defined
In Asia, Pomeroy and colleagues (2001) found that the individual fishers or households with rights to fish in the bounded fishing area, to participate in management, and to be a member of an organization should be clearly defined. The numbers of fishers or households should not be so large as to restrict effective communication and decision making. In the Caribbean, Pomeroy and colleagues (2004) found that membership should be clearly defined to include only those who really have a stake in the fishery.

Participation by Those Affected
Most individuals affected by the co-management arrangements are included in the group that makes decisions about the arrangements and can change them (Pomeroy et al. 2001). In South Africa, Hauck and Sowman (2003) found that fundamental to the concept of co-management is the active participation and involvement of resource users and their commitment to the co-management process. Without the commitment and willingness of resource users to participate in the co-management process, sharing of management responsibility cannot be achieved. Khan and colleagues (2004) found that in Africa, the active participation of all resource users can bring about legitimization of laws and harmonization of traditional and modern management and enforcement systems.

In evaluating experiences with participatory planning and management in the Caribbean, the Caribbean Natural Resources Institute (CANARI 1999) found that initiatives that incorporate all relevant stakeholders from the outset are likely to be the most enduring. Pomeroy and colleagues (2004) found that participation in co-management in the Caribbean is constrained because, in many cases, fishers expect government to do things for them and they are reluctant to get involved in management. White and colleagues (1994) state that all stakeholders need to participate in the co-management process in order to ensure a politically neutral process. They also state that there needs to be ongoing feedback of information on the co-management process to sustain and increase community participation.

Leadership
Leaders set an example for others to follow, set courses of action, and provide energy and direction (Pomeroy et al. 2001). While a community may

already have leaders, they may not be the correct or appropriate leaders for co-management. Local elites may not be the most appropriate leaders, and new leaders may need to be identified and developed. Hauck and Sowman (2003) state that one or two people often become involved in the co-management process as "champions," facilitating communication and interaction among stakeholders. White and colleagues (1994) found that organizational formation is strategic in identifying and developing leaders. Sverdrup-Jensen and Nielsen (1998), in an analysis of case studies on co-management in eight African countries, found that traditional leadership systems, often having a high legitimacy with local people, should be reflected in the design of co-management arrangements. Despite the importance of local leaders for co-management, Pomeroy and colleagues (2004) found that there is a lack of effective leadership among fishers in the Caribbean to guide change and the co-management process.

Empowerment, Capacity Building, and Social Preparation
Individual and community empowerment is a central element of co-management (Pomeroy et al. 2001). Empowerment is concerned with building the capability of individuals and the community in order for them to have greater social awareness, to gain greater autonomy in decision making, to gain greater self-reliance, and to establish a balance in community power relations. Empowerment is enhanced by capacity building through education and training that raise the level of knowledge and information of those involved in the co-management process. Hauck and Sowman (2003) found that in South Africa, empowerment and capacity building are important in order for resource users to understand the concepts and principles of sustainable resource use and co-management. CANARI (1999) states that true participation can be achieved only when participants are provided with the information required to make decisions. McConney and colleagues (2003) found that in the Caribbean, the building of stakeholder capacity is essential for participants' engagement in co-management. White and colleagues (1994) caution that education and training alone are not sufficient to change major behavioural patterns that have consequences for people's livelihoods. Changes in behaviour are bounded by community values. Pomeroy and colleagues (2004) report that effective communication among stakeholders, brought about through capacity building, can improve the success of co-management. Capacity must be built so that local management institutions remain flexible in order to address changing needs and conditions as co-management matures over time.

Community Organizations
The existence of a legitimate (as recognized by the local people) community or people's organization is vital for representing resource users and

other stakeholders and for influencing the direction of policies and decision making (Pomeroy et al. 2001). These organizations must have the legal right to exist and make arrangements related to their needs. They must be autonomous from government. Geheb and Sarch (2002) found that for the inland fisheries of Africa, traditional pre-existing management organizations and institutions should be a part of any new management structure. CANARI (1999) states that in the Caribbean, participation in fisheries and coastal resource management requires the existence and support of effective local organizations. McConney and colleagues (2003) state that community organizing and the establishment of stakeholder organizations is a critical component in the process of co-management in the Caribbean. Authorities need to support community organizing instead of just steering it towards management roles. Pomeroy and colleagues (2004) found, however, that organizational capacity to engage in co-management is weak in the Caribbean. White and colleagues (1994) state that co-management is not possible in the absence of community organizations.

Long-Term Support of the Local Government Unit and Political Elites
The cooperation of the local government unit and the local political elite is important to co-management (Pomeroy et al. 2001). Local government can provide a variety of technical and financial services and assistance to the co-management process. There must be local political will to share benefits, cost, responsibility, and authority with the community members. In Africa, Geheb and Sarch (2002) found that there is a strong role for local government in co-management, including enforcement, sanctions, extra-community issues, extension, and information. McConney and colleagues (2003) found that in the Caribbean, the inclusion of the government as a partner is essential for establishing and sustaining co-management. White and colleagues (1994) state that local government can provide appropriate support for co-management, which the community members cannot, such as local ordinances to support management measures and enforcement. CANARI (1999) reports that participation in co-management requires changes in the attitude of government staff and political elites towards co-management and towards other stakeholders in the process. There needs to be an awareness that powerful stakeholders may circumvent participatory processes when it serves their interest to do so. McConney and colleagues (2003) state that co-management is likely to redistribute power and to be resisted by those who want to avoid losing or sharing power. Geheb and Sarch (2002) state that new co-management initiatives may be used by one or more stakeholders to improve or consolidate their power or position. In designing new co-management systems, it must be assumed that such struggles will affect the outcome of any intervention, and the objective becomes one of trying to ensure that any resulting social or economic disequilibria are minimized.

Property Rights over the Resource

Property rights, either individual or collective, should address the legal ownership of the resource and define mechanisms (economic, administrative, and collective) and the structures required for allocating use rights to optimize use and ensure conservation of resources; they should also address the means and procedures for enforcement (Pomeroy et al. 2001). Without legally supported property rights, resource users have no standing to enforce their claims over the resource against outsiders. Hauck and Sowman (2003) state that while co-management arrangements in South Africa have focused on increased user participation in management, a fundamental problem has been the need to clarify and secure property rights to resources. McConney and colleagues (2003) state that in the Caribbean, partners in co-management are unlikely to contribute significantly to the effort over the long term if they do not expect to be able to maintain or increase the benefits of their investment in participation. A key to success is to reduce the open-access nature of marine resources through the establishment of property rights. Pomeroy and colleagues (2004) report that in the Caribbean, legislation providing property rights over marine and coastal resources is absent.

Adequate Financial Resources/Budget

Pomeroy and colleagues (2001) report that co-management requires financial resources. Funds are needed to support various operations and facilities related to planning, implementation, coordination, monitoring, and enforcement, among other activities. Funding, especially sufficient, timely, and sustained funding, is critical to co-management. Hauck and Sowman (2003) report that in South Africa, limited funding and unrealistic time frames impose constraints on co-management. It is critical to recognize the time and resources required to develop and implement co-management arrangements. Unreliable funding can create significant obstacles to collaborative working relationships between stakeholders. Khan and colleagues (2004) report that in Africa, the provision of adequate financial and technical resources are key to any sustainable co-management. In the Caribbean, CANARI (1999) states that the implementation of participatory decisions and management actions requires not only political support but also adequate technical and financial resources.

Partnerships and Partner Sense of Ownership of the Co-Management Process

Pomeroy and colleagues (2001) report that in Asia, active participation of partners in the co-management planning and implementation process is directly related to their sense of ownership and commitment to the co-management arrangements. Partners involved in co-management need to feel that the process benefits them, and to have a strong sense of participation in, commitment to, and ownership of the process. Partnerships must grow out of a mutual sense of trust and respect among the partners.

McConney and colleagues (2003) reiterate that trust and respect among partners is necessary for successful co-management in the Caribbean context. White and colleagues (1994) also state that trust and respect between community workers, outside organizations, and community members must be established and maintained. They further state that communities respond to an intervention when they believe that it is needed, that it will be effective in meeting their needs, and that they "own" the intervention process.

Accountability

Co-management means having a process in which business is conducted in an open and transparent manner (Pomeroy et al. 2001). All partners must be held equally accountable for upholding the co-management agreement. There need to be accepted standards for monitoring and evaluating the management objective and outcomes. White and colleagues (1994) state that monitoring with community participation can provide information that helps the community understand what is happening in the co-management process and maintains the openness of the process. Hauck and Sowman (2003) state that resource users must establish a local-level institution that provides a voice for their contribution to management and that is accountable to them.

Conflict Management Mechanism

Arbitration and resolution of disputes are imperative when conflicts arise over co-management. If resource users are to follow rules, a mechanism for discussing and resolving conflict and infractions is needed (Pomeroy et al. 2001). Sverdrup-Jensen and Nielsen (1998) report that mechanisms for conflict resolution need to be given high priority in the design of co-management arrangements, and management approaches that minimize conflict should be adopted wherever feasible. Geheb and Sarch (2002) state that a co-management structure needs to be established based on forums within which negotiation and conflict management can occur.

Clear Objectives from a Well-Defined Set of Issues

The clarity and simplicity of objectives help to steer the direction of co-management (Pomeroy et al. 2001). Clear and simple objectives based on an understanding of the issues by the stakeholders are essential for successful co-management. Fundamental to co-management is a common understanding of the situation, comprehension of the root causes of the problems and the issues, and an agreement on appropriate solutions to the identified problems. Hauck and Sowman (2003) state that the objectives of co-management must be agreed upon by all parties. Co-management originates as a result of varying objectives. People who are affected by management decisions must be involved in developing the objectives and setting the parameters to be achieved. In the Caribbean, Pomeroy and colleagues (2004) found that clear objectives for co-management need to be defined by the stakeholders based on the problems and the stakeholders' interests. White and colleagues (1994) state that clear, salient objectives and issues are crucial early on, because many people need to know, early on, where the co-management process is headed. Identification of the issues and clear objectives are key to motivating individuals and organizations to engage in co-management.

Management Rules Enforced

In Asia, Pomeroy and colleagues (2001) found that the enforcement of management rules was very important for the success of co-management. Rules must be simple and enforceable. Vigorous, fair, and sustained rule enforcement requires the participation of all partners. Hauck and Sowman (2003) found that resource users should be consulted and actively involved when rules are developed, to bring about greater legitimacy. There is a need for mutual agreement on what constitutes legitimate rules as a means of fostering trust and increasing compliance. Monitoring for enforcement should be an integral part of the co-management process, should involve local resource users, and should be backed up with government support. McConney and colleagues (2003) report that weak enforcement undermines co-management by increasing the uncertainty of resource sustainability and decreasing the returns on participation. Pomeroy and colleagues (2004) found that in the Caribbean, the success of co-management is enhanced when management rules are enforceable by both resource users and the management authority.

Knowledge of Resource

McConney and colleagues (2003) report that co-management is more likely to succeed if the resource is one that stakeholders have a good knowledge of. The integration of good traditional knowledge, practices, and tenure systems must be given a high priority and made a part of the co-management process (White et al. 1994). Geheb and Sarch (2002) state that if communities of resource users are to assume or retain responsibilities for controlling access to the fisheries, then their knowledge about and perception of the resources need to be understood.

Individual and Household Level

Individual Incentive Structure

Pomeroy and colleagues (2001) state that the success of co-management hinges on an individual incentive structure (economic, social, political) that induces individuals to participate in the process. CANARI (1999) states that co-management efforts that appeal to the motivations (most often economic) of the stakeholders are most likely to secure their participation. White and colleagues (1994) state that individuals who are not dependent upon a finite resource will not respond quickly to co-management. Sverdrup-Jensen and Nielsen (1998), in a summary of findings from eight co-management case studies in Africa, report that when stakeholders' expectations are high, unmet expectations can lead to an unwillingness to participate in co-management. McConney and colleagues (2003) report that incentives may not always work in favour of co-management unless there is some level of personal gain from participation.

Benefits Exceed Costs
Hauck and Sowman (2003) state that while it is difficult to measure benefits and costs to individuals engaged in co-management because they are measured in different ways, and some factors are intangible and unmeasureable, there must be clear benefits that outweigh costs or disadvantages. McConney and colleagues (2003) state that co-managers need to be concerned about benefits or incentives for all the participating stakeholders, to ensure that motivation is sustained, especially in the early stages of co-management. Individual stakeholders have their own real costs and need real benefits for themselves, often to justify participation to a larger constituency that they represent or interact with. Hauck and Sowman (2003) further state that only when benefits become tangible can people afford to adopt a long-term view and commitment to using resources sustainably.

Adaptive Co-Management
A key feature of adaptive co-management is the combination of the iterative learning dimension of adaptive management and the linkage dimension of collaborative management, in which rights and responsibilities are jointly shared. Although with co-management much of the focus is on the local scale, where issues of management performance are felt most directly, adaptive co-management is a flexible system for environment and resource management that operates across multiple levels and with a range of local and non-local organizations (Chapter 1). Key features of adaptive co-management include a focus on learning-by-doing, integration of different knowledge systems, collaboration and power sharing among community, regional, and national levels, and management flexibility (Olsson et al. 2004).

The analysis of conditions for successful co-management in Asia, Africa, and the wider Caribbean undertaken in this chapter did not explicitly identify the iterative learning dimension of adaptive management as a condition. However, the integration of different knowledge systems (see "Knowledge of Resource" above), collaboration across different scales (see "Alliances and Networks" above), and management flexibility (see "Empowerment, Capacity Building, and Social Preparation" above) are all identified.

This is not to say that the features of adaptive co-management are not mentioned in the various studies. For example, Hauck and Sowman (2003, 335) state: "Success is more likely to be achieved if stakeholders involved in these various co-management initiatives share experiences, learn from past mistakes and are willing to modify their management strategies and rules to suit changing circumstances and management capabilities." For their part, McConney and colleagues (2003, 11) state: "One approach is to manage by trial and error, without paying much attention to accumulating knowledge about the systems. A better approach is to learn through adaptive management ... It involves institutional learning where all of the co-management stakeholders share information and record conclusions or decisions about the human and natural resource systems. By careful analysis and documentation, the co-management institution, as a whole, learns together for improvement."

Discussion

A number of studies in Asia, Africa, and the wider Caribbean, published in recent years, have identified key conditions that help to account for the success and sustainability of co-management. These conditions show both similarities and differences between regions. It should be noted that these are generalized conditions for the region and that the key conditions may vary for individual countries within the region, or even for localities within a country. They must be viewed in the distinct political, biological, cultural, technological, social, and economic context of that region and the individual countries within the region. We also need to bear in mind the role these unique characteristics play in shaping the process and implementing co-management in the region. In Asia, where the use of co-management is more mature, there is more delegated co-management (government lets formally organized users/stakeholders make decisions) (Pomeroy and Viswanathan 2003). In Africa and the Caribbean, where co-management is still a relatively new concept, there is more consultative co-management (government interacts often with users/stakeholders but makes most decisions) (Sverdrup-Jensen and Nielsen 1998; Hara and Nielsen 2003).

It is important to note that adaptive management is not explicitly mentioned as a key condition for successful co-management in any of the studies, although several individual features of adaptive co-management (integration of knowledge systems, collaboration across scales, and management flexibility) are identified as key conditions. The iterative learning dimension of adaptive co-management is discussed in several papers as an important element in the co-management process. The lack of acknowledgement of adaptive co-management in the papers may be due to a lack of formal recognition of adaptation and learning in the co-management process or the relative newness of the approach.

Several of the key conditions are more common across the regions than others, including participation by those affected by the co-management arrangements, empowerment and capacity building, community organizations, and individual incentive structure.

Some of the conditions can be met by using attributes internal to the community, while others require external support. The number and variety of conditions indicate that the planning and implementation of co-management must be conducted at several levels. These levels include the individual (individual incentive structure; benefits exceed costs); the stakeholder (participation by those affected; empowerment and capacity building; community organizations); the local government (long-term support of the local government unit and political elites); the national government (enabling policies and legislation); the external agent; the resource (appropriate scale and boundaries); and the overall co-management process (clear objectives from a well-defined set of issues; management rules enforced; adequate financial resources).

None of the conditions exists in isolation; each supports and links to another to make the complex process and arrangements for co-management work. In addition, all the stakeholders (resource users, external agents, government) have different but mutually supportive roles to play. The fulfillment of these complementary roles is crucial to the operation and sustainability of co-management.

Implementation often requires a balancing act to meet these conditions, as timing and linkages in the co-management process and arrangements are important. For example, empowerment and capacity building are needed to support community organization development. Development of trust between partners is associated with effective communication. The recognition of resource management problems is associated with the development of clear objectives from a set of well-defined issues.

There is a need to transform co-management into adaptive co-management. Many of the key conditions for adaptive co-management have already been identified in previous studies. The essential step now is for co-management practitioners and communities to explicitly recognize the importance of adaptation and learning and to integrate them into the process of co-management.

References
Berkes, F. 1994. Co-management: Bridging the two solitudes. *Northern Perspectives* 22 (2-3): 18-20.
Berkes, F., H. Fast, and M.K. Berkes. 1996. *Co-management and partnership arrangements in fisheries resource management and in Aboriginal land claims agreements*. Winnipeg: University of Manitoba.

Berkes, F., R. Mahon, P. McConney, R. Pollnac, and R. Pomeroy. 2001. *Managing small-scale fisheries: Alternative directions and methods.* Ottawa: International Development Research Centre.

CANARI (Caribbean Natural Resources Institute). 1999. *Evaluation of Caribbean experiences in participatory planning and management of marine and coastal resources.* St. Lucia: CANARI.

DeCosse, P.J., and S.S. Jayawickrama. 1998. Issues and opportunities in co-management: Lessons from Sri Lanka. In *Communities and conservation: Natural resource management in South and Central Asia,* ed. A. Kothari et al., 112-21. New Delhi: Sage Publications.

Geheb, K., and M.-T. Sarch, eds. 2002. *Africa's inland fisheries: The management challenge.* Kampala, Uganda: Fountain Publishers.

Hara, M., and J.R. Nielsen. 2003. Experiences with fisheries co-management in Africa. In *The fisheries co-management experience: Accomplishments, challenges, and prospects,* ed. D.C. Wilson, J.R. Nielson, and P. Degnbol, ch. 5. Dordrecht, Netherlands: Kluwer Academic Publishers.

Hauck, M., and M. Sowman, eds. 2003. *Waves of change: Coastal and fisheries co-management in Southern Africa.* Lansdowne, South Africa: University of Cape Town Press.

Hoefnagel, E., and W. Smit. 1996. *Co-management experiences in the Netherlands.* The Hague: Fisheries Department, Agricultural Economics Research Institute.

ICLARM (International Center for Living Aquatic Resources Management)/IFM (Institute for Fisheries Management and Coastal Community Development). 1996. *Analysis of fisheries co-management arrangements: A research framework.* Manila, Philippines: ICLARM; Hirtshals, Denmark: North Sea Center, IFM.

Jentoft, S., and T. Kristofferson. 1989. Fishermen's co-management: The case of the Loftoten fishery. *Human Organization* 48 (4): 355-65.

Khan, A.S., H. Mikkola, and R. Brummett. 2004. Feasibility of fisheries co-management in Africa. *NAGA, Worldfish Center Quarterly* 27 (1 & 2, January-June): 60-64.

McConney, P., R. Pomeroy, and R. Mahon. 2003. *Guidelines for coastal resource co-management in the Caribbean: Communicating the concepts and conditions that favor success.* Barbados: Caribbean Conservation Association.

Normann, A.K., J.R. Nielsen, and S. Sverdrup-Nielsen, eds. 1998. *Fisheries co-management in Africa: Proceedings from a regional workshop on fisheries co-management research.* Fisheries Co-management Research Project, research report no. 12. Hirtshals, Denmark: Institute for Fisheries Management and Coastal Community Development.

Olsson, P., C. Folke, and F. Berkes. 2004. Adaptive co-management for building resilience in socio-ecological systems. *Environmental Management* 34 (1): 75-90.

Ostrom, E. 1990. *Governing the commons: The evolution of institutions for collective action.* Cambridge: Cambridge University Press.

–. 1992. *Crafting institutions for self-governing irrigation systems.* San Francisco: Institute for Contemporary Studies Press.

–. 1994. Institutional analysis, design principles and threats to sustainable community governance and management of commons. In *Community management and common property of coastal fisheries in Asia and the Pacific: Concepts, methods and experiences.* ICLARM Conference Proceedings 45, ed. R.S. Pomeroy, 34-50. Manila, Philippines: International Center for Living Aquatic Resources Management.

Pinkerton, E., ed. 1989. *Co-operative management of local fisheries: New directions for improved management and community development.* Vancouver: UBC Press.

–. 1993. *Local fisheries co-management: A review of international experiences and their implications for salmon management in British Columbia.* Vancouver: School of Community and Regional Planning, University of British Columbia.

–. 1994. Summary and conclusions. In *Folk management in the world's fisheries,* ed. C.L. Dyer and J.R. McGoodwin, 317-37. Boulder: University of Colorado Press.

Pollnac, R.B., 1998. *Rapid assessment of management parameters for coral reefs.* Coastal Management Report no. 2205 and ICLARM Contribution no. 1445. Narragansett: Coastal Resources Center, University of Rhode Island.

Pomeroy, R.S., and R. Rivera-Guieb. 2006. *Fishery co-management: A practical handbook.* Wallingford, UK: CABI Publishing; Ottawa: International Development Research Centre.

Pomeroy, R., and K. Viswanathan. 2003. Experiences with fisheries co-management in Southeast Asia and Bangladesh. In *The fisheries co-management experience: Accomplishments, challenges, and prospects,* ed. D.C. Wilson, J.R. Nielson, and P. Degnbol, ch. 6. Dordrecht, Netherlands: Kluwer Academic Publishers.

Pomeroy, R., B. Katon, and I. Harkes. 2001. Conditions affecting the success of fisheries co-management: Lessons from Asia. *Marine Policy* 25: 197-208.

Pomeroy, R., P. McConney, and R. Mahon. 2004. Comparative analysis of coastal resource co-management in the Caribbean. *Ocean and Coastal Management.* 47: 429-47.

Sen, S., and J.R. Nielsen. 1996. Fisheries co-management: A comparative analysis. *Marine Policy* 20 (5): 405-18.

Smith, A.H., and R. Walters. 1991. Co-management of the white sea urchin resources of St. Lucia. Paper presented at the International Development Research Centre workshop on Common Property Resources, Winnipeg. *CANARI Communication.* 38: 1-12.

Sverdrup-Jensen, S. and J.R. Nielsen. 1998. Co-management in small-scale fisheries: A synthesis of Southern and West African experiences. Hirtshals, Denmark: North Sea Center, Institute for Fisheries Management and Coastal Community Development.

White, A.T., L.Z. Hale, Y. Renard, and L. Cortesi. 1994. *Collaborative and community-based management of coral reefs.* West Hartford, CT: Kumarian Press.

Part 3: Challenges

10
Communities of Interdependence for Adaptive Co-Management
John Kearney and Fikret Berkes

An increasingly important question for natural resource management is whether the notion of community is relevant in heterogeneous, complex societies that are usually composed of competing interest groups, significant degrees of social differentiation, and cultural pluralism. At the same time, societies and ecosystems are connected to global processes perhaps more than ever before, making them vulnerable to pressures and incentives that may originate at other levels of social and political organization. Thus, one might question the usefulness of the notion of community in a consideration of adaptive co-management.

Agrawal and Gibson (1999, 640) critique the existence of the "mythic" community of "small, integrated groups using locally evolved norms to manage resources sustainably and equitably" that is often presented as the rationale for community-based management. The mythic community does not account for the differences in social status, resource access, and political power that usually exist in communities. But the popularity of the mythic community among many development practitioners is understandable as a reaction to the dominance of what Polanyi (2001 [1944]) termed "utopian" economics: "Our thesis is that the idea of a self-adjusting market implied a stark utopia. Such an institution could not exist for any length of time without annihilating the human and natural substance of society." Today's globalized, liberal economy is based on such a utopian view of individuals finding their freedom through the contractual relationships they form in the marketplace: relationships that are arm's-length, strategic, and calculating. This market, however, cannot take into account the full complexity of human relations or the full process of social development (Kerans and Kearney 2006). While the market economy has brought increased prosperity to a global minority, Polanyi's thesis is realized in the rapidly deteriorating condition of the earth's environment, widespread poverty, and sharp inequalities in wealth.

Thus, the mythic community and the utopian economy share a reductionist view of society and a one-size-fits-all methodology with respect to resource management. One is based on the homogeneous group's acting in unison, the other on the autonomous individual's achieving satisfaction through the market. A corrective to these reductionist views, one based on group dependence, the other on individual independence, is the notion of interdependence. As described by the philosopher Charles Taylor (1989), we become autonomous persons only within a field of meaning that is provided in the community around us. This community gives us our sense of direction and a set of values around which we form our identity. Modern culture, contrary to the hierarchical structure of ancient civilizations, and before it was hijacked by utopian economics, was based on the principles of equality, mutual respect, and mutual service among individuals in society (Taylor 2002). In this interdependent culture, we further ourselves by helping others. This vision can serve as a corrective to both the mythic community and utopian economics: a vision of autonomous free persons, living in communities of belonging and caring, sharing and solidarity, reflection and service.

While there is a wealth of scientific literature describing the importance of interdependence in human and social development (for a summary, see Kerans and Kearney 2006), it has not been systematically applied to our understanding of natural resource management. This notion of interdependence in community is very different from the mythic community and most other notions of community in community-based management. The community of interdependence celebrates diversity as enriching and recognizes the existence of excessive power differentials as a potential threat to community. Like the mythic community, the community of interdependence in resource management will usually be geographically based. It is not synonymous, however, with the geographical delimiters known as a village or town. People may refer to a village as a "community," but that does not mean that it is a community of interdependence. The most likely scenario is that the village contains within its borders some combination of a mythic community, a utopian economy, and communities of interdependence. In these circumstances, the critical questions for resource management then become: (1) Why is a community of interdependence important for resource co-management? and (2) How does one build a community of interdependence?

This chapter will elaborate on the importance of an interdependent community as a corrective to reductionist approaches by examining its relationship to the building of resilience in adaptive co-management systems. Resilience is the capacity of a system to adapt to or tolerate changes or disturbances without collapsing into a qualitatively different state (Gunderson and Holling 2002). It is proposed that this adaptive capacity stems from the existence or creation of institutions that:

- embody the meanings and purpose of the community
- are capable of responding to the complexity of ecological and social circumstances of the community
- take into account a wide variety of external drivers
- create cross-scale linkages across geographical space and levels of organization
- establish spaces for learning and knowledge generation.

To build such resilience and communities of interdependence, there is a need to re-examine the relationship between the notions of exclusion and inclusion in common property theory. It will be useful to begin with a specific case study that helps illustrate the five points above.

Case Study: The Bay of Fundy Fisheries

From time immemorial, the Mi'kmaq, Maliseet, and Passamaquoddy First Nations fished along the shores of the Bay of Fundy, a marine body of water located between the boundaries of what are today known as the state of Maine in the United States and the provinces of New Brunswick and Nova Scotia in Canada.

Europeans first settled the Bay of Fundy region beginning in 1604. These settlers, the French "Acadians," were primarily agriculturalists. In 1755, the Acadians were deported by the British, and those who were able to return had to forsake their former agricultural lands and begin life anew as fishers along the coast of the Bay of Fundy. They were joined in great numbers by British Loyalists fleeing the American Revolution in the late eighteenth century. This larger-scale settlement coincided with the Golden Age of Sail. The Bay of Fundy region prospered, as it never has since, as one of the main points on the triangular trade route between Europe, North America, and the Caribbean. Fishing was primarily an offshore bank fishery, and the area was renowned for the skill of its sea captains and crew.

The small-boat, inshore fishery was largely oriented towards providing bait, such as herring, for the large, offshore fishing vessels as well as supporting some subsistence and commercial activities (Kearney 1993).

The inshore was radically transformed in the late nineteenth century with the collapse of the offshore cod fishery. Unemployed fishers from the sailing ships turned to fishing shellfish, groundfish, and pelagics in small boats close to shore. This multi-species fishery became the "traditional" inshore fishery of the Maritime economy, supporting scores of small fishing villages. Social relations were characterized by an egalitarian ethic, kin- and acquaintance-based labour processes, and equitable sharing of revenues among fishing partners. Youth (primarily male) entered the fishery through an informal apprenticeship system. Access and fishing effort were regulated by a combination of informal customary mechanisms and by government regulation. In the lobster fishery, in particular, fishers and the federal government established as early as the 1880s the basic framework for lobster management that exists up to the present (Kearney 1993).

The Bay of Fundy and adjoining areas in southwest Nova Scotia were unique relative to other coastal areas of Atlantic Canada. In most areas, the merchant class of the offshore cod fishery evolved into the merchant class buying the fish and extending credit to the inshore fishers. In these same areas, as the fishery industrialized after the Second World War, the merchants became, were replaced by, or co-existed with the owners of the large fish-processing companies. In southwest Nova Scotia and the Bay of Fundy, the fish buying and processing sector was characterized by a very large number of small, village-based enterprises. Large-scale processors were the exception. This contributed to considerable competition for the supply of fish coming from fishers and, perhaps, even competitive port market prices. In any case, it appears that Bay of Fundy fishers exercised considerably more economic control over their fishing enterprises than their counterparts in other regions (Clement 1986; Apostle and Barrett 1992; Kearney 1993).

During the years 1950-80, the fishing communities of the Bay of Fundy underwent rapid modernization and industrialization, resulting in growing prosperity and social differentiation, greatly increased participation of women in the labour force, enhanced ethnic pride and identity, over-exploitation of fish stocks, dramatic resource declines, and habitat degradation (Kearney 1993). By 1980, there was an ever-building pressure to introduce utopian economics and reshape the traditional inshore fishery along corporate industrial lines through new fishing technologies, market-based access rights, and deregulation by government.

The first fishery to conform to this model of development was the herring fishery. Initially, it appeared that government was moving in the opposite direction, for in 1976 the Minister of Fisheries and Oceans initiated the first co-managed, non-Aboriginal commercial fishery in Canada (Kearney 1984). The minister supported the fishing captains in maintaining the independent (non-processor) ownership of the herring purse seine fleet by offering subsidies, market incentives, and their own individual fish quota. The resulting higher prices also sparked a boom in herring fishing for the smaller boats using gillnets. Within four years, however, the oligopsonistic herring processors gained control of a portion of purse seine fleet ownership by offering advantageous contractual arrangements to selected skippers. By 1981, a new minister made the individual quotas transferable. The herring purse seine fishery thus became the first fishery in Canada with market-regulated access through individual transferable quotas (ITQs). The result was a virtual takeover of the purse seine fleet by the processing sector, which could offer high prices for the purchase of quotas, and a withering away of the small-boat herring gillnet fleet.

The privatization of resource access by means of market-driven ITQs continued with offshore groundfish in 1983, offshore scallops in 1986, inshore groundfish draggers (otter trawlers) in 1991, and inshore scallops in 1996. Each time, ownership of the fleet by processing companies (through quota purchase) was consolidated to a considerable degree.

In 1996, fearing an imposition of ITQs on their fleet, inshore fixed-gear (hook-and-line and gillnet) groundfish fishers sought to gain greater collective control over fishing allocations and rules through community-based management. After forcing the federal government to concede to their demands for an alternative to resource privatization by staging demonstrations and occupations of government offices, they established ten community boards for the management of the fixed-gear groundfishery (Kearney 2005). Since the federal government did not provide legislative support for these boards, which were organized according to geographical clusters of fishing communities in Nova Scotia and New Brunswick, the management boards enforced compliance with their rules by initiating their own legal framework through contract law. The fishers thus created their own management space by offering fish harvesters the opportunity to fish under conventional government management or under a community regime that met government requirements for conservation but set its own allocation and fishing rules to better satisfy local ecological conditions and community and household interests. Within two years, 98 percent of all active fixed-gear fishers were fishing under a community management plan. By 1996 and subsequently, however, the groundfish resource had declined so precipitously that revenues from this fishery accounted for a relatively small percentage of the annual income for most inshore fishers.

In contrast, lobsters rose in abundance while the other traditional components of the inshore fishery – groundfish, scallops, and herring – declined. By the end of the twentieth century, lobster accounted for 80-100 percent of annual enterprise incomes in what remained of a multi-species fishing strategy. Scientists are not certain why lobster populations have increased. Favourable environmental conditions and the absence of groundfish predators are the most likely reasons. Nonetheless, the contribution of the management efforts of the lobster fishers cannot be dismissed. They have been constantly vigilant and, at times, militant in their promotion and protection of the lobster fishery. They have supported a wide array of biological and effort control measures over the lobster fishery (closed seasons and areas, return of juvenile and egg-bearing females to the sea, and gear and vessel limits). They continue to convince the government to keep the inshore lobster fishery free from quotas, to disallow any fishing technology other than the lobster trap or the use of any vessel over 13.7 metres in length, to limit the growth of an offshore lobster fishery, and to maintain lobster management decision making at the local level. For example, there are four lobster management areas in the Bay of Fundy alone. This situation stands in stark contrast to almost every other fishery on the Canadian Atlantic coast.

Lobster fishers have also been staunch supporters of the federal government's owner-operator policy requiring licence holders in the inshore sector to operate their fishing vessels. This policy has been undermined in recent years by fish processors, buyers, and more affluent agents, who have found the means to obtain economic control over these licences through trust agreements with retiring fishers and their daughters and sons. According to federal Department of Fisheries and Oceans' (DFO) licensing documents, these fishers own and operate the boats but, in reality, they have no economic or political decision-making authority over the management of those fishing enterprises. Instead, decisions are made by the processors and buyers, or the lawyers representing them, who have purchased from the fisher a contractual legal control over the fishing enterprise. This problem has come about and been exacerbated by the escalating costs of the investment required in establishing a lobster-fishing enterprise.

In 1967, the lobster fishery became the first limited-entry fishery in Canada, that is, a fishery where an incoming fisher must replace an existing one by buying the licence of the retiring fisher. At that time, the average initial investment for a lobster fisher was $2,480 (Canadian), about the same as it was during the 1940s (DeWolf 1974). By 1990, the required initial investment was around $500,000, and in 2005, over $1 million. More than half of this cost goes towards the purchase of a licence. This escalation in licence costs is likely due to a number of reasons, including current lobster abundance and various government-sponsored licence buyout programs that increased licence prices in general, coupled with the fact that limited-entry licences are, like ITQs, a market-driven form of resource access.

Such investments are beyond the means of the incoming generation of fishers, and thus they or their parents are forced to strike a deal with a buyer or processor. They remain fishers but at the cost of the household's losing economic control of the enterprise. Reports on the ground indicate that close to 30 percent of the lobster licences in the Bay of Fundy and southwest Nova Scotia are now under the control of buyers or processors. At the time that limited-entry licensing was introduced in 1967, that figure stood at 1 percent (DeWolf 1974). The lobster fishers are now engaged in a new militancy to convince the federal government to find a means both to effectively enforce the owner-operator policy and to undo existing agreements, all in the hope of maintaining the control of fishing households over fishing enterprises in the last bastion of the inshore fishery.

Fundy Fishing Communities and Commons Theory

In returning to a discussion of a community of interdependence, it is necessary to examine its relationship to commons theory. Commons theory has undergone a major transformation since the 1960s, from the "tragedy of the commons," with its prognosis of gloom and doom, to the idea that resource users are capable of self-organization and self-regulation. A great deal of research in the last three decades has focused on commons institutions and defining the conditions that lead to the solution of the tragedy of the commons. It is important to point out that the fishery was seen as a prime example of the tragedy of the commons at a very early date (Gordon 1954).

The new commons theory was developed mainly through the study of communities and community-based resource management cases. Small-scale common property systems were often chosen because these relatively simple systems could be used as "laboratories" to build theory. For example, Ostrom (1990, 29) comments that her strategy was to study small-scale common property situations "because the processes of self-organization and self-governance are easier to observe in this type of situation than in many others."

The work since the 1980s has led to increasingly more precise definitions of the issues and their solutions. Common property (common-pool) resources share two characteristics: (1) exclusion or the control of access of potential users is difficult, and (2) each user is capable of subtracting from the welfare of all other users (Feeny et al. 1990). These two universal characteristics of the commons are referred to as the exclusion problem and the subtractability problem, respectively. Thus, Ostrom and colleagues (1999) define common-pool resources as "those in which (i) exclusion of beneficiaries through physical and institutional means is especially costly, and (ii) exploitation by one user reduces resource availability for others."

"Exclusion" refers to the ability to exclude people other than the members of a defined group. In the Bay of Fundy case study, exclusion mechanisms prior to 1967 were embedded in a broad spectrum of formal and informal social institutions such as territorial use rights, social norms, kinship, apprenticeship, and government regulation. After 1967, utopian economics exerted its influence as exclusion was achieved primarily through a market mechanism. In some fisheries, such as herring, scallops, and groundfish dragging, exclusion was achieved through the use of ITQs. In other cases, such as lobster and fixed-gear groundfish, exclusion was exercised through another market mechanism: limited-entry licensing.

"Subtractability" refers to the ability of social groups to design a variety of mechanisms to regulate resource use among members. The ITQ regime is governed by one main rule: do not exceed your individual quota. But is it that simple? One of the major reasons for the collapse of groundfish stocks on the Atlantic coast was the massive discarding of lesser-quality fish (including immatures) at sea, since only the fish landed at the wharf were counted against the quota (Angel et al. 1994). In addition, the science on which the quota figure is based can proceed from the wrong assumptions, as was the case for Atlantic groundfish stocks (Finlayson 1994). Reductionist thinking and socially disembedded management contributed to the very tragedy it was designed to deal with. (See also Chapter 5.)

In the case of the inshore lobster fishery, subtractability was based on a century or more of locally determined management measures designed in a diversity of ways to conserve lobster stocks, maintain economic control of fishing by households, and ensure some level of equitable distribution of the catch among those households. The fixed-gear groundfish fishers, by establishing the community management boards, attempted to re-embed quota management within the social and ecological context of their local region. By that time, however, groundfish were already in decline, and the boards were too late to capture much economic benefit for the fixed-gear sector. In the case of lobster, management has proven to be ecologically sustainable over the long term, but the fishers did not foresee that limited-entry licensing would result in their own children and the youth of the community being excluded from becoming independent owner-operators like themselves. The economic benefits of sustainable lobster management are increasingly captured by a much smaller group within their community: the fish buyers and processors.

If we examine exclusion and subtractability through the lens of the community of interdependence, it becomes apparent that we must look not only at the mechanisms of exclusion but also at the processes of inclusion. The ideals of personal freedom through mutual service would require an attempt to tailor the design of fisheries access and management to meet the needs of as many community members as possible within a framework of sustainable and economically viable resource use.

Utopian economic critics would be quick to point out that pre-1967 fisheries, open to all, had become "the employer of last resort" where no one could make an adequate livelihood. This critique has been soundly refuted by Béné (2003), who demonstrated that throughout the world, poverty in fishing communities is usually the result of exploitation of the weaker members of the community by the more powerful. This kind of exploitation, along with political manipulation, was equally true for Atlantic Canada throughout the nineteenth and twentieth centuries (Kearney 2004). Moreover, utopian economics has resulted in the extreme impoverishment of fisheries resources. A recent study shows, for example, that cod biomass on the ocean shelf off the coast of Nova Scotia has fallen from 1.26 million metric tonnes in 1852 to less than 50,000 metric tonnes today, with only 3,000 tonnes being adult fish (Rosenberg et al. 2005).

The argument being advanced here is not meant to advocate a return to pre-1967 conditions. Rather, it is a questioning of the utopian economic model that has taken the fishery to its current state. The lobster fishery is an example of where the community of interdependence has survived and evolved to a considerable extent. However, it has still not incorporated all the elements necessary to continue that survival and further develop a community of interdependence. A number of enabling conditions are important to the success of commons institutions, and it is necessary to consider this complexity.

Communities as Complex Systems Embedded in Larger Systems
Unlike the mythic community, communities are not simple or homogeneous entities but show some of the characteristics of complex systems: they may be multi-level in structure and include competing groups and different interests by social and ethnic group, as well as differentiation by gender and age. Hence, community heterogeneity is the norm rather than the exception. The notion of community is often used without an adequate critique of its geographical, political, and normative dimensions.

These complex communities are embedded in larger complex systems and global processes. What were once remote communities are being integrated into increasingly privatized, individualized, and commoditized socio-economic systems. These are not new or even necessarily recent trends, but one can argue that the speed of change has been accelerating (Folke et al. 2002). The upshot is that these changes have been influencing property rights dynamics at the local level, the role of traditional governance, and social values. The general shift from subsistence and livelihood use of local resources towards the pursuit of economic accumulation and international markets has been creating rifts within communities and conflicts with the outside world. The interests of communities have been colliding with the interests of a larger system of resource users. As the spatial scale of resource use increases, heterogeneity of users also increases, and commons governance becomes multi-scale and multi-jurisdictional.

Under these circumstances, it is not surprising to hear the practitioners of community-based management in the Bay of Fundy speak words of discouragement when they see community disintegrating around them due to the pervasiveness of economic and market-based approaches. To achieve the goals of personal freedom and human development, it will be necessary to create new institutions that, as Polanyi (2001 [1944], 262) wrote, "are embodiments of human meaning and purpose." Communities of interdependence need to develop social institutions that can deal with complexity, embody the meaning sought by community members, and help to achieve their goals.

Bay of Fundy fixed-gear fishers established community management boards because they saw the history of co-management and ITQs in their region and realized that they would not last long in the fishery if these were implemented in their case. It was, in the first instance, an act of survival. In developing an alternative, however, the fishers eschewed reductionist thinking and, with time, began taking steps to re-embed a spectrum of social considerations in their decision making. The extent to which this was done was uneven from one community board to the next, but throughout, there were remarkably similar attempts to build participatory, democratic, transparent, and accountable mechanisms into decision making. For example, most boards established a sanctioning process that was based on quantitatively verifiable offences, offered ample opportunity for violators to speak to their case, and assured anonymity to both offenders and judges until a final decision was reached, including the completion of an appeal process. Another example of re-embedding the fishery in social institutions was the increasingly visible and important role played by women in the operations of the community boards and in fisheries management in general (see, for example, Guysborough County Women's Fishery Enhancement Association 2001).

External Drivers

As defined by the Millennium Ecosystem Assessment (2003), a driver is "any natural or human-induced factor that directly or indirectly causes a change." Bay of Fundy communities have had to respond to various environmental drivers over the years, including habitat degradation, pollution, biotic impoverishment, altered biotic composition, climate change, and perhaps reduced ecological resilience (Wells et al. 2004; Ollerhead et al. 1999). There have also been sweeping changes due to numerous social and cultural drivers resulting from rapid industrialization and the increasing influence of government, many of which have already been discussed. Social scientists have been particularly struck by the impact of the introduction of groundfish dragging (trawling), initially with the support of both federal and provincial governments (Davis 1991; Kearney 1993). A confidential social psychiatric study of the region during the 1940s to 1960s (reported in Kearney 1993) documented the social stress created by the introduction of the groundfish dragger and predicted that it would be one of the most important drivers of social change in the decades ahead. The full realization of this prediction was not evident until the 1990s, when the then greatly expanded dragger fleet was rationalized through ITQs, which, combined with resource declines, resulted in the loss of many fishing jobs and the closure of fish-processing plants as fishers sold their quotas to other, often distant, communities. At the same time, many fixed-gear groundfish fishers laid the blame for their reduced catches on what they saw as the highly exploitative and wasteful practices of the dragger fleet.

Another significant external driver was the Marshall decision of the Supreme Court of Canada in 1999, recognizing the right of the Mi'kmaq people to a commercial fishery. Over the decades, the Mi'kmaq of the Bay of Fundy area had been excluded from mainstream fisheries development, and the court decision required major adjustments on the part of the non-Aboriginal fishers to accept the Mi'kmaq back into the fishery.

Identifying the impacts of external drivers on a community is not easy because of the confounding effects of multiple drivers of social and cultural change, such as "imported" or non-local values, the formal educational system, TV and mass media, as well as environmental drivers, economic drivers such as market forces, and government policy. External drivers not only insert a high degree of additional complexity into communities but demonstrate as well that this complexity is not static.

Cross-Scale Governance

Commons research has often sought the simplicity of community-based systems to develop theory. In reality, however, resources tend to be used by competing communities and user groups, and the scope of inquiry needs to be broadened by dealing with cross-scale linkages between communities, interest groups, and other levels of governance. It is difficult to find a resource management system that does not have some linkages and drivers at different scales (Berkes 2002).

Using the terminology of Young (2002), "institutional interplay" draws attention to the linkages among institutions, both at the same level of social and political organization and across levels. It includes the linkage of institutions *horizontally* (across geographical space) and *vertically* (across levels of organization).

In the Bay of Fundy fisheries, we see two types of vertical linkages (Figure 10.1). The first and most common one is the participation of fisher organizations in government-initiated consultative bodies for particular fisheries. Each of the fisheries described in this chapter has a corresponding body that advises government on fisheries conservation and management. The fishers have no decision-making powers, however, and their function is strictly advisory. Despite the use of the term "co-management" to characterize these consultations, there is little indication of the sharing of any meaningful authority with inshore fisher organizations, with the possible exception of the inshore lobster fishery. Over the decades, the federal government has closely followed the advice of the fishers in the various lobster management areas of the Bay of Fundy and southwest Nova Scotia, albeit sometimes after considerable militancy on the part of the fishing organizations. In recent years, however, lobster fishers have sensed a diminution in the influence of their advice to government, and, in the spring of 2005, they formed a lobster management board separate from the government. The function and direction of this board are only beginning to emerge at the time of this writing.

Figure 10.1

Formal cross-scale linkages in the Bay of Fundy fixed-gear groundfishery. The diagram does not include informal horizontal and vertical linkages with First Nations, environmental organizations, and community groups.

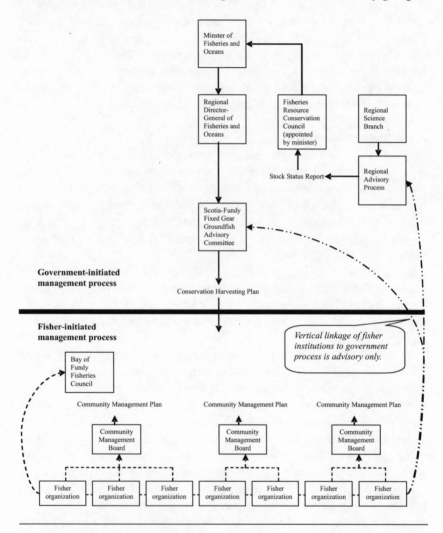

The second kind of vertical linkage in the Bay of Fundy is exemplified by fisher-initiated management processes. Local fisher organizations that had traditionally cooperated across geographical areas (horizontal linkages) formed community management boards to develop and enforce fixed-gear groundfish management plans for their combined areas (vertical linkage). The fishing organizations comprising the three community management boards with fishing activities in the Bay of Fundy then formed the Bay of Fundy Fisheries Council to make management decisions on a bay-wide basis for all inshore fisheries (additional vertical linkage). The council helped to mitigate the impact of fishing gear on marine mammals and was effective in stopping a proposed experimental krill fishery (as krill are important at the base of marine food webs).

On the whole, however, fishers feel frustrated in their own management efforts due to their lack of strong vertical linkages with government. Their community management plans must conform to the annual "conservation harvesting plan" developed by government through a top-down process in which the fishers play only an advisory role. They have compensated for this weak linkage with government by forming strong vertical and horizontal linkages among themselves and with First Nations, community groups, and fishers in New England and the west coast of Canada and the United States, and in developing countries. For example, in 2003 non-Aboriginal fishers and Mi'kmaq fishers participated together in a bus tour through the Bay of Fundy region and New England, conducting workshops and press conferences on community-based management (Milsom 2003). Through these horizontal linkages, fishers hope to gain the knowledge, political base, and experience to increase their capacity to strengthen vertical linkages in the future.

As can be seen from these examples, cross-scale governance deals with management at multiple levels. It has also played a strong role in shifting the focus of fishers from exclusionary processes to inclusive ones. Out of the crisis created by the Marshall decision, the non-Aboriginal fishers, who were on the brink of embracing a violent solution, began a dialogue with Mi'kmaq leaders. Through this dialogue, they began to see their mutual concerns and interdependencies: how they both depended on the health of marine ecosystems, their shared values around the importance of community and household control over resource use, and their frustrations with federal government paternalism. It became obvious that they would have a greater chance of achieving their purposes through mutual respect and mutual service. In the end, the Mi'kmaq were peacefully accepted into the lobster fishery. In one case, non-Aboriginal lobster fishers pressured the government to stop dragging its heels in allowing one First Nation access to the lobster fishery, and provided the Mi'kmaq with some of the fishing gear required to begin their fledgling fishery (see also Stiegman 2003).

Building Adaptive Capacity to Deal with Change

The many impacts and rapid changes affecting local communities raise an important question about adaptations: is it possible to investigate the various ways in which one can help build adaptive capacity at the local level to increase resilience in the face of change? The concept of resilience is a promising tool for dealing with change because it provides a way of analyzing the dynamics of how systems persist, transform themselves, or collapse. Resilience is the capacity of a system to tolerate impacts of drivers without irreversible change in its output and structure, or to tolerate disturbance without flipping into a qualitatively different state, a different equilibrium (Gunderson and Holling 2002). The failure of groundfish stocks to rebuild to historical levels in the Bay of Fundy despite conservation efforts may indicate this kind of flip or a lack of capacity on the part of humans to take the appropriate actions, or both.

The notion of anticipating future change and building adaptive capacity to deal with it has been discussed by Folke and colleagues (2002), who argue that such planning could be done in part through the creation of flexible multi-level governance systems that can learn from experience and generate knowledge to cope with change. As applied to the Bay of Fundy, building adaptive capacity may mean strengthening local institutions, fostering international institutions, and building cross-scale linkages from the local level to the international.

To expand on the foregoing, such measures may build resilience in three ways (Berkes and Folke 1998; Gunderson and Holling 2002). First, improving the ability to deal with shocks and stresses depends on developing coping and adaptive strategies, retaining "memory" to be able to reorganize after a perturbation, and making use of opportunities created by processes of change. In the Bay of Fundy, the multi-species fishing strategy and occupational pluralism were important adaptive strategies for dealing with fluctuations in resource and economic conditions. The former has been severely weakened by privatization of resource access because of quotas, and the latter, by the participation requirements of various licensing and professionalization programs. However, fishers have begun to retain memory through various participatory research programs that document past and current knowledge and practice (see, for example, Graham et al. 2002).

Second, improving capability for self-organization requires capacity building and institution building at various levels. It requires healthy community institutions for collective action. Here, the policy challenge is to strengthen community institutions (which may involve reversing current trends) while at the same time building new institutions at other levels and creating cross-scale linkages among them. Shortly after its first year of operation, one of the fixed-gear groundfish management boards, the Fundy Fixed Gear Council, along with a local community development agency, initiated the formation of the Bay of Fundy Marine Resource Centre. The centre is a community-governed capacity-building organization that serves not only fishers but all marine industries and organizations interested in community-based approaches to development. Its success has sparked the formation of three other centres in the Bay of Fundy region.

Third, improving the capacity for learning and adapting requires the creation of political space for community-based management so that people can learn from their own successes and failures. Rather than following the prescriptions of conventional top-down management, local managers and co-managers need to be encouraged to generate a diversity of experiments. The Bay of Fundy Fisheries Council conducted an experiment by holding an extended series of consultations with fishers in which they rewrote the rules of fisheries management from scratch. From this, the fishers devised a set of principles to guide their actions in relation to current management practices (Bay of Fundy Fisheries Council 2000).

The recent formation of an inshore lobster management board is an exciting development, and the board should be provided the political space for experimentation. The groundfish community management boards have now reached a level of maturity such that inviting community residents other than licence holders to participate in decision making could enhance their experiments in inclusiveness. All of these initiatives by inshore fishers are in a fragile state and tax the time and financial resources of their organizations and members. Their ongoing success may well depend on the inclusion of many other groups, as well as government policy support.

Nurturing and building social institutions for communities of interdependence require the creation of flexible multi-level governance systems that can learn from experience (adaptive management) and generate knowledge to cope with change by combining different kinds of knowledge, both local and scientific. Resilience thinking is in many ways a corrective to reductionist thinking, and is consistent with celebrating the diversity that will strengthen communities of interdependence and create the conditions for social health in a globalized world.

Conclusion

Through an examination of the Bay of Fundy fisheries, we have shown that resource management, to the extent that it strives towards full human and social development, should avoid reductionist thinking that overemphasizes market-based approaches. Resource management can benefit from building communities of interdependence that foster inclusive as well as exclusive processes. Such communities are more suited to dealing with social and ecological complexity at multiple levels, and carry much promise for building resilience for the fishery as an integrated system of people and the marine ecosystem. Building resilience requires the establishment of institutions that address the five areas discussed in this chapter: institutions that embody the meanings and purpose of the community, are capable of responding to the complexity of ecological and social circumstances of the community, take into account a wide variety of external drivers, create cross-scale linkages across geographical space and levels of organization, and establish spaces for learning and knowledge generation. Thus, communities of interdependence not only are relevant to adaptive co-management but may in fact be essential in maintaining healthy and resilient social and ecological systems.

References

Agrawal, A., and C.C. Gibson. 1999. Enchantment and disenchantment: The role of community in natural resource conservation. *World Development* 27 (4): 629-49.

Angel, J.R., D.L. Burke, R.N. O'Boyle, F.G. Peacock, M. Sinclair, and K.C.T. Zwanenburg. 1994. *Report of the workshop on Scotia-Fundy groundfish management from 1977 to 1993.* Canadian Technical Report of Fisheries and Aquatic Sciences, no. 1979. Dartmouth, NS: Department of Fisheries and Oceans.

Apostle, R., and G. Barrett. 1992. *"Emptying their nets": Small capital and rural industrialization in the fishing industry of Nova Scotia.* Toronto: University of Toronto Press.

Bay of Fundy Fisheries Council. 2000. *Writing the rules of ecological fisheries management in the Bay of Fundy.* Frederickton: Bay of Fundy Marine Resource Centre and Conservation Council of New Brunswick.

Béné, C. 2003. When fishery rhymes with poverty: A first step beyond the old paradigm on poverty in small-scale fisheries. *World Development* 31 (6): 949-75.

Berkes, F. 2002. Cross-scale institutional linkages for commons management: Perspectives from the bottom-up. In *The drama of the commons,* ed. E. Ostrom, T. Dietz, N. Dolsak, P.C. Stern, S. Stonich, and E.U. Weber. Washington, DC: National Academy Press.

Berkes, F., and C. Folke, eds. 1998. *Linking social and ecological systems: Management practices and social mechanisms for building resilience.* Cambridge: Cambridge University Press.

Clement, W. 1986. *The struggle to organize: Resistance in Canada's fishery.* Toronto: McClelland and Stewart.

Davis, A. 1991. *Dire straits: The dilemmas of a fishery, the case of Digby Neck and the Islands.* St. John's, NL: ISER Books.

DeWolf, A.G. 1974. The lobster fishery of the Maritime provinces: Economic effects of regulations. *Bulletin of the Fisheries Research Board of Canada* 187: 1-59.

Feeny, D., F. Berkes, B.J. McCay, and J.M. Acheson. 1990. The tragedy of the commons: Twenty-two years later. *Human Ecology* 18: 1-19.

Finlayson, C. 1994. *Fishing for truth: A sociological analysis of the northern cod stock assessments from 1977-1990.* St. John's, NL: ISER Books.

Folke, C., S. Carpenter, T. Elmqvist, L. Gunderson, C.S. Holling, B. Walker, J. Bengtsson, et al. 2002. *Resilience and sustainable development: Building adaptive capacity in a world of transformations.* International Council for Science, ICSU Series on Science for Sustainable Development, no. 3. http://www.sou.gov.se/mvb/pdf/resiliens.pdf.

Gordon, H.S. 1954. The economic theory of a common property resource: The fishery. *Journal of Political Economy* 62: 124-42.

Graham, J., S. Engle, and M. Recchia. 2002. *Local knowledge and local stocks: An atlas of groundfish spawning in the Bay of Fundy.* Antigonish, NS: Centre for Community-Based Management, Extension Department, St. Francis Xavier University.

Gunderson, L.H., and C.S. Holling, eds. 2002. *Panarchy: Understanding transformations in human and natural systems.* Washington, DC: Island Press.

Guysborough County Women's Fishery Enhancement Association. 2001. *Women working together and making a difference: A story of women's participation and leadership in enhancing local fisheries.* Antigonish, NS: Centre for Community-Based Management, Extension Department, St. Francis Xavier University.

Kearney, J. 1984. The transformation of the Bay of Fundy herring fisheries, 1976-1978: An experiment in fishermen-government co-management. In *Atlantic fisheries and coastal communities: Fisheries decision-making case studies,* ed. C. Lamson and A.J. Hanson, 165-203. Halifax: Dalhousie Ocean Studies Programme.

–. 1993. Diversity of labour process, household forms, and political practice: A social approach to the inshore fishing communities of Clare, Digby Neck, and the Islands. PhD thesis, Anthropology, Université Laval, Quebec.

–. 2004. Extreme makeover: The restructuring of the Atlantic fisheries. *Acadiensis* 34 (1): 156-63.

–. 2005. Community-based fisheries management in the Bay of Fundy: Sustaining communities through resistance and hope. In *Natural resources as community assets: Lessons from two continents,* ed. B. Child and M.W. Lyman, 83-100. Madison, WI: Sand County Foundation; Washington, DC: Aspen Institute.

Kerans, P., and J. Kearney. 2006. *Turning the world right side up: Science, community and democracy.* Halifax: Fernwood Publishing.

Millennium Ecosystem Assessment. 2005. *Ecosystems and human well-being: Synthesis.* Washington, DC: Island Press.

Milsom, S. 2003. Tour highlights zeal of small-scale fisheries. *Gulf of Maine Times* 7 (4). http://www.gulfofmaine.org/times/winter2003/tour.asp.

Ollerhead, J., P.G. Hicklin, P.G. Wells, and K. Ramsey. 1999. *Understanding change in the Bay of Fundy ecosystem: Proceedings of 3rd Bay of Fundy science workshop.* http://www.bofep.org/workshop/work99/index.html.

Ostrom, E. 1990. *Governing the commons: The evolution of institutions for collective action.* Cambridge: Cambridge University Press.

Ostrom, E., J. Burger, C.B. Field, R.B. Norgaard, and D. Policansky. 1999. Revisiting the commons: Local lessons, global challenges. *Science* 284: 278-82.

Polanyi, Karl. 2001 [1944]. *The great transformation.* Boston: Beacon Press.

Rosenberg, A.A., W.J. Bolster, K.E. Alexander, W.B. Leavenworth, A.B. Cooper, and M.G. MacKenzie. 2005. The history of ocean resources: Modeling cod biomass using historical records. *Frontiers in Ecology and Environment* 3 (2): 78-84.

Stiegman, M. 2003. United we fish. *Alternatives* 29 (4): 38-41.

Taylor, C. 1989. *Sources of the self: The making of modern identity.* Cambridge, MA: Harvard University Press.

–. 2002. Modern social imaginaries. *Public Culture* 14 (1): 91-124.

Wells, P.G., G.R. Daborn, J.A. Percy, J. Harvey, and S.J. Rolson, eds. 2004. *Proceedings of the 5th Bay of Fundy science workshop and coastal forum,* vol. 21. Environment Canada, Atlantic Region Occasional Reports. Environment Canada.

Young, O.R. 2002. *The institutional dimensions of environmental change.* Cambridge, MA: MIT Press.

11
Adaptive Co-Management and the Gospel of Resilience
Paul Nadasdy

Two new environmental management paradigms have emerged in the past few decades: cooperative management (co-management) and adaptive management. Although the two arose largely independently of one another, some scholars and resource managers have recently begun advocating a new approach integrating the two: *adaptive co-management*. They view this strategy as potentially offering solutions to some of the problems identified by critics of more standard forms of co-management. Indeed, the title of this volume suggests that the fusion of adaptive and cooperative strategies might be the key to overcoming some of the problems of co-management. In this chapter, I consider how adaptive co-management fares against one set of critiques that have been levelled at standard co-management: that despite the rhetoric of local empowerment that generally accompanies such processes, they often actually serve to perpetuate colonial-style relations by concentrating power in administrative centres rather than in the hands of local/Aboriginal people (Cruikshank 1998; Feit 1998; Nadasdy 2003). To this end, I examine the political and cultural assumptions implicit in the project of adaptive management, particularly the key concept of *resilience*. I begin with a brief look at the principles of adaptive management before considering how these principles play out in a co-management context.

The Principles of Adaptive Management
Although there is no simple way to characterize the body of theories and practices that fall under the rubric of "adaptive management," it is safe to say that adaptive management grows out of attempts to apply the insights of what Scoones (1999) dubs the "new ecology" to the practice of resource management. The new ecology refers to a revolution in ecological science brought about in the 1970s by the realization among ecologists that there is not, in fact, any natural tendency for ecosystems to develop towards a state of maturity (characterized by an increase in either biomass stabilization, diversification of species, cohesiveness in plant and animal communities,

and/or homeostatic regulation), as had long been supposed (Botkin 1990; Scoones 1999). This overturned the long-standing assumption that ecological systems are characterized by a single state of stable equilibrium to which ecosystems can return following a disturbance. Instead, ecosystem scientists came to realize that what they had conceived of as "the environment" must be viewed as a set of nested non-linear social-environmental systems of great complexity. The relations between various processes in such systems are so complex that the system's overall behaviour is unpredictable. As a result, cause and effect are not easily linked. Indeed, the notion of "cause" itself becomes highly problematic in complex non-linear systems. All this had profound implications for the practice of environmental management.

Conventional scientific resource management was developed over a hundred years ago, when it made sense to talk about designing strategies to maintain and enhance the stability of ecosystems. In the new ecology, this no longer makes sense. Adaptive management as a field of applied science owes much to the work of C.S. Holling (1978, 1986; Holling and Goldberg 1981), who argued that conventional resource management does not work because it is rooted in a set of outmoded assumptions about the environment and the nature of environmental change. And indeed, by the mid-1970s, many scholars and resource managers were beginning to realize that conventional resource management, rooted as it is in equilibrium-based models of the environment, was simply not working very well. Some turned to the new ecology for possible solutions.

Designing a management strategy based on the new ecology is no easy feat, however. Indeed, the new ecology represents something of a crisis for the very idea of environmental management. To begin with, the new ecology renders the concept of "management" deeply problematic. The linked social-environmental systems of the new ecology are characterized by a fundamental uncertainty (resulting from extreme dependence on initial conditions, a non-linear relationship between cause and effect, and the complex interdependence of multiple scales). This makes it extremely difficult – if not impossible – to predict the consequences of any particular action, including those initiated by would-be managers (Winterhalder 1994, 38-39).

Proponents of adaptive management claim that, as a result, management regimes need to be flexible enough to adapt to changing circumstances and, most importantly, managers need to be able to learn from experience if they are to manage complex systems effectively. As the consequences of particular management practices change (in response to changes in the social-environmental system), management institutions need to be able to respond appropriately. Management can no longer be based on static environmental models; instead, managers and management institutions must monitor and learn from the effects of their actions. This notion of "learning-by-doing" is the hallmark of adaptive management (Berkes and Folke 1998, 10).

Even the idea of learning-by-doing, however, is problematic in the context of the uncertainty associated with complex non-linear systems. As Holling himself notes, "what a complex system is *doing* seldom gives any indication of what it *would do* under changed conditions" (1978, 4). Since social-environmental systems are constantly evolving, what one learned by doing in the past may no longer be valid under current, even only slightly changed, conditions. To get around this problem, proponents of adaptive management have embraced Holling's concept of "resilience." Resilience is "the ability of a system to maintain its structure and patterns of behavior in the face of disturbance," and it is distinguished from stability, which is the "propensity of a system to attain or retain an equilibrium condition of steady state or stable oscillation ... resist any departure from that condition and, if perturbed, return rapidly to it" (Holling 1986, 296). Unlike stability, resilience "emphasizes non-equilibrium events and processes, variability, and adaptive flexibility. From a resilience perspective, incremental change may not reliably signal its effect. If a boundary [around the domain of attraction] is reached, the effect will be abrupt, unpredicted, and disproportionate to the cause – a surprise" (Winterhalder 1994, 37).

Rather than assuming the existence of a stable equilibrium and designing management programs to help maintain that stability, as in conventional management, proponents of adaptive management advocate managing for resilience – sometimes at the expense of short-term stability.[1] Holling (1995) has noted that conventional management, associated as it so often is with capitalist resource extraction and agro-industry, tends to focus on maintaining the stability of some part of the managed ecosystem – almost always for socio-economic purposes. The goal is typically to reduce the variability of some element of the system whose normal fluctuations pose problems for user groups (e.g., logging companies, fishers, ranchers, and so on). Such management practices necessarily also cause changes to the larger social-ecological system, however, and generally, the more "successful" the stability-based management practices, the greater such changes. These changes are seldom beneficial to the system as a whole: "The very success in managing a target variable for sustained production of food or fiber apparently leads inevitably to an ultimate pathology of less resilient and more vulnerable ecosystems, more rigid and unresponsive management agencies, and more dependent societies. This seems to define the conditions for gridlock and irretrievable resource collapse" (Holling 1995, 8).

According to this view, then, the secret to avoiding nasty environmental surprises and the collapse of social-environmental systems is to eschew the economically induced temptation to manage for a reduction in the natural fluctuation of important resources and instead allow regular minor disturbances to lead to the sorts of natural variation that enhance resilience. As a result, proponents of adaptive management call for the development of more flexible institutional structures and of mechanisms for social learning within those institutions. The idea is that flexible institutions that can learn will be better able to adapt to changes and so forestall catastrophic system shifts.[2]

Adaptive Co-Management and Its Legitimacy

The recognition that management institutions and practices need to be flexible enough to adapt to constant changes in social-environmental systems has led some proponents of adaptive management to look to the practices of indigenous peoples – who, in many cases, successfully adapted to their environments over millennia – for evidence of (and inspiration for) adaptive management. Increasingly, those who do so are declaring that indigenous people have been practising adaptive management all along (Armitage 2003; Berkes 1999; Berkes et al. 2000, 2003; *Ecology and Society* 2004; Olsson et al. 2004). One such study, for example, claims that "adaptive management can be seen as the rediscovery of traditional systems of knowledge and management" (Berkes et al. 2000, 1260), while another refers to a set of indigenous beliefs and practices as "traditional adaptive management strategies," claiming that this "traditional resource management system and local knowledge framework *premised on principles of adaptive co-management* continues to be used" in the region under study (Armitage 2003, 81 [emphasis added]). Of course, in making such statements, proponents of adaptive co-management do not claim that indigenous peoples developed the scientific theories and experimental practices of academic adaptive management. Rather, they argue that "adaptive management may be viewed as the scientific analogue of Traditional Ecological Knowledge because of its integration of uncertainty into management strategies and its emphasis on practices that confer resilience" (Berkes et al. 2000, 1260).

Proponents of adaptive co-management, however, are hardly the first to claim that the scientific management practices they espouse are merely a rediscovery of ancient indigenous knowledge and practices. As long as a hundred years ago, Gifford Pinchot, the founder and first head of the US Forest Service and one of the most influential early advocates for scientific resource management in North America, believed that he and others were merely reinventing what "Indian" people had already been practising before Europeans arrived on the continent (Miller 2001, 377-78). Since then, advocates of scientific management have regularly made claims that, in effect, they are merely rediscovering the land-based knowledge and practices of indigenous people. Even the co-management literature is replete with claims, such as Hobson's, that "Traditional Knowledge *Is* Science" (1992, 2).

What are we to make of the fact that scientific resource managers have claimed to be reinventing indigenous knowledge and practices for over a hundred years now – in spite of dramatic changes in the assumptions, techniques, goals, and practices of scientific resource management itself over the same period? Given the legitimizing power of the term "science" in contemporary Euro-American society, it is hardly surprising that anyone wishing to take indigenous knowledge and practices seriously would first need to label them as "science" (see Nadasdy 2003, 138-39). This is clearly part of what is going on when scientific managers claim that traditional knowledge and practices *are* science (or adaptive management). But indigenous knowledge and practices represent a powerful symbolic currency in their own right; they, too, can confer legitimacy on other practices with which they become associated. Numerous scholars have noted this phenomenon, and many have begun their analysis of it with what Redford (1991) dubbed the image of the "ecologically noble savage."[3]

This common stereotype is based on the assumption that indigenous people are the "original conservationists," whose ecological wisdom and spiritual connections to the land can serve as a model for more sustainable human/environment relations. Even critics of this stereotype admit that it has great symbolic power and has long proven to be an effective device for criticizing dominant Euro-American beliefs and practices. Those who successfully manage to link themselves to the mythic figure of the ecological Indian tap into its symbolic power and thereby legitimize their own environmentalist positions (Conklin and Graham 1995). Because the ecologically noble Indian represents a symbolic ideal rather than any actual set of beliefs and practices, the stereotype is extremely malleable; anyone can invoke the image to bolster his or her own particular vision of the ideal human/environment relationship. And, indeed, environmentalists of all stripes – many of whom have disagreed profoundly with one another – have attempted to associate themselves and their agendas with the ideal of the ecologically noble Indian (Nadasdy 2005b).

But why should proponents of adaptive co-management – who are building on the latest scientific theories to manage resources for the benefit of all – feel the need to appeal to this stereotype to legitimate their position? To answer this, we need to situate adaptive co-management in its proper social and historical context.

Adaptive Management as a Social Project

Geographer David Harvey (1993, 25) notes that "all ecological projects (and arguments) are simultaneously political-economic projects (and arguments) and vice versa. Ecological arguments are never socially neutral any more than socio-political arguments are ecologically neutral." Environmental management is nothing if not a socio-political undertaking. Environmental historians and anthropologists alike have noted that the development of the institutions and practices of state wildlife management at the beginning of the twentieth century was inextricably bound up with the expansion of state power. In many parts of the world (including North America), it was the imposition of state wildlife management and conservation programs that first brought not only land and wildlife but also local and Aboriginal people under the effective control of central governments (see, for example, Feit 1998; Jacoby 2001; Marks 1984). Wildlife management, they have shown, is "very much a social activity serving needs and interests of specific groups, and not simply those of wildlife or of society in general" (Feit 1998, 133). In fact, resource management has often been a very unpopular and controversial undertaking, entailing, as it does, the establishment of elaborate government bureaucracies and regulatory regimes for restricting people's access to and use of the environment. Although adaptive management differs in some important ways from conventional resource management, proponents of adaptive co-management, too, like their predecessors, advocate particular social objectives having to do with access to and control over resources. The social and institutional changes proposed by adaptive managers are often every bit as controversial as those imposed by conventional managers a century ago; as a result, they face stiff opposition – not least from within now-entrenched (conventional) resource management bureaucracies themselves.

The fact that adaptive management is situated within a particular set of beliefs and social relations should not be surprising, but it compels us to attend to the socio-political interests and agendas that both shape and are reflected in adaptive management. To do so, we need to consider the nature of the management project itself. Environmental management is a normative endeavour; it is based on the presumption that some ecological (or, in the case of adaptive management, social-ecological) states are more desirable than others. Indeed, the goal of all management is to promote or maintain certain desired ecological states as opposed to others. The equilibrium-based concept of nature that was dominant until the 1970s lent itself well for use as a model for the social-environmental "good," because it provided a clear basis for evaluating environmental states: anything that contributed to equilibrium, stability, and coherence of the ecosystem was good, while anything that detracted from them was bad (e.g., Leopold's now classic discussion of a "land ethic" [1949, 201-26]). From its beginnings, the equilibrium-based science of ecology inspired social criticism and was used as the basis for political action (Worster 1979, 198-209). It was a powerful force in shaping the views of most environmental activists and organizations (including the institutions of conventional management), and it is still evident in much of their rhetoric and practice.

It is for this reason that some environmental scholars and activists view the rise of the new ecology with some trepidation. Environmental historian

Donald Worster (1993), for example, sees the new ecology as a grave threat to the environmental movement precisely because it undermines the movement's ethical foundations. Without the notion of ecosystem balance to guide us, there is no longer any foundation for an ecological ethic upon which to base political/environmental action. After all, if the environmental consequences of one's actions are ultimately unforeseeable, how then is one supposed to judge between one environmental practice and another? Worster argues that these developments in the science of ecology are merely one aspect of post-modernism, a broad cultural shift away from the emphasis on stability, production, and progress that characterized modernity to a focus on disequilibrium, information, and non-linear change in nearly all aspects of contemporary Euro-American society; and he views the rise of the new ecology as at least in part a reaction against the political ideals and implications of equilibrium-based ecology (1993, 166-67).

Worster's pessimism does not seem completely justified, however. In the first place, as Harvey (1993, 10-15) so convincingly argues, values do not inhere in nature, but rather emerge from particular sets of beliefs and social relations. So, although some may indeed embrace the new ecology as a means of opposing environmental activism, there is nothing *inherently* anti-environmentalist about a non-equilibrium ecology. Second, I would argue that the rise of adaptive management itself should be viewed at least in part as an effort to reconstruct a "land ethic" in the context of the post-modern emphasis on disequilibrium and change. The great majority of scholars contributing to the literature on adaptive management advocate managing *for* resilience; so, that which contributes to resilience is "good" while anything that detracts from it is "bad." In place of the "balance of nature," we now have "resilience" as the ecological ideal against which to judge social-environmental action.

A few scholars, however – particularly those studying degraded social-ecological systems that have already flipped into highly resilient but undesirable states (e.g., Carpenter et al. 2001; Walker et al. 2002) – recognize that resilience in and of itself is not always desirable. These scholars have developed a more sophisticated concept of resilience,[4] one that does not easily lend itself to use as the basis for an environmental ethic. In the process, however, these scholars do not abandon the search for an ecological ethic; they simply replace the concept of *resilience* with *sustainability* as the absolute social-ecological "good" for which managers should strive. Carpenter and colleagues (2001, 766), for example, note that, unlike resilience, which is neither inherently good nor bad, "sustainability is an overarching goal that includes assumptions or preferences about which system states are desirable" (see also Walker et al. 2002, 19).[5] Unfortunately, even though they recognize that sustainability, like resilience, has many meanings (Carpenter et al. 2001, 765), they make no effort to define the term, except in the broadest generalities.[6] Even so, it is clear from the context in which they use it that their notion of "sustainability" remains closely linked to that of "resilience." Indeed, for them, sustainability seems to refer to the resilience of the *desired* equilibrium configuration of a social-ecological system (as opposed to the resilience of the undesirable ones) (e.g., see Carpenter et al. 2001, 778; Walker et al. 2002, 19, 24). Thus, these scholars continue to advocate managing *for* resilience – with the caveat that "where an SES [social-ecological system] is already in an undesirable configuration, resilience management involves reducing the resilience of this configuration as well as enhancing the resilience of desired ones" (Walker et al. 2002, 20).[7]

Although the rise of a post-modern land ethic may be good news for environmentalists and environmentally minded resource managers, it also highlights the fact that adaptive management is rooted in a particular set of social beliefs and values. Why, for instance, in the context of complex systems with multiple equilibrium states, should resilience be seen as an absolute good? When a social-ecological system is perturbed enough to push it into a new domain of attraction, the system as a whole is likely to experience massive disruption and change. But the consequences of such a shift for any individual species are difficult to predict. While dominant species may suffer catastrophic declines, other (previously marginal or absent) species will flourish and become dominant. The same holds for people and institutions; while a system shift may render previous economic activities unsustainable and bring about social and institutional collapse, other economic/ecological possibilities will emerge to take their place, along with corresponding systems of social organization.

When proponents of adaptive management valorize resilience, then, they necessarily also valorize one particular set of social-ecological relations (those that characterize the domain of attraction within which the social-ecological system is currently functioning). But why should the current equilibrium state – which is but one workable possibility – be viewed as intrinsically better than all others? Better for whom? This is fundamentally a political question. Unfortunately, merely substituting "sustainability" for "resilience," as Carpenter and colleagues do, does not solve this problem. Managing for this type of sustainability, like managing for resilience, assumes that one equilibrium configuration is better than all the others (although perhaps not the current one). It does not answer, nor even ask, the question: Better for whom? If a person's notion of sustainability (i.e., the social-ecological good) is influenced by his or her position within the social-ecological system, we cannot assume that there will be agreement about which equilibrium state is most desirable. So, although substituting sustainability for resilience may enable us to avoid the trap of assuming that the current configuration is necessarily good, it fails to help us address a crucial political issue: that is, who gets to decide what the "desired" social-ecological configuration is? And, just as important, what happens if there is disagreement over what is desirable?[8]

How one evaluates resilience and/or the current configuration of the social-ecological system necessarily depends on one's position within that system. The more one has invested (ecologically, socially, or economically) in existing social-ecological relations and institutions, the more one is likely to view resilience as "good." Those who are marginalized or excluded are less likely to view a collapse of existing social/institutional structures as an unmitigated disaster. Indeed, they may even embrace the kind of radical socio-ecological change brought about by a system shift. The valorization of resilience, then, represents a decision – at least implicitly – to endorse the socio-ecological status quo.

Proponents of adaptive management may object to this, asserting that, in fact, they do call for quite substantial reforms to the institutions and practices of environmental management. This is true; as we have seen, they have issued a clear call for the development of more flexible institutional structures and mechanisms for social learning within those institutions. For all their attention to institutional change, however, proponents of adaptive management have largely ignored the broader political and economic context within which environmental management institutions are themselves embedded. This is not to say that they ignore politics altogether; on the contrary, some proponents of adaptive management (Lee 1993) have described in detail the extraordinary political complexity of adaptive management arrangements, while others (Walters 1997; Pinkerton 2003) have identified numerous obstacles to successful adaptive/cooperative management, many of which are of a political nature. All of these scholars, however, take for granted the broader political/economic context of capitalism/colonialism that gave rise to the notion of and need for resource management institutions in the first place. Thus, although proponents of adaptive management clearly recognize that it is the economic imperatives of modern extractive and agro-industries that are the root cause of the management "pathologies" that lead to decreased resilience and ultimate collapse (Colding et al. 2003; Holling 1986, 1995), their proposed solutions do not address these larger issues at all. The focus on building flexible management institutions that can learn is fine as far as it goes, but it ignores the political economy of resource extraction that drives management in the first place. Indeed, it is my experience that scientific resource managers are among the first to complain that science often plays too small a role in resource management decisions. As often as not, their scientifically generated management recommendations are ignored by politicians in the face of pressures exerted by powerful special interests in resource extraction and agro-industry. In such a context, changes in the mindsets of managers and in the structure of management institutions – not to mention the science underlying them – are almost beside the point.

Environmental managers may now prefer to manage for resilience – even at the expense of short-term stability – but powerful interests in the extractive and agricultural industries do not have that luxury. Capitalist production *demands* a degree of short-term stability. Companies must have access to reliable supplies of necessary resources if they are to recoup their investments in capital and labour (not to mention raise investment capital in the first place). It is, as proponents of adaptive management themselves recognize, precisely this dynamic that leads to overexploitation and system collapse. Indeed, it could be argued that it is largely because of this dynamic that conventional resource management even exists. It is certainly the reason conventional resource managers developed and continue to use concepts like maximum sustainable yield, so despised by proponents of adaptive management (for example, see Chapter 5). As long as this capitalist dynamic exists, the pressure to make management decisions based on the stability of one or two key resources will remain enormous. In such a context, it is hard to imagine how management institutions – however flexible and "smart" they may be – will be able to avoid the kinds of pathologies proponents of adaptive management attribute to conventional management.

There are also theoretical problems associated with ignoring the context of capitalism. Adaptive management proponents' failure to take into account the broader political/economic context within which environmental management actually takes place renders a thorough analysis of social-ecological systems impossible. As Harvey (1993, 28) points out:

> Money flows and commodity movements ... have to be regarded as fundamental to contemporary ecosystems ... because these flows form a coordinating network that keeps contemporary ecosystems reproducing and changing in the particular way they do. If these flows ceased tomorrow, then the disruption within the world's ecosystems would be enormous. And as the flows shift and change their character, so the creative impulses embedded in any socio-ecological system will also shift and change in ways that may be stressful, contradictory or harmonic as the case may be.

To the extent that they fail to take such flows into account, proponents of adaptive management necessarily adopt an impoverished view of the social-ecological systems that they purport to study.

Capitalism simply cannot be viewed as a set of social processes and relations that play themselves out on a neutral landscape. Rather, present-day social-ecological systems are themselves the products of capitalist processes and social relations. As human geographers, environmental historians, and ecological anthropologists have repeatedly demonstrated, resource extraction and agro-industry have literally remade global and regional ecosystems (e.g., Cronon 1991; Crosby 1986; Smith 1990; White 1996; Worster 1979). Because of the dialectical link between social and environmental processes, contemporary environments must be viewed as integral aspects of the capitalist relations and processes that shaped them. Thus, in an important sense, the relations of capitalism are "embodied" in contemporary social-ecological systems. As Harvey (1993, 27) put it, "created ecosystems tend to both instantiate and reflect ... the social systems that give rise to them" so that "the very design of the transformed ecosystem is redolent of its social relations."

This should hardly come as a surprise to proponents of adaptive management, who themselves argue that environment and society are inextricably linked. Yet, it means that their focus on resilience – on *maintaining* the existing social-ecological system in more or less its current state – has the implicit goal of maintaining the social-ecological relations of capitalist resource extraction and agro-industry. Nor does the strategy employed by some ecosystem scientists (e.g., Carpenter et al. 2001; Walker et al. 2002) of substituting the goal of sustainability for resilience help practitioners avoid this problem, especially given the vagueness surrounding their use of the term "sustainability."[9]

The implications of this are especially problematic where indigenous peoples are concerned (i.e., in much adaptive co-management) because it is precisely the relations of capitalist resource extraction and agro-industry that are most responsible for the marginalization of indigenous peoples and the dispossession of their lands and resources. Historian William Cronon (1983), for example, has shown how English colonists' importation of diseases, plants, and animals to New England, along with their imposition of particular forms of governance, property relations, and strategies for capital accumulation, so radically altered the regional ecology as to deprive indigenous peoples of the ecological basis for their way of life. This was a social-ecological system shift if ever there was one. Yet, while this shift was disastrous for many indigenous species, including people, it clearly benefited European colonists and their biological imports. So, although indigenous people may indeed engage in flexible and adaptive practices that seem on the surface to qualify as adaptive management, the social and political assumptions upon which they are based are completely different. Indigenous people, who are often politically and socially marginalized within existing social-ecological systems (shaped as they have been by capitalist dynamics), have far less invested in maintaining the resilience of those systems than do resource managers.

Nor does the strategy of substituting sustainability for resilience prevent ecosystem scientists from treating the landscape of capitalism as a given. In their analysis of degraded rangelands in Australia, for example, Carpenter and colleagues (2001) take for granted the eviction and replacement of Aboriginal peoples (who historically maintained the land in the desired grassy state through burning) by European ranchers engaged in wool production for the world market. Taking the economic/ecological relations of ranching as their baseline, these scholars identify ranchers' weak property rights and the vagaries of the market (rather than the dispossession of Aboriginal people and the cessation of burning) as two of the principal factors leading to the loss of resilience of the grassy state (Carpenter et al. 2001, 776). Thus, they cast social-ecological restoration as a technical problem that should be solvable by strengthening ranchers' property rights over heretofore public lands and encouraging ranchers to diversify economically. Such a view clearly takes for granted the dispossession of Aboriginal people. As long as we are considering the restoration of an ecological system that – by the authors' own admission – is unlikely to occur, why not consider the restoration of Aboriginal land rights and regular burning, the only practice that we *know* enhanced the resilience of the desirable grassy state? Undoubtedly, there are all kinds of problems, political and otherwise, with this suggestion, but the fact that Carpenter and colleagues do not even discuss such a possibility (even if just to discount it) indicates the degree to which they take the colonial relations of capitalism as a given in their analysis. They also fail to consider the potential social impacts of their suggested solutions for increasing sustainability (e.g., strengthening of ranchers' property rights) – especially for any remaining Aboriginal people in the region who might be hunting or gathering on the public lands they would privatize.

Given the legacy of social-ecological system shifts like that which occurred in colonial New England and the embeddedness of notions about resilience in relations of capitalist exploitation, we should not be surprised when indigenous people refuse to embrace these ideas and even actively oppose adaptive co-management. This is precisely what happened in an effort to adaptively co-manage Dall sheep in the southwest Yukon. Below, I provide a brief description of this effort and show that it was the political and economic assumptions underlying the proposed adaptive co-management project that led First Nations people to reject it.

Adaptive Co-Management in the Ruby Range
The Ruby Range Sheep Steering Committee (RRSSC) was created in 1995 and charged with the task of developing a set of recommendations for managing Dall sheep in the southwest Yukon's Ruby Range.[10] RRSSC representatives were chosen from a wide range of groups with interests in the sheep, including government biologists, affected outfitters, and members of the Kluane First Nation, Aboriginal inhabitants of the area. It soon became apparent that different members of this co-management body had radically different ideas about the magnitude of the decline in the sheep population,

the reasons for this decline, and potential management solutions. Biologists and outfitters sitting on the RRSSC saw the population decline as relatively minor, a temporary fluctuation caused by several years of unusually bad weather. Significantly, neither biologists nor outfitters felt that hunting by humans had contributed to the sheep decline. As a result, they opposed any restrictions on hunting, the outfitters adamantly so.

By contrast, Kluane First Nation members saw the decline in the sheep population as long-term and catastrophic. They argued that the population had been declining steadily since the 1960s and that the situation had now reached a crisis. They vehemently disagreed with biologists and outfitters about the role of weather and the significance of human hunting. Indeed, Kluane people identified hunting – especially by outfitters – as the single most important factor leading to the decline of the sheep population and advocated a ban on sheep hunting in the region (or, failing that, imposition of a quota).

The members of the RRSSC all agreed that more information was needed to determine which factors were having the greatest effect on the sheep population, so they decided to develop a comprehensive research plan. As it turned out, however, committee members were unable to reach an agreement on this plan. Since biologists did not see the problem as an emergency requiring immediate action, they advocated a policy of adaptive management. Rather than just doing anything that might work to help the sheep (i.e., manipulating any and all relevant variables simultaneously in an emergency effort to save the sheep), biologists wanted to manage a limited number of variables and monitor the effects of their management practices closely, so they could alter their strategy in response to the effects it was having on the sheep. As one biologist put it: "The assumption was that the actions (both management and monitoring) should be designed to test predictions about the effects of these actions and to measure and compare population and behavioral parameters in sheep exposed to different human actions. In this way, the relative influence of different influences on the sheep could be assessed. This applies more of an adaptive management paradigm" (Nadasdy 2003, 286). A crucial part of this approach involved leaving part of the population completely unmanaged to serve as a control group. Biologists felt that, in the long run, this adaptive approach would enable people to manage sheep much more effectively. They saw the Ruby Range situation as an opportunity to learn about sheep management rather than simply as a case of sheep needing to be saved.

Because the RRSSC had no mandate to deal with anything other than sheep, it was somewhat hamstrung in its ability to manage for ecosystem resilience; it was clear, however, that the biologists had resilience in mind. Although none of them ever used the word during a meeting, they were clearly disdainful of conventional management concepts like "maximum sustainable harvest" (RRSSC 1996a, 12). They steadfastly refused to place an absolute limit on the number of sheep that should be killed each year, preferring instead a management strategy flexible enough to adapt not only to ecological uncertainties (e.g., fluctuations in the size of the sheep population) but also to socio-economic ones (e.g., in the price and number of hunts that outfitters could sell and in the success of those hunts).

Although Kluane elders and hunters agreed with biologists on the need to maintain flexibility (RRSSC 1996b, 4) and were generally not averse to scientific studies of the sort advocated by biologists (but see Nadasdy 2003, 199-210), they felt that the sheep crisis was so acute that the RRSSC could not afford to "waste time" taking the kinds of half-measures the biologists were proposing. Indeed, Kluane people for the most part viewed the biologists' approach as self-serving; several of them told me they felt that biologists were more concerned with maintaining their jobs (by generating yet another series of scientific studies) than with saving the sheep.

The disagreement over how to conduct research also had obvious political and economic dimensions. Dall rams, with their large, curving horns, are a prized trophy animal for big game hunters all over the world. As trophy animals, Dall sheep represent a significant potential income for big game outfitters as well as for the territorial government, which sells hunting licences and collects trophy fees and taxes. Because of outfitters' considerable political power in the Yukon, it would have been difficult for the biologists to implement any management initiatives opposed by them (such as a ban on hunting), regardless of any recommendations by the RRSSC. This is not to say that it would have been *impossible*, but at the very least, wildlife managers would have needed convincing evidence (to Yukon politicians) supporting such action. And, despite rhetoric about the value of traditional ecological knowledge, this still means evidence produced by biologists, *not* the uncorroborated testimony of First Nations elders, especially if that testimony contradicts the biological evidence. To prove that human hunting was a relevant factor in the decline of the sheep population (and so obtain the biological evidence essential to ban hunting), however, any adaptive management program would have had to treat human hunting as a variable. That is, biologists would have had to *ban* hunting in at least part of the research area to observe how sheep fared there compared with non-hunted areas. Politically, this was simply not an option. Kluane people were understandably less than enthusiastic about participating in a research program that would not be studying the effects of human hunting, the factor they believed to be the principal cause of decline in the sheep population.

Although the strategy advocated by biologists may in some ways have been a novel approach to managing/researching sheep in the region, it was perfectly consistent with the existing social and political relations underlying the management of sheep. In the first place, it took for granted the bureaucratic and institutional structures of wildlife management in the territory. Indeed, it would clearly have enhanced the role of Yukon government biologists in the management of Ruby Range sheep in that it would have united experimentation, monitoring, and policy making. Second, the biologists' plans for adaptive management were clearly geared towards enhancing the resilience of the existing socio-ecological system, *including* the activities of outfitters, the very group that Kluane people saw as the source of the problem. By avoiding research questions that might ruffle political feathers (such as an inquiry into the effects of outfitter hunting on sheep populations), not to mention overtly political questions (such as who should have the right to hunt sheep in the first place, and who should have jurisdiction over their management), the biologists' program took for granted the broader political and economic context in which sheep are managed in the Yukon.

By contrast, the kinds of actions supported by Kluane people (including perhaps policy-based research on the effects of human hunting) directly challenged existing social and political relations underlying sheep management in the territory. After more than fifty years of oppression by government officials in the name of wildlife conservation (Nadasdy 2003, ch. 1), Kluane people can be excused for being wary of changes that strengthen the hands of government wildlife managers, especially when they viewed the latter as being more interested in creating future work for themselves than in saving sheep. And Kluane people's insistence that future research look into the effects of human hunting, which in turn would have called into question who was doing the hunting and who was benefiting from it, questioned the socio-political context of sheep hunting/management in the territory and threatened those with powerful vested interests in the status quo.

In the end, RRSSC members were unable to agree on even the outlines of a research program, adaptive or otherwise (Nadasdy 2003, 206-7), and research on Ruby Range sheep ground nearly to a halt. The RRSSC was disbanded in 1998, and few of its recommendations were ever implemented. Kluane people had lost faith in the process and chose to pursue their interests in Ruby Range sheep through the more overtly political process of land-claim negotiations.[11]

Conclusion

The preceding discussion demonstrates that while a flexible co-management institution pursuing a robust adaptive strategy might well have solved some of the problems of managing Dall sheep in Kluane country, it is unlikely that such an institution could have addressed the political/economic inequities that lie at the heart of Kluane people's concerns about the sheep.

What is more, had Kluane people agreed to participate in the adaptive management process, they would have become complicit in their own marginalization, because the process itself took for granted a political context within which they were already marginalized. The problem is that the equitable treatment of marginalized peoples is simply not a management issue (cooperative, adaptive, or otherwise); it is a political issue. "Management" itself, as a concept, is based on a set of underlying assumptions about the world that are rooted in the political and economic context of capitalist resource extraction. Since management efforts, adaptive or otherwise, are explicitly designed to be carried out within that context, those who engage in management have no choice but to take that context for granted. The practices and complex institutional structures of "management" are not neutral, but instead constrain thought and action in ways that end up reinforcing existing political and economic inequalities. Because managers necessarily take for granted existing relations of inequality and exploitation, they tend to view the project of management itself as a relatively straightforward exercise that involves identifying a series of "problems" (some of them perhaps political) that stand in the way of management, finding technical solutions to those problems, and implementing those solutions. This view of management necessarily obscures the relations of political and economic inequality and exploitation that are the root causes of such problems in the first place (see Nadasdy 2005a).

If we are to take seriously one of the central insights of adaptive management – that social and environmental systems are inextricably linked to one another – we must expand our analysis of socio-ecological systems to include not only the nature and workings of management institutions but also the embeddedness of those institutions (however flexible they may be), and indeed of management itself, in the relations of capitalist production. Because of that embeddedness, it is extremely unlikely that analysis and reform at the institutional level will by themselves lead to the equitable treatment of local and indigenous peoples in the management process. Adaptive co-management, like all environmental management, is an inherently political undertaking, not simply a technical one. The kinds of recommendations adaptive managers make (whether for institutional reform or the strengthening of ranchers' property rights) and even the questions they do or do not ask (such as whether human hunting affects Dall sheep populations in the Ruby Range) are deeply political. We must not, therefore, view adaptive co-management simply as a means for the enlightened use of resources and empowerment of local people – a means that is, unfortunately, beset by various problems. Rather, we must consider the fact that even "successful" adaptive co-management may, like conventional management, be part of the larger project of colonialist resource extraction.

Acknowledgments
To begin with, I would like to thank Derek Armitage, Fikret Berkes, and Nancy Doubleday for organizing the adaptive co-management symposium that spawned this volume and for all their hard work editing the manuscript. Every one of the participants at the symposium and the follow-up authors' meeting provided me with helpful comments, criticism, and feedback that enabled me to improve this chapter considerably. I also received helpful comments from Marina Welker, Derek Johnson, and two anonymous reviewers. As always, I acknowledge the help and friendship of the people of Burwash Landing, Yukon, without whom this chapter could never have been written. Thanks, too, to the members of the Ruby Range Sheep Steering Committee for allowing me to attend their meetings, especially Barney Smith, who – despite our differences – has always been very generous with his time and willing to discuss the difficulties of co-management. Finally, the research on which the case study section of this chapter is based was carried out with the support of the National Science Foundation (grants 9614319 and 0233914) and the Wenner Gren Foundation for Anthropological Research.

Notes
1 But see below.
2 Also, given the ultimate inevitability of such shifts, flexible institutions are regarded as ideal for taking advantage of the productive creativity of the collapse and reorganization phases of non-linear system change (Holling 1986).
3 As Shepard Krech (1999) has pointed out, however, this is little more than a (marginally) new twist on the age-old stereotype of the noble savage, and its use is vulnerable to many of the same criticisms.
4 See especially Carpenter et al. 2001 for a lucid discussion of the multiple possible meanings of "resilience" and of the ways in which the concept depends upon one's spatial, temporal, and social perspective.
5 Even these scholars, however, are less than consistent in their use of the term "resilience." At times they seem to slip back into a more standard use of the term, one in which it appears to be a desirable goal in and of itself (e.g., Walker et al. 2002, 17). In other works (e.g., Folke et al. 2002), some of these same scholars revert completely to an unproblematized concept of resilience.
6 Walker and colleagues (2002, 24), for example, refer to sustainability as "the continued well-being of the economy, society, and the natural resource base."
7 The language of "managing for resilience" is so entrenched in the field that these scholars sometimes speak about the improvement of degraded social-ecological systems as an increase in the resilience of the desired configuration – even though that configuration no longer exists! (For example, see Carpenter et al. 2001, 773.)
8 It might be objected that this is exactly what scenario planning is for (e.g., Chapter 15); yet the literature on scenario planning deals inadequately, if at all, with questions of representation (i.e., who gets to represent whom at the scenario-planning exercise?) and control (who designs, chooses, presents, and interprets the scenarios – which, like models, are simplifications of complex realities based upon assumptions and best guesses?). Nor do proponents of scenario planning generally say how they intend to proceed in the face of fundamental disagreements among participants over their preferred scenario.
9 I have not examined the concept of sustainability in this chapter, except for its use by some ecosystem scientists as a stand-in for resilience. In its general use, however, sustainability is a notoriously slippery concept, with so many meanings that it is in danger of becoming an empty buzzword. Yet, because no one wants be seen as opposing something that on its face seems so beneficial, the term "sustainability" – now embraced by the political right as well as the left – has proven a remarkably effective tool for justifying the expansion of control by central management bureaucracies and the maintenance of global and regional inequalities (Kearney 1996, 107; Sachs 1992; Escobar 1995, 192-211). Indeed, some of these scholars have noted that the concept of sustainability not only takes for granted the dynamics of capitalist development but has actually helped rehabilitate that dynamic in the eyes of many erstwhile critics (Sachs 1992).

10 See Nadasdy 2003 for a more complete discussion of the structure of the RRSSC, the political context in which it functioned, and how it worked.
11 As of the summer of 2006, no new research plan had been put in place. Sheep research in the Ruby Range continues, but it has been scaled back dramatically. During the years leading up to the creation of the RRSSC and while it was in existence (1992-97), the Yukon Government Fish and Wildlife Branch carried out aerial sheep surveys of the region every year. Since then, however, they have conducted only two such surveys (in 2001 and 2004), both of which indicated a continuing, though slight, decline in the total population. Kluane First Nation negotiators were unsuccessful in their efforts to establish a special sheep management area in the Ruby Range as part of the First Nation's land-claim agreement (which was signed in 2004), and many Kluane people remain convinced that the sheep will ultimately disappear from the Ruby Range.

References

Armitage, D. 2003. Traditional agroecological knowledge, adaptive management and the socio-politics of conservation in Central Sulawesi, Indonesia. *Environmental Conservation* 30 (1): 79-90.

Berkes, F. 1999. *Sacred ecology: Traditional ecological knowledge and resource management.* Philadelphia: Taylor and Francis.

Berkes, F., and C. Folke. 1998. Linking social and ecological systems for resilience and sustainability. In *Linking social and ecological systems: Management practices and social mechanisms for building resilience,* ed. F. Berkes and C. Folke, 1-25. Cambridge: Cambridge University Press.

Berkes, F., J. Colding, and C. Folke. 2000. Rediscovery of traditional knowledge as adaptive management. *Ecological Applications* 10 (5): 1251-62.

–. 2003. *Navigating social-ecological systems: Building resilience for complexity and change.* Cambridge: Cambridge University Press.

Botkin, D. 1990. *Discordant harmonies.* New York: Oxford University Press.

Carpenter, S., B. Walker, J.M. Anderies, and N. Abel. 2001. From metaphor to measurement: Resilience of what to what? *Ecosystems* 4: 765-81.

Colding, J., T. Elmqvist, and P. Olsson. 2003. Living with disturbance: Building resilience in social-ecological systems. In *Navigating social-ecological systems: Building resilience for complexity and change,* ed. F. Berkes, J. Colding, and C. Folke, 163-85. Cambridge: Cambridge University Press.

Conklin, B., and L. Graham. 1995. The shifting middle ground: Amazonian Indians and eco-politics. *American Anthropologist* 97 (4): 695-710.

Cronon, W. 1983. *Changes in the land: Indians, colonists, and the ecology of New England.* New York: Hill and Wang.

–. 1991. *Nature's metropolis: Chicago and the Great West.* New York: W.W. Norton.

Crosby, A. 1986. *Ecological imperialism: The biological expansion of Europe, 900-1900.* Cambridge: Cambridge University Press.

Cruikshank, Julie. 1998. Yukon Arcadia: Oral tradition, indigenous knowledge, and the fragmentation of meaning. In *The social life of stories: Narrative and knowledge in the Yukon Territory,* ed. Julie Cruikshank. Lincoln: University of Nebraska Press.

Ecology and Society. 2004. Special issue: Traditional knowledge in social ecological systems. 9 (3). http://www.ecologyandsociety.org/vol9/iss3

Escobar, A. 1995. *Encountering development: The making and unmaking of the Third World.* Princeton, NJ: Princeton University Press.

Feit, H.A. 1998. Reflections on local knowledge and wildlife resource management: Differences, dominance and decentralization. In *Aboriginal environmental knowledge in the North,* ed. L.-J. Dorais, M. Nagy, and L. Müller-Wille, 123-48. Québec: GÉTIC.

Folke, C., S. Carpenter, T. Elmqvist, L. Gunderson, C.S. Holling, and B. Walker. 2002. Resilience and sustainable development: Building adaptive capacity in a world of transformations. *Ambio* 31 (5): 437-40.

Harvey, D. 1993. The nature of the environment: The dialectics of social and environmental change. *Socialist Register* 29: 1-51.

Hobson, G. 1992. Traditional knowledge is science. *Northern Perspectives* 20 (1): 2.

Holling, C.S. 1978. Overview and conclusions. In *Adaptive environmental assessment and management,* ed. C.S. Holling, 1-37. Chichester and New York: John Wiley and Sons.

–. 1986. The resilience of terrestrial ecosystems: Local surprise and global change. In *Sustainable development of the biosphere,* ed. W.C. Clark and R.E. Munn, 292-317. Cambridge: Cambridge University Press.

–. 1995. What barriers? What bridges? In *Barriers and bridges to the renewal of ecosystems and institutions,* ed. L.H. Gunderson, C.S. Holling, and S.S. Light, 3-34. New York: Columbia University Press.

Holling, C.S., and M.A. Goldberg. 1981. Ecology and planning. In *Contemporary anthropology: An anthology,* ed. D.G. Bates and S.H. Lee, 78-93. New York: Alfred Knopf.

Jacoby, K. 2001. *Crimes against nature: Squatters, poachers, thieves, and the hidden history of American conservation.* Berkeley: University of California Press.

Kearney, M. 1996. *Reconceptualizing the peasantry: Anthropology in global perspective.* Boulder, CO: Westview Press.

Krech, S. 1999. *The ecological Indian: Myth and history.* New York: W.W. Norton.

Lee, K.N. 1993. *Compass and gyroscope: Integrating science and politics for the environment.* Washington, DC: Island Press.

Leopold, A. 1949. *A sand county almanac, and sketches here and there.* New York: Oxford University Press.

Marks, S. 1984. *The imperial lion: Human dimensions of wildlife management in Central Africa.* Boulder, CO: Westview Press.

Miller, C. 2001. *Gifford Pinchot and the making of modern environmentalism.* Washington, DC: Island Press.

Nadasdy, P. 2003. *Hunters and bureaucrats: Power, knowledge, and Aboriginal-state relations in the southwest Yukon.* Vancouver: UBC Press.

–. 2005a. The anti-politics of TEK: The institutionalization of co-management discourse and practice. *Anthropologica* 47 (2): 215-32.

–. 2005b. Transcending the debate over the ecologically noble Indian: Indigenous peoples and environmentalism. *Ethnohistory* 52 (2): 291-331.

Olsson, P., C. Folke, and F. Berkes. 2004. Adaptive co-management for building resilience in social-ecological systems. *Environmental Management* 34 (1): 75-90.

Pinkerton, E. 2003. Toward specificity in complexity: Understanding co-management from a social science perspective. In *The fisheries co-management experience: Accomplishments, challenges, and prospects,* ed. D.C. Wilson, J.R. Nielson, and P. Degnbol, 61-77. Dordrecht, Netherlands: Kluwer Academic Publishers.

Redford, K. 1991. The ecologically noble savage. *Cultural Survival Quarterly* 15 (1): 46-48.

RRSSC (Ruby Range Sheep Steering Committee). 1996a. Minutes from the meeting of the Ruby Range Sheep Steering Committee, 10-11 January. Prepared by Paul Nadasdy. Burwash Landing, YT.

–. 1996b. Minutes from the meeting of the Ruby Range Sheep Steering Committee, 8 May. Prepared by Paul Nadasdy. Haines Junction, YT.

Sachs, W. 1992. Environment. In *The development dictionary: A guide to knowledge as power,* ed. W. Sachs, 26-37. London: Zed Books.

Scoones, I. 1999. New ecology and the social sciences: What prospects for a fruitful engagement. *Annual Review of Anthropology* 28: 479-507.

Smith, N. 1990. *Uneven development: Nature, capital, and the production of space.* Oxford: Basil Blackwell.

Walker, B., S. Carpenter, J. Anderies, N. Abel, G. Cumming, M. Janssen, L. Lebel, J. Norberg, G. Peterson, and R. Pritchard. 2002. Resilience management in social-ecological systems: A working hypothesis for a participatory approach. *Conservation Ecology* 6 (1): 14.

Walters, C. 1997. Challenges in adaptive management of riparian and coastal ecosystems. *Conservation Ecology* 1 (2): 1.

White, R. 1996. *The organic machine: The remaking of the Columbia River.* New York: Hill and Wang.

Winterhalder, B. 1994. Concepts in historical ecology: The view from evolutionary ecology. In *Historical ecology: Cultural knowledge and changing landscapes,* ed. C. Crumley, 17-41. Santa Fe, NM: SAR Press.

Worster, D. 1979. *Dust bowl: The southern Plains in the 1930s.* New York: Oxford University Press.

–. 1993. *The wealth of nature: Environmental history and the ecological imagination.* New York: Oxford University Press.

12
Culturing Adaptive Co-Management: Finding "Keys" to Resilience in Asymmetries of Power
Nancy Doubleday

Since the first international co-management conference twenty years ago (Pinkerton 1989), interest in co-management, both as theory and as practice, has grown globally. The adaptive potential of co-management has encouraged efforts to link social and ecological systems thinking (Berkes and Folke 1998; Gunderson and Holling 2002; Westley et al. 2002) to create "adaptive co-management systems" (Olsson et al. 2004). In turn, social/cultural/ecological linkages stimulate perceptions of the adaptive potential of co-management as a source of new approaches to governance and sustainability.

While initial interest has focused on "formal" co-management and on the interface of people and resources, complex systems thinking and learning theory is encouraging wider exploration of the "informal" dimensions and of the processes by which social-ecological change occurs. One of the emerging poles of increasing interest in this widening circle is that of culture and identity. As a result, a dilemma exists for a social-ecological "systems" approach: how do we frame the interpretation of the role and significance of culture in relation to the nature of resilience in human systems, when culture serves as a source of diversity and difference (Doubleday 2004, 2005b, 2005c, 2005d)? Here I argue that such framing is crucial to both understanding complex social-ecological systems subject to co-management (Westley et al. 2002) and to relating to analyses of power in co-management (Nadasdy 2003).

If we are to understand social-ecological change in intercultural environments, and become successful practitioners of adaptive co-management in a new approach to governance (Armitage et al. 2005), we need a better understanding of the contributions of individuals and social groups within and outside organizations. Increasingly, social theorists are recognizing the need for an informed praxis (Gibson-Graham 2003). When working across an interface of cultural difference in attempting co-management, as is the case of management of renewable resources in Canada's North, we need to actively consider the role of culture in adaptive practice. If we look at co-management itself as an adaptive process, one that is both dynamic and evolving, we can fit elements of the adaptive cycle described by Holling to patterns of change and development in relations within adaptive co-management (Doubleday 2005b, 2005c, 2005d). Such an approach allows for embedding an *expectation* of change in the outlook of participants, and thus the process of adaptive co-management becomes inherently forward-looking in the sense used by Westley (2002).

The importance of culture to resilience in ecosystem management (Gunderson and Holling 2002; Doubleday 2004; Berkes et al. 2005), to adaptive co-management (Berkes and Folke 1998), and to social capital (Chapter 4) is underscored by arguments for holistic approaches to management of social-ecological systems (Westley et al. 2002; Berkes and Seixas 2005). Folke and colleagues (2003) highlight four categories of factors for building resilience: (1) learning to live with (accept) change and uncertainty; (2) nurturing diversity as a means of ensuring greater options for renewal and reorganization; (3) combining knowledge types to enhance learning; and (4) creating conditions and opportunities for self-organization. All of these categories can be seen as having a cultural dimension. This framework complements the four "key ingredients for a sustainable nature-human interaction" of Scheffer and colleagues (2002, 239) and emphasizes the significance of learning and adaptive processes, among others, as keys to resilience in social-ecological systems.

Another approach to addressing culture is taken by Westley and colleagues (2002, 110), who draw parallels between the function of remembrance in adaptation in nature and consciousness and reflexivity in self-organizing human systems. They also comment on culture and human systems, but in the context of "popular" culture associated with globalization and mass consumption. In this chapter, culture is viewed through a different lens, recognizing that diversity is inherent in the concept of culture. But "culture" may not be sufficiently visible to be disentangled, except where co-management occurs within an intercultural context. This difference in interpretation of culture can be attributed to research locality, defined by differences in the geographical and historical context. Nonetheless, consciousness and reflexivity are hallmarks of self-organizing human systems that can be expected to transcend specific situations.

Previous related work (Doubleday 2005a, 2005b, 2005c, 2005d) examined co-management itself as an adaptive process, using the adaptive cycle of Holling (Holling and Gunderson 2002, 34) as a metaphor for describing and modelling linked and nested iterations of learning and adaptation in the context of policy related to Aboriginal land claims in northern Canada. This chapter flows from this framework and presumes an inherent adaptive capacity intrinsic to self-organizing, complex human and natural systems (Westley et al. 2002) as a basis for examining culture and its role in the cycle of adaptation related to co-management. The significance of individuals and groups as *agents* of culture having adaptive capacity themselves must also be recognized, however, in order to understand how people envision alternative futures (Gibson-Graham 2003; Westley et al. 2002) and what such visions have to do with successful adaptive co-management (Chapter 14).

Although the role of culture in adaptive co-management has not been well defined, its significance and potential have been recognized (e.g., Berkes and Folke 1998, 433; Folke et al. 2003). To make this role more visible, I have chosen a case study that emphasizes social and cultural considerations. We will see that, for a dominantly indigenous community, negotiating the social and cultural practices of daily life can be just as difficult as negotiating the harvest of natural resources when management issues are being considered, and that the relevant collective rights can be equally contested. Besides documenting struggle, however, I also sketch the partial outline of adaptive capacity and resilience.

To explore the role of culture in the context of adaptive co-management, I draw on a case study of community justice in Cape Dorset, Nunavut. Although other analyses of adaptive co-management in this volume centre on natural resources, if we are to appreciate the contribution of culture to adaptation in the context of adaptive co-management, focusing on a culture-centred co-management problem can highlight important lessons. These lessons are then potentially transferable to other complex adaptive co-management situations in which culture plays a prominent role, including those addressing natural resources, particularly where livelihoods are contingent upon resilient ecosystems.

One factor that continues to perturb analyses of co-management is power, particularly asymmetries of power that may impede co-management in practice. Nadasdy (2003) has found inequalities rooted in power relations and cultural difference an almost insurmountable obstacle to co-management. Berkes (Chapter 2) has, on the other hand, adopted a broad construction of co-management as partnership that converges with adaptive management. Here, I suggest that culture and culture-derived identity serve as *extra-formal* drivers or power bases, in the sense of being inherent properties of cultural/social/ecological systems, and differ from negotiated formal powers. Whereas Nadasdy's analysis focuses on inequality as disempowering, here, I look at cultural expressions of difference and diversity as potentially empowering.

This chapter triangulates within a social/cultural/ecological system in order to locate individual and collective agency and to examine the relationship of culture to adaptation, self-efficacy (Bandura 1986, 1997), resilience (Gunderson and Holling 2002; Berkes and Fast 2005), and visioning (Chapter 14) or "forward looking expectation behaviour" (Westley 2002).

This analysis is grounded in the recognition that all social-ecological systems ultimately connect and in the documentation of the lived experience of people engaged in imperfect co-management relations with respect to community justice issues in Cape Dorset. When examining the situation in Cape Dorset, I use the broadest definition of adaptive co-management compatible with the continuum of Berkes (Chapter 2). By this I mean a directed yet changing relationship between partners, whereby a "developmental co-management spectrum" exists. This co-management spectrum is capable of giving standing to social facts of power beyond those embedded in structural governmentality. Where intercultural contexts form the basis for co-management, as in the case of relations between different peoples, particularly in the context of post-colonial relations in the Canadian North, there is reason to expect that culture must play a part in co-management, in terms of power, practice, and norms. Further, it is reasonable to anticipate that culture may drive adaptation. A dynamic view of co-management as a behavioural form that *is both adaptive and participatory* is useful. Arguably, it offers an alternative to a fixation on asymmetries of power as obstacles to the emergence of co-management. It appears to be a valid interpretation of specific experience and practice in Cape Dorset.

Cape Dorset: Community Justice and Adaptive Co-Management

Cape Dorset is a community of approximately 1,150 people, located along the southern coast of Baffin Island, Nunavut.[1] Most residents are beneficiaries of the Nunavut Land Claim Agreement (NLCA) of 1993. Inuit in this place are people living close to the land; many are also sophisticated providers of commodities emblematic of traditional life, in the form of highly prized – and priced – carvings and prints. This trade engages the globalized world and has an impact that has left traces from Afghanistan to the British Columbia Winter Olympic logo, and from the United Nations Headquarters in New York to Moscow (Doubleday et al. 2004). Beyond this external success, the community has also shown itself competent to address many internal needs, including providing a culturally appropriate daycare facility and addressing personal development as a pathway to healing. As is the case in most northern communities, there are educational and health facilities run by government, in this case, the Government of Nunavut. There is also a Royal Canadian Mounted Police (RCMP) facility, under federal jurisdiction, as well as regional and municipal offices of the Government of Nunavut, offering support and advice and employing many, including development, tourism, and wildlife officers. The Hunters and Trappers Committee (HTC), created under the NLCA, is the local community body devoted to wildlife issues. Similarly, there are local committees for education, health, and justice, with varying degrees of formality. Given the intimate association of social, cultural, and environmental practices in Cape Dorset, knit together through cultural practices such as hunting, gathering, and fishing, it is not surprising that many key individuals play active roles in more than one community committee. From a whole systems perspective, it is reasonable to expect that social learning in one "substantive" context is readily transferable, and transferred, to others (Diduck et al. 2005). What informs decision making by the HTC is very likely to mobilize decision making in the education or health or justice domains, and vice versa.

Institutional Dimensions and Formal Elements of Justice Co-Management

The realities of the legal framework of the criminal justice system in Cape Dorset are as follows. The criminal justice system is defined by the Criminal Code of Canada and works through the Territorial Court System and courts of superior jurisdiction to punish offenders. Nunavut Justice has authority over the administration of justice in the territory. The Community Justice Committee (CJC) exists formally under the Native Community Justice Program, created in 1993 by an agreement between the federal and territorial governments. It has a legally recognized mandate to offer alternative justice services to the community. To participate in the alternative processes of community justice, however, the "offender" must be diverted from the court system to the CJC by the RCMP. This fact is the crux of the asymmetry of power in the co-management of justice in Cape Dorset.

The community participates actively in the Community Justice Program (CJP), which was created by a formal agreement with the federal Department of Justice and the Government of Nunavut. Under the CJP, a Community Justice Committee has a mandate to address justice matters locally. In terms of participation, the Cape Dorset CJC is drawn from respected members of the community and includes many elders, mature men and women, and younger adults. The process employed in addressing issues is one of thoughtful discussion and consensus building. A Community Justice Coordinator supports the CJC. Regional Justice Co-ordinators serve the Baffin Region as well. The commitment of the members and the coordinators to holistic approaches to understanding justice issues as rooted in social, cultural, and ecological conditions was evident in their actions. For example, in order to address issues of youth and respect, elders and youth were hosted by the CJC during travel on the land dedicated to conveyance of culture-specific values.

An Interview-Based Case Study from Cape Dorset: Views from the Community

Between 2001 and 2004, a series of guided interviews were conducted in Cape Dorset, using a common set of questions intended to invite free expression of views by the participants concerning sustainability, identity, culture, and *Inuit Quajimaqatuqangit* (IQ) (Inuit traditional knowledge) with respect to wildlife and community justice issues. Time was also made available to participants to discuss other related matters of concern to them.

Those interviewed comprised a heterogeneous group of women and men, young adults, and elders from various backgrounds, including waged, unwaged, and self-employed people, office holders, hunters, artists, and other community members. A few long-term residents who were non-Inuit also participated. As this study was designed to determine community perceptions of the community justice process rather than the formal justice delivery and arrangements, interviews focused on community members rather than the RCMP. Future work addressing RCMP perceptions of both the formal system and the Community Justice Committee would be a useful contribution.

Analysis of the interview responses highlighted a number of common themes and recurring issues, revealing a high degree of shared concern among community members. Key themes included:

- perceived reluctance of authorities to engage the CJC and the community justice system, shown by less than optimal use of power to divert individuals from the criminal justice system to the CJC
- insensitivity by RCMP to Inuit cultural norms concerning relations between offenders and victims
- lack of understanding of the impact of criminalization of community members on the community, and of their physical removal on those left behind
- need for more community control over everyday life, including justice
- need for greater inclusion of IQ in the administration of justice at all levels
- concern for the consequences of incarceration, including brutality and isolation experienced in southern jails, lack of rehabilitation, and return of unprepared criminal offenders to equally unprepared communities
- concern for community well-being, and risks associated with the potential for recurring violence
- need to link opportunities for social and economic development (particularly for at-risk groups) to alleviate downward spirals of despair, antisocial behaviour, and violence.

In addition, the social impact of the criminal justice system and of the stigma created by a criminal record was of concern. During the period of this study, a community in another region of Nunavut made headlines in southern media when the postmaster alleged that no local staff could be found for federal jobs because the people available had criminal records and consequently could not be hired.

Discussion

The reported reluctance within the criminal justice system to engage with the CJC is supported by evidence of reduced numbers of offenders being diverted by the RCMP to the CJC since Nunavut was created (Clark 2004). This indicates to the community that there may be a lack of trust on the part of the RCMP, in spite of formal agreements between the federal Department of Justice and the Government of Nunavut to establish the Native Community Justice Program and the CJCs. One of the areas of contention is the RCMP policy that interprets "restorative justice" practices to include mandatory participation by the victim of a crime where the offender is referred to an alternative process. This policy requirement violates Inuit precepts of customary law that make such involvement by victims discretionary.

The opportunity for increased diversion presented by CJCs was not readily availed of by the RCMP. The reasons are not clear. Possible interpretations include a higher level of commitment to internal policies and approaches. It may also mean that the value of contributing to the development of community justice alternatives, in terms of deployment of resources and promotion of cultural integrity and community responsibility, is not well understood. This is important: the overrepresentation of Aboriginal people in the criminal justice system is well known, and the return to the community of offenders who have not been rehabilitated is a clear concern. For example, John Vandoremalen (1998), director of communications of the National Parole Board, stated: "Aboriginal people are widely overrepresented in federal corrections. While they represent about 3% of Canada's total population, they account for nearly 15% of the incarcerated population. That proportion is even higher in the Prairie Provinces, where Aboriginal offenders represent about 40% of the inmate population." It should be noted that this represents a 6 percent increase in the incarcerated Aboriginal population compared with statistics reported in 1977 (Government of Canada 1980, 37).

The case of community justice in Cape Dorset poses interesting questions for understanding the potential for adaptive co-management when formal co-management does not function as intended. First, is the situation still amenable to being understood as an example of adaptive co-management? The answer to this question appears to be yes, provided that three conditions are met: (1) we need to recognize "formal" adaptive co-management as situated within an informal system of community care and concern, underlying which is a deeper cultural context; (2) we need to understand the continuum of adaptive co-management (Chapter 2) as including hybrid adaptive co-management models (meaning that a formal sphere of adaptive co-management may relate to an informal sphere having a measure of autonomy [Table 12.1]); and (3) we need to take seriously a forward-looking stance, including aspirations for the future, and so enable the workings of reflexivity and cultural resilience to become visible.

Table 12.1

Continuum of co-management spheres applicable to community justice in Cape Dorset

	Formal	Inter-systemic	Autonomous
	RCMP, Criminal Code	*Community Justice Agreement*	*Community Justice Committee (CJC)*
Degree of external rule specification	High; may be legislated; applies to jurisdiction, procedures	Negotiated, agreed upon	Low
Mandate/focus	Prescribed/ inward	Negotiated/ between	Self-directed/ outward
Goals	Uniform	Shared	May be diverse
Discretion	Minimal	Negotiated	High
Relationships	Prescribed	Negotiated	Self-defined, self-regulatory
Values	Certainty, control	Mutuality, flexibility, social learning	Individual and epistemic group processes and outcomes

Second, what is the impact of inequality in co-management relations? From the standpoint of a power-based analysis (e.g., Nadasdy 2003), it might be tempting to dismiss the situation of Cape Dorset due to the evident asymmetry of power favouring the RCMP. If, however, we are to take up the challenge posed at the beginning of this chapter, to learn more about the role of culture in relation to resilience in social systems, it may not be enough to stop at the boundaries of the formal sphere of adaptive co-management when assessing how people engage in forward-looking behaviour under adaptive co-management. Rather, I would argue, the four "categories of factors" of Folke and colleagues (2003) that are key to resilience are present here, but they find expression beyond the formal sphere, in the work of individuals, epistemic groups, and the CJC in the community.

A fundamental social convention, such as the law of colonial successor states, inevitably contributes to the production of "western" models of social-ecological interactions, including power relations, just as the more mechanistic conventions of western science do (Berkes and Folke 1998).

Similarly, the discourse of customary law or "folk law" can be understood to parallel the discourse of traditional ecological knowledge (TEK). This is not to imply that western legal systems cannot adapt. Indeed, there are many arguments as to the evolutionary capacity inherent in these systems (e.g., Weeks 1986; Doubleday 1989a, 1989b; Bankes 2005; Milsom 2005). Rather, this is to point out that, as in the case of the long process of negotiating a "space" (*sensu* Olsson et al. 2004) for TEK in wildlife management through land claims and policy change, a similar structural problem awaits with respect to addressing community concerns for justice. However, this does not negate the adaptive capacity of either the community or of adaptive co-management practices, and where cultural difference includes a source of collective wisdom, such experiences of contestation and negotiation may actually fuel informal adaptive co-management arrangements.

We should not overlook, however, the frustration experienced by the Community Justice Committee as a result of the lack of response from the formal system. Some community members question the belief that effective partnership with the criminal justice system is workable in the current co-management model. This loss of faith in the formal co-management system is also coupled with other concerns about the administration of justice. As the level of dissatisfaction with the formal system increases, that system itself stands to lose credibility. It is also clear that these concerns exist outside contemporary "formal" systems of governance or co-management. Refusal by the criminal justice system to engage beyond its own definition of restorative justice implies rigidity and, perhaps, lack of adaptive capacity on its part. In any event, such a stance by a major partner within the formal co-management system imposes the added cost of loss of a prime opportunity for social learning. The rigidity of the formal system and its failure to embrace cultural differences and conflicts as learning opportunities forces these concerns into the informal system. Evidently, this increases the dissatisfaction of the community with the formal system.

However, the void in the formal adaptive co-management sphere (created by the asymmetry of power and lack of cooperation) can also be seen as a window of opportunity for the greater community. The CJC has begun to engage in creative practices, such as organizing community workshops with experts that it invites and brings into the community. In qualitative terms, these actions reflect key dimensions of resilience (see Table 12.2).

Although the Cape Dorset experience may not correspond to an ideal of successful cooperative interaction between co-management partners, it enables us to develop a deeper understanding of the role of culture in co-management in relation to adaptation and adaptive capacity. It does this by making more visible both the tensions and the windows of opportunity that can occur when co-management crosses cultural boundaries. Although many of these tensions can be understood as fundamentally rooted

Table 12.2

Resilience criteria and cultural expression in the Cape Dorset community justice case study

Categories of factors important for resilience* and forward-looking behaviour**	Keys to resilience evident in relevant Cape Dorset responses
Learning to live with change and uncertainty	Taking action to heal, to build skills, and to gain new knowledge
Nurturing diversity for reorganization and renewal	Linking youth and elders for diversion Linking justice programs, criminal law, and healing in the community
Combining different kinds of knowledge	*Inuit Quajimaqatuqangit* and western law Inuit and non-Inuit ideas about healing
Creating opportunities for self-organization	Ability to see what can be done despite limitations of formal systems (e.g., camping with elders and youth; travelling for hunting, fishing, and gathering)
Envisioning new realities	Creating new norms and realities
Practising "thick co-management"	Asserting views and initiating events to bring about change

* After Folke et al. (2003); Berkes and Seixas (2005).
** Westley et al. (2002); Olsson (2006).

asymmetries of power, the interplay among culture, resilience, and adaptive co-management at the community level is both mirrored and nurtured by interactions of identity, citizenship, and self-efficacy in relation to individual capacity for adaptation. I pursue these ideas below.

Resilience in Social Systems: Community Visions, Desires, and Goals
The ethos of community justice in Cape Dorset is rehabilitation and restoration of healthy relationships in the community so that the offender can successfully reintegrate. From a social resilience perspective, these objectives appear to be fully in accord with factors related to resilience (Folke et al. 2003). The broader desires and concerns of the community, as expressed in the words of the community members interviewed during the course of this research, include the following visions:

- "Inuit knowledge and values could be used more to work for sustainability ... they are not used enough at present."
- "People are concerned about justice and about wildlife – especially about the impact of the southern laws on community practices."

- "Having the Government of Nunavut is an important step," but "the community also has a big role to play in the future."
- "Inuit expect more recognition of Inuit knowledge, values and practices in the areas of wildlife and justice now that Nunavut is in place."
- More "local participation" is needed.
- The community wants "opportunities of all kinds" to ensure "better lives for all."

From these summary statements, it is quite clear that the community is interested in change and has a strong sense of what changes are desirable and also that these changes are culturally referenced to a large degree, whether in the domain of sustainability or wildlife or justice. This may seem surprising, given the extent to which the formal systems responsible for management (Government of Nunavut) and co-management (Nunavut Land Claim Agreement) have already brought changes to Nunavut. Significantly, community members are clear in their perception of a role for the community itself, beyond the formally constituted arrangements that currently exist in relation to Nunavut. The other important feature, from the perspective of social dimensions of resilience, is that so many of these views concern the future, and these forward-looking expectations are very clear.

"Thick" Citizenship, Co-Management, and Culture

While it appears that the cultural context within which co-management takes place is critical to understanding the outcomes of adaptive co-management, in this case conditions affecting the agency of individuals are also significant.

Corresponding to the treatment of "citizenship education" by Williams and Humphrys (2003, 11) as "thin" and "thick," the dominance of state-driven, legal norms and passive citizen reactions taken to describe "thin citizenship education" can also be used to describe minimal efforts at formal co-management. Similarly "citizen-defined, cross-scale, trans-age, value-clarifying and active participation" are elements of "thick citizenship education" and can equally be applied to describe complex and rich social relations in "thick" adaptive co-management.

To be explicit, one possibility is to understand formal co-management in its barest and least successful form as "thin" co-management, when the degree of regulation and control is high, the degrees of freedom are low, and the system is relatively rigid. A parallel view of "thick" co-management positions it not in the limited social space of governmental control but rather in a participatory governance space where "thick" values are among the key features. Here participation becomes a matter of choice, but also a matter of responsibility; as a result, thick co-management offers the opportunity for a high degree of participation and for the possibility of self-governance.

In the case of community justice in Cape Dorset, the persistence of the participants can be seen as a commitment to thick co-management, beyond the reach of the formal system. The resistance of the formal justice system to engaging with the community on the community's terms more closely resembles thin co-management. So it appears that a "thick" response (community perseverance) is possible even where formal co-management interactions are "thin." From the perspective of resilience, this can also be seen as an instance of collective "self-reference" (Westley 2002, 342), which in the context of complexity theory, creates greater capacity for seeing alternatives and making choices in the face of chaos and change.

Experience from Cape Dorset suggests that culture similarly serves as a self-referenced framework for adaptation in the context of frustrated formal co-management.

Individuals, Self-Efficacy, and Adaptive Capacity
The focus on the individual as an agent of adaptive management raises questions about the nature and source of adaptive capacity at the level of the individual and the community in relation to social learning (e.g., Westley 2002). An important aspect of Westley's case study (2002, 360) of "Lake Algonquin" (pseudonym) is the role of "citizen scientists," described as capable of moving an "experiment" from one stage to another (358). Here we see a link between individual capacity and community potential for adaptation relevant to resilience in adaptive co-management: change starts with people who have the capacity to envision realistic alternatives and some reinforcing experience in implementation.

One explanation for the community desire for change is found in an application of social theory of self-efficacy. As Bandura (1986, 1995, 1997) and others (e.g., Pajares 1996) have shown, beliefs about self-efficacy influence individual and collective capacity and outcomes in an almost prescriptive fashion:

> People change their lives for the better not only through self-development but by acting together to alter adverse institutional practices. If the practices of social systems impede or undermine the personal development of some sectors of society, then a large part of the solution lies in changing the adverse practices of social systems through the *exercise of collective self-efficacy.* To shape their social future, *people must believe themselves capable of accomplishing significant social change,* which rarely comes easily ... personal and social change are complementary (Bandura 1997, 33).

The capacity of community members in Cape Dorset to make change and to adapt can be seen as an "exercise of collective self-efficacy" that is consistent with the keys to resilience described above.

When we ask deeper questions about the nature and origin of the source of inspiration and beliefs underlying the "exercise of collective self-efficacy" and the values enabling self-reference and adaptive capacity, are we not in essence asking where the wellsprings of resilience in social/cultural/ ecological systems are? For Inuit, who have succeeded in the past thirty years in their claims for lands, resources, territories, and self-government, including constitutional protection of these rights, to varying degrees in different regions, these struggles and successes undoubtedly fuel a sense of self-efficacy and resilience (Doubleday 2005d). The bedrock from which these wellsprings of self-efficacy and resilience flow in Cape Dorset is clearly embodied in culture.

I argue here that one of the ways that we can theorize co-management behaviour and experience as adaptive is to adopt a vision of the participants as agents with the power to choose a future different from their past (Gibson-Graham 2003). We can then see self-efficacy as a transferable property acquired through self-referenced success that is learned, experienced, and consciously embodied through performance (Bandura 1997). Greater self-efficacy leads to greater control (Pinkerton 1991) and autonomy. The fact is that the role of culture in this process of self-referencing for *performing differently* is not well understood in adaptive co-management (although it is recognized as a factor in other literatures, e.g., Mackenzie 2001) and is further evidence of the need for additional research in adaptive co-management emphasizing social systems.

One of the links between the practices of community competence and the theoretical framing of self-efficacy by Bandura can be seen in the self-referencing of individuals in the community to those local bodies established to address particular issues of concern, such as the CJC and the Hunters and Trappers Committee. This self-referencing to community bodies is done both positively, in terms of what people believe they can achieve on their own, and negatively, such as when legally mandated but unaccountable authority is seen to prevent the exercise of community autonomy in solving problems.

Members of the community of Cape Dorset have a high degree of self-awareness and interest in making changes to improve the quality of their lives. Examples include actions, visions, and plans, such as:

- examining the past and clearing up matters that concern people (e.g., "learn to heal from abuse, so we can stop it")
- finding new ways of bringing healthy opportunities for education, employment, recreation, and creativity that are in keeping with the quality of life that people want (e.g., "train and hire local Inuit for local jobs")
- living in harmony *within* the environment (e.g., livelihoods that respect Inuit cultural values)

- combining life, work, and health through holistic approaches (e.g., "people in the past planned community hunts," providing food and improving communication; "likewise, today, we could have more consultation with community stakeholders in making plans for future").

These statements are courageous and forward-looking. They are congruent with high levels of self-efficacy (Bandura 1997) and conform to the four characteristics of social/cultural/ecological resilience (Folke et al. 2003). They are also articulated in terms of culturally specific cross-references. This again prompts a fundamental question as to the source of the self-efficacy, resilience, and community desire for autonomy. To understand this, it is necessary to recognize the integrated totality of social/cultural/ecological forces shaping identity (Doubleday 2003) as well as the roles of the individual and of groups in imagining alternative futures and in seeing themselves as having choices.

For those in communities that have been disempowered by external forces, the process of renewal of their capacity to adapt and thrive can be as straightforward as learning to see themselves as having choices and then taking action to choose (Gibson-Graham 2003; Doubleday 2004; Doubleday et al. 2004). When formal systems become dysfunctional, community members can take action and engage in collective practices of self-efficacy (Bandura 1997, 33), contributing to social and cultural resilience (Berkes et al. 2005). This is precisely what we see happening in Cape Dorset, and it highlights the centrality of the thick, informal system in understanding adaptive co-management.

The connection between increased levels of community control, increased self-efficacy, and reduced social frustration has thus empowered the Community Justice Committee. I return, therefore, to the argument raised at the outset, that asymmetry in power does not inevitably negate adaptive co-management in theory or in practice. Depending on contextual and intrinsic cultural and personal factors, individuals, epistemic groups, and formal organizations may be capable of working autonomously to adapt and create future conditions.

We expand our capabilities for understanding culture as a creative source and driver of adaptive co-management when the perspectives and practices of engaged community members can be seen to express *and produce* resilience, thereby increasing self-efficacy and enhancing adaptive capacity in social systems through self-referencing to culture, regardless of structural rigidity.

Self-Efficacy and Culture
When individuals respond creatively and with some autonomy in an intercultural context, despite apparently dysfunctional or otherwise inadequate

formal co-management regimes, we have to wonder – and look more closely. One possibility is that culture offers the self-referencing needed to inspire individuals to become those architects, teachers, and nurturers needed for enhanced adaptive capacity, enabling the self-empowered individual or epistemic group to become an agent of change. This offers a basis for situating more precisely the "human wellsprings" of both resistance and resilience within arguments for a culturally grounded adaptive co-management (Doubleday 2004).

Pursuing the view that the complexity of social-ecological systems requires more than an additive approach (partly in order to accommodate the future-oriented capacity of humans), the role of culture in creating diverse visions of desirable futures should not be underestimated. Notwithstanding the critique that socially produced knowledge includes virtual reality that is experienced as being "real" (Westley et al. 2002, 110), and the corollary that management systems are also constructions of reality, the formulation of complex systems *capable* of supporting aspirations for a future different from the past is clearly distinct from deterministic models based on hindcasting.

Here, self-efficacy may be seen as an emergent cultural property in social systems that is analogous to ecological resilience in ecological systems. Arguably, adaptive co-management offers a context for adaptation in complex social/cultural/ecological systems here by *accommodating* emergent properties and self-referent frames.

One clear analogy between Westley's study of fishery management and this Cape Dorset study is the significance in both of designated agents within the formal system and of epistemic community groups (Westley 2002, 334). In Westley's study, both types of agency played critical roles, advancing the practice of co-management in a specific situation from a tenuous and fragile position to one of robust practice. This corresponds to the previous analogy of thick citizenship and thick co-management. In Cape Dorset, there are significant examples of agency at the level of the individual and also of an informed epistemic group ("citizen customary law authorities," in this case elders rather than "citizen scientists"), but the situation is made inherently more complex by the intercultural nature of the context. The community justice participants are predominantly but not wholly Inuit, and their cultural context is clearly Inuit culture. The formal justice system, meaning the criminal justice system, is equally clearly dominated by the RCMP, and its culture is western criminal legal culture.

This cultural dimension finds expression in the focus of the community on a long-term, resilient, holistic vision of community well-being that engages historical injustices, as well as in contemporary concern with the practices of the formal justice system. Further evidence for the reality of this vision as a reflection of Inuit culture at the scale of Nunavut has been discussed elsewhere (Doubleday 2003). At the scale of a community, this is a significant qualitative difference in the context of co-management in Cape Dorset as compared with that of the "Lake Algonquin" case (Westley 2002).

In conceptual terms, by adopting a stance open to envisioning new futures in relation to the practice of adaptive co-management in contexts of asymmetries of power, to the idea of a partnership continuum of adaptive co-management (Chapter 2), and to the further expansion of social capital to include adaptive capacity (Chapter 4), it is possible to understand the practice of community justice in Cape Dorset not only as a case in which culture creates a window of opportunity but also one that fosters the adaptive capacity or collective self-efficacy necessary for action. Empowered individuals and groups then act within this "opportunity space." By working with engaged individuals in this research, and informed by empowerment theorized as self-efficacy, we begin to see more clearly the emergence of adaptive capacity in social/cultural/ecological systems as an analogue to ecological resilience within ecosystems. We also see adaptation in action in the changing relations among individuals and groups within the social/ cultural/ecological system, comparable to physical/ecological drivers of adaptive cycles described in ecological analyses.

Conclusions
Conflict and cooperation, adaptation and change, and social systems and ecological systems form pairs of interdependent states, co-evolving and informing one another in the context of co-management. In this sense, the axes and poles constructed from these characteristics of what is, after all, one integrated reality produce the perception of difference. More importantly, when adopting an evolutionary perspective of the adaptive process of co-management in complex systems, we begin to see that *adaptive co-management as a process* is also capable of creating the gaps or opportunities within which adaptation can occur and change can arise. More significantly, from the perspective of this analysis of the role of culture in adaptation, we see that adaptive capacity can also be understood as an important cultural property analogous to resilience in ecological terms.

Experience in Cape Dorset confirms this: it seems quite clear that community norms have survived, personified in individuals who experience self-efficacy and who continue to seek recognition of their views and adapt to new challenges in doing so. The community finds expression through the community justice system, although the RCMP largely ignores it. The criminal justice system is often inconsistent with Inuit cultural norms and practices and, as a result, returns damaged individuals to the community – persons who are often still in conflict and at odds with the community.

Neither the individual nor the community is healed in this situation. The inability of the RCMP to engage in a constructive relationship with the community, which would lead to diversion of more offenders from the criminal justice system, may ultimately fuel further desires for autonomy. Individuals and epistemic groups capable of functioning autonomously experience growing self-efficacy and demonstrate greater resilience and greater adaptive capacity as a result of persisting in spite of asymmetries of power and dysfunctional formal co-management relationships.

As an alternative to the pessimistic adoption of conventional views of power in the context of adaptive co-management, this analysis leads me to propose an agenda for adaptive co-management research and practice that embraces the process of re-envisioning and refocusing of effort beyond formal, institutional, rights-based contestation and resistance, towards adaptive, learning-based nurturance and cultivation, committed to valuing cultural as well as biological diversity as a source of resilience. Here, strength is manifested as self-efficacy rather than as negotiated authority, and culture emerges as a source of adaptive capacity, self-reference, and resilience.

In the case of large social/cultural/ecological systems and their processes of renewal, social and institutional learning are likely to be an important element of adaptation. Thus, given our view that adaptive co-management constitutes in part a response to desires for "innovative governance," I propose three further additions to our research agenda to move us towards envisioning an emergent, adaptive co-management as well as sustainable futures. First, we might consider the adoption of a long-term, developmental approach to adaptive co-management linked to evolving norms of social and ecological sustainability, recognizing cultural resilience as an important emergent property of complex and diverse social/cultural/ecological systems. Second, we need to clarify the potential of culture as well as "citizenship" for creating windows of opportunity. Third, we need to know more about the adaptive potential of co-management as a process for enabling transformational learning and nurturing self-efficacy in these complex systems.

This study from Cape Dorset is but a very modest beginning. Further intercultural studies of adaptive co-management are needed to explore the role of culture in relation to social-ecological resilience and to examine the role of the individuals and groups who, as keepers of the keys of resilience, are also midwives to adaptation through culture.

Acknowledgments
I thank the people of Cape Dorset who participated in this research, and the Social Sciences and Humanities Research Council for the funding that made it possible. Shawn Donaldson and Pootoogook Elie assisted in the field. I also thank the reviewers and my co-editors for supportive suggestions in preparing this chapter.

Notes
1 http://www.capedorset.ca/en/community.asp.

References
Armitage, D., F. Berkes, and N. Doubleday. 2005. Symposium rationale. Paper prepared for the Moving beyond the critiques of co-management: Theory and practice of co-management symposium, Wilfrid Laurier University, Waterloo, ON, 4-5 February.
Bandura, A. 1986. *Social foundation of thought and action: A social cognitive theory.* Englewood Cliffs, NJ: Prentice Hall.
–, ed. 1995. *Self-efficacy in changing societies.* Cambridge: Cambridge University Press.
–. 1997. *Self-efficacy: The exercise of control.* New York: W.H. Freeman.
Bankes, N. 2005. Exploring the roles of law and hierarchy in ideas of resilience: Regulating resource harvesting in Nunavut. In *Breaking ice: Renewable resource and ocean management in the Canadian North,* ed. F. Berkes, R. Huebert, H. Fast, M. Manseau, and A. Diduck, 291-318. Calgary: University of Calgary Press.
Berkes, F., and H. Fast. 2005. Introduction. In *Breaking ice: Renewable resource and ocean management in the Canadian North,* ed. F. Berkes, R. Huebert, H. Fast, M. Manseau, and A. Diduck, 1-19. Calgary: University of Calgary Press.
Berkes, F., and C. Folke, eds. 1998. *Linking social and ecological systems: Management practices and social mechanisms for building resilience.* Cambridge: Cambridge University Press.
Berkes, F., and C.S. Seixas. 2005. Building resilience in lagoon social-ecological systems: A local-level perspective. *Ecosystems* 8: 967-74.
Berkes, F., R. Huebert, H. Fast, M. Manseau, and A. Diduck, eds. 2005. *Breaking ice: Renewable resource and ocean management in the Canadian North.* Calgary: University of Calgary Press.
Clark, S. 2004. *Review of the Nunavut Community Justice Program.* Final report. Ottawa: Scott Clark Consulting for the Department of Justice, Government of Canada.
Diduck, A. 2005. Unpacking social learning in social-ecological systems: Case studies of polar bear and narwhal management in northern Canada. In *Breaking ice: Renewable resource and ocean management in the Canadian North,* ed. F. Berkes, R. Huebert, H. Fast, M. Manseau, and A. Diduck, 269-90. Calgary: University of Calgary Press.
Doubleday, N.C. 1989a. Aboriginal subsistence whaling: The right of Inuit to hunt whales and implications for international environmental law. *Denver Journal of International Law and Policy* 17 (2): 373-93.
–. 1989b. Co-management provisions of the Inuvialuit Final Agreement. In *Co-operative management of local fisheries: New directions for improved management and community development,* ed. E. Pinkerton, 209-27. Vancouver: UBC Press.
–. 2003. The nexus of identity, Inuit autonomy and Arctic sustainability: Learning from Nunavut, community and culture. *British Journal of Canadian Studies, Special Issue on Environment, Community, Resources* 16 (2): 297-308.
–. 2004. Finding human well-springs: In search of roots of resistance, sources of resilience? Environmental Studies Association of Canada, Panel on Resilient Livelihoods and Community Based Resource Management, University of Manitoba, Winnipeg, 3-5 June.
–. 2005a. Adaptive co-management and the integration of cultural, social, ecological and geocryological knowledge for mitigation of environmental impacts of Arctic climate change. Poster presented at the International Conference on Arctic Research Planning (ICARP II) Copenhagen, Denmark, 9-13 November. http://www.icarp.dk/Posters/1-5.jpg.
–. 2005b. From dialectic to praxis: Adaptive co-management, participatory action learning and community-based research opportunities. Paper presented at the Moving beyond the Critiques of Co-management: Theory and Practice of Adaptive Co-Management Symposium, Wilfrid Laurier University, Waterloo, ON, 4-5 February.
–. 2005c. From dialectic to praxis: Adaptive co-management as mid-wife to change? Paper presented at the Moving beyond the Critiques of Co-management: Theory and Practice of Adaptive Co-management author's workshop, Ottawa, 25-26 May.
–. 2005d. Inuit culture, justice and adaptive co-management: Midwife to change? Paper presented at the Ocean Management Research Network national conference, Ottawa, 30 September.

Doubleday, N., A. Mackenzie, D. Fiona, and S. Dalby. 2004. Reimagining sustainable cultures: Constitutions, land and art. *Canadian Geographer* 48(4): 389-402.

Folke C., J. Colding, and F. Berkes. 2003. Synthesis: Building resilience and adaptive capacity in socio-ecological systems. In *Navigating social-ecological systems: Building resilience for complexity and change,* ed. F. Berkes, J. Colding, and C. Folke, 352-87. Cambridge: Cambridge University Press.

Gibson-Graham, J.K. 2003. An ethics of the local. *Rethinking Marxism* 15: 49-74.

Government of Canada. 1980. *Indian conditions: A survey.* Ottawa: Queen's Printer.

Gunderson, L.H., and C.S. Holling, eds. 2002. *Panarchy: Understanding transformations in human and natural systems.* Washington, DC: Island Press.

Holling, C.S., and L.H. Gunderson. 2002. Resilience and adaptive cycles. In *Panarchy: Understanding transformations in human and natural systems,* ed. L.H. Gunderson and C.S. Holling, 25-62. Washington, DC: Island Press.

Mackenzie, A.F.D. 2001. On the edge: "Community" and "sustainability" on the Isle of Harris, Outer Hebrides. *Scottish Geographical Journal* 117: 219-40.

Milsom, S.F.C. 2005. *A natural history of the common law.* New York: Columbia University Press.

Nadasdy, P. 2003. *Hunters and bureaucrats: Power, knowledge, and Aboriginal-state relations in the southwest Yukon.* Vancouver: UBC Press.

Olsson, P., C. Folke, and F. Berkes. 2004. Adaptive co-management for building resilience in social-ecological systems. *Environmental Management* 34 (1): 75-90.

Pajares, F. 1996. Self-efficacy beliefs and mathematical problem-solving of gifted students. *Contemporary Educational Psychology* 21: 325-44.

Pinkerton, E., ed. 1989. *Co-operative management of local fisheries: New directions for improved management and community development.* Vancouver: UBC Press.

–. 1991. Locally based water quality planning: Contributions to fish habitat protection. *Canadian Journal of Fisheries and Aquatic Sciences* 48: 1326-33.

Scheffer, M., F. Westley, W.A. Brock, and M. Holmgren. 2002. Dynamic interaction of societies and ecosystems: Linking theories from ecology, economy and sociology. In *Panarchy: Understanding transformations in human and natural systems,* ed. L.H. Gunderson and C.S. Holling, 195-240. Washington, DC: Island Press.

Vandoremalen, J. 1998. Pushing the envelope of human rights through innovation and creativity in Aboriginal corrections. *Let's Talk* 23 (4): 18-19. http://www.npb-cnlc.gc.ca/infocntr/aborig_e.htm.

Weeks, N.C. 1986. National parks and Native peoples: A study of the experience of selected other jurisdictions with a view to co-operation in northern Canada. In *Contributions to circumpolar studies: Uppsala research reports in cultural anthropology,* ed. Hugh Beach, 7: 83-150. Uppsala, Sweden: University of Uppsala.

Westley, F. 2002. The devil in the dynamics: Adaptive management on the front lines. In *Panarchy: Understanding transformations in human and natural systems,* ed. L.H. Gunderson and C.S. Holling, 333-60. Washington, DC: Island Press.

Westley, F., S.R. Carpenter, W.A. Brock, C.S. Holling, and L.H. Gunderson. 2002. Why systems of people and nature are not just social and ecological systems. In *Panarchy: Understanding transformations in human and natural systems,* ed. L.H. Gunderson and C.S. Holling, 103-19. Washington, DC: Island Press.

Williams, M., and G. Humphrys. 2003. Introduction. In *Citizenship education and lifelong learning: Power and place,* ed. M. Williams and G. Humphrys, 1-18. New York: Nova Science Publishers.

Part 4: Tools

13

Novel Problems Require Novel Solutions: Innovation as an Outcome of Adaptive Co-Management

Gary P. Kofinas, Susan J. Herman, and Chanda Meek

Soon after signing the Canadian Porcupine Caribou Management Agreement in 1985, community representatives and agency managers of the western Canadian Arctic began establishing co-management protocols for joint community/agency decision making. Among the Porcupine Caribou Management Board's (PCMB) early tasks was the development of a "management plan" for the herd. Board members recognized that most agency-written wildlife management plans were finished, shelved, and of little value to future decision making. Working outside the typical conventions of bureaucratically organized resource management, members of the PCMB assessed the opportunity provided by the new arrangement to explore and test novel ideas for wildlife planning. The board members designed a structured yet dynamic planning process that would articulate the concerns of managers and resource users, identify possible solutions, and make explicit the accountability of government agencies for board-recommended actions (Table 13.1). The PCMB plan departed from previous wildlife management plans by using artwork and as few words as possible to facilitate communication with the greater public. When printed, the plan was formatted in a large size so that it would be difficult to file and forget. To improve the responsiveness of the co-management board, the PCMB approached its management plan as a living document, revisiting its prescribed actions every six months based on emerging conditions and reflections by the board on past experience (Kofinas 1998).

For more than a decade, this management plan served the PCMB as a scoping and tracking device for joint decision making and coordinated board/agency actions. In those transactions, the plan's structure provided space and time for reflection and responsiveness, and generated countless operational innovations that drew from individual and collective interests and the knowledge of those involved. After fifteen years, however, the use of the plan was discontinued. The terms of several First Nations' self-government and land claim agreements, settled in the 1990s, created inconsistencies

Table 13.1

Matrix guiding the Porcupine Caribou Management Board co-management plan process

Issue areas*	Physical condition	Herd population	Habitat	Co-management communications	Culture and education	Tourism activities	Industry activities
Status (current)	What is the current status of the caribou resource vis-à-vis the issue areas? What are the current programs to address past initiatives?						
Concerns about management area	Are there problems associated with the status of each area?						
Solutions to concerns	What should be done about those concerns?						
Actions for coming year and parties responsible	What are the action items and who will take responsibility for completing each item?						
Actions for year 2 and parties responsible	What are the action items and who will take responsibility for completing each item?						
Actions for year 3 and parties responsible	What are the action items and who will take responsibility for completing each item?						

* Issue areas include focused topics of discussion by the board. Addressing each topic, board members use the questions to assess the status of conditions and public concerns, and identify solutions and short- and long-term action items, with government agencies assigned responsibility for completing the tasks.
Source: Revised from Kofinas (1998, 191).

with the older 1985 caribou agreement. These inconsistencies involved the representation of those First Nations governments at the co-management table and new expectations of their greater role in caribou management. As the board works to reconcile these issues, its leadership expects that the management plan process will be revised, redesigned, and reinitiated in the future.

Innovation Solutions through Co-Management

The creation, implementation, and later rethinking of the strategic planning process of the PCMB is one of several examples from this and other co-management arrangements that suggests the need to explore more carefully the hypothesis that co-management provides unique opportunities for innovative thinking and action, and that the innovative outcomes of co-management are important elements for building social-ecological resilience. In this chapter, we examine innovation as an outcome of co-management with the intent of moving beyond an apparent schism among students of co-management – those who focus on the apparent power imbalances that persist after the implementation of formal co-management agreements (e.g., Nadasdy 1999, 2003; Natcher et al. 2005; Spak 2001) and those who focus on the functional contributions of power-sharing institutions to sustainability (e.g., Berkes and Folke 1998; Kendrick 2003; Pinkerton 1994). Moving beyond this schism, we assume that issues of power and questions of social-ecological resilience through power sharing are interrelated (Adger et al. 2005; Gunderson 1999). We also note that social learning and co-management innovation are in some cases the consequence of tense political conflict. Following from these assumptions, we seek to explore whether, how, and when innovation through co-management can enhance the adaptive capacity of social-ecological systems.

Understanding the factors that contribute to social-ecological resilience is especially critical in the northern latitudes, where climate change, the expansion of industrial development and human infrastructure, and socioeconomic, cultural, and political transformations are bringing new levels of uncertainty and complexity, resulting in a new set of challenges for local communities and resource managing agencies alike (Berkes and Jolly 2001; Chapin et al. 2004; Hinzman et al. 2005; Krupnik and Jolly 2002; Peterson and Johnson 1995). The conditions of rapid and unprecedented change in the North are well documented (ACIA 2004; AHDR 2004; Ulvevadet and Klokov 2004), but the mechanisms for humans' coping with rapid change are not well understood. Consequently, many northerners are investigating how best to study and organize for increasing complexity, greater uncertainty, and inevitable surprises (Kofinas et al. 2005).

Evidence shows that the capacities of local communities to be responsive to change, to interact and coordinate their actions with others, to learn from experience and incorporate feedback, and to revise strategies in a self-organized manner are important measures of sustainability (Folke et al. 2002). This responsiveness is achieved in part through the autonomy exercised by local subunits in experimenting with institutional rules for incorporating new information on environmental change and responding to that information (Dietz et al. 2003) and also through coordination of efforts and broad social learning networks at the regional scale. An effective adaptive co-management process, then, must facilitate not only the sharing of information across scales but also learning from those interactions in ways that stimulate new insights and new discoveries (Berkes 2002).

We recognize that achieving an effective adaptive co-management process is far from simple. The fusion of the concepts of *co-management* – the sharing of power between local communities of resource users and state governments in governance over natural resources (Pinkerton 1989a) – and *adaptive management* – a strategy for limiting, anticipating, and seeking the incidents of surprise (Lee 1993) – provide foundational thinking in understanding the potential and challenges associated with adaptive co-management (Berkes et al. 2005).

Given the high rate and novelty of global social-ecological change in the North (and beyond), we suggest that those involved in co-management must increasingly scan the environment to detect change, understand it in ways that are meaningful to decision making, and ultimately achieve robust policy responses that sustain the properties of social-ecological systems deemed desirable by society. Facing novel conditions, future co-managers must also think beyond political agendas and reflect more carefully about alternative solutions to novel problems and the processes by which novel solutions are readily discovered and tested. It is this aspect of adaptive co-management that concerns our chapter, particularly the process by which local communities and resource management agencies together generate, implement, and experiment with novel solutions to regional problems. We view innovative change through co-management as analogous to the survival of a firm in a highly uncertain and quickly changing economy. In making this analogy, however, we note that co-management arrangements are embedded in an environment of diverse sets of political actors who commonly employ contentious power strategies (Adger et al. 2005). How, then, are the combined conditions of cultural diversity, power sharing, and power politics of northern resource management related to the production of innovative solutions and social-ecological resilience?

Innovation Defined

Innovation is an act or process of inventing or introducing something new and/or taking a new approach to an old problem. The study of innovation is a vast and ongoing field that addresses the types and sources of innovation, the stages of its development, and its economic, technological, and social implications. Rogers' classic work (2003) of sociology on the diffusion of innovation, for example, considers the role of social networks in promoting innovation and its potential consequences, both positive and negative (e.g., the innovation by Nestlé of introducing the use of milk formula to mothers of the developing world, ostensibly to affect the problem of malnourished infants). The literature of business management is replete with prescriptions for how best to organize for innovation (e.g., HBS 2003), and much of the literature on sustainability of for-profit firms emphasizes the importance of innovation as a viable path for achieving a balanced ecological and economic human/environment relationship (Nattrass and Altomare 1999).

The interest in innovation related to natural resources management has focused almost exclusively on innovative forms of governance (i.e., new institutional arrangements) and how they foster greater public participation, conflict resolution, and problem solving (e.g., Wondolleck and Yaffee 2000). With co-management being an innovative institutional arrangement, we focus on the process by which community/state power sharing stimulates innovative thinking, ideas, and action. Following Pinkerton (1989b), we also assume that prospects for successful innovation through co-management are not automatic but situational and dependent upon a set of facilitating conditions.

We acknowledge from the outset that our investigation of innovation as an outcome of adaptive co-management is in its exploratory stage. As a result, we pose more questions than we answer. We hope, however, that our discussion will generate a greater interest in the study of innovation as a critical dimension of adaptive co-management and resilience building. Below, we identify several cases of innovative co-management outcomes, leading to a preliminary set of conditions that we hypothesize foster innovative co-management thinking and action.

Increased Complexity and Change Require Innovation

The need for innovation through co-management follows, in part, from two emergent conditions – increased complexity and rates of change (Figure 13.1). In a simple social-ecological system with a relatively stable and homogeneous set of actors and somewhat constant ecological conditions, the need for innovation is less critical. Some have asserted that innovation in "primitive societies" was perceived as a threat to group survival (see North 1991). In contrast, a system with multi-level interactions of local communities, state agencies, and non-governmental organizations (NGOs), along with multiple and interacting forces for change, adds complexity and a special demand for innovation. In the context of northern co-management, such complexity is increasing through processes of globalization (i.e., economic, technological, and political changes) that have led to greater interdependence of organizations involved in northern resource management, both vertically and horizontally. Whereas in the past local Arctic communities had to cope with the effects of change in relative isolation from others (for example, during the Little Ice Age of 1560-1850), today they face the combined and interacting effects of climate change, industrial development, greater participation in the cash economy, urbanization, and loss of indigenous language (AHDR 2004).

Figure 13.1

Rate of change and level of complexity in a system as related to the need for innovative thinking and action

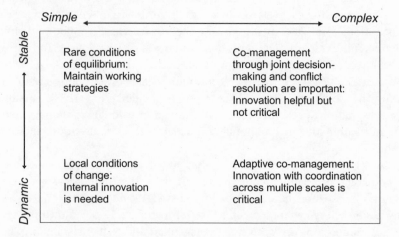

We argue that rapid change and complexity in the North pose special challenges, pressing those responsible for recommending, coordinating, and implementing resource policy to be skillful and creative in inventing novel solutions. Given the continued trajectories of change, we anticipate that future co-managers will have shorter response times and more limited evidence for understanding causality in ecosystems that are already associated with high uncertainty. Political conflicts will be more difficult to resolve as greater connectivity among groups provides more players the capacity to engage in the policy process. Decision makers will also face novel social-ecological change as multiple forces interact in complex and surprising ways. While there is no guarantee that innovation will always support resilience, it is clear that maintaining traditional approaches may result in the inability of local communities or residents of a region to cope with emergent conditions. The absence of innovation can result in the application of inappropriate and ineffective solutions, a lack of preparedness, and/or high social costs. The consequences may be significant and possibly fatal, leading to abrupt disorganization and even collapse (Tainter 1992).

The "Adaptive Cycle" of Gunderson and Holling (2002) provides a model of social-ecological change as it follows from phases of exploitation, release, reorganization, and renewal. Innovation in the Adaptive Cycle is described as a response by a social-ecological system in disorganization to establish stability when emergent change outpaces the effectiveness of former strategies. Collapse is avoided when innovation provides for reorganization while simultaneously retaining the critical governing properties of the system in question. In the event of collapse, innovation has the potential to restore and/or reorganize components of the former system. The model of change in the Adaptive Cycle is metaphorical, not deterministic, and thus raises the question of whether innovation must be cyclical or whether it is possible to facilitate and perhaps sustain the process of innovation through a set of adaptive institutional and organizational design principles. Interest in this question has also been the subject of studies focused on the "reinvention of government" and the role of innovation in public administration (Light 1998). Considered in the politically charged and culturally diverse context of northern co-management, we contemplate the extent to which innovation can be cultivated and sustained over time.

Examples of Innovative Outcomes from Co-Management

The Porcupine Caribou co-management planning process mentioned in the introductory vignette of this chapter provides one example of innovation by a co-management governing body that made an effort to self-organize for reflective learning through a structured process. As we find from a cursory accounting of several co-management innovations (Table 13.2), such novel solutions come from a number of sources, take several forms, and have a multiplicity of effects.

As noted, innovation can be *institutional,* changing rules in use. Dramatic institutional innovations are typically slow to emerge because of the high transformational costs associated with their negotiation and implementation (North 1990; Ostrom 1990), and these sorts of changes are not typically outcomes of co-management processes. More common and readily implemented in co-management are *operational* innovations, which establish new ways of doing business within an existing set of process rules, such as an innovation in a communication strategy for engaging communities. Holding meetings in local communities on a rotating basis (instead of urban centres where government offices are located) was an early innovation by several northern co-management boards in the 1980s, undertaken with the hope of building awareness and legitimacy of co-management in local communities and sensitizing agency managers to the concerns of communities through greater contact time. More subtle but important operational innovations in communication include the quarterly multilingual newspaper *Caribou News,* produced by the Beverly Qamanirjuaq Caribou Board, the monthly radio bulletins of the Porcupine Caribou Management Board, and the community tour of several Inuvialuit organizations and co-management bodies. While these innovations may seem like simple good business practices, they have the potential to produce a sea change for government

Table 13.2

Examples of innovation from co-management

Arrangement	Problem	Innovation	Implications
Yukon Fish and Wildlife Management Board	Conflict in traditional system of social control and state fish and wildlife enforcement approach Recognized need for better monitoring	Establishment of a "Game Guardians" program that creates a role for community members to provide oversight and guidance in harvesting practices and ecological monitoring, and leadership in stewardship	Stronger system of culturally appropriate social and ecological monitoring
Co-management of Porcupine Caribou through the Canadian Porcupine Caribou Management Agreement	Changing issues and concerns Accountability problem of follow-through with multiple tasks Limited institutional memory	A strategic planning approach to wildlife management that formally revisits co-management concerns, solutions, and actions assumed by responsible parties	Responsiveness to new problems Better accountability of parties Systematic issue tracking Enhanced institutional memory
Beverly Qamanirjuaq Caribou Management Board	Communications with communities about caribou issues and activities of caribou co-management process	Production of *Caribou News*, a newspaper produced quarterly in several languages that reports on status of herd and current issues	Higher profile of the board among some community members
Mayo Renewable Resource Council	Finding time to reflect on management decisions and plan ahead	Organization of annual river float trip for council members to discuss conditions and needed activities	Stronger sense of group for council members More thorough process of decision making
Fortymile Caribou Planning Group	Restoring a low caribou population with public opinion against a wolf control program	Use of alternative method for sterilization of alpha male and female wolves Relocation of wolf pups	Increased herd population Increased hunting opportunities

agencies, which often act in path-dependent ways and typically lack incentives to innovate (Light 1998). For example, before the period of co-management, the failure of many centralized resource regimes to regulate or even understand harvest patterns in the North was rarely mentioned as a reason to foster transparency in research and decision making.

Other forms of innovation are related to research and its technology. One of the most well known and classic examples of *technological/methodological* innovation in northern resource management is the Alaska Bowhead Whale case, in which indigenous whalers challenged the methods used previously for conducting whale stock assessments by suggesting new methods that would lead to more accurate results (Freeman 1989). The innovation of taking an existing technology (sonar technology) and applying it to a new situation (counting whales in Alaska) followed from the traditional knowledge of Iñupiat whalers and led to a higher stock assessment, a better understanding of whale ecology, and the eventual reversal of the International Whaling Commission's bowhead hunting moratorium on the Alaskan Iñupiat. This innovative thinking and action on the part of the Iñupiat and the scientists who co-managed the research eventually led to the formal establishment of the Alaska Eskimo Whaling Commission as the primary regulatory body for the Iñupiat whaling. Another example is the proposal for the sterilization of alpha wolf males to aid in the restoration of the international Fortymile Caribou Herd (Boerje and Gardner 2000). This novel idea was generated in 1995 through an international planning process for the herd that involved user groups, biologists, and managers who together searched for an alternative to a publicly unacceptable wolf kill program. The idea proved highly successful, with herd numbers continuing to increase (Susan Todd, pers. comm.).

Several examples of innovations appear in social-ecological monitoring, a key component of any adaptive management program. The community-based monitoring program of the Arctic Borderlands Ecological Co-op is a regional innovation facilitating the integration of local and science-based observations (Kofinas et al. 2002a). Another example is the "Game Guardians" program of Yukon First. The innovation here is a product of the Yukon Fish and Wildlife Management Board's deliberations, and it represents a departure from government wildlife enforcement policing in its use of local observers, who serve as resource stewards, educators, and monitors of local social behaviour.

As reflected in this short list of examples, innovation through co-management may be manifested as old ideas or practices applied to a new context or a mix of ideas from different points of view or bases of experience. It may arise in reaction to a crisis situation or from a hope of avoiding the crisis, or it may surface from sources of human creativity and inspiration. As described in the introductory vignette, innovation can also follow from structured processes designed to stimulate novel thinking and action. As we compiled these examples, we realized that we could just as easily provide a list of failures in power sharing and their absence of innovation. Given this variance in co-management experience, what then are the conditions facilitating innovation?

Co-Management Conditions Facilitating Innovative Outcomes

Drawing on these observations and other documented case studies, we provide a list of eight propositions that characterize the conditions that facilitate anywhere from modest to major innovation in co-management. Again, we note that this list is in no particular order; it is preliminary and intended to be a starting point for developing hypotheses for future research.

Periods of institutional transformation provide a unique opportunity for novel change

As noted in the introductory vignette, nascent institutions may be perceived by actors in a co-management arrangement as opportunities for change, prompting key individuals to think in new ways and consider adopting new approaches. In the PCMB case, the newfound freedom to innovate grew out of discussions by an agency board representative and a co-management board staff person who recognized that in order for co-management to meet its stated objectives, there would need to be a change in the systems of accountability, and that the best time for making such a change was at onset of the board's organizational life. These times of transition may come with few pre-established protocols and may be periods of perceived optimism.

Accessing institutional memory is a critical aspect of gleaning benefits during times of transition. As co-managers develop new protocols, they can consider new solutions based on the past mistakes of previous processes, such as those of agencies and communities working in isolation or in protracted conflict. Experiences of failure by government agency personnel who feel trapped in their conventional modes of doing business have been a source of innovation at these junctures (D. Urquhart, pers. comm.), as have the memories of community members who understand firsthand the consequence of top-down resource management failure.

Our general observations of co-management through time show that although processes can become routine and idea generation can stagnate, periodic upheavals can also occur, such as changes in personnel (i.e., changes in a board's membership and in community leadership), and these may bring with them a revision of rules and rethinking of conventions. Clearly, it is not desirable that formal institutions for co-management collapse and be reinvented regularly, but periodic change and reorganization can be helpful in capturing opportunities to improve the system through new approaches.

Interdependency and social capital are the basis for creative engagement
The interdependency of groups – i.e., sharing a common definition of the "problem domain" (Gray and Wood 1991) – and the presence of sufficient social capital to engage actors' creative energies in problem solving are facilitating conditions that are noted in the literature of co-management (Hanna et al. 1996; Singleton 1998). Agreement on basic management objectives by key actors is also noted as critical to the success of an adaptive management process (Lee 1999). As noted by institutionalists, social capital follows from specified property rights, which ensure that basic entitlements are secure. In the case of co-management, this security is found in the perceived legitimacy of power sharing and the effectiveness of the regime in addressing concerns. The willingness of individuals or groups to stand their ground in a debate, express their perspectives clearly, consider the problem from angles beyond their own interest, and concurrently trust that others will work towards a solution are basic conditions for innovative outcomes.

Appropriate levels of heterogeneity and productive friction provide for novel solutions
Whereas it is important to have sufficient levels of social capital among actors, we note that both heterogeneity and appropriate levels of conflict are also important. This assertion is significant when we consider that institutional economists (e.g., Coase 1960; Williamson 1993) explain human decision making in terms of transaction costs and cost avoidance, and co-management scholars focus on the cultivation of social capital as a means of lowering those costs (Hanna 1994; Taylor and Singleton 1993). Elsewhere, Kofinas (1998) argued that the transaction costs of northern wildlife co-management are considerable for local communities, and these costs may also be transformational, reshaping traditional community management systems into ones that are more bureaucratic and more dependent on western science (Kofinas 2005; Nadasdy 1999). Those arguments, however, do not account for how conflict may have benefits in the co-production of innovative solutions.

Here we suggest that the costs of power sharing may also come with a type of "productive friction" that accelerates innovation through the interaction of differing perspectives (Brown and Hagel 2005). Brown (1983) studied the phenomenon of conflict at the inter-organizational interface to consider how varying levels of conflict may have different results, ranging from cultural homogenization to full dysfunction. Following this assessment, we view innovation from co-management as resulting in part from the healthy tension of differing worldviews, interests, and needs. An active program of public participation and active engagement with agencies by those operating at the board level are important in generating such conflict and maintaining that healthy tension. Conversely, co-management boards that isolate themselves from public debate may be less inspired to engage in creative thinking and, as a result, may be less resourceful in problem solving.

A culture that is open to new ideas and that promotes risk taking promotes innovation

The cultural dimensions of innovation include groups' norms and beliefs about taking risks. Mahler (1997) argues that the more ambiguous a particular problem, the more organizational culture will affect social learning and adaptation geared to overcome it. Given the high levels of ambiguity that typically surround northern social-ecological problems, we view the cultural dimension of risk taking as a key variable. When the work environment of a partner organization celebrates and rewards risk taking instead of penalizing failure, experimental thinking is more likely to lead to innovation (Light 1998).

Organizational culture is relevant to state management agencies as well as traditional indigenous communities. For example, state agencies may have strong informal organizational norms limiting the consideration of indigenous knowledge as a legitimate source of information (Pomeroy and Berkes 1997). Similarly, local communities may focus exclusively on their traditional ways to the exclusion of novel and viable scientifically based approaches. Norms for communication within and between groups are a key aspect of this process, affecting the willingness and manner in which a group interacts with non-group members. The willingness to consider information and ideas across organizational boundaries, the willingness to look at novel ideas open-mindedly, the willingness to keep options open long enough to generate sufficient ideas all depend on a culture in which key stakeholder groups are more invested in problem solving than in maintaining their own status.

The vision and skill of individuals (leaders) promote and guide innovative problem solving

Leadership is a critical variable in resource management (Wondolleck and Yaffee 2000), ecosystem co-management (Pinkerton 1997), and government and non-profit innovation (Light 1998). While institutions may design the incentives, the ability of leaders to see beyond the known and consider the unexplored may be equally important (Light 1998). Leadership for innovation is also related to managing a process that seeks a balance between structure and freedom. For example, the directives of a co-management board chairperson when running a meeting may limit or enhance the nature of discussions and the production of novel ideas. A leader's wisdom in knowing when to abandon old models and champion new ones, and possession of the transformational skills needed to sell novel ideas to those within a co-management process, may also prove vital. For example, the PCMB co-management planning process initially met with great resistance from a high-status and powerful agency manager, who was fearful that the new approach would be received by colleagues and the greater public as folly, thus threatening his and his agency's credibility. It was only through the skillful manoeuvring and negotiations of key entrepreneurs of co-management that the innovative management plan was accepted, ultimately implemented, and later hailed in the region as an important contribution to co-management.

Finding endorsement from opinion leaders outside the direct co-management process may also be critical. In some cases, informal leadership by individuals who maintain the trust of all participants and do not have a stake in any particular organization's interest (e.g., convenors, support staff, and consultants) can play a prominent and influential role in championing a particular innovation to realization. Leaders who have a vested interest can also develop quid quo pro arrangements among organizations that foster the interests of one without undermining the interests of the others. The ability of leaders to communicate novel ideas in a way that makes the groups feel ownership contributes to the acceptance and ultimate success of an innovation.

Innovation and reflective learning take time

The day-to-day work of co-management does not stop while a group innovates, yet feedback learning by co-managers requires an allocation of time during which practitioners can reflect on experience and contemplate alternative actions. For most northern co-management boards, there is little time for reflection because of crowded meeting agendas, multiple mandates, and multiple impending political crises. It takes time to determine what the actual problems are and to develop alternative solutions. It takes additional time to implement and then evaluate the success of those ideas, in order to innovate further. The regular work must continue concurrently with the work of being creative in identifying problems and solutions. Systems need to be developed to allot adequate time for these dual tracks to work successfully. In such conditions, time for innovation may need to be found in periodic pauses from the day-to-day decision making, or there may be a need for alternative structures such as a planning retreat or a separate task force to develop initial innovations that can later be refined at the full board and public review levels. The planning process of the PCMB included a one- to two-day meeting every three years to scan the environment, discuss emergent conditions, review current status, generate concerns and solutions, and assign action items. During most two-day workshops, there were moans of frustration by board members who felt that the board's time on the plan was not well spent and that other issues were more pressing. Additional time was needed at regular meetings to track the status of action items.

To ensure focused attention by members, the Renewal Resource Council of Mayo, Yukon, has instituted a process of reflective action by taking all members on an annual river trip to be close to the land while discussing the council's future plans and actions. Co-management processes that do not allot adequate time for innovation (in the interests of saving time) may paradoxically consume greater time grappling with serious problems that could have otherwise been avoided.

Decision support tools stimulate creative thinking about novel alternatives

Decision support tools are structured systems that guide thinking and facilitate problem solving (e.g., Chapter 15). Use of brainstorming, Delphi models, scenarios, interactive gaming, and simulation models are examples of tools that offer the possibility of stimulating innovation in co-management. Using computer simulation models for decision support is a common practice in adaptive management but is not employed regularly in northern wildlife co-management processes, for good reason. Computational models are overly mechanistic and can be perceived as black boxes that provoke fear among many and come with the potential of alienating and disempowering local community members.

In 2002, university researchers used simulation models of the Porcupine Caribou herd population with PCMB members and additional harvesters from Alaska to discuss possible futures under conditions of a rapidly declining herd (Kofinas et al. 2002b). The timing of the workshop coincided with reports that the herd had declined dramatically since 1989. The rich discussions about the need for research to address data gaps of the model and to assess the population status of the herd and future trajectories of population levels were followed by a gaming exercise in which three scenarios projected a continued decrease of the herd. As a part of that exercise, small groups were asked to develop and evaluate policy responses. Through this gaming exercise, users and managers of the region discussed, for the first time, specifics of how the board would respond to a caribou population crash crisis. The results of the gaming scenarios were striking, with groups of participants producing sets of novel policy solutions addressing education, research, and methods of allocation, and discussing the implications of those policies for communities and management agencies.

When properly delivered, decision support tools have the potential to capture the imagination of a group, provide mental pathways for managing crisis, and stimulate innovative responses. In many respects, the use of formal computer models in adaptive co-management is similar to the management planning of the PCMB in providing a structured process for generating innovative policy alternatives and considering their implications. Clearly, more research is needed in the application of decision support tools, especially in a setting that involves indigenous subsistence harvesters and professional resource managers.

Prior experience with successful innovation builds confidence to experiment and learn in the future

Ultimately, it may be the ongoing experience of co-managers and the public at large with successful innovation that makes the most significant difference, by building the confidence and capacity of those involved to try new things and experiment creatively again in the future. Where innovations fail or succeed only partially, there must be sufficient stock taking, as well as support and acknowledgment of the learning involved in such situations. In this respect, engagement in an adaptive co-management process that strives towards innovation requires a type of willingness that differs from the actors' trust in cooperating in problem solving, as described in the first condition (interdependency and social capital are foundational requirements) since it also requires a willingness to be creative and reflect openly on past experience to derive lessons for the future.

With this final proposition, we suggest a possible feedback effect – that in time, co-managers will begin to identify with the novelty of their problem solving, and that groups that are more distant to co-management decision making may be less resistant to innovative ideas. How and when these changes in attitude may emerge in adaptive co-management is another topic worthy of investigation.

Discussion

We have explored the hypothesis that co-management produces innovative outcomes and that the degree of innovation depends on a number of conditions; we have also argued that the need for innovation is a consequence of increasing social-ecological complexity and rapid change. The production of innovative ideas and actions through formal co-management are only parts of an adaptive co-management process that includes testing of those ideas and reflection on their performance. While much of the discussion in this chapter has focused on board-level transactions and how they may generate novel solutions, adaptive co-management involves broader social learning networks or "communities of practice" (Cummings and Zee 2005) that are critical to the resilience of a social-ecological system. We have also argued that embedded in this process is the dialectic of power politics and power sharing, two interacting realities of co-management that need to be considered in tandem. As we have noted, differing perspectives and conflict interacting on a foundation of social capital are important elements in the production of innovation, but not all innovations are appropriate or beneficial for all groups. As agencies, communities, and co-management boards consider innovation that ventures closer to social engineering than adaptation and common problem solving, they will face moral and ethical hazards, which demand introspection and careful evaluation (Kofinas 2005).

The work presented in this chapter is only a small beginning of the exploration that is needed. We have not compared the relative potency of each proposition. We have not considered phases of innovation thinking, reflection, and action. We have not considered how co-management arrangements in their early to later stages of development differ in their capacity to retain their creative thinking and, conversely, the extent to which they are likely to become routinized in new patterns, becoming more rigid and less innovative over time. Nor have we considered the lateral diffusions of innovations that commonly occur across regimes throughout the North and beyond. As well, we have neither explored the factors that stimulate partner organizations (agencies or communities) to be open to innovation and idea testing, nor considered how innovation may support the testing of models and questioning of underlying assumptions of management, which are fundamental to adaptive management.

As we move forward with future research in this area, however, we propose that the production of innovation through co-management be a significant indicator in assessing the effectiveness of adaptive co-management. Significant innovation will provide evidence that actors are working to resolve novel problems in imaginative ways, whereas limited to no innovation may be equally telling, identifying when a co-management regime is in a state of stagnation or protracted unproductive conflict.

Our exploration brings us back to the question of whether innovation can be sustained or whether it is inherently part of a cyclical adaptive process. We conclude that it is both – that human responsiveness to emergent problems is alerted through the waxing and waning of impending crisis, while the quality of our responses is enhanced by the development of our capacity to innovate.

Conclusion

As rapid changes confront residents of the higher latitudes, resource management decision makers at all levels will increasingly face novel conditions that require novel solutions. Conditions of rapid social, ecological, technical, and economic change allow limited time to address emergent problems or test in systematic ways for the "right solution." At the heart of our interest in co-management innovation is the extent to which formal co-management can address this increasingly complex set of challenges. Today formal co-management arrangements are common in the northern regions of North America and, when effective, they are key components of an adaptive co-management learning network. Examples of innovative thinking and action through co-management are evident, and vary widely in their sources, types, and effects. The Porcupine Caribou Management Board management plan is one example in which a co-management board intentionally institutionalized a reflective learning process that stimulated innovative outcomes. The suspension of the management planning process fifteen years later illustrates that these processes, even when used and well regarded, can be abandoned as structural, political, economic, and social problems dictate.

In this chapter, we drew on several cases to generate eight proposed conditions that facilitate innovation. We view this set as a starting point and encourage more research that both compares experiences in co-management innovation and assesses adaptive co-management processes at multiple levels. We leave unanswered the question of how rapid change and increased complexity will affect northerners' ability to engage in innovative thinking and action. We only recognize that the need is likely to increase rather than abate, and since co-management itself was in the recent past a dramatic and extraordinary innovation, we anticipate continued research, lively debate, and informative results.

Acknowledgments
We wish to thank the US National Science Foundation for supporing this research and the Porcupine Caribou Management Board for its help with the management planning case study. This chapter benefited from the helpful comments of Paul Nadasdy, Evelyn Pinkerton, the editors of this volume, and members of the Adaptive Co-Management Symposium in Waterloo in 2005. Special thanks also to Doug Urquhart and Susan Todd for their co-management insights. The ideas in this chapter are solely those of the authors.

References
ACIA (Arctic Climate Impact Assessment). 2004. *Impacts of a warming Arctic: Arctic Climate Impact Assessment.* Cambridge: Cambridge University Press.

Adger, W.N., K. Brown, and E.L. Tompkins. 2005. The political economy of cross-scale networks in resource co-management. *Ecology and Society* 10: 9. http://www.ecologyandsociety.org/vol10/iss12/art19/.

AHDR (Arctic Human Development Report). 2004. Akureyri, Stefansson Arctic Institute.

Berkes, F. 2002. Cross-scale institutional linkages: Perspectives from the bottom up. In *The drama of the commons,* ed. E. Ostrom, T. Dietz, N. Dolsak, P.C. Stern, S. Stonich, and E.U. Weber, 293-321. Washington, DC: National Academy Press.

Berkes, F., and C. Folke. 1998. Linking social and ecological systems for resilience and sustainability. In *Linking social and ecological systems: Management practices and social mechanisms for building resilience,* ed. F. Berkes and C. Folke, 1-25. Cambridge: Cambridge University Press.

Berkes, F., and D. Jolly. 2001. Adapting to climate change: Social-ecological resilience in a Canadian Western Arctic community. *Conservation Ecology* 5 (2): 18. http://www.ecologyandsociety.org/vol5/iss2/art18/.

Berkes, F., R. Huebert, H. Fast, M. Manseau, and A. Diduck, eds. 2005. *Breaking ice: Renewable resource and ocean management in the Canadian North.* Calgary: University of Calgary Press.

Boerje, R.D., and C.L. Gardner. 2000. The Fortymile caribou herd: Novel proposed management and relevant biology 1992-1997. *Rangifer* 12: 17-38.

Brown, D.L. 1983. *Managing conflict at organizational interfaces.* Reading, MA: Addison-Wesley.

Brown, J.S., and J. Hagel III. 2005. Productive friction: How difficult business partnerships can accelerate innovation. *Harvard Business Review* (February): 82-91.

Chapin, F.S.I., G. Peterson, F. Berkes, T.V. Callaghan, P. Angelstam, M. Apps, C. Beier, et al. 2004. Resilience and vulnerability of northern regions to social and environmental change. *Ambio* 33: 344-49.

Coase, R.H. 1960. The problem of social cost. *Journal of Law and Economics* 3: 1-44.

Cummings, S., and A.V. Zee. 2005. Communities of practice and networks: Reviewing two perspectives on social learning. *KM4D Journal* 1: 8-22.

Dietz, T., E. Ostrom, and P.C. Stern. 2003. The struggle to govern the commons. *Science* 302: 1907-12.

Folke, C., S. Carpenter, T. Elmqvist, L. Gunderson, C.S. Holling, B. Walker, J. Bengtsson, et al. 2002. *Resilience and sustainable development: Building adaptive capacity in a world of transformations.* International Council for Science, ICSU Series on Science for Sustainable Development, no. 3. http://www.sou.gov.se/mvb/pdf/resiliens.pdf.

Freeman, M.M.R. 1989. The Alaska Eskimo Whaling Commission: Successful co-management under extreme conditions. In *Co-operative management of local fisheries: New directions for improved management and community development,* ed. E. Pinkerton, 137-54. Vancouver: UBC Press.

Gray, B., and D.J. Wood. 1991. Collaborative alliances: Moving from practice to theory. *Journal of Applied Behavioral Sciences* 27: 3-22.

Gunderson, L. 1999. Resilience, flexibility and adaptive management: Antidotes for spurious certitude? *Conservation Ecology* 3 (1): 7. http://www.ecologyandsociety.org/vol3/iss1/art7/.

Gunderson, L.H., and C.S. Holling, eds. 2002. *Panarchy: Understanding transformations in human and natural systems.* Washington, DC: Island Press.

Hanna, S. 1994. Co-management. In *Limiting access to marine fisheries: Keeping the focus on conservation,* ed. K.L. Gimbel, 233-42. Washington, DC: Center for Marine Conservation; World Wildlife Fund US.

Hanna, S.S., C. Folke, and K.-G. Maler. 1996. *Rights to nature: Ecological, economic, cultural, and political principles of institutions for the environment.* Washington, DC: Island Press.

HBS (Harvard Business School). 2003. Managing creativity and innovation. Boston: Harvard Business School Press.

Hinzman, L., N. Bettez, F.S. Chapin, M. Dyurgerov, C. Fastie, B. Griffith, R.D. Hollister, A. Hope, H.P. Huntington, et al. 2005. Evidence and implications of recent climate change in terrestrial regions of the Arctic. *Climate Change* 72 (3): 251-98.

Kendrick, A. 2003. Caribou co-management in Northern Canada: Fostering multiple ways of learning. In *Navigating social-ecological systems: Building resilience for complexity and change,* ed. F. Berkes, J. Colding, and C. Folke, 241-68. Cambridge: Cambridge University Press.

Kofinas, G. 1998. The costs of power sharing: Community involvement in Canadian Porcupine Caribou co-management. PhD dissertation, University of British Columbia.

–. 2005. Hunters and researchers at the co-management interface: Emergent dilemmas and the problem of legitimacy in power sharing. *Anthropologica* 47 (2): 179-96.

Kofinas, G., Aklavik, Arctic Village, Old Crow, and F. McPherson. 2002a. Community contributions to ecological monitoring: Knowledge co-production in the US-Canada Arctic borderlands. In *The earth is faster now: Indigenous observations of Arctic environmental change,* ed. I. Krupnik, and D. Jolly, 54-91. Fairbanks: ARCUS.

Kofinas, G., C. Nicolson, M. Berman, and P. McNeil. 2002b. Proceedings of a workshop on caribou harvesting strategies and sustainability, Inuvik, NT, April 15-16, 2002. NSF Sustainability of Arctic Communities Project (Phase II).

Kofinas, G., B. Forbes, F. Berkes, M. Berman, H. Beach, T. Chapin, Y. Csonka, et al. 2005. A research plan for the study of rapid change, resilience and vulnerability in social-ecological systems of the Arctic. *CPR Digest of the International Association for the Study of Common Property* (June): 1-7.

Krupnik, I., and D. Jolly, eds. 2002. *The earth is faster now: Indigenous observations of Arctic environmental change.* Fairbanks: ARCUS.

Lee, K.N. 1993. *Compass and gyroscope: Integrating science and politics for the environment.* Washington, DC: Island Press.

–. 1999. Appraising adaptive management. *Conservation Ecology* 3 (2): 3. http://www.ecologyandsociety.org/vol3/iss2/art3/.

Light, P.C. 1998. *Sustaining innovation: Creating nonprofit and government organizations that innovate naturally.* San Francisco: Jossey-Bass.

Mahler, J. 1997. Influences of organizational culture on learning in public agencies. *Journal of Public Administration Research and Theory* 7: 519-40.

Nadasdy, P. 1999. The politics of TEK: Power and the "Integration" of knowledge. *Arctic Anthropology* 36: 1-18.

–. 2003. *Hunters and bureaucrats: Power, knowledge, and Aboriginal-state relations in the southwest Yukon.* Vancouver: UBC Press.

Natcher, D.C., S. Davis, and C.G. Hickey. 2005. Co-management: Managing relationships, not resources. *Human Organization* 64: 240-50.

Nattrass, B., and M. Altomare. 1999. *The natural step for business: Wealth, ecology and the evolutionary corporation.* Gabriola Island, BC: New Society Publishers.

North, D.C. 1990. *Institutions, institutional change and economic performance.* New York: Cambridge University Press.

–. 1991. Institutions. *Journal of Economic Perspectives* 5: 97-112.

Ostrom, E. 1990. *Governing the commons: The evolution of institutions for collective action.* Cambridge: Cambridge University Press.

Peterson, D.L., and D.R. Johnson. 1995. Human ecology and climate change at northern latitudes. In *Human ecology and climate change: People and resources in the Far North,* ed. D.L. Peterson and D.R. Johnson, 3-14. Washington, DC: Taylor and Francis.

Pinkerton, E. 1989a. *Co-operative management of local fisheries: New directions for improved management and community development.* Vancouver: UBC Press.

–. 1989b. Introduction: Attaining better fisheries management through co-management – prospects, problems, and propositions. In *Co-operative management of local fisheries: New directions for improved management and community development,* ed. E. Pinkerton, 3-33. Vancouver: UBC Press.

–. 1994. Summary and conclusions. In *Folk management in the world's fisheries,* ed. C.L. Dyer and J.R. McGoodwin, 317-37. Niwot: University Press of Colorado.

Pinkerton, E.W., D. Moore, and F. Fortier. 1997. A model for First Nation leadership in multi-party stewardship of watersheds and their fisheries. In *Royal Commission on Aboriginal Peoples. For seven generations: An information legacy of the Royal Commission on Aboriginal peoples.* Ottawa: Libraxus. [CD-ROM].

Pomeroy, R.S., and F. Berkes. 1997. Two to tango: The role of government in fisheries co-management. *Marine Policy* 21: 465-80.

Rogers, E.M. 2003. *Diffusion of innovations.* New York: Free Press.

Singleton, S. 1998. *Constructing cooperation: The evolution of institutions of comanagement.* Ann Arbor: University of Michigan Press.

Spak, S. 2001. *Canadian resource co-management boards and their relationship to indigenous knowledge: Two case studies.* Toronto: University of Toronto.

Tainter, J.A. 1992. *The collapse of complex societies.* Cambridge: Cambridge University Press.

Taylor, M., and S. Singleton. 1993. The communal resource: Transaction costs and the solution of collective action problems. *Politics and Society* 21: 195-214.

Ulvevadet, B., and K. Klokov. 2004. *Family-based reindeer herding and hunting economies, and the status and management of wild reindeer/caribou populations: A report to the Sustainable Development Working Group of the Arctic Council.* Tromsø, Norway: Centre for Saami Studies, University of Tromsø.

Williamson, O.E. 1993. Transaction cost economics and organizational theory. *Industrial and Corporate Change* 2: 107-55.

Wondolleck, J.M. and S.L. Yaffee. 2000. *Making collaboration work: Lessons from innovation in natural resource management.* Washington, DC: Island Press.

14

The Role of Vision in Framing Adaptive Co-Management Processes: Lessons from Kristianstads Vattenrike, Southern Sweden

Per Olsson

Adaptive co-management relies on collaboration among a diverse set of actors operating through social networks. These collaborations cross social and political levels, from local users to municipalities, to regional and national or supranational organizations. In this chapter, I use the definition of adaptive co-management by Olsson and colleagues (2004a), which is developed from the work of Folke and colleagues (2003) and Gadgil and colleagues (2000). It states that adaptive co-management systems are tailored to specific places and situations and supported by, and working with, various organizations at different levels. Adaptive co-management combines the dynamic learning characteristic of adaptive management with the linkage characteristic of collaborative management.

These systems draw on a variety of sources of information and knowledge and avoid set prescriptions of management that may be superimposed on a particular place, situation, or context. Important components of adaptive co-management are monitoring, interpreting, and responding to ecosystem feedback (Folke et al. 2003). Adaptive co-management allows for a participatory approach to management that gives local resource users the opportunity to influence decisions regarding the future of the environment in which they live and operate (Borrini-Feyerabend et al. 2004). It also supports flexible organizations and institutions that can strengthen our capacity to deal with uncertainty and change and to sustain ecosystem services.

Adaptive governance enables adaptive co-management of social-ecological systems (Folke et al. 2005). Using the distinction between management and governance made by Stoker (1998) and Lee (2003), "management" is about strategies for dealing with ecosystems, whereas "governance" addresses the broader social contexts of creating the conditions for social coordination that enable adaptive co-management. Adaptive governance relies on polycentric institutional arrangements, which are nested, quasi-autonomous decision-making units operating at multiple scales (Ostrom 1996; McGinnis 1999; Dietz et al. 2003). Spanning local to higher organizational levels, polycentric institutions provide a balance between decentralized and centralized control (Imperial 1999). Lee (2003) refers to such adaptive systems of governance as the "new governance," and defines it as a form of social coordination in which actions are coordinated voluntarily by individuals and organizations with self-organizing and self-enforcing capabilities.

Adaptive governance relies on networks that connect individuals, organizations, agencies, and institutions at multiple organizational levels (Folke et al. 2005). Boyle and colleagues (2001) have suggested a triad of activities, where governance is the process of resolving trade-offs and providing a vision and direction for sustainability, management is the realization of this vision, and monitoring provides feedback and synthesizes the observations to a narrative of how the situation has emerged and might unfold in the future.

In this chapter, I focus on the role of visioning processes in framing and directing adaptive co-management of Kristianstads Vattenrike, a wetland landscape in southern Sweden. Others have addressed the role of vision in nature conservation (Wiesman et al. 2005), natural resource collaborations (Kofinas and Griggs 1996; Wondolleck and Yaffee 2000; Walker and Hurley 2004), and environmental planning (Singleton 2002), and assessments (Armitage 2005). I also focus on the role of visioning in transforming the social-ecological system of Kristianstads Vattenrike towards adaptive governance that enabled adaptive co-management. Others address the role of vision in transformative change towards ecosystem management (Westley 1995; Danter et al. 2000) and watershed management (Bressers and Kuks 2004).

The capacity to adapt to and shape change is an important component of social-ecological system resilience (Berkes et al. 2003). Olsson and colleagues (2004a) have proposed that adaptive co-management of ecosystems has the potential to build resilience in social-ecological systems. Social-ecological resilience refers to the capacity of these systems to absorb disturbance and reorganize while undergoing change so as to retain essentially the same function, structure, identity, and feedbacks (Walker et al. 2004). The ability to reorganize and renew a desired social-ecological system state following disturbance and change strongly depends on the states and dynamics at scales above and below (Gunderson and Holling 2002). Hence, resilience reflects the degree to which a social-ecological system is capable of self-organization, and the degree to which the system can build and increase the capacity for learning and adaptation (Carpenter et al. 2001). In this sense, social features of governance systems can provide sources of resilience for adaptive co-management systems.

In this chapter, I analyze visioning processes in two key components of social-ecological resilience: *adaptability* and *transformability*. In a social-ecological system with high adaptability, actors have the capacity to sustain the system in desired trajectories in response to changing conditions and disturbance events. Transformability is the capacity to create a fundamentally new system when ecological, economic, or social (including political) conditions make the existing system untenable (Walker et al. 2004). Transformability means defining and creating novel system configurations by introducing new components and ways of governing social-ecological systems, thereby changing the state variables, and often the scales of key cycles, that define the system. Transformations fundamentally change structures and processes that alternate feedback loops in social-ecological systems.

I begin with a brief background of the social-ecological system of Kristianstads Vattenrike. Sections that follow trace the development of the adaptive co-management approach for the area. The discussion argues that visioning and adaptability can help sustain the system in a desired trajectory of adaptive co-management and provide a social source of resilience in social-ecological systems. It describes how visioning relates to transformability and how it helped change the social features of the governance system at one scale so that adaptive co-management was enabled at another scale.

The Study Area: Kristianstads Vattenrike

The town of Kristianstad is situated in northeast Scania County (Skåne Län), southern Sweden. The town is the administrative centre of the Municipality of Kristianstad, with 73,000 inhabitants. The vast wetlands surrounding the town, also known as Kristianstads Vattenrike, has long been appreciated for its cultural and natural values. Kristianstads Vattenrike roughly translates as "the Kristianstad Water Realm," but *rike* also means riches; the double meaning of the title both defines the catchment area and reflects its rich natural values. Kristianstads Vattenrike covers an area of 110,000 hectares. Since June 2005, it has been a Biosphere Reserve under the Man and the Biosphere Programme of the United Nations Educational, Scientific and Cultural Organization (UNESCO).

The social-ecological system of Kristianstads Vattenrike is defined by hydrological and political borders. It includes the Helgeå River catchment area and the coastal regions of Hanö Bay within the Municipality of Kristianstad (Figure 14.1). The natural hydrological regime of the lower Helgeå River is highly dynamic, with an annual average water level fluctuation of 1.4 metres in central Kristianstad, which creates extensive floodplains. Kristianstads Vattenrike is therefore characterized by wet ecosystems, including rivers, streams, wetlands, and lakes. There are also other ecosystems, including sandy grasslands and beech forests.

Besides providing ecosystem services such as high biodiversity, unique habitats, and aesthetic landscape, it is one of Sweden's most productive agricultural areas. It also holds the largest groundwater reserve in northern Europe, which is used for drinking water and irrigation. Other ecosystem

Figure 14.1

The lower Helgeå River catchment, showing the Ramsar Convention Site, Kristianstads Vattenrike, and the Municipality of Kristianstad

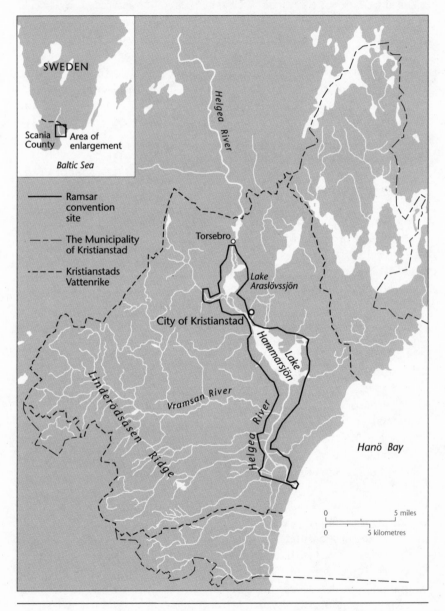

services include flood buffering, nutrient retention, recreation, fodder production for farm animals, pollination, timber production, meat production, fish production, and seed dispersal (L. Schultz et al., 2007).

The abundance of ecosystem services generated in the area is also reflected in the range of actors representing different interests and land uses. They include the County Administrative Board, Kristianstad University, the Kristianstad Tourism Board, World Wildlife Fund Sweden, local environmental conservation organizations, the Bird Society of Northeastern Scania, tour operators, individual landowners, local fishing and hunting associations, and farmers' associations (L. Schultz et al., 2007). There are real and potential conflicts among different users of ecosystem services.

Adaptive Co-Management in Kristianstads Vattenrike

Since 1989, a flexible collaborative approach to the management of the values of Kristianstads Vattenrike has been in place. It promotes management that treats humans as part of ecosystems and includes social, economic, and ecological dimensions. The local organization Ecomuseum Kristianstads Vattenrike (EKV) plays a key role as a facilitator and coordinator of local collaboration processes, which involve international associations, national, regional, and local authorities, researchers, non-governmental organizations, and landowners (Hahn et al. 2006). The EKV was established in 1989 to support the Municipality of Kristianstad in managing Kristianstads Vattenrike, which was defined as the area of focus for the new management approach. The EKV has a staff of five and is part of the municipality's organization. It reports directly to the municipal executive board and is similar to a municipal administration, but has no power to make or enforce formal rules. It relies on several funding sources, including the Municipality of Kristianstad, the County Administrative Board, and the Swedish Environmental Protection Agency. The EKV is also involved in initiating and conducting inventories and producing follow-up reports and updates for specific areas. It is also a body to which proposed measures for the area are referred for consideration. The EKV has also played a vital role in developing a shared vision for the system, as described in the next section.

The EKV provides leadership for social coordination by visioning, maintaining, and facilitating key conditions for adaptive co-management. At the moment, it coordinates and facilitates approximately twenty projects in Kristianstads Vattenrike. It directs the adaptive co-management of Kristianstads Vattenrike by a vision that is "to preserve and develop the natural and cultural values of Kristianstads Vattenrike, while at the same time making careful and sustainable use of these values, and thus set a good example that can help promote the region." Key conditions include trust building, sense making, identification of common interests, learning, vertical and/or horizontal collaboration, and conflict management (Hahn et al.

2006). In this way, the EKV serves as a bridging organization, facilitating collaborations between local actors and between local actors and non-governmental and governmental bodies at other organizational levels. As an integral part of the adaptive governance of social-ecological systems, bridging organizations such as the EKV provide social incentives by rewarding and creating space for collaboration, value formation, and innovation (Hahn et al. 2006).

Adaptive co-management in Kristianstads Vattenrike builds on voluntary participation. There are no new rules or legislation created specifically for the adaptive co-management processes in order to regulate the interaction between people or force people to participate. Instead, the EKV has served to change people's perceptions and behaviours and has attained collaboration through encouragement and engagement. This creates a challenge since there are always people who are opposed to adapting new management approaches and changing their behaviour. The EKV has therefore developed a set of strategies for initiating collaboration processes.

For example, the wetlands around the City of Kristianstad are important resting sites for migrating cranes. In the spring, the arrival of the cranes often coincides with the farmers' spring tillage and the cranes often cause damage to the crops, especially potatoes. In the late 1990s, the crane population increased in Kristianstads Vattenrike, and one of the EKV staff observed a potential conflict of interests and a pending crisis down the road. Through his frequent contact with farmers, he had observed a growing discontent. To forestall the conflict and collaboratively seek solutions, the EKV initiated and facilitated the formation of the "Crane Group." This group consists of local landowners and farmers and representatives from the Swedish Farmers' Federation, the Bird Society of Northeastern Scania, the Swedish Nature Conservancy, the Municipality of Kristianstad (through the EKV), and the County Administrative Board. A first meeting between the Bird Society of Northeastern Scania and the EKV took place in October 1997. It was decided to contact farmers from Lake Hornborgarsjön and invite them to Kristianstads Vattenrike.

Lake Hornborgarsjön is one of the most popular birdwatching places in Sweden, and residents have experience of how cranes and farmers can co-exist and how to minimize crop damage. At a meeting in December 1997, farmers from the lake presented their experiences, and strategies for Kristianstad were discussed. Three local farmers participated, including the chairman of the local division of the Federation of Swedish Farmers (LRF), together with three representatives from the Bird Society of Northeastern Scania and two from the EKV. The Crane Group was formed at this meeting. Since then, the Crane Group has collaboratively sought solutions to the problem and has engaged in various activities to gain new knowledge, including, in 2002, a study trip to the Rügen-Bock area of north Germany which is a popular resting site for cranes. It has also explored different ways to feed the cranes at specific sites. The group monitors the cranes and has produced a list of recommendations for farmers if cranes land on their fields. It has appointed a contact person who can provide devices to frighten cranes and assess damage.

As illustrated by this example, the EKV starts with individuals who are open to new ideas and are genuinely interested in and positively disposed towards the project. Hence, the EKV is careful about who is invited to participate in the early stage of a project. It avoids bringing people together for large unconditional meetings, since there is a genuine risk that sensitive issues will be aired and that different interests and stakeholders will position themselves against each other, causing a deadlock. After the first stage of bringing positive actors together and starting the project, the process is expanded gradually and others are invited. The EKV staff is aware that sooner or later they have to face the more negative actors, and it is easier if their peers who are already on board convince them. The EKV staff argues that it is better to show a real example of the processes that they want to create than to describe them in theory to the actors. The vision is used as a guiding star and as a tool for engaging and encouraging actors to participate in these processes.

The strategy of starting small and expanding gradually that is used by the EKV in specific projects to solve particular problems is also used to expand the adaptive co-management processes to incorporate new projects in Kristianstads Vattenrike. Although the initial work focused primarily on flooded meadows, the EKV has gradually widened the scope of management and has initiated new projects to address a broader set of issues related to ecosystems processes across temporal and spatial scales. Management expands from individual actors, to group of actors, to multiple-actor processes. Organizational and institutional structures evolve as a response to the broader set of environmental issues. Knowledge of ecosystem dynamics develops as a collaborative effort and becomes part of the organizational and institutional structures. Social networks develop that connect institutions and organizations across levels and scales. These networks facilitate information flows, identify knowledge gaps, and create nodes of expertise that are of significance for ecosystem management.

The Crane Group is one example among many similar project-oriented collaboration groups in Kristianstads Vattenrike. Together with the EKV, these groups form a flexible organizational structure that has been referred to as an "adhocracy" (Hahn et al. 2006), wherein organizations emerge to deal with particular problems in the area. These organizations may exist for only as long as the problem persists, and subsequently dissolve. This pulsing relies on a dormant or latent set of connections in a social network of actors involved in the management of Kristianstads Vattenrike (Olsson et al., 2007). These connections have developed around the EKV over the years, and can be seen as "sleeping links" that are triggered by exogenous events such as the arrival of migrating cranes or extreme floods. These links connect actors within and across organizational levels at critical times and help tune social and ecological dynamics by monitoring, combining knowledge, developing management practices, and responding to environmental change and impending conflicts. Each new project is potentially a good example that could be used to convince new actors and continue the expansion of adaptive co-management in the landscape.

Another organization in Kristianstads Vattenrike is the Consultancy Group for Nature Conservation. It has twenty-five members, including representatives from the EKV who represent a variety of interests in the area. The members meet several times a year, and the organization provides a forum for information and discussion. It also makes recommendations and advises the municipal executive board on land use plans. The group was formed by a key individual, Sven-Erik Magnusson, in the early 1990s, within the nature conservancy section of the EKV, and was meant to mitigate conflict and produce mechanisms for conflict management. The purpose was to gather representatives who were involved in activities that had links to the water of Kristianstads Vattenrike and who had not met earlier in a common forum. The only time they had been in contact with each other before was during a conflict arising on the letters page of the local newspapers (Olsson et al. 2004b). In the early days of this group, the EKV led the process of identifying common interests and discussing differences of opinion in a constructive way. The idea was to build trust among the representatives, which is essential to the success of the collaboration process. Magnusson argues that starting to discuss collaboration during a conflict situation is not a good strategy.

In this section, I have described the adaptive co-management system in Kristianstads Vattenrike. In the next section, I will describe the transformative changes that were needed to enable the emergence of the adaptive co-management approach.

The Emergence of Adaptive Co-Management
The transformation of the Kristianstads Vattenrike social-ecological system towards adaptive governance in the late 1980s was preceded by the emergence of a social network for managing the lower Helgeå River at the catchment level. A number of individuals from various local organizations observed declining bird populations, decreasing water quality, nuisance plant growth in lakes, and decreasing use of flooded meadows for haymaking and grazing (Olsson et al. 2004b). They anticipated an ecological crisis down the road, and there was growing discontent with the prevailing management of these values.

Originally trained as a geologist, Sven-Erik Magnusson was employed by the Kristianstads County Museum at the time, first as an assistant and eventually as the curator of the department of natural history. He was among those who were concerned about the loss of ecological and cultural values.

Magnusson recognized that the problems arising in the area were interrelated. He was also aware of the diversity of actors at different organizational levels involved in ongoing activities in the area, such as inventory and monitoring programs, restoration projects, and programs for improved land use and management practices. These activities were narrow in focus, and the people engaged were often not aware of each other. Magnusson began to connect key individuals from ongoing projects in order to build knowledge for creating integrated solutions and matching the scale of the solutions to the scale of the problems. This self-organized process was aimed at finding integrated landscape-level solutions to the problems.

The new network included individuals from local groups, such as environmental organizations, the Bird Society of Northeastern Scania, and local farmers' associations. It also included actors at other organizational levels, such as the Municipality of Kristianstad, the County Administrative Board, WWF Sweden, the National Museum of Natural History, and a national research council (Forskningsrådsnämnden, or FRN). These individuals became nodes of expertise in the emerging network.

Beyond connecting people, the process involved trust building and sense making, which are about synthesizing a variety of information into what Waltner-Toews and colleagues (2003) refer to as a coherent collective narrative. Such trust building and sense making created a platform for conflict management and for sharing of information between groups. In this way, the network tied together a number of sources of knowledge and experience, which increased the knowledge pool for decision making and helped develop practices for ecosystem management. To frame and give direction to this process, Magnusson developed and communicated a vision of ecosystem management for the area and managed to mobilize broad support for the new management approach, including support from key individuals. He also developed a relationship with local media in order to build public support for the idea. Thus, he provided leadership functions such as connecting key individuals, developing and communicating a vision, and engaging with others to establish direction. He aligned, motivated, and inspired people to invest in an alternative approach, thereby building broad support for change. At this stage, Magnusson coined the term "Kristianstads Vattenrike" and developed the idea of the EKV as a bridging organization.

In Kristianstads Vattenrike, social change and ecological crises at one scale triggered a transformation of the governance of the social-ecological systems at another scale. Two key circumstances are believed to have placed the management of Kristianstads Vattenrike on the municipal political agenda and affected the political will to adopt the new governance approach currently in use (Olsson et al. 2004b). First, local politicians were keen to find a new profile for the municipality, which had been a centre for military training. Second, environmental questions had been emphasized during the national Swedish election in September 1988, probably heightened by reports of red tides and viral disease killing a vast number of seals along the Swedish coasts.

At the time, the ecosystem approach for integrated landscape-level solutions to environmental problems in Kristianstads Vattenrike existed within the network that Magnusson had initiated. With support from a wide range of actor groups at various organizational levels, Magnusson took the opportunity to bring the idea to two municipal politicians and make them aware of the emerging problems in Kristianstads Vattenrike and the need for action. Using this vision of ecosystem management, he linked the proposal to other goals such as regional development, and managed to change the perception of these politicians from seeing the wetlands as a problem ("water sick") to seeing it as a valuable resource ("water rich"). The politicians in turn convinced the municipal executive board to support the idea. The vision also called for the creation of a bridging organization, the EKV, and the development of a flexible and collaborative approach for managing the wetland landscape.

Although there were many potential projects, Magnusson concentrated efforts on the flooded meadows because of a widespread sense of urgency among a number of actors concerning the threat, and because of awareness and appreciation of these meadows among the public. This project had a good chance of succeeding and produced a good example of the management approach that had been developed in the proposal. The example was highly valuable, since it attracted the attention and funding needed to take on other projects.

In summary, the transformation towards adaptive governance involved changes in a number of social features. These features include perception and meaning, network configurations, social coordination, and associated institutional arrangements and organizational structures. Sven-Erik Magnusson used the vision described earlier to produce these changes. The consequences for the management of Kristianstads Vattenrike are shown in Table 14.1.

Discussion

Visioning and Adaptability
The EKV has deliberately chosen a flexible organizational structure to increase its ability to respond to environmental feedback and to develop new knowledge and understanding for dealing with uncertainty and change

Table 14.1

The social features of governance in Kristianstads Vattenrike and the changes in these after the establishment of the Ecomuseum Kristianstads Vattenrike

Social feature	Before	After
Perception and meaning	The wetlands around the City of Kristianstad were seen as a problem and the area as "water sick." Dredging and draining of the wetlands were common. In the 1960s, the city dump was situated in the wetlands.	The wetlands are seen as a potential resource that generates a variety of ecosystem services and the area as "water rich." The wetlands are a part of the identity of Kristianstad and are used to promote the region.
Social network configurations	Patchy networks were organized around projects on specific issues and interests. Hence, these projects were often narrow in focus.	Social networks with vertical and horizontal links connect projects and actors with different interests. They also link actors at different organizational levels, including governmental agencies, non-governmental organizations, the municipality, and landowners.
Social coordination	Projects in the area were fragmented, with poor coordination among these at the landscape level.	There is coordination for an integrated landscape solution to problems using trust building, negotiation, sense making, and conflict management.
Institutional arrangements and organizational structures	No local management body managed Kristianstads Vattenrike. No mechanisms or strategies were developed that secured participation of local resource users.	Ecomuseum Kristianstads Vattenrike (EKV) acts as a bridging organization implementing participatory planning processes and arenas for adaptive co-management.

Note: "Before" and "after" refers to the year 1989, when the EKV was established and the new management approach implemented.

(Olsson et al. 2004b). Since the EKV has no formal mandate to lead, adaptive co-management builds on voluntary participation. The flexible self-organizing structure of Kristianstads Vattenrike requires good leadership, and the EKV staff needs to have the trust of the various actors to lead these processes. This means that the EKV can direct these processes as long as people like what EKV is doing and a trust relationship is maintained. Apart from leadership,

I have identified three factors that helped frame and direct adaptive co-management: a visioning process, maintenance of certain key conditions for adaptive co-management, and the availability of good examples to follow.

It is the ability to combine these factors that is the strength of the EKV's leadership and capacity to direct the adaptive co-management processes in Kristianstads Vattenrike. It is not enough to have one without the others. For example, key conditions for adaptive co-management include trust building, sense making, identification of common interests, learning, vertical and/or horizontal collaboration, and conflict management. But without a vision of where the process is going, it is hard to know how you are doing. Without good examples, it can be difficult to convince people to engage and participate in adaptive co-management processes. Strategies that secure the combination of these three factors enhance adaptability.

Kofinas and Griggs (1996) divide collaborations into two categories, those induced by conflict and those motivated by a shared vision. They also point out the difficulties of the first form, which is often burdened with the struggles of actors advocating their separate interests. Furthermore, these authors present two advantages of collaboration oriented towards the realization of shared visions. First, actors are not entering into a bargaining arena to negotiate over a single issue. Second, actors are less likely to be hindered by the expectations of their constituency or the need for formal ratification of decisions. The form of collaboration used in Kristianstads Vattenrike corresponds to the shared vision, as exemplified in the crane project, where EKV staff were on the lookout for potential conflict and initiated a dialogue between farmers and ornithologists to forestall conflict before it happened. Sven-Erik Magnusson argues that engaging and encouraging actors to participate and share their ideas and experiences creates a positive atmosphere that serves to mitigate conflict.

The vision guides the process that has been referred to as "framed creativity" (Folke et al. 2003). Kofinas and Griggs (1996) also note that the shared vision form of collaboration is characterized by an expansive exploration of ideas and creativity, while the other form is more structured and is characterized by the often tense interaction of negotiation. In a similar way, Wondolleck and Yaffee (2000) argue that a vision statement and common goals can provide a guiding mission and focus to diverse groups of actors and help facilitate the problem-solving process. The adaptive co-management in Kristianstads Vattenrike is characterized by "adhocracy" and self-organization, and can be viewed as a messy but creative process that makes use of diverse sources of knowledge and ideas for solving the problems that emerge. These sources include both local ecological knowledge and scientific knowledge.

Adaptive co-management increases the need for good leadership, a finding consistent with Danter and colleagues (2000, 554), who argue that "ecosystem management demands continuous agency change, in that stable, linear, and predictable organizational processes will be replaced by adhocracy. For this reason, after implementation of ecosystem management, agency governance must be more leadership oriented than was previously required under earlier resource management models." Envisioning the future together can create a sense of ownership of the processes. As the EKV matures, it continues to develop values and build motivation among actors for continued adaptive co-management of Kristianstads Vattenrike. In this way, the EKV staff provides leadership.

Developing a vision does not guarantee successful adaptive co-management, however. There is also a risk that the creation of a vision may stimulate other actor groups to develop competing visions (Singleton 2002; Wiesman et al. 2005). Hurley and Walker (2004) describe how efforts to realize particular visions through a land use planning program called the "Natural Heritage 2020: A Vision for Nevada County" triggered competing visions for the future of the local environment among some social groups. This led to a bitter conflict between actor groups, which, in turn, caused a collapse of the program less than a year after it was initiated. The EKV is well aware of the potential problem of competing visions and therefore developed the strategy to start with a few people and expand gradually. Another way to avoid the problem of competing visions in this context is scenario building and the creation of alternative futures together (Baker et al. 2004; Peterson et al. 2003).

The dependence of the adaptive co-management approach on leadership and trust makes the social-ecological systems of Kristianstads Vattenrike vulnerable to different threats. There are several possible threats, including loss of public support due to undeservedly bad publicity in the media, loss of key individuals, conflict, and loss of trust. In addition, collaborations can get derailed and arenas hijacked by specific interests, becoming what Walker and Hurley (2004) describe as an "avenue of power that social groups use to achieve broader political ends."

Bridging organizations such as the EKV can contribute to adaptability by providing social sources of resilience in the form of strategies that reduce the vulnerability of the adaptive co-management approach that emerged in Kristianstads Vattenrike. These strategies include engaging in dialogue with actors, scanning for discontent and potential conflict, creating good relations with the media, diversifying leadership, maintaining social networks for knowledge and problem-solving skills, and cultivating a variety of funding sources.

Visioning and Transformability

The transformation towards adaptive governance and the emergence of adaptive co-management did not involve the creation of new institutions (rules and regulations) but rather reorganization within existing institutional frameworks. This reorganization was guided by a shared vision and involved connecting and coordinating ongoing activities. This means that the change in behaviour that was observed among actors in the area was due not to the enforcement of rules and regulations but to the creation of incentives for individual action and engagement.

Kotter (1995) and Bass (1990) refer to transformational leadership, which Kotter defines as "a process to establish direction, align people, motivate and inspire – with the ultimate goal of producing movement or change." In Kristianstads Vattenrike, Sven-Erik Magnusson identified places where the interests of actor groups coalesce in order to find starting points for dialogue and collaboration. This was a first step towards changing the perceptions of key individuals and overcoming resistance to transformational change. Transformational leadership therefore includes recognizing windows of opportunity, and identifying and transforming constraints and barriers such as conflicts of interest, values, and opinions.

Such qualities are critical for reducing the resilience of undesired trajectories and building up a momentum for moving into new trajectories. Westley (1995) argues that visionary leaders can appear in times of crisis, to forge new alliances between knowledge and action when the paradigms that forged old bridges have proven bankrupt as a platform for the effective management of ecosystems. The problems and pending crisis in Kristianstads Vattenrike stimulated Magnusson to develop and communicate a vision of ecosystem management that framed the self-organizing processes. Visionary leaders forge new and vital meanings, overcome contradictions, create new syntheses, and forge new alliances between knowledge and action (Westley 1995; Olsson et al. 2006).

Kotter (1995) identifies eight important steps in organizational transformations, three of which focus on vision: (1) creating a vision, (2) communicating the vision, and (3) empowering others to act on the vision. In Table 14.2, I compare these steps with Sven-Erik Magnusson's work in Kristianstads Vattenrike, which helped stake out a new trajectory for adaptive co-management. The transformational leadership that he provided helped change the perception of key actors and guided the transition towards adaptive co-management.

Conclusions

This chapter has used the insights gained from study of the Kristianstads Vattenrike social-ecological system to explore the role of vision in framing and directing adaptive co-management processes. The EKV helps develop values and builds motivation for ecosystem management among actors by envisioning the future together and developing, communicating, and building support for this vision. Key factors for the success of this process are dialogue, trust building, and sense making. The vision defines an arena for

Table 14.2

How Sven-Erik Magnusson's work in Kristianstads Vattenrike compares with three of J.P. Kotter's steps (1995) in organizational transformations

Steps	The work in Kristianstads Vattenrike
Developing a vision	Sven-Erik Magnusson developed a vision for Kristianstads Vattenrike that is attractive to a wide variety of actors and interests. The vision also included an alternative organizational structure for managing the area.
Communicating the vision	Magnusson communicates the vision one-on-one, focusing on key individuals who can make a change.
Empowering actors to act on the vision	The participatory planning processes initiated by Magnusson empower local resource users to act on the vision.

---

collaboration, frames the adaptive co-management processes, and fosters the development of social networks and interactions among actors, including those dealing with conflict resolution. Visioning processes can therefore be as important as implementation of rules and regulations for framing and directing adaptive co-management.

Developing and communicating a vision is important both in the creation of new organizations for ecosystem management and in their continuing development. The adaptive co-management approach emerged as a response to an anticipated ecological crisis, and Sven-Erik Magnusson organized information into a comprehensible framework and presented local political leaders with a vision for changing the management approach for Kristianstads Vattenrike. The vision contributed to a shift in local political leaders' perception of the values of the wetland landscape and to the subsequent shaping of local policy. The vision also called for the creation of a bridging organization, the Ecomuseum Kristianstads Vattenrike, and the development of adaptive co-management of the area. This reorganization was guided by the development of a shared vision among diverse actors across several levels of society. Magnusson, as the key individual, provided leadership throughout this process.

Visioning is, in itself, no guarantee of successful adaptive co-management. It needs to be combined with the maintenance of key conditions of adaptive co-management and the provision of good examples that can inspire actors to participate. In Kristianstads Vattenrike, Magnusson and the staff at the EKV are important in the process of expanding management structures to meet new challenges of matching social and ecological dynamics. Such expansion is needed when prevailing management structures become insufficient to address functional links in the landscape, for example, between sandy grasslands and flooded meadows. It requires skills and strategies that are not all that common in conventional environmental management and planning. For example, the approach used in Kristianstads Vattenrike – that of starting the visioning process with a small number of people and expanding gradually – should be examined seriously by anyone thinking of using and leading adaptive co-management processes.

The adaptive co-management approach used in Kristianstads Vattenrike, which builds on trust and good leadership, also makes it vulnerable to change. The period of transition was a vulnerable phase; if Magnusson had moved away or for some other reason disappeared at that point, the direction of management would have been highly uncertain, and the transformation might have followed other paths. In this sense, the current regime's strength in the management of Kristianstads Vattenrike is also its most vulnerable aspect; sustaining the EKV vision depends on substantive and continuous dialogue and personal linkages. The EKV, as a bridging organization, can build capacity to increase resilience and reduce the vulnerability of the social-ecological system.

This chapter has shown how visioning processes are important in moving to trajectories with the capacity to govern social-ecological systems for sustainability and human well-being. It has also shown how novel ideas and places in which to explore new configurations of the social-ecological system are crucial for transforming governance regimes from ones that mask environmental feedbacks to ones with effective feedback loops.

References

Armitage, D.R. 2005. Collaborative environmental assessment in the Northwest Territories, Canada. *Environmental Impact Assessment Review* 25: 239-58.

Baker, J.P., D.W. Hulse, S.V. Gregory, D. White, J. van Sickle, P.A. Berger, D. Dole, and N.H. Schumaker. 2004. Alternative futures for the Willamette River Basin, Oregon. *Ecological Applications* 14: 313-24.

Bass, B.M. 1990. From transactional to transformational leadership: Learning to share the vision. *Organizational Dynamics* 18: 19-31.

Berkes, F., J. Colding, and C. Folke, eds. 2003. *Navigating social-ecological systems: Building resilience for complexity and change.* Cambridge: Cambridge University Press.

Borrini-Feyerabend, G., M. Pimbert, M.T. Farvar, A. Kothari, and Y. Renard. 2004. *Sharing power: Learning-by-doing in co-management of natural resources throughout the world.* Teheran: IIED, IUCN/CEESP, Cenesta.

Boyle, M., J. Kay, and B. Pond. 2001. Monitoring in support of policy: An adaptive ecosystem approach. In *Encyclopedia of global environmental change*, ed. T. Munn, 4: 116-37. New York: John Wiley and Sons.

Bressers, H., and S. Kuks, eds. 2004. *Integrated governance and water basin management: Conditions for regime change towards sustainability.* Dordrecht, Netherlands: Kluwer Academic Publishers.

Carpenter, S.R., B. Walker, J.M. Anderies, and N. Abel. 2001. From metaphor to measurement: Resilience of what to what? *Ecosystems* 4: 765-81.

Danter K.J., D.L. Griest, G.W. Mullins, and E. Norland. 2000. Organizational change as a component of ecosystem management. *Society and Natural Resources* 13: 537-47.

Dietz, T., E. Ostrom, and P. Stern. 2003. The struggle to govern the commons. *Science* 302 (5652): 1907-12.

Folke C., J. Colding, and F. Berkes. 2003. Synthesis: Building resilience and adaptive capacity in socio-ecological systems. In *Navigating social-ecological systems: Building resilience for complexity and change,* ed. F. Berkes, J. Colding, and C. Folke, 352-87. Cambridge: Cambridge University Press.

Folke, C., T. Hahn, P. Olsson, and J. Norberg. 2005. Adaptive governance of social-ecological systems. *Annual Review of Environment and Resources* 30: 441-73.

Gadgil, M., P.R. Seshagiri Rao, G. Utkarsh, P. Pramod, A. Chatre. 2000. New meanings for old knowledge: The people's biodiversity registers programme. *Ecological Applications* 10: 1307-17.

Gunderson, L.H., and C.S. Holling, eds. 2002. *Panarchy: Understanding transformations in human and natural systems.* Washington, DC: Island Press.

Hahn, T., P. Olsson, C. Folke, and K. Johansson. 2006. Trust-building, knowledge generation and organizational innovations: The role of a bridging organization for adaptive co-management of a wetland landscape around Kristianstad, Sweden. *Human Ecology* 34: 573-92.

Hurley P.T., and P.A. Walker. 2004. Whose vision? Conspiracy theory and land-use planning in Nevada County, California. *Environment and Planning A* 36: 1529-47.

Imperial, M.T. 1999. Institutional analysis and ecosystem-based management: The institutional analysis and development framework. *Environmental Management* 24: 449-65.

Kofinas, G.P., and J.R. Griggs. 1996. Collaboration and the BC Round Table on the Environment and the Economy: An early-stage analysis of a "better way" of deciding. *Environments Journal* 23 (2): 17-40.

Kotter, J.P. 1995. Leading change: Why transformational efforts fail. *Harvard Business Review* (March-April): 59-67.

Lee, M. 2003. Conceptualizing the new governance: A new institution of social coordination. Paper presented at the Institutional Analysis and Development Mini-Conference, 3-5 May, Indiana University, Bloomington.

McGinnis, M.D., ed. 1999. *Polycentric governance and development: Readings from the workshop in political theory and policy analysis.* Ann Arbor: University of Michigan Press.

Olsson, P., and C. Folke. 2001. Local ecological knowledge and institutional dynamics for ecosystem management: A study of Lake Racken watershed, Sweden. *Ecosystems* 4: 85-104.

Olsson, P., C. Folke, and F. Berkes. 2004a. Adaptive co-management for building resilience in social-ecological systems. *Environmental Management* 34: 75-90.

Olsson, P., C. Folke, and T. Hahn. 2004b. Social-ecological transformation for ecosystem management: The development of adaptive co-management of a wetland landscape in southern Sweden. *Ecology and Society* 9 (4): 2. http://www.ecologyandsociety.org/vol9/iss4/art2.

Olsson, P., L.H. Gunderson, S. Carpenter, P. Ryan, L. Lebel, C. Folke, and C.S. Holling. 2006. Shooting the rapids: Navigating transitions to adaptive governance of social-ecological systems. *Ecology and Society* 11 (1): 18. http://www.ecologyandsociety.org/vol11/iss1/art18.

Olsson, P., V. Galaz, C. Folke, T. Hahn, L. Schultz. 2007. Enhancing the fit through adaptive co-management: Creating and maintaining bridging functions for matching scales in the social-ecological systems of Kristianstads Vattenrike, Sweden. *Ecology and Society* 12 (1): 28. http://www.ecologyandsociety.org/vol12/iss1/art28.

Ostrom, E. 1996. Crossing the great divide: Coproduction, synergy, and development. *World Development* 24: 1073-87.

Peterson, G.D., G.S. Cumming, and S.R. Carpenter. 2003. Scenario planning: A tool for conservation in an uncertain world. *Conservation Biology* 17: 358-66.

Schultz, L., C. Folke, and P. Olsson. 2007. Enhancing ecosystem management through social-ecological inventories: Lessons from Kristianstads Vattenrike, Sweden. *Environmental Conservation* 34: 140-52.

Singleton, S. 2002. Collaborative environmental planning in the American West: The good, the bad and the ugly. *Environmental Politics* 11: 54-75.

Stoker, G. 1998. Governance as theory: Five propositions. *International Social Science Journal* 50: 17-28.

Walker, B., C.S. Holling, S.R. Carpenter, and A. Kinzig. 2004. Resilience, adaptability and transformability in social-ecological systems. *Ecology and Society* 9 (2): 5. http://www.ecologyandsociety.org/vol9/iss2/art5.

Walker, P.A., and P.T. Hurley. 2004. Collaboration derailed: The politics of "community-based" resource management in Nevada County. *Society and Natural Resources* 17: 735-51.

Waltner-Toews, D., J.J. Kay, C. Neudoerffer, and T. Gitaud. 2003. Perspective changes everything: Managing ecosystems from the inside out. *Frontiers in Ecology and the Environment* 1: 23-30.

Westley, F. 1995. Governing design: The management of social systems and ecosystems management. In *Barriers and bridges to renewal of ecosystems and institutions,* ed. L.H. Gunderson, C.S. Holling, and S.S. Light, 391-427. New York: Columbia University Press.

Wiesman, U., K. Liechti, and S. Rist. 2005. Between conservation and development: Concretizing the first World Natural Heritage Site in the Alps through participatory processes. *Mountain Research and Development* 25: 128-38.

Wondolleck, J.M., and S.L. Yaffee. 2000. *Making collaboration work: Lessons from innovation in natural resource management.* Washington, DC: Island Press.

15
Using Scenario Planning to Enable an Adaptive Co-Management Process in the Northern Highlands Lake District of Wisconsin

Garry Peterson

Adaptive co-management aims to integrate adaptive environmental management and co-management. Adaptive management is an approach to ecological management that focuses on the synthesis of new management concepts and their experimental testing (Holling 1978; Walters 1986; Lee 1993). Co-management is a type of ecological governance wherein responsibility for ecological management is shared between state and local ecosystem user institutions (Pinkerton 1989; Pomeroy and Berkes 1997; Borrini-Feyerabend et al. 2000). There have been many locations where some form of adaptive management or co-management has been adopted, but few places have integrated adaptive management with co-management (Olsson et al. 2004a).

The successful implementation of adaptive management appears to depend upon the development of trust and a shared understanding of the system being managed among the people involved in management (Holling 1978; Walters 1997). However, in many situations in which co-management is being attempted or where it would be beneficial, there has been little trust between groups and a lack of a shared understanding of the system. In this chapter, I describe how scenario planning was used to build connections among separate groups and to start a dialogue about the functioning of the managed social-ecological system. I describe and reflect upon a scenario-planning process that attempted to build capacity for adaptive co-management by stimulating shared understanding and cooperation in the Northern Highlands Lake District (NHLD) of Wisconsin, a region where nature-oriented tourism threatens to undercut the ability of the region to continue supplying the ecosystem services that support tourism. This chapter examines the use of scenario planning to build the potential for adaptive co-management, the application of this approach in northern Wisconsin, and the lessons that this experience suggests.

Ecological Management

Ecological management needs to be sensitive to the social-ecological situation in which it occurs. Most ecological management theory has been developed for situations in which uncertainty is low and controllability is high, as shown in Figure 15.1 (Peterson 2005). Funtowicz and Ravetz (1993) have argued that uncertainty, the presence of multiple legitimate perspectives, and alternative values characterize many modern environmental problems. While ecosystem users frequently have sophisticated understandings of specific aspects of ecological behaviour, people are very uncertain about the long-term sustainability of specific social-ecological systems due to their ecological and social complexity. Furthermore, in many situations, managers have only weak, partial control over ecological dynamics and people's interactions with ecosystems. Ecosystems are complex systems whose behaviour emerges from the interaction of adapting components; consequently, their behaviour is frequently non-linear, sometimes resisting large perturbations, while becoming transformed at other times due to small perturbations (Levin 1999). Social-ecological systems are even more complex, with unexpected changes and transformations occurring frequently. These complex dynamics increase uncertainty and decrease controllability (Gunderson and Holling 2002).

Figure 15.1

The appropriateness of different approaches to ecological management varies according to the relative uncertainty and controllability of an ecological management situation

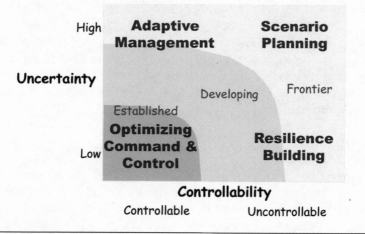

Source: Adapted from Peterson (2005).

Uncertainty

Ecological management depends upon decisions that are expected to improve a situation. Choosing from among alternative actions requires evaluating implicitly or explicitly the expected outcomes of such actions. People derive their expected futures from models of how management works. These models may be tacit or formal, but they shape management action.

Formal approaches to ecological management use mathematical models to cope with uncertainty. Mathematical models are fit to data and compared with competing models to discover which ones predict future behaviour better than others. This approach can be effective if the system being modelled continues to operate in a similar fashion; however, if the system has the potential to reorganize, for example, following the introduction of a new species, models based upon past behaviour will often fail to predict reorganization (Peterson et al. 2003b). Because all possibilities cannot be considered, management approaches should expect predictions to occasionally fail and surprises to occur (Holling 1986).

Social dynamics are even more difficult to predict than ecological dynamics due to the diversity of human values, the rapid pace of social change, and the reflexive nature of people (Westley et al. 2002). Ecological policy is often based on existing technologies and values, or the continuation of existing trends. Frequently, however, new inventions change the way people impact ecosystems. For example, protected areas established prior to the Second World War were not designed to incorporate snowmobiles or all-terrain vehicles, which did not exist at the time. Now, many of these areas are struggling to develop new regulations to reduce the ecological impact of people's using these machines (Vail and Heldt 2004). Furthermore, humans are reflexive and therefore consider the consequences of their, and other people's, future behaviour before making a decision. This reflexivity can make predictions self-fulfilling and self-negating, which makes predicting future behaviour more complex. For example, people's behaviour changes based upon their beliefs about other people's behaviour. The social nature of belief means that, while norms of behaviour are frequently reinforced, they can also change rapidly (Kuran 1989).

Controllability

Controllability of ecological processes by management action depends on both the nature of the ecological processes involved and the organization of the society being managed. Available knowledge and technology strongly influence management control of both aspects of controllability.

Ecological processes vary in their controllability depending upon three factors: novelty, visibility, and connections across spatial and temporal scales. First, the uniqueness of a given ecological situation makes control more difficult, because control techniques are more easily transferred between analogous situations. For example, there are fewer analogs to the Florida Everglades than to a small boreal forest lake. Second, the ease with which a system's dynamics can be understood depends upon the ease with which ecosystem functional relationships can be detected and separated from environmental variation. This process is difficult when: (1) ecological change occurs slowly, as in the case of the accumulation of phosphorus in soil; (2) when there are long time lags between action and environmental change, as in the effect of deforestation on groundwater dynamics; or (3) when ecological processes are technically challenging to measure or observe, as in oceanic fish populations (Walters 1986). Third, the controllability of a system being managed is decreased if processes external to it strongly influence the system's dynamics. For example, attempts to restore salmon to a section of river will be influenced by dam management, runoff from surrounding land, changes in fishing techniques, and the ocean temperature patterns in the North Pacific.

Along with these ecological features of controllability, society also strongly influences what type of control is possible in a given location. The degree to which people are able to agree upon how to manage a shared resource influences the degree of control people can exert over ecological dynamics. Attributes of ecological management institutions can help or hinder the ability to respond to change. It has been suggested that the four attributes of institutions that impact the effectiveness of ecological management are (1) shared ecological understanding, (2) a match between scales of organization and ecological processes, (3) effectiveness of collective action, and (4) effectiveness of past conflict resolution. Shared understanding among actors of how the natural world works is important because it determines whether people can agree upon an intervention in the system (Holling 1978). The fit between institutional and ecological scales represents the degree to which management institutions function at the scales at which important ecological change occurs (Folke et al. 1998; Young 2002). Effectiveness of collective action is the degree to which organized groups of people can implement new policies (Bromley 1989). The legitimacy of past conflict resolution shapes the ability of an institution to address new issues (Hoff 1998). Governments have frequently expropriated resources from local people only to see attempts at management fail due to passive or active resistance to management policies from these people (Scott 1998). Consequently, the controllability of a social-ecological system is determined, to a large extent, by the group of people involved with using and managing it (Ostrom 1990).

Technology, along with social organization, determines the controllability of an ecosystem. Depending on the technology available to managers, different ecological processes are more or less easy to control. For example, technological advances have enabled fishers to access previously inaccessible fish populations (Pauly et al. 2002). Similarly, a stream is cheaper to monitor and regulate than is groundwater. Technology can shift these relationships. For example, satellites and transponders lower the cost of monitoring fishing and enforcing regulations, potentially increasing the controllability of an offshore fishery.

By working to increase controllability and reduce uncertainty, people make social-ecological situations more manageable. Increasing social agreement can increase the ability of people to control a system, as can ecological engineering interventions. Similarly, social learning processes such as co-management, as well as complex systems approaches that allow the useful simplification of complex situations, can increase understanding.

Cross-Scale Social-Ecological Dynamics and Adaptive Co-Management
Co-management commonly occurs in a complex cross-scale context that includes many more connections than just those between the local community and state organizations (Berkes 2002; Adger et al. 2005). Local communities commonly have horizontal linkages with their neighbours and other communities that are involved in common resource management situations. Communities also frequently have linkages with other civil society groups, such as advocacy organizations, non-governmental organizations (NGOs), media, and scientists. Similarly, state organizations exist within a complex of other state organizations, similar organizations within other states, and media, scientific, and international organizations. Such linkages provide extra capacity to both local and state organizations to manage ecosystems in a world of pervasive change. By bridging local knowledge and scientific knowledge, adaptive co-management aims to increase the social-ecological capacity of management and achieve goals that are shared by both state and local actors (Olsson et al. 2004a).

Adaptive co-management has the potential to partially resolve a fundamental problem facing ecological management, namely, that property rights are defined at specific scales, while ecological processes span scales. Ecological processes therefore connect property rights held by many different actors at many different scales, and this problem cannot be escaped by reorganizing property rights. Rather, ecological management needs to bridge scales. Most traditional approaches fail to do this, but this is the potential strength of adaptive co-management. Co-management provides a mechanism for bridging scales by representing the interests of local and non-local stakeholders; for example, the James Bay and Northern Québec agreement brings together Aboriginal communities of people who live in an area used for hydropower generation by the Canadian province of Québec (Berkes 2002). This cross-scale linkage is complemented by adaptive management, which provides a method of coping with change (Figure 15.2).

Figure 15.2

Adaptive co-management attempts to bring together social and ecological knowledge from both local and general knowledge for management

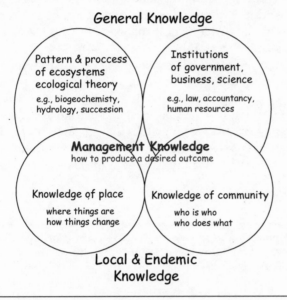

General Knowledge

Pattern & proccess
of ecosystems
ecological theory

e.g., biogeochemisty,
hydrology, succession

Institutions
of government,
business, science

e.g., law, accountancy,
human resources

Management Knowledge
how to produce a desired outcome

Knowledge of place

where things are
how things change

Knowledge of community

who is who
who does what

Local & Endemic
Knowledge

Approaches to Building Capacity for Adaptive Co-Management

Adaptive co-management cannot be simply implemented in a region. Cooperation between different people, organizations, and types of management requires mechanisms for linking local social and ecological knowledge, such as the history of land use practices in a wetland, with more universal knowledge, such as the dynamics of biogeochemical cycles. Doing this requires that participants have some minimal level of trust in one another, and that they have some shared vision of the management issues that they face (see Chapter 14). In northern Wisconsin, a variety of cross-scale ecological issues, such as the spread of invasive species, a limited degree of control, and a lack of regional ecological management suggested that there was a substantial opportunity for adaptive co-management; however, the region lacked trust and mechanisms for linking local and more general social-ecological knowledge. Ecological management was occurring in a context that was both uncontrollable and uncertain.

Beginning in 2000, a group of researchers organized through the University of Wisconsin's Center for Limnology, which has worked in the region for more than a century, decided to attempt to see whether a scenario-planning exercise could be used to enhance the opportunities for regional adaptive co-management. The project aimed to build regional ecological management capacity, create a shared understanding of management issues, develop a mental model of the region and changes facing it, and facilitate collaborations (Peterson et al. 2003a). This project was initiated by ecologists, including this author, but expanded to include other environmental and social scientists with experience in remote sensing, rural sociology, and economics, as well as a wide diversity of people involved in ecological management in northern Wisconsin.

To develop scenarios in northern Wisconsin, we used a scenario-planning approach that has been influenced by adaptive environmental management (Peterson et al. 2003c). Scenario planning, like adaptive environmental management (Holling 1978), examines alternative models of how the world might work and seeks to develop policies that are robust to this uncertainty (van der Heijden 1996; Wollenberg et al. 2000). The key feature distinguishing them is their relative ability to engage in management experiments.

Figure 15.3

The scenario-planning process is an iterative process of identifying a problem, synthesizing knowledge, identifying alternatives, creating scenarios, and using the scenarios

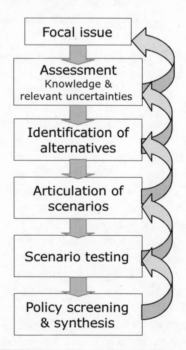

Source: Based on Peterson et al. (2003c).

When experimental manipulation is possible, adaptive management approaches are effective at answering questions. Scenario planning is most useful when there is a high level of uncertainty about the system of interest, and system manipulations are difficult or impossible (van der Heijden 1996). The lack of agreement about how the world works in northern Wisconsin meant that there was little agreement over what type of future the region could experience. The scenario process was intended to be a mechanism for stimulating dialogue about external pressures and internal dynamics of the region, to help build capacity for ecological management. The scenario-planning approach we adopted begins by bounding a problem, synthesizing existing knowledge, identifying alternative development paths or uncertainties that could shape the future, and then creating a set of scenarios that capture a set of important alternatives (Peterson et al. 2003c). These scenarios are then revised based upon various checks of their plausibility, before being used to examine policy alternatives (Figure 15.3).

Northern Highlands Lake District

The Northern Highlands Lake District (NHLD) covers 5,300 square kilometres of the extreme northern part of the state of Wisconsin. It contains thousands of natural lakes that make up about 13 percent of the region (Figure 15.4). Since the Second World War, this region has been a focus of lake-centred tourism.

The NHLD has been sparsely occupied for thousands of years. In the seventeenth century, European fur traders entered the region and transformed the lives of Native Americans, its original inhabitants. In the nineteenth century, the expansion of the United States led Native Americans into a series of contested treaties with the US government, which included some Native American hunting and fishing rights (Loew 2001). The old-growth forest of the NHLD was extensively logged in the late nineteenth and early twentieth centuries. By the 1930s, much of the Northern Highlands had been clear-cut. At the beginning of the twenty-first century, about 80 percent of the region was mixed conifer and deciduous forest (Peterson et al. 2003a).

Since 1990, the population of the region has grown fourfold, while the summer population has grown tenfold. Population growth has accelerated over the past three decades (Peterson et al. 2003a). Recreation and tourism are major components of the economy, and there has been substantial development of housing around lakes (Schnaiberg et al. 2002). The region lies within a day's drive of several major urban centres – Chicago, Milwaukee, and Minneapolis-Saint Paul. In recent decades, highway improvements have increased the accessibility of the region by decreasing the travel time from these cities.

The Northern Highlands Lake District's location within North America (a) and land cover (b)

a)

CANADA

WI

USA

MEXICO

0 300 600 km

b)

N

Land cover type
- forest
- wetland, grass, or agriculture
- urban
- water

0   20   40
kilometres

Ecological Management in NHLD

Regional ecological management is determined by several important actors, including governmental natural resources agencies, Native American tribes, other property owners, participants in outdoor recreation, and various business groups that encourage economic development, such as realtors, construction companies, and tourism operators. Lakeshore development for tourism and second homes is increasingly altering the region's lake ecosystems, undercutting their ability to provide the ecosystem services that are currently the region's chief attraction.

Ecological management has been slow to adjust to ecological and social changes in this area. Most of the major management changes have been driven by crisis. For example, the redistribution of fisheries and wildlife resources between tribal and state users occurred only after the settlement of a federal lawsuit in 1991 (Nesper 2002). Similarly, changes in zoning and water regulations have occurred only after most of the traditional lakeshore has been manipulated and changed (Schnaiberg et al. 2002). There is no integrated ecological management in the region, and state enforcement of laws is weak, due to low levels of staffing, which makes it difficult to police the region.

Social Learning

The lack of an integrated concept of the Northern Highlands is a barrier to social learning. There has been a focus on maintaining the past rather than attending to what the future could bring or what changes have occurred. This has resulted in a reactive management approach. The fragmented society of the region has produced fairly separate bodies of knowledge.

There is a long history of scientific research in the region. Such research has been undertaken by the University of Wisconsin (represented in the NHLD by the Trout Lake Biological Station and by an extension unit), the Wisconsin Department of Natural Resources (WDNR), and the Great Lakes Indian Fish and Wildlife Commission (GLIFWC). In particular, the region has a long history of studies of lake ecology. There has been a long-term ecological research (LTER) site in the region for about thirty years (Beckel 1987; Magnuson et al. 2005). This project initially studied only the ecology of the lakes in the NHLD, but over the past decade, it has expanded to include the landscape surrounding the lakes and the social forces that changed that landscape. This research has brought international expertise to northern Wisconsin and has increased scientific understanding of social-ecological change in the region. For example, research has shown that the average duration of ice cover has decreased about twelve days over the past century (Magnuson et al. 2000).

The WDNR maintains a long-term fisheries research program that has studied the fish populations of a variety of lakes. It frequently meets with the GLIFWC, which also researches fish populations and quality. The University of Wisconsin has collaborated with the GLIFWC and the WDNR. It is unusual for a rural, sparsely populated region to possess such a high-quality information base. Despite this wealth of information, however, there is no integrated view of the ecological issues facing the region.

Locally, separate sets of ecological management knowledge have been developed by the Lac du Flambeau tribe and other lakeshore residents. The Lac du Flambeau tribe has legal rights to a different set of ecosystem services than other residents of the area. They collaborate with the GLIFWC to engage in studies of fish populations, but have informal and formalized systems of transmitting local ecological knowledge. The history of colonization and the extensive and occasionally violent conflict over fishing rights in the 1980s led to a lack of trust between Lac du Flambeau and other people in the region (Loew 2001; Nesper 2002). Knowledge produced by local fisheries management experiments is kept within tribal governance and management organizations. Minor briefing activities occur during information meetings organized by University of Wisconsin Extension or the WDNR, or through informal connections among individuals.

Lakeshore property owners have organized into lake associations and, in some cases, lake districts to develop coordinated programs of ecological management. Lake associations have existed in Wisconsin for over a century, but expanded after the state passed a 1974 law to support them and increase their status. Lake associations usually belong to larger groups of lake associations, such as the Wisconsin Association of Lakes. There are also other groups, such as the Vilas County Lakes Association, that focus on regional water management. This network of lake associations disseminates information among its members, mostly lakeshore property owners. Both the WDNR and the University of Wisconsin Extension Service work with these organizations, but lake associations have little interaction with either the GLIFWC or the Lac du Flambeau tribal council.

While there are some connections among different groups in the NHLD, it is striking how little communication and learning occurs between different groups. Barriers to communication are likely due to a tense conflict over aboriginal fishing rights in the 1980s that divided the native and non-native community (Reimer 2004), and the rise of tourism that has divided the district between absentee, older new migrant, well-off lakeshore property owners, and poorer non-lakeshore year-round residents.

Scenario Planning in the NHLD
Scenario planning in the Northern Highlands Lake District aimed to integrate an extensive body of research findings from the social and natural sciences and on-the-ground experience of people living in the region to

create a sense of the alternative trajectories the region could take. These alternative visions of the future were meant to engage people with a stake in the region and provide them with a tool for reflecting on the forces driving change in the region, what those changes could bring, and what people could do to shape their futures.

The scenario-planning project was initiated in 2000 by a group of researchers at the University of Wisconsin. It has undergone a number of iterations, alternating between the synthesis of this accumulated scientific data and participatory assessments. I co-organized a workshop in 2001, which included a diverse set of people concerned with ecological management, from within and outside northern Wisconsin, to discuss the issues facing the region. This workshop developed an initial definition of the problems facing the region and an initial assessment.

The initial assessment focused on the key ecosystem services that attract people to the region – the production of sport fish, attractive lakes, wildlife, and clean drinking water. It characterized the history of the region as a social-ecological system and the resilience of these services. From this assessment, two key uncertainties facing the region were identified: the extent to which the region's ecosystems were vulnerable to development and the size of future population growth.

Following this workshop, a small group of scientists at the University of Wisconsin created a set of three scenarios that addressed these uncertainties. This process involved data collection, analysis, and synthesis, as well as discussion with various social and natural scientists who had expert knowledge of demographic and ecological change in northern Wisconsin.

To broaden and deepen the scope of the scenarios, a second participatory workshop reanalyzed the region in 2002. At this workshop, a broader group of local people, resource managers, and academics reoriented the issues addressed by the scenarios to include people's livelihoods and the region's social capital. This redefinition was used to identify a broader set of alternatives facing the region. A large number of alternative scenarios were quickly created during the workshop, a set of key trade-offs and issues were identified, and these were then used to distill four new scenarios. These scenarios had some elements in common with the initial three but explored an expanded set of issues. Following this meeting, the scenarios were further developed. A series of cartoon illustrations were made to show how the landscape would look in each scenario. Short versions of the scenarios and the illustrations were combined in a report, which was widely distributed in the region and made freely available on the Internet (Figure 15.5).

The Northern Highlands Lake District scenarios consider the interactions of three groups: lakeshore property owners, Native Americans of Lac du Flambeau, and other permanent residents. Lakes in the region vary from

Figure 15.5

Visual representations of Northern Highlands Lake District scenarios, illustrating changes in settlement, use of ecosystem services, and changes in ecological structure possible by 2025

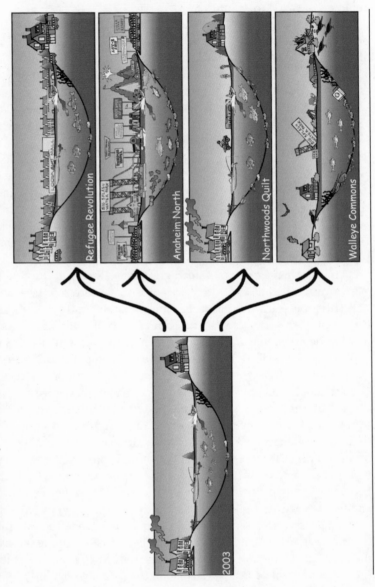

Source: Adapted from Carpenter et al. (2003).

Box 15.1
Northern Highlands Lake District scenarios

Anaheim North
The expansion of highway access to the region brings more part-time and full-time residents to the NHLD. The combination of population increase and little local control over land use change results in more conflicts over lake and land use, and degradation in water quality. Larger lakes that are lower on the landscape have extensive tourist development, which includes tourism water parks and resorts. In a search for more quiet areas, new residents build large homes on previously more remote and less accessible lakes. Many local lodges, restaurants, and stores are replaced or are bought by large international chains. The Lac du Flambeau casino grows, but the tribe is caught up in regional conflicts over fishing rights and the spread of invasive species. While private reserves provide quality fishing and hunting experiences to those who can afford it, fishing is poor and invasive species are abundant in most of the region's lakes.

Walleye Commons
Ecological disruption due to the spread of invasive species decreases the quality of fishing, swimming, and boating opportunities across the region. These changes lead to an economic decline in which out-migration, business closures, tourism decline, and declining property values reinforce one another. The tourism that remains centres on ethno-tourism to Lac du Flambeau. A museum and Indian sweat lodges provide novel experiences for tourists. The lakes contain a variety of undesirable species. While regional governance is limited, the Native Americans of Lac du Flambeau play an increasingly central role. Residents who remain regret the lower incomes and lack of convenient shopping, but they enjoy having the region to themselves.

Northwoods Quilt
In response to local problems, the state government devolves regulatory power to a diversity of local management groups. This leads to a patch-work of regulations being applied across the region's lakes. Some lakes permit motorized sports, while others restrict motorized access. While many residents are unhappy with regional changes, most feel that their lakes are well managed. Tourism continues to grow, despite local conflicts over issues that involve connections among lakes, such as road building, boating, fishing, water quality, and the spread of invasive species. Water quality is generally good, except in some of the larger, shallower lakes near towns. Fishing quality is poor across the entire region, however, with the exception of some lakes that have been effectively privatized by local regulations.

Refugee Revolution
Fear of terrorism in Chicago leads many summer home owners to move to northern Wisconsin and live there year-round, transforming the region from a tourist to a working ecosystem. All levels of government reorganize in response to this change, resulting in decisions being increasingly made by state and federal regulators. The areas around towns develop rapidly and become more densely settled as people move to be near schools, churches, and other services. Areas used for production, such as forest plantations, cranberry bogs, and fish hatcheries, expand. Lac du Flambeau does well economically and is relatively successful in managing development on tribal lands. Water pollution is regulated, but water quality is low near towns.

small acidic lakes high in the region's watershed to large, settled lakes lower in the watershed. The consequences for these groups across this diverse landscape are explored in scenarios of the next twenty-five years that address uncertainties about lake governance, migration to and from the region, and ecological vulnerability. The four scenarios are briefly described in Box 15.1, and their social and ecological aspects are compared in Table 15.1 (Carpenter et al. 2003).

The scenarios envision substantially different futures for the NHLD. Demographic change in the region is driven largely by external factors that could produce either a population decline or explosion. The scenarios highlight how the use of ecosystem services in the region could shift from fish and cultural services to a more diverse set of provisioning services. Furthermore, the importance of regulating services will likely increase as the population and number of buildings increase. However, ecological surprises due to invasive species plus the consequences of poor nutrient management from sewage, lawns, and erosion have the potential to reduce the region's attractiveness as a tourism destination (Table 15.1).

To generate a wider discussion of the scenarios, a combined online and mail survey was used to evaluate residents' responses to the scenarios and the issues they raised (Peterson et al., in prep.). The results of the survey matched the results of workshops and showed that there was agreement among NHLD residents about the threats facing the region, with only minor differences in what the goals of management should be, but that there were major differences in preferred approaches. A substantial majority felt that there was a need for preservation or sustainable environmental management. When considering the scenarios, people preferred Northwoods Quilt over Walleye Commons, both of which were preferred over Anaheim North and Refugee Revolution, but they felt that Northwoods Quilt and Anaheim North

Table 15.1

Comparison of Northern Highlands Lake District scenarios

Characteristic	Base 2003	2025			
		Anaheim North	Walleye Commons	Northwoods Quilt	Refugee Revolution
Population	43,000 2× summer	60,000 2× summer	12,000 1.5× summer	55,000 1.5× summer	120,000 1.25× summer
Economic	Mild recession after decade of growth Growth of tourism Rising property values	More inequity in wealth and property values Stagnation after decade of growth No economic diversification	Economic decline Reduced property values Economy somewhat diversified	Uneven economic growth but diversification of economy Generally increased property values	Substantial growth of economy Diversification of economic opportunities away from tourism
Landscape	Lake-centred Sprawl near some towns Large public conservation and reservation lands	More lake development More sprawl Public lands and reservations similar	Less lake development Expanded tribal land ownership	Varied development around lakes Sprawl near large towns	Extensive development of lakes and uplands Heavy use of public lands

▼ Table 15.1

Characteristic	Base 2003	2025			
		Anaheim North	Walleye Commons	Northwoods Quilt	Refugee Revolution
Water quality (including nutrients, toxins)	Good (some mercury; some eutrophication risk)	Moderate to poor (more metals, road salt, and eutrophication)	Moderate but variable (some mercury and toxic algae) Other lakes good or recovering	Good but variable with some degraded lakes	Moderate and variable More water extraction Declining ground-water table
Fisheries, habitat, and aquatic invasions	Good Some overfishing Some habitat loss Some invasions	Moderate and declining	Variable and improving Some invaders persist Some lakes recover slowly from fish diseases	Good Some invasions	Moderate and variable but recovering Aquaculture in lakes
Forests and wildlife	Good Little old growth Rotational harvesting Deer overpopulation Some exotics	Similar but heavier use Increased deer populations Increased exotics	Good and improving Deer population decimated Small moose herd	Similar but heavier use Expanded hunting to control deer	Working forests Heavier harvesting Closely regulated deer population

were equally likely. This pattern was surprisingly consistent among various groups (e.g., property owners versus non-property owners, residents versus non-residents, motor sport enthusiasts versus silent sport enthusiasts). People also shared the belief that they had little power to shape the future of their region. There were major differences, however, in what respondents viewed as problems facing the region and how those problems should be confronted. Some people saw people's moving to the region as a threat, while others saw development as a threat. Many saw increased planning and/or land use zoning as a solution, while a small minority saw any form of government regulation as a threat. The next step in the scenario-planning process will be to experiment with games that combine the scenarios with computer models to test and develop regional policies with groups of decision makers.

Discussion

The scenario-planning process revealed previously unconsidered opportunities and vulnerabilities of the region. Opportunities for enhanced learning and collaboration exist between lake associations and the Native Americans of Lac du Flambeau, who have complementary lake management expertise and experience. The analysis revealed that there were great opportunities to increase the spread of knowledge and understanding among people from different lakes within the region, and within the region as a whole. Due to the radically different demographic characteristics of different groups, traditional places where people meet and discuss events, such as churches, bars, sports teams, and schools, divide rather than unite different groups. In other regions, the creation of networks that bridge such disparate groups has been a key part of developing new ecological management approaches (Olsson et al. 2004b). These successes suggest that efforts to establish networks of individuals that bridge these groups could increase the opportunities to address the larger-scale processes that are changing the region. In particular, the NHLD is vulnerable to region-wide ecological changes in fish stocks and the spread of invasive species due to the connections that fishing and the movement of motorboats have established between lakes.

The region is strongly influenced by changes in the outside world, which alter the relative attractiveness of the region to tourist and second-home dwellers, as well as by the various ecological problems that impact the region from outside, such as mercury, climate change, and invasive species. While the region does not have the ability to control these processes, people and organizations within the region can adopt strategies that reduce their vulnerability to undesired changes and take advantage of opportunities. Doing this requires a better understanding of how external social changes interact with the society and ecology of the region. The region could benefit from forging partnerships with external organizations and governments that can help address these larger-scale issues. Time will tell how successful ecosystem management is in the NHLD, but there have recently been positive steps towards the development of cross-cutting networks (e.g., a recent inclusive workshop on invasive species hosted by the Native Americans of Lac du Flambeau, and towards a shared integrated mental model of the region (as indicated by extensive discussion of the scenarios described earlier) (S. Carpenter, pers. comm.).

The experience of working with scenario planning in northern Wisconsin suggested some general lessons about the use of scenario planning as a tool to facilitate adaptive co-management. Scenario planning has provided a mechanism for a diverse group of people to discuss and imagine the future of a region. It has helped establish new connections among people in the NHLD, as well as provide people with new tools for ecological management and a new, integrated understanding of the social-ecological changes taking place in the region. The scenarios that have been created provide a means for a larger group of people to discuss and reflect upon the future of a region they care about. This progress occurred over several years, however; like other inclusive approaches to environmental management, scenario planning takes time. Dialogue between different groups requires time to arrange and to occur. The dialogue requires multiple iterations of the scenario process, multiple passes through a process of defining questions, assembling data, conducting synthesis, and screening policy.

Scenario planning provides a forum for social learning, which does not require agreement on technical issues or experimental management. It is narrative-based, which allows scenarios to be retold in a variety of ways, easing the process of translating scenarios between different contexts and increasing the speed with which people challenge a scenario detail or propose alternative scenarios. This accessibility enables people to articulate and communicate using a set of alternative models of the future. While this process is not without confusion or opportunities for misunderstanding, it is far more accessible and generally understandable than alternative approaches that rely on statistics or computer models for projecting the future. Shared understanding can be increased by social learning processes that permit the useful simplification of complex situations in a way that allows meaningful creation and consideration of management alternatives. If the process of dialogue and the establishment of bridging networks help build trust, discussing the future can also increase the controllability of an ecological management situation. Both increased understanding and controllability increase the potential for ecological management to effectively accomplish its social and ecological goals (Figure 15.6). Thus, if it is used to provide an accessible, non-mathematical, dialogue-oriented process for discussing the future of a region, scenario planning has the potential to help build the trust and shared mental models that may contribute to the success of adaptive co-management.

Figure 15.6

Reduction of uncertainty in ecological management through development of theory and learning, and increase in social and ecological controllability through development of agreement and ecological engineering ability

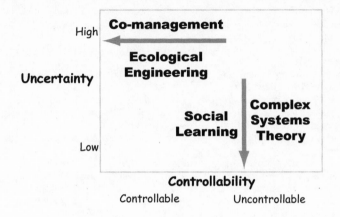

Acknowledgments

This chapter is based on my collaboration with Steve Carpenter, Elena Bennett, T. Doug Beard, Liz Levitt, and Graeme Cumming, and on discussions with the participants of workshops and planning meetings in northern Wisconsin. Thanks to Line Gordon, Gary Kofinas, Fikret Berkes, two anonymous reviewers, and participants in the Ottawa adaptive co-management meeting for comments on the text. This research was funded by a grant to the Resilience Alliance from the MacDonnell Foundation and the Canada Research Chair in Social-Ecological Modelling.

References

Adger, N., K. Brown, and E. Tompkins. 2005. The political economy of cross-scale networks in resource co-management. *Ecology and Society* 10 (2): 9. http://www.ecologyandsociety.org/vol10/iss2/art9/.

Beckel, A., ed. 1987. *Breaking new waters: A century of limnology at the University of Wisconsin.* Transactions of the Wisconsin Academy of Sciences, Arts and Letters, Madison, WI.

Berkes, F. 2002. Cross-scale institutional linkages: Perspectives from the bottom up. In *The drama of the commons,* ed. E. Ostrom, T. Dietz, N. Dolsak, P.C. Stern, S. Stonich, and E.U. Weber, 293-321. Washington, DC: National Academy Press.

Borrini-Feyerabend, G., A. Kothari, and M.P. Pimbert. 2000. *Co-management of natural resources: "Learning by doing" throughout the world.* Gland, Switzerland: International Union for the Conservation of Nature and Natural Resources.

Bromley, D. 1989. *Economic interests and institutions: The conceptual foundations of public policy.* New York: Basil Blackwell.

Carpenter, S.R., E.A. Levitt, G.D. Peterson, E.M. Bennett, D. Beard, J.A. Cardille, and G.S. Cumming. 2003. *Scenarios for the future of the Northern Highlands Lake District.* Madison: Center for Limnology, University of Wisconsin.

Folke, C., L. Pritchard Jr., F. Berkes, J. Colding, and U. Svedin. 1998. *The problem of fit between ecosystems and institutions.* IHDP Working Paper 2, International Human Dimensions Program, Global Environmental Change, Washington, DC.

Funtowicz, S. and R. Ravetz. 2003. Science for the post-normal age. *Futures* 25: 739-55.

Gunderson, L.H., and C.S. Holling, eds. 2002. *Panarchy: Understanding transformations in human and natural systems.* Washington, DC: Island Press.

Hoff, M.D., ed. 1998. *Sustainable community development: Studies in environmental, economic and cultural revitalization.* St. Lucie, FL: CRC Press.

Holling, C.S., ed. 1978. *Adaptive environmental assessment and management.* New York: John Wiley and Sons.

–. 1986. The resilience of terrestrial ecosystems: Local surprise and global change. In *Sustainable development of the biosphere,* ed. W.C. Clark and R.E. Munn, 292-317. Cambridge: Cambridge University Press.

Kuran, T. 1989. Sparks and prairie fires: A theory of unanticipated political revolution. *Public Choice* 61: 41-74.

Lee, K.N. 1993. *Compass and gyroscope: Integrating science and politics for the environment.* Washington, DC: Island Press.

Levin, S.A. 1999. *Fragile dominion: Complexity and the commons.* Reading, MA: Perseus Books.

Loew, P. 2001. *Indian nations of Wisconsin.* Madison: Wisconsin Historical Society Press.

Magnuson, J.J., T.K. Kratz, and B.J. Benson, eds. 2005. *Long-term dynamics of lakes in the landscape: Long-term ecological research on north temperate lakes.* New York: Oxford University Press.

Magnuson, J.J., D.M. Robertson, B.J. Benson, R.H. Wynne, D.M. Livingstone, T. Arai, R.A. Assel, et al. 2000. Historical trends in lake and river ice cover in the Northern Hemisphere. *Science* 289: 1743-46.

Nesper, L. 2002. *The Walleye war: The struggle for Ojibwe spearfishing and treaty rights.* Lincoln: University of Nebraska Press.

Olsson, P., C. Folke, and F. Berkes. 2004a. Adaptive comanagement for building resilience in social-ecological systems. *Environmental Management* 34: 75-90.

Olsson, P., C. Folke, and T. Hahn. 2004b. Socio-ecological transformation for ecosystem management: The development of adaptive co-management of a wetland landscape in southern Sweden. *Ecology and Society* 9 (4): 2. http://www.ecologyandsociety.org/vol9/iss4/art2.

Ostrom, E. 1990. *Governing the commons: The evolution of institutions for collective action.* Cambridge: Cambridge University Press.

Pauly, D., V. Christensen, S. Guénette, T.J. Pitcher, U.R. Sumaila, C.J. Walters, R. Watson, and D. Zeller. 2002. Towards sustainability in world fisheries. *Nature* 418: 689-95.

Peterson, G.D. 2005. Ecological management: Control, uncertainty, and understanding. In *Ecological paradigms lost: Routes to theory change,* ed. K. Cuddington and B. Beisner, 371-95. New York and London: Academic Press.

Peterson, G.D., D. Beard, B. Beisner, E. Bennett, S. Carpenter, G. Cumming, L. Dent, and T. Havlicek. 2003a. Assessing future ecosystem services: A case study of the Northern Highlands Lake District, Wisconsin. *Conservation Ecology* 7 (3): 1. http://www./ecologyandsociety.org/vol7/iss3/art1/.

Peterson, G.D., S.R. Carpenter, and W.A. Brock. 2003b. Uncertainty and the management of multistate ecosystems: An apparently rational route to collapse. *Ecology* 84: 1403-11.

Peterson, G.D., G. Cumming, and S.R. Carpenter. 2003c. Scenario planning: A tool for conservation in an uncertain world. *Conservation Biology* 17: 358-66.

Pinkerton, E., ed. 1989. *Co-operative management of local fisheries: New directions for improved management and community development.* Vancouver: UBC Press.

Pomeroy, R.S., and F. Berkes. 1997. Two to tango: The role of government in fisheries co-management. *Marine Policy* 21: 465-80.

Reimer, J. 2004. Chippewa spearfishing, lake property owner/anglers, and tourism: A case study of environmental social conflict. *Sociological Spectrum* 24: 43-70.

Schnaiberg, J., J. Riera, M.G. Turner, and P.R. Voss. 2002. Explaining human settlement patterns in a recreational lake district: Vilas County, Wisconsin, USA. *Environmental Management* 30: 24-34.

Scott, J.C. 1998. *Seeing like a state: How certain schemes to improve the human condition have failed.* New Haven, CT: Yale University Press.

Vail, D., and T. Heldt. 2004. Governing snowmobilers in multiple-use landscapes: Swedish and Maine (USA) cases. *Ecological Economics* 48: 469-83.

van der Heijden, K. 1996. *Scenarios: The art of strategic conversation.* New York: John Wiley and Sons.

Walters, C. 1997. Challenges in adaptive management of riparian and coastal ecosystems. *Conservation Ecology* 1 (2): 1. http://www.consecol.org/vol1/iss2/art1.

Walters, C.J. 1986. *Adaptive management of renewable resources.* New York: McGraw-Hill.

Westley, F., S.R. Carpenter, W.A. Brock, C.S. Holling, and L.H. Gunderson. 2002. Why systems of people and nature are not just social and ecological systems. In *Panarchy: Understanding transformations in human and natural systems,* ed. L.H. Gunderson and C.S. Holling, 103-19. Washington, DC: Island Press.

Wollenberg, E., D. Edmunds, and L. Buck. 2000. Using scenarios to make decisions about the future: Anticipatory learning for the adaptive co-management of community forests. *Landscape and Urban Planning* 47: 65-77.

Young, O.R. 2002. *The institutional dimensions of environmental change: Fit, interplay, and scale.* Cambridge, MA: MIT Press.

16
Synthesis: Adapting, Innovating, Evolving
Fikret Berkes, Derek Armitage, and Nancy Doubleday

Resource management is at a crossroads. Problems are complex, values are in dispute, facts are uncertain, and predictions are possible only in a limited sense. The scientific system that underlies resource management is facing a crisis of confidence in legitimacy and power. Top-down resource management does not work for a multitude of reasons, and the era of expert-knows-best decision making is all but over (Holling and Meffe 1996; Ravetz 2003).

Some of the new directions that have been proposed include adopting learning-based approaches in place of set management prescriptions (Lee 1993), using a broader range of knowledge (Berkes and Folke 1998), dealing with resilience and complexity (Gunderson and Holling 2002), and sharing management power and responsibility. As Pahl-Wostl and Hare (2004, 193) put it, "management is not a search for the optimal solution to one problem but an ongoing learning and negotiation process where a high priority is given to questions of communication, perspective-sharing and the development of adaptive group strategies for problem solving."

This volume contributes to a deeper understanding of the issues surrounding the sharing of management power and responsibility (co-management) and, more specifically, to the evolution of co-management into adaptive co-management through communication, perspective sharing, problem solving, trust building, and learning. We combine the perspectives of co-management (e.g., Pinkerton 1989) with those of adaptive management (e.g., Lee 1993), and the resulting synthesis is different from either perspective (Table 16.1). We recognize that co-management and adaptive management have been evolving towards common ground, but we find that the results of the convergence open up some additional opportunities.

Take co-management. Complexities of co-management have emerged gradually, unfolding over the years. For example, the initial Pacific salmon co-management arrangement described by Pinkerton (1992) was about harvest allocation. It set the stage for a complex multi-stakeholder resource

Table 16.1

Differences and similarities between co-management, adaptive management, and adaptive co-management

Characteristic	Co-management	Adaptive management	Adaptive co-management
Focus on establishing linkages	Establishing vertical institutional linkages	Learning-by-doing in a scientific and deliberate way	Establishing horizontal and vertical linkages to carry out joint learning-by-doing
Temporal scope	Short- to medium-term: tends to produce snapshots	Medium- to long-term: multiple cycles of learning and adaptation	Medium- to long-term: multiple cycles of learning and adaptation
Spatial scope	Bridging between local level and government level(s)	Focus on managers' needs and relationships	Multi-scale, across all levels, with attention to needs and relationships of all partners
Focus on capacity building	Focus on resource users and communities	Focus on resource managers and decision makers	Focus on all actors: "two (or more) to tango"

management exercise, however, and subsequently led to complex multi-jurisdictional integrated management in the Pacific Northwest. Several other co-management arrangements show this kind of stepwise evolution and of learning to move on to tackle larger problems (Chapter 2). What makes this possible is social learning and the building of social capital (Chapter 3).

The expansion of the scope of co-management to include trust building, institution building, and social learning introduces an evolutionary dimension. Earlier studies did not focus on developmental aspects of co-management because the experience to support such an analysis was not available. With the accumulation of experiences and cases, including many described in the chapters of this volume, it is now clear that the success of co-management ultimately depends on the development of human relationships and institutional arrangements. Facilitating such social interactions presents a formidable challenge, as most resources tend to be contested by multiple stakeholders with diverse interests and values, and relationships are complex. If co-management is viewed as a process, then co-managers need to understand that failure to facilitate social interactions may result in failure of the co-management process itself (Chapter 3). Hence, there is a need to develop capacity and institutions that can handle such co-management arrangements (Chapter 2).

A view of co-management as a complex process has implications for common property theory as well. Commons or common property theory informs much of co-management. Commons research of the 1980s and 1990s often sought the simplicity of community-based systems and single-use resource management to work out the basic principles, but many of these systems in reality are multi-level. The analysis of complex, multiple-use commons helps us understand the dynamics of multiple stakeholders and build better commons theory (Edwards and Steins 1999). Co-management, as it has been evolving over the last two decades, calls attention to such complexity and the ways in which complexity can be addressed (Chapter 2).

Take adaptive management. Learning-by-doing in practice requires the input of the people who have the practical knowledge of the systems being managed. The principle of user participation is commonsense and is increasingly recognized in some of the most comprehensive efforts to manage integrated social-ecological systems (e.g., Millennium Ecosystem Assessment 2005; World Resources Institute 2005; Timmer and Juma 2005). But adaptive management has technocratic roots (Holling 1978; Walters 1986). At its purest, it seeks to conduct field experiments from which it can learn, without much regard to whether or not this interferes with the livelihoods of the people who depend on the ecosystems that generate those resources. This is at odds with pragmatic adaptive management, which has little alternative but to seek consensus and bring users on board (Brunner et al. 2005). Lee (1999) explains the dilemma:

Adaptive management is a mode of learning. It is one [that is] attractive to natural scientists, drawn to the trustworthiness of experimentation as a way to establish reliable knowledge. Practitioners of adaptive management are moving the method toward the pragmatics of trial and error learning, while seeking to preserve the rigor of scientific logic ... Adaptive management has been framed so as to win favor with those who are nominally in charge of stewardship – typically government managers or harvest regulators and private landowners. When these stewards' legitimacy is under attack, adaptive management has at times appeared to be a way to deflect criticism by opening the way to trying novel ideas. But unless those novel ideas turn out to command a consensus within a short time of adoption, adaptive management is no more than a way to justify trial and error in the midst of a political free-for-all.

In this chapter, we discuss the larger significance and particular findings of the research reported in this volume, in combining the perspectives of co-management and adaptive management. As highlighted in Chapter 1, a number of emerging themes provide a reference point from which the different authors explore key concepts and interpret lessons from experience, limitations, and evolving tools and ideas in adaptive co-management. The emerging themes are: complex systems thinking; adaptive capacity and resilience; institutional design for adaptive co-management; partnerships and power sharing; conditions of success and failure; learning, knowledge, and social capital; and policy implications. We discuss each in turn.

Complex Systems Thinking

One of the characteristics of the evolving field of adaptive co-management is the prevalence of complex systems thinking, with attention to scale, self-organization, uncertainty, resilience, and other characteristics of complex adaptive systems. Such an approach is seen, for example, in Chapters 2, 4, 5, 10, 12, 13, and 15. Scale is an important theme, as a number of chapters illustrate, not only because it highlights the advantages of making decisions as close to the user as possible (the subsidiarity principle) but also because of the necessity of matching the scale of ecological systems and those of governance systems. It is easy to criticize the one-size-fits-all approach to resource management: the misfit between the scale of institution and resource systems (Folke et al. 2005) is a major reason for management failure in the cases considered in Chapters 5, 8, 10, and 11. Related to this conclusion are a number of insights that emerge from the chapters.

For instance, unpacking complex adaptive system characteristics and the challenge of scale help reveal the multiple variables and processes that need to be addressed. In this context, attention to cross-scale interplay (Young 2002) becomes an important dimension of adaptive co-management because it highlights the self-organization and feedback inherent in collaboration and learning (Chapters 2 and 4). The study of change processes requires attention to drivers of change, which often originate outside the local or regional system to be managed. The findings from the chapters here are that vertical linkages help deal with some of the external drivers but that, although they are necessary, they are insufficient to solve the problems. Vertical and horizontal linkages can build interdependence that creates empowerment, while the absence of linkages can mean disempowerment (Chapter 10).

The scrutiny of the structures (formal and informal) and processes of cross-scale interaction is necessary because the outcomes of those interactions are unlikely to be socially or politically neutral and may result in unexpected winners and losers (Chapters 11 and 12). Finally, social learning itself is a complex phenomenon. The interaction of social learning, social capital, and adaptive co-management is both a source and a product of inherent complexity in social systems (Chapter 3), implying that new tools such as scenario planning and visioning will be key to making complexity more tractable in an adaptive co-management process (Chapters 14 and 15).

Adaptive Capacity and Resilience

The experience explored in this volume illustrates the co-evolutionary nature of adaptive co-management, whereby changes in one part of the system lead to changes in another and vice versa. It is these changes in the complex system itself that facilitate or hinder adaptive co-management. Success comes as a result of learning, adaptability, and flexibility, rather than prediction, certainty, and controllability. Highlighting this point, Chapter 5 refers to the *illusion of certainty* and the *fallacy of controllability,* and proceeds to discuss policies that can help deal with the problems of uncertainty and lack of control. Of course, adaptive management was itself designed to deal precisely with these problems, providing a systematic way of testing, exploring, and learning in an uncertain world.

Several chapters of the volume offer insights for building adaptive capacity and resilience as a way of dealing with uncertainty. For example, building adaptive capacity will require a diverse portfolio of strategies, resource management tools, and greater attention to the broader social and institutional context in which adaptation emerges (Chapters 4, 5, and 10). Efforts to build adaptive capacity, moreover, have to occur at multiple levels. Singular attention to scale-specific issues of adaptive capacity may result in the neglect of the multi-layered relationships that influence adaptive capacity and of the linkages that enhance self-organization (Chapters 4 and 10). As observed by Armitage and Johnson (2006), the idea of scale provides a bridge between resilience and external drivers such as the effects of globalization.

Resilience thinking draws attention to nested scales ("panarchy," in resilience jargon [Gunderson and Holling 2002]) in the way drivers should be assessed.

Building adaptive capacity and resilience is clearly a long-term social process rather than a technical challenge. If so, these concepts are connected to the domain of learning, the role of culture as a wellspring of values, the acknowledgment of scientific uncertainty, the incorporation of local and traditional knowledge, and the importance of social capital (Chapters 3, 7, and 12). The tools mentioned above, like scenario planning and visioning (Chapters 14 and 15), emerge again as important because they help to frame and direct adaptive co-management, and help to identify the strategies required to build adaptive capacity and mediate contested ideas about the meaning of resilience.

Innovation in resource management systems, finally, is an outcome of efforts to build adaptive capacity and resilience. It is important to highlight this last point because it gets at a key concept in resilience analysis. Resilience is not only a measure of the capacity of a system to absorb disturbance but also a measure of the capacity of a system to "reorganize while undergoing change" (Walker et al. 2004). Hence, resilience is not about preserving a static condition; it is about living with change and making appropriate use of windows of opportunity – periods in time when actors are able to see and respond to situations in ways that build transformative learning potential – created by change (Gunderson and Holling 2002). The hypothesis of Chapter 13 is that co-management produces innovative outcomes and that co-management itself has been an extraordinary innovation. Recognition that the building of adaptive capacity and resilience, in turn, require innovation closes the cycle.

Institutional Design for Adaptive Co-Management

Co-management, by definition, straddles two or more levels of organization. If the management of a particular resource or set of resources involves multiple levels of governance, then users and managers of the resource need to devise institutions that straddle those levels. The issue is addressed by Dietz and colleagues (2003), who identified three strategies for addressing governance problems at the level of regional and global commons: analytic deliberation among all parties; nested, redundant, and layered institutions; and a variety of institutional types. These three items can be stated as principles and are consistent with an adaptive co-management framework, if the diversity of institutional types also serves to facilitate experimentation and learning.

The first principle of Dietz and colleagues (2003), about the critical importance of analytic deliberation among all the parties in a co-management case, is supported by virtually all the chapters in this volume. If the institutional design does *not* involve key participants, fails in building trust, and does not produce consensus on governance rules, the end result is going to be failed co-management, as described in Chapter 11. Atlantic fisheries co-management cases (Chapters 5 and 10) also indicate some of the consequences of a lack of informed discussion of governance rules among the parties.

The second principle, that "institutional arrangements must be complex, redundant, and nested in many layers" (Dietz et al. 2003, 1910), finds support in Chapters 5, 6, 7, 8, 13, and 14. Chapter 14 is of particular importance here because of the key role of bridging organizations, or what Cash and Moser (2000) would call "boundary organizations." The local interpretive centre, the Ecomuseum Kristianstads Vattenrike (EKV), serves as an interface among organizational layers, facilitating collaboration among local actors and between local actors and governmental bodies. The Fisheries Joint Management Committee (FJMC), the co-management agency, similarly serves as a boundary organization, facilitating the interaction of local and regional Inuit organizations and governmental bodies, as described in Chapter 7.

The third principle, that "governance should employ mixtures of institutional types (e.g., hierarchies, markets, and community self-governance)" (Dietz et al. 2003, 1910), primarily addresses incentives, monitoring, and compliance. Although all co-management cases in this volume have two of the three institutional types mentioned in the principle, the use of market institutions is underrepresented in the cases. Chapter 10 finds that, in the Bay of Fundy experience, quota management has been a barrier to the development of adaptive co-management, at least from the point of view of small-scale fishers. Nevertheless, there is a great deal of theoretical and practical interest in the use of individual transferable quotas (ITQs) and tradable environmental allowances in general (Rose 2002). Such regimes can have a mix of market mechanisms, community self-governance, and the regulatory supervision of larger legal institutions, demonstrating an expanded kind of co-management.

Partnerships and Power Sharing

Although we have described co-management as a continuum of power-sharing arrangements (Chapters 1 and 2), most agree that mere consultation is not co-management. True partnerships devolve power to communities and local-level resource users, as was done, for example, in the cases described in Chapters 7, 13, and 14. A large number of factors work against the devolution of power and the development of partnerships, however. These include systemic political/economic inequities (Chapter 11); cultural differences (Chapter 12); the historic role of government bureaucracies in management (Chapters 5, 6, and 12); agency structure and function (Chapter 8); the inability of local users to influence external drivers (Chapter 10); and low levels of political and financial support, and lack of traditions of cooperation (Chapter 6).

Chapter 11 examines power as a determinant factor and posits that embedded historical and colonial relations, transformed through science into relations within management, adaptive or otherwise, dictate that issues of equity manifested in management are fundamentally political issues and must be addressed as such. In this chapter, Paul Nadasdy argues that inequities lie at the heart of the failure of wildlife co-management with this Yukon indigenous group; "what is more, had the Kluane people agreed to participate in the adaptive management process, they would have become complicit in their own marginalization." Chapter 12 looks at asymmetrical power relations in a case study of justice in a Northern indigenous community and concludes that where a community vision persists, in this case, traceable to cultural/social/ecological relations and individual and collective properties such as self-efficacy, inequalities may drive adaptation.

Chapter 8 examines partnerships in which cross-scale factors and unequal power relations are complicated by adherence to different visions of management. In the case study of the West Coast Vancouver Island Aquatic Management Board, local approaches, rooted in a holistic understanding of ecological and social systems, engage with governmental mandates based on segmental approaches. Chapter 6 identifies trust and respect as critical aspects of co-management partnerships in the Caribbean, and notes that additional investigation of power and political factors as potentially confounding forces in co-management is needed, especially in the context of post-colonial governance.

Partnerships and power sharing take on different meanings in the multilevel globalized world. In moving from a two-player co-management scenario to a public/private/government partnership (Rhodes 1997), power sharing becomes a much more complicated affair. There is added emphasis on the roles of the partners, involving a search for the relative advantages of each partner. Each actor in the arrangement brings certain strengths; some roles are more suitable for some parties (Cash and Moser 2000). For example, the local partner has relative strengths in monitoring the resource and enforcing rules; the government partner can devolve management rights, strengthen local controls, and provide legal backing for local enforcement. Examples in this volume do not provide clear cases for such power sharing that pays attention to relative strengths in a division of labour. A case in point is the comparative role of local-level controls versus multi-scale regulation of the impacts of mobile fishing fleets and mobile buyers ("roving bandits") in their ever-expanding search for products for rapidly developing, globalized markets.

What makes roving banditry different from most commons dilemmas is the new dynamic of globalized markets developing so rapidly that the speed of resource exploitation overwhelms the ability of existing institutions to respond. What are the relative advantages of each partner in an adaptive co-management arrangement to deal with roving bandits? Berkes and colleagues (2006) suggest that the local level is key because local resource users can see the problem and monitor the results of exploitation long before government agencies can respond. But the problem must be addressed at multiple scales, with global, regional, and national bodies monitoring trade and resource trends; disseminating information that stimulates problem solving consistent with local practices; and strengthening local governance and environmental stewardship.

Conditions of Success and Failure

In a wide-ranging review, Chapter 9 uses three categories to identify contextual variables contributing to the success of adaptive co-management: supra-community or external factors; community-level or internal factors; and factors residing at the individual and household levels. Supra-community factors include elements such as external agents, networks and coalitions, legislation, and sharing of power with government. At the level of the community, physical and social characteristics become important, such as demarcation of boundaries, definition of group membership, recognition of property rights, and user knowledge of the resource. Chapter 9 also considers that management-related variables such as clear objectives, accountability, enforcement, adequate fiscal support, and conflict resolution arrangements contribute to success. At the individual and household level, benefits must exceed costs for co-management to succeed, and individuals must have incentives for participation.

Both Chapters 6 and 7 identify a set of conditions for success, overlapping with those in Chapter 9, and emphasize trust, respect, and leadership. Chapter 7 also points out that the response of the resource itself to measures instituted under co-management may be critical, especially early in the process. Favourable outcomes help build the confidence of fishers, scientists, and managers in the co-management process, increasing the level of trust and reinforcing additional cooperative measures. On the other hand, apparent failure of the measures can have the opposite effect.

The role of individuals in leadership, sense making, and vision is emphasized in Chapters 12 and 14. According to Per Olsson in Chapter 14, the emergence of adaptive co-management requires "transformation towards adaptive governance" (Folke et al. 2005). At the community level, the corollary is the flexible self-organizing network, shaped around trust, voluntarism, and leadership. Three factors are identified as key: visioning processes, maintenance of the conditions identified above, and the use of good examples ("best practices").

Supplementing Robert Pomeroy's analysis of conditions of success in Chapter 9 is Evelyn Pinkerton's list of "behavioural biases" (or "bureaucratic rationality") of resource management agencies (Chapter 8). Recognizing that the conditions for failure may be embedded in the practices and "biases" of these agencies, she examines them in the light of her case study and identifies a number of ways in which these biases may be overcome, in collaboration with a co-management body. These analyses suggest a very interesting dynamic: not only do the co-managers learn from the ongoing co-management experience, but the very act of engagement in adaptive co-management has the potential to change the way that the dominant management agencies have always conducted their business, challenging their biases and creating windows of opportunity for new leadership to emerge from within those agencies.

Learning, Knowledge, and Social Capital

Learning is a defining feature of adaptive co-management, with a focus on learning-by-doing through iterative, reflexive practice, evaluation, problem solving, and action modification. Theory-driven and case-based chapters draw attention to learning in its myriad dimensions, as a goal, an outcome, and a process, and highlight several key considerations.

For example, there are many different types of learning and learning outcomes in adaptive co-management. Social learning, or transformative learning in which actors jointly revise the assumptions and worldviews that shape practice, represents an often desirable, although occasional, outcome (Chapter 3). More commonly, actors engage in instrumental learning that may enhance the efficiency of management practice (Chapter 6). In either case, the conditions and essential ingredients required for the production of learning varies considerably with context, highlighting the importance of active social facilitation, beyond conventional management by managers, in the learning process (Chapters 3, 7, and 8).

Learning, then, must be cross-scale and must occur simultaneously among different actors, particularly where transformative learning is a desired outcome. Too often, attention is directed towards the learning requirements and responsibilities of local resource users and user groups. In complex, multi-dimensional systems, however, responsibility for learning and the capacity required to support learning must be distributed equitably (Chapter 4). Cross-scale dimensions of learning thus draw attention to the iterative relationship between social learning and social capital formation through networks, and the importance of trust building among actors at different levels (Chapters 2 and 3). In this regard, there is increasing awareness of the role of the informal and voluntary sectors in learning and adaptation, where voluntary participation, facilitated by bridging organizations (boundary organizations) that foster collaboration through encouragement and engagement, can lead to changes in perceptions and behaviour (Chapter 14). This conclusion is consistent with Agrawal (2005), who examined community-based forest management in the Kumaon Hills of northern India and traced the change in individual people's mentalities when they have the power and knowledge to deal with a problem.

Not surprisingly, the role of knowledge sharing and integration is an important theme throughout this volume. The existence and application of multiple knowledge sources, including indigenous knowledge, are recognized as providing the opportunity for enhanced learning and collaboration (Chapters 5, 9, and 10), and as a condition for participatory action learning (Chapter 6). Rather than offering a blueprint or strategies for knowledge integration, however, the authors highlight the fact that integration of knowledge depends on a shared commitment, and that awareness of strengths and limitations of different types and sources of knowledge is embedded in processes of social learning and social capital formation. Other recent volumes deal with this particular issue in more detail (e.g., Reid et al. 2006).

Finally, the formalization of adaptive co-management systems also has important implications for learning, the corollary development of social capital, and integration of knowledge. For instance, the degree of formalization can have an influence on the emergence of critical windows of opportunity. Finding these spaces is an important aspect of learning in the transformation of governance from environmental command-and-control to social-ecological response and adaptive feedback (Chapters 12 and 14). Codification of co-management systems can enhance stability, develop positive working relationships, and enable adaptive management (Chapter 7). Codification may, however, also increase rigidity and serve to fix in time and place the existing power inequities among social actors at different levels (Chapter 11). Nevertheless, windows of opportunity for transformative learning can also emerge from culturally based informal arrangements that foster resilience in the context of change and despite the rigidity of formal co-management (Chapter 12).

Policy Implications

The chapters in this volume provide theory and insights for natural resource management policy. These theories and insights are not always easily translatable into the language of policy makers or the process of policy development. This is problematic because, as a novel governance approach for conditions of complexity and uncertainty, the socio-economic, institutional, and legal requirements of adaptive co-management should be actionable.

Highlighting the relationships among adaptive co-management theory, practice, and policy is thus a task requiring ongoing attention. Throughout this volume, there is an implicit assumption that adaptive co-management will lead to better policy. Good policy is a clear destination or goal of adaptive co-management (Chapter 4). Many of the chapters, however, also highlight the fact that certain policy conditions are required to enable adaptive co-management. Cases of resource collapse or conflict and non-adaptive policy indicate that adaptive co-management may not always prevail by reason, and that competing approaches to policy and management can themselves present barriers to adaptation (Chapters 5 and 8).

An enabling policy environment for adaptive co-management will require some level of commitment from higher-order institutions, a commitment to public involvement in governance beyond merely consultation, and an openness on the part of authority to change and to active citizen engagement, both as individuals and in formal and informal organizations (Chapter 9). In stressing the importance of these policy conditions for adaptive co-management, however, it is clearly necessary to recognize the historical context of contemporary power relations, where root questions of equity have not always been adequately addressed (Chapters 10 and 11). As documented in this volume, however, even where asymmetries of power exist, windows of opportunity for learning and adaptation can and do emerge (Chapter 12).

From a policy perspective, it is paramount that adaptive co-management be recognized as a process-based approach (Chapter 2) and not an aggregation of governance structures and mechanisms. Adaptive co-management enables learning over the mid to long term, as social capital accumulates, and will bear interest in the form of trust, mutual respect, and cooperative relationships. Transaction costs associated with this process-oriented approach may appear high in the short term, but long-term benefits associated with the development of policy and resource management decisions are more likely to emerge (Chapters 7 and 8), especially with significant and targeted investments in capacity building across the range of actors involved (Chapters 4 and 6).

The policy process is often seen as adversarial, pitting stakeholder groups against one another. The chapters in this volume show policy development as an iterative learning process, with devolution of responsibility, that enables community resilience and optimism in the face of adversity (Chapters 6 and 7). For policy makers and managers, there is merit in considering how adaptive co-management intersects with issues of risk – political, economic, and institutional. Where adaptive co-management emerges in structure and spirit, there can be an important element of risk diffusion for policy makers and managers (Chapters 7 and 8).

Box 16.1 recaps some of the practical lessons from the consideration of these seven themes. It provides some guiding questions and do's and don'ts that can be applied by policy people and resource managers to adaptive co-management cases. The table is speculative, of course, because such factors are highly context-dependent and will vary from case to case. As a practical tool, Box 16.1 supplements Box 2.1 in Chapter 2 (which outlines a six-step iterative problem-solving schema) and the analysis, in Chapter 8, of how managers can counteract behavioural biases that constrain adaptive co-management.

Conclusions

We began this volume by suggesting that there is a range of definitions of co-management and adaptive co-management, and that such fuzziness accommodates different historical, cultural, political, and geographical contexts in which adaptive co-management occurs. The diversity of experiences is humbling for the scholar trying to formulate principles. There is no agreement, even among experts, on the question of whether co-management can be forged, or whether it is an emergent property, that is, an arrangement emerging spontaneously through feedback learning from simple systems of management. Both arguments may be correct in part, and the cases in this volume provide evidence for both positions. Perhaps more important, they provide evidence for the importance of the *interaction* of institutional design and emergence.

The implicit message of the volume is that co-management as a power-sharing arrangement has served a certain purpose. Adaptive co-management, however, means that the actors in co-management have moved to a different plane and are involved in learning and transformational processes. Adaptive co-management has a number of characteristics that are different from those of both co-management and adaptive management (Table 16.1). For example, in adaptive co-management, the capacity-building focus is on actors from both the community and the government side, and not on one or the other.

To emphasize the importance of capacity and institution building, not only at the community level but also at the government level, Pomeroy and Berkes (1997) invoked the metaphor of "two to tango." However, recognizing that there are multiple actors and often more than two levels, the tango is clearly inadequate. A Filipino or Turkish folk dance may be a more apt metaphor. With adaptive co-management, to push the metaphor further, one may talk about successive rounds of dances in which the dancers will build social capital and learn to be more and more in step with one another. Dancing to different accompaniments and different moods, they may come together in different combinations to tackle different themes. Unlike folk dancing, however, adaptive co-management appears to lack appropriate measures of performance.

Box 16.1

A prescriptive guide for adaptive co-management practitioners

Complex systems thinking
- Pay attention to scale and other complexity considerations.
- Bring decisions as close to the user as possible.
- Match the scale of governance systems to the scale of ecological systems; don't use a "one-size-fits-all" approach.
- Allow for pluralism by recognizing a mix of perspectives.
- Pay attention to drivers of change that originate outside the local or regional system to be managed.
- Use a variety of modes of communication, processes of group deliberation, and scenario-planning and visioning exercises to deal with complexity.

Adaptive capacity and resilience
- Use adaptive management approaches to encourage systematic learning.
- Focus on learning, adaptability, and flexibility.
- Avoid an overemphasis on prediction, certainty, and controllability (e.g., basing management decisions on MSY and similar quota assumptions).
- Use a mix of methodological approaches, tools, and techniques that allow for broad participation of partners.
- Acknowledge scientific uncertainty and incorporate local and traditional knowledge.
- Build adaptive capacity at multiple levels (capacity building is not just a local issue).
- Approach adaptive capacity and resilience as a long-term social process, rather than as a technical challenge.
- Apply resilience thinking to facilitate "living with change" and to make appropriate use of windows of opportunity, and not to preserve a static condition.

Institutional design for adaptive co-management
- Make use of existing institutions, especially at the local level, rather than designing them from scratch.
- Design layered institutions (i.e., those that straddle multiple levels) if the management of a resource or area requires multiple levels of governance.
- Make sure institutional design includes all of the key players.
- Build or foster institutions (boundary organizations) that can facilitate, mediate, and translate information and meanings among partners.
- Encourage the use of a mix of institutional types, including hierarchies, markets, and community self-governance, as appropriate.

Partnerships and power sharing
- Devolve power to communities and local-level resource users; don't just consult.
- Create incentives for partners to engage in new ways of sharing power.
- Actively deal with barriers to adaptive co-management, including systemic inequities, colonial legacies, and lack of traditions of cooperation.
- Recognize that different visions of management may be rooted in different worldviews.
- Seek appropriate roles for the partners, and search for the relative strengths they can bring to the partnership.
- Recognize that local resource users can see problems long before government agencies can respond.

Conditions of success and failure
- Seek an understanding of local rules and definition of group membership.
- Ensure clear objectives, accountability, enforcement, and adequate fiscal support.
- Engender platforms for negotiation and conflict resolution.
- Facilitate the building of mutual trust and respect between holders of different kinds of knowledge.
- Allow for enough time to build mutual trust and respect.
- Build flexible self-organizing networks, shaped around trust, voluntarism, and leadership.
- Recognize that there are a number of ways in which behavioural biases or bureaucratic rationality may be overcome.

Learning, knowledge, and social capital
- Focus on learning-by-doing through iterative, reflexive practice, evaluation, problem solving, and action modification.
- Incorporate multiple kinds of knowledge and ways of knowing as sources of opportunity for enhanced learning and collaboration.
- Focus on instrumental learning to enhance the efficiency of management practice.
- Foster transformative learning, in which actors jointly revise the assumptions and worldviews that shape practice.
- Question standard operating procedures so as to consider a broader range of options (double-loop learning).
- Create information clearinghouses to build a shared understanding.
- Take advantage of the synergies of mutual learning.

Policy considerations
- Create an enabling policy environment with some level of commitment from higher-order institutions.
- Treat adaptive co-management as a process (rather than an endpoint) focused on problem solving.
- Recognize that a process-oriented approach may have high transaction costs in the short term but benefits in the long term.
- Reward risk taking and experimentation with creative solutions.
- Foster development of new skills among partners, particularly those usually marginalized.
- Recognize that the emergence of adaptive co-management in structure and spirit provides an important element of risk diffusion for policy makers and managers.

One of the findings of this volume is that both co-management and adaptive co-management appear to lack consistent methodological approaches. Further, very few studies appear to have had success with outcome measures or metrics. Performance evaluation has been difficult, given the diversity of contextual factors in the various co-management examples and the propensity of some apparently "successful" co-management cases to fall apart. However, the accumulation of experience over the last twenty or so years indicates that there are sets of indicators by which one can at least identify different maturity stages of adaptive co-management.

Inspired by the work of Pretty and Ward (2001), Table 16.2 distinguishes three stages in the maturity of an adaptive co-management arrangement, based on ten criteria. The criteria follow many of the factors discussed in this volume, and suggest that a mature adaptive co-management arrangement will have a number of characteristics that range from the degree of trust (not easily measurable) to the number of key partners and linkages (relatively easy to measure). Some of these factors, such as the degree of power sharing, have been used to evaluate co-management; others, such as shared vision building, are relatively new. Some of the criteria cover large and complex areas, and finding simple measures may be difficult. One example is the use of knowledge. The availability of a greater range of knowledge appears to be a relatively commonsense objective for improving resource management (Berkes and Folke 1998), but how different knowledge systems can be bridged – or whether they should be bridged – is a much more complicated issue (Nadasdy 1999; Reid et al. 2006).

The lack of measures and criteria of success is one major conclusion and challenge for further research. A second major challenge based on the

Table 16.2

Three stages in the maturity of an adaptive co-management arrangement

Criterion	Early stage	Middle stage	Mature stage
Reason for being	Initiated by top-down intervention or self-organized in response to crisis	Successful self-organization to respond to management challenges	Adaptive co-management to address a series of challenges, including those not originally in the mandate
Degree of power sharing	Little or none, or only as formally mandated	Moving from two-way information exchange to decision-making partnership	Partnership of equals in formulating the management problem and solution options, testing them, and making decisions
Worldview and sense making	Reacting to past events and resource crises	Making sense of new realities and beginning to look forward and to develop a consensus	Shaping reality by looking forward, planning, and developing a shared vision of the future
Rules and norms	Tend to be externally imposed, often with a disconnect between formal and informal rules	Beginning to develop own rules and norms, both formal and informal	Rules and norms tested and developed as needed; complementary relationship between formal and informal rules
Trust and respect	Relationships relying on formal arrangements rather than on mutual trust and respect	Learning to exercise mutual trust and respect, typically through high and low points in the relationship	Well-developed working relationships with trust and respect, involving multiple individuals and agencies
Horizontal links and networks	Few links and informal networks	Increasing number of links and information sharing	Many links with partners with diverse functions; extensive sharing of knowledge through networks

Vertical links	Only as formally mandated	Sorting out of roles and functions of other levels; realization that information can flow upward as well as downward	Robust and redundant links with other levels of management authority, with two-way information flow
Use of knowledge	Uncritically using available technical and scientific data or local information	More attention to different kinds of knowledge and how to use them together	Valuing local and traditional knowledge; combining different kinds of knowledge and co-producing knowledge
Capacity to experiment	Little or no capacity or willingness to experiment	Willingness to experiment; developing capacity to plan, carry out, and learn from experiment	Experimentation leading to adaptation and innovation through several cycles
Learning	Instrumental learning	Building on the experience of instrumental learning; developing flexibility; recognizing uncertainty	Double-loop or transformative learning; "learning to learn" to deal with uncertainty

findings of this volume concerns partnerships. Almost all of the cases involve co-management linkages and partnerships with communities and civil society actors on the one hand and government bodies and agencies on the other. Others have argued that adaptive co-management could include not only community/government partnerships but also public/private partnerships. And yet, we have very few such examples in the area of resource management (Carlsson 2003) and none in this book.

Some of the governance and business management literature has been emphasizing public/private partnerships (e.g., Rhodes 1997), and commons theory would predict potentially viable joint management arrangements involving any combination of the three kinds of institutions – communal, private, and governmental (Rose 2002). For example, Dietz and colleagues (2003) point out that market-based management instruments and community-based systems appear to have opposite strengths and weaknesses. This would suggest that a tradable permit system, in combination with a community-based system for monitoring and enforcement, may be particularly robust. By contributing new perspectives to these and other research questions, the adaptive co-management approach may prove useful for identifying innovative new strategies, as well as providing a way of thinking about the dynamic interplay between co-management and adaptive learning.

References

Agrawal, A. 2005. *Environmentality: Technologies of government and the making of subjects.* Durham, NC, and London: Duke University Press.

Armitage, D.R., and D. Johnson. 2006. Can resilience be reconciled with globalization and the increasingly complex conditions of resource degradation in Asian coastal regions? *Ecology and Society* 11 (1): 2. http://www.ecologyandsociety.org/vol11/iss1/art2/.

Berkes, F., and C. Folke, eds. 1998. *Linking social and ecological systems: Management practices and social mechanisms for building resilience.* Cambridge: Cambridge University Press.

Berkes, F., T.P. Hughes, R.S. Steneck, J.A. Wilson, D.R. Bellwood, B. Crona, C. Folke, et al. 2006. Globalization, roving bandits and marine resources. *Science* 311: 1557-58.

Brunner, R., T. Steelman, L. Coe-Juell, C. Cromley, C. Edwards, and D. Tucker. 2005. *Adaptive governance: Integrating science, policy and decision making.* New York: Columbia University Press.

Carlsson, L. 2003. The strategy of the commons: History and property rights in central Sweden. In *Navigating social-ecological systems: Building resilience for complexity and change,* ed. F. Berkes, J. Colding, and C. Folke, 116-31. Cambridge: Cambridge University Press.

Cash, D.W., and S.C. Moser. 2000. Linking global and local scales: Designing dynamic assessment and management processes. *Global Environmental Change* 10: 109-20.

Dietz, T., E. Ostrom, and P. Stern. 2003. The struggle to govern the commons. *Science* 302 (5652): 1907-12.

Edwards, V.M., and N.A. Steins. 1999. A framework for analyzing contextual factors in common pool resource research. *Journal of Environmental Policy and Planning* 1: 205-21.

Folke, C., T. Hahn, P. Olsson, and J. Norberg. 2005. Adaptive governance of social-ecological systems. *Annual Review of Environment and Resources* 30: 441-73.

Gunderson, L.H., and C.S. Holling, eds. 2002. *Panarchy: Understanding transformations in human and natural systems.* Washington, DC: Island Press.

Holling, C.S., ed. 1978. *Adaptive environmental assessment and management.* New York: John Wiley and Sons.

Holling, C.S., and G.K. Meffe. 1996. Command and control and the pathology of natural resource management. *Conservation Biology* 10 (2): 328-37.

Lee, K.N. 1993. *Compass and gyroscope: Integrating science and politics for the environment.* Washington, DC: Island Press.

–. 1999. Appraising adaptive management. *Conservation Ecology* 3 (2): 3. http://www.consecol.org/vol3/iss2/art3/.

Millennium Ecosystem Assessment. 2005. *Ecosystems and human well-being: Synthesis.* Washington, DC: Island Press.

Nadasdy, P. 1999. The politics of TEK: Power and the "Integration" of knowledge. *Arctic Anthropology* 36: 1-18.

Pahl-Wostl, C., and M. Hare. 2004. Processes of social learning in integrated resources management. *Journal of Community and Applied Social Psychology* 14: 193-206.

Pinkerton, E., ed. 1989. *Co-operative management of local fisheries: New directions for improved management and community development.* Vancouver: UBC Press.

–. 1992. Translating legal rights into management practice: Overcoming barriers to the exercise of co-management. *Human Organization* 51: 330-41.

Pomeroy, R.S., and F. Berkes. 1997. Two to tango: The role of government in fisheries co-management. *Marine Policy* 21: 465-80.

Pretty, J., and H. Ward. 2001. Social capital and the environment. *World Development* 29: 209-27.

Ravetz, J. 2003. The post-normal science of precaution. *Futures* 36: 347-57.

Reid, W.V., F. Berkes, T. Wilbanks, and D. Capistrano, eds. 2006. *Bridging scales and knowledge systems: Linking global science and local knowledge in assessments.* Washington, DC: Millennium Ecosystem Assessment and Island Press.

Rhodes, R.A.W. 1997. *Understanding governance: Policy networks, governance, reflexivity and accountability.* Buckingham, UK: Open University Press.

Rose, C.M. 2002. Common property, regulatory property, and environmental protection: Comparing community-based management to tradable environmental allowances. In *The drama of the commons,* ed. E. Ostrom, T. Dietz, N. Dolsak, P.C. Stern, S. Stonich, and E.U. Weber, 233-57. Washington, DC: National Academy Press.

Timmer, V., and C. Juma. 2005. Biodiversity conservation and poverty reduction come together in the tropics: Lessons from the Equator Initiative. *Environment* 47 (4): 24-47.

World Resources Institute. 2005. *World resources 2005: The wealth of the poor – managing ecosystems to fight poverty.* Washington, DC: World Resources Institute, United Nations Development Programme, United Nations Environment Programme, and the World Bank. http://www.wri.org.

Walker, B., C.S. Holling, S.R. Carpenter, and A. Kinzig. 2004. Resilience, adaptability and transformability in social-ecological systems. *Ecology and Society* 9 (2): 5. http://www.ecologyandsociety.org/vol9/iss2/art5.

Walters, C.J. 1986. *Adaptive management of renewable resources.* New York: McGraw-Hill.

Young, O. 2002. *The institutional dimensions of environmental change: Fit, interplay and scale.* Cambridge, MA: MIT Press.

Glossary

Adaptation: A response to social-environmental change, whether anticipatory or reactive, that enables humans to cope by altering social, ecological, or economic variables.

Adaptive capacity: The ability of social actors or systems to cope with change or disturbance and/or learn through uncertainty.

Adaptive co-management: A process whereby institutional arrangements and ecological knowledge are tested and revised in an ongoing, self-organized, and dynamic process of learning-by-doing.

Adaptive management: A strategic learning-by-doing or quasi-experimental approach to the management of natural resources encouraged by institutional flexibility.

Capacity building: The sum of efforts needed to nurture, enhance, and utilize the skills and capabilities of people and institutions at all levels towards a particular goal.

Collaborative/participatory management: Arrangements through which government and civil society share rights and responsibilities for effective environmental management.

Co-management: A resource management partnership in which local users and other stakeholders share power and responsibility with government agencies.

Commons theory: Theory about the management of common-pool (common property) resources; understanding of the conditions under which user groups at multiple levels and governments may regulate resource access and make rules for resource use.

Community: A social group possessing shared beliefs and values, stable membership, and the expectation of continued interaction.

Community of practice: A social group or learning network that develops around shared interests or activities.

Complex systems thinking: Thinking that highlights the complex interactions among variables in social-ecological systems and takes into account interconnected networks of components that cannot be described by simple rules.

Complexity: A feature of systems that comprise diverse components among which there are many interactions, the resulting implications of which are often unpredictable.

Country food: Wild or traditional food that is harvested primarily (but not always) for subsistence, often by Aboriginal hunters and gatherers.

Cross-scale/multi-level linkages: Social, institutional, or ecological connections that link actors or entities. Such linkages may be horizontal (e.g., across geographical space) or vertical (e.g., across different levels of organization).

Decision support tools: Structured systems used to inform and guide thought processes and decision making for environmental management, such as brainstorming, Delphi models, scenarios, interactive gaming, and simulation models.

Devolution: The delegation of decision-making authority and financial responsibility to lower administrative levels (e.g., communities, community-based organizations, municipalities).

Double-loop learning: A process in which existing worldviews and underlying values are challenged (e.g., the shared reconsideration of the goals of management), allowing for or resulting in fundamental changes in stakeholder behaviour.

Driver: Any natural or anthropogenic factor that causes change within a system, whether through direct or indirect means, regardless of whether it is internal or external to the system.

Ecosystem-based management: Resource management that takes account of interactions of a given resource with other components in the ecosystem of which it is a part.

Emergent property: A characteristic of a complex adaptive system that cannot be predicted or understood simply by examining the components of the system.

Empowerment: Having the power and responsibility to do something; the ability of a person or a group of people to control or to have an input into decisions that affect their livelihoods.

Feedback loops: The process by which system outputs are returned to the system as an input, either to oppose the initial input (negative feedback) or to enhance it (positive feedback).

Governance: Consideration of all public and private interactions undertaken to generate societal opportunities and address societal challenges. Governance thus includes the development and application of the principles, rules, norms, and enabling institutions that guide public and private interactions.

Indicator: A variable, pointer, or index. Its fluctuation reveals the variations in key elements of a system.

Indigenous knowledge: Local knowledge held by a group of indigenous people, or local knowledge unique to a given culture or society; traditional ecological knowledge is a subset of indigenous knowledge.

Innovation: The creation or introduction of something new, or the application of a new approach to resolve an existing problem. In co-management, innovation can be institutional (changing rules in use), operational (establishing new ways of doing business within an existing set of process rules), or technological/methodological (changing the type of technology or method, or the manner in which these are applied).

Institution: The formal (rules, laws, constitutions, organizational entities) and informal (norms of behaviour, conventions, codes of conduct) practices that structure human interaction.

Integrated management: An approach to management through which multiple actors collaborate and share risk in defining, analyzing, and resolving social-ecological challenges for the common good. This approach moves beyond conventional single-species management to consider the implications of species interactions, habitat and ecosystem linkages, and cumulative effects.

Livelihood: The strategies undertaken by individuals or social groups to create or maintain a living. Outcomes are often determined by the manner in which available capital assets (natural, financial, physical, social, and human) are mobilized.

Monitoring: The collection of information for the purpose of assessing progress and impacts.

Multi-party arrangements: An organizational structure that includes a range of stakeholders in the environmental decision-making process.

Participatory action research: Collaborative research that evolves in conjunction with a community of stakeholders who participate in all stages of the process. This type of research is designed to incorporate a social justice component and promote learning, and often results in applied management outcomes.

Policy: The course of action for an undertaking adopted by a government, a person, or another party.

Precautionary principle: A principle applied in managing complex environmental systems, which states that if the consequences of an action or decision are potentially severe and if knowledge about impacts is uncertain, decision making should err on the side of caution and the burden of proof should lie with those advocating the activity.

Property rights: Claim to a benefit stream that is collectively protected, in most cases by the state.

Quota management: A tool commonly applied for managing fisheries and wildlife, by means of which the total allowable catch or harvest for a management unit is divided into quotas, which are then allocated to resource users.

Resilience: The ability of a system to absorb or rebound from disturbance without shifting to another, fundamentally different system configuration.

Robust management: Management that is designed to ensure an acceptable level of performance despite conditions of elevated scientific uncertainty and limited control over exploitation.

Scenario planning: A management tool used to determine a range of possible alternative futures within a specific context where uncertainty is high. This mechanism can be used to stimulate dialogue among stakeholders who have conflicting ideas about how the system may or should develop.

Self-organization: In adaptive co-management, self-organization involves the emergence of actors working in a collaborative and creative process, often drawing on a range of knowledge sources and ideas, to resolve issues and move forward in response to disturbance.

Single-loop learning: The identification of alternative strategies or actions (e.g., harvesting techniques) to resolve specific problems and improve outcomes (e.g., improved incomes, higher yields).

Social capital: The social norms, networks of reciprocity and exchange, and relationships of trust that enable people to act collectively.

Social learning: The collaborative or mutual development and sharing of knowledge by multiple stakeholders through learning-by-doing.

Social-ecological systems: Integrated, coupled systems of people and environment.

Stakeholders: Individuals or groups (including governmental and non-governmental institutions, communities, research institutions, development agencies, etc.) with an interest or claim.

Sustainability: Management that promotes resource stewardship and builds or maintains system resilience over the long term.

Threshold: The critical boundary (e.g., spatial, temporal) where the attraction of a system to a new equilibrium or configuration supersedes the system's attraction to its current state.

Traditional/local knowledge: A cumulative body of knowledge, practice, and belief, evolving by adaptive processes and handed down through generations by cultural transmission, about the relationship of living beings (including humans) with one another and with their environment.

Transformability: The ability of a system to switch into a completely new state with new structures and processes when change or disturbance inhibits the persistence of current conditions.

Uncertainty: The extent to which actors are unable to understand, predict, or control how system components, relationships, and processes will interact, and what outcomes will result.

Visioning: A process by which actors collaboratively develop a shared notion of their preferred future system state, which can then guide the determination of appropriate management strategies.

Vulnerability: The degree to which a system is susceptible to the impacts of change or disturbance.

Contributors

Derek Armitage is Associate Professor in the Department of Geography and Environmental Studies and the Cold Regions Research Centre at Wilfrid Laurier University, Waterloo. His current research focuses on the relationships among livelihoods, social-ecological change, and adaptive co-management, with a particular emphasis on coastal and marine contexts in Southeast Asia and Northern Canada. He has published in such journals as *Society and Natural Resources*, *Ecology and Society*, *Ecological Economics*, *Canadian Journal of Development Studies*, and the new *International Journal of the Commons*. He has served as a consultant with a range of national and international organizations, such as Fisheries and Oceans Canada, World Bank/Global Environmental Facility, and the Inter-American Development Bank. Email: darmitag@wlu.ca

Burton G. Ayles received his BSc and MSc in zoology and genetics from the University of British Columbia and his PhD in fisheries genetics from the University of Toronto. He worked for twenty-five years for the federal Department of Fisheries and Oceans as a research scientist and manager, retiring in 1998 as Regional Director General for the Central and Arctic Region. Dr. Ayles is currently a Canada Member of the Canada/Inuvialuit Fisheries Joint Management Committee. This agency, with the Department of Fisheries and Oceans and the Inuvialuit Game Council, is responsible for management of fisheries and marine mammal management in the western Canadian Arctic. As a Canada member, Dr. Ayles is involved in a range of activities related to the co-management of fisheries and marine mammal populations in the western Canadian Arctic. Recent activities related to adaptive co-management include participation in the development of Arctic char integrated management plans and development operational planning structures for a proposed Marine Protected Area in the Mackenzie River Delta.

Robert Bell is a biologist and partner in Norplan Consulting, a firm based in Blaine Lake, Saskatchewan, that has had a long involvement with the environmental impact assessment process. Mr. Bell holds a BSc and an MSc (Limnology) from the University of Manitoba. Prior to joining Norplan in 1986, Mr Bell spent twenty years in the Northwest Territories, first as a teacher and education administrator, and later, in renewable resource administration, as Director of Wildlife Management for the NWT. In that capacity, he chaired the Canadian Polar Bear Administration Committee and helped to develop both the Beverly-Kaminuriak and the Porcupine Caribou Management Agreements. Mr. Bell served two terms as member of the Canadian Environmental Assessment Research Council, a council that provided advice to the Minister of the Environment, and was a panel member on the federal Rafferty Alameda Environmental Review Panel. Email: robert.bell@sasktel.net

Fikret Berkes is Professor at the Natural Resources Institute at the University of Manitoba, Winnipeg. He holds the Canada Research Chair in Community-Based Resource Management, and the title of Distinguished Professor. He has published extensively. His work combines social and natural sciences, and has been mainly in the areas of commons theory and the interrelations between societies and their resources. Email: berkes@cc.umanitoba.ca

Anthony Charles is Professor of Management Science and Environmental Studies at Saint Mary's University, Halifax. His work focuses on the sustainability and resilience of natural resource systems, particularly in regard to fishery and coastal management, including ecosystem-based approaches, protected areas, and participatory, community-based management. Holder of a Pew Fellowship in Marine Conservation, Dr. Charles is a past member of the Fisheries Resource Conservation Council and the Atlantic advisory body to Canada's Minister of Fisheries and Oceans. He is the author or co-author of a wide range of publications, including the books *Sustainable Fishery Systems* and *Canadian Marine Fisheries in a Changing and Uncertain World*. Email: Tony.charles@smu.ca

Nancy Doubleday is Associate Professor in the Department of Geography and Environmental Studies at Carleton University, Ottawa. Her research deals with social-cultural-ecological change in complex systems, with a particular emphasis on temporal and spatial aspects of long-term environmental change and the role of culture in adaptation and resilience. Current interests include biodiversity, land use and climate change, and applications of adaptive co-management to planning and development decision-making. Email: Nancy_Doubleday@carleton.ca

John FitzGibbon is Professor of Planning at the School of Environmental Design and Rural Development at the University of Guelph. His current research is in the area of community-based environmental and resources management and in the area of network governance as applied to environmental management. He is also the chair of the Ontario Farm Environment Coalition. E-mail: jfitzgib@uoguelph.ca

Susan J. Herman is Professor of Management in the School of Management and Director of the Northern Leadership Center at the University of Alaska, Fairbanks. Her research has examined environmental leadership, inter-organizational relations, and the effectiveness of small non-profits. Email: ffsjh@uaf.edu

Andrea Hoyt is a Resource Biologist with the Canada/Inuvialuit Fisheries Joint Management Committee in Inuvik, Northwest Territories. She has a BSc (Biology) from Acadia University and a Master of Natural Resources Management (Interdisciplinary) from the Natural Resources Institute, University of Manitoba. Her current projects include community habitat monitoring, Inuvialuit student mentoring, and various species-specific and broader ecosystem planning processes. E-mail: fjmc-rp@jointsec

John Kearney is a social anthropologist and consultant residing in Nova Scotia. For twenty-eight years, he has worked for fishery, community, and First Nation organizations in community-based resource management in Asia, the United States, and Canada. Email: john.kearney@ns.sympatico.ca

Gary P. Kofinas is Associate Professor of Resource Policy and Management and director of the Resilience and Adaptation Graduate Program at the University of Alaska, Fairbanks. His research focuses on the social-ecological resilience of indigenous subsistence-based communities and, in particular, the effects of climate change and industrial development on Human-Caribou Systems. Email: gary.kofinas@uaf.edu

Robin Mahon is Professor of Marine Affairs and Director at the Centre for Resource Management and Environmental Studies (CERMES) at the University of the West Indies, Cave Hill Campus, Barbados. His current research and publications relate to governance of marine resources at multiple scales and factors contributing to and ways of coping with complexity in man-in-nature systems. Email: rmahon@caribsurf.com

Patrick McConney is Senior Lecturer in the Centre for Resource Management and Environmental Studies (CERMES) at the University of the West Indies, Cave Hill Campus, Barbados. He works mainly on marine resource management and planning, including co-management and other forms of governance with emphasis on small-scale fisheries and marine protected areas. This includes outreach and capacity-building in collaboration with non-governmental and community-based organizations. Email: patrick.mcconney@cavehill.uwi.edu

Chanda Meek lives in Fairbanks, Alaska, and studies the human dimensions of resource management through the Department of Resources Management at the University of Alaska. She is PhD fellow in the Resilience and Adaptation Program. Her dissertation research compares two resource agencies in their approach to co-management of marine mammals in Alaska, using aspects of adaptive co-management as indicators of resilience management. Email: chanda.meek@uaf.edu

Paul Nadasdy is Associate Professor of Anthropology and American Indian Studies at the University of Wisconsin, Madison. He is the author of *Hunters and Bureaucrats: Power, Knowledge, and Aboriginal-State Relations in the Southwest Yukon* and numerous scholarly articles on the politics of co-management. His research interests include the anthropology of science and knowledge, ecological anthropology, the changing nature of aboriginal-state relations, and the politics of wildlife management and its role in the constitution of state power. Email: penadasdy@wisc.edu

Per Olsson is a researcher at the Stockholm Resilience Centre, Stockholm University. His primary research interest is in interconnected social-ecological system dynamics and resilience. Current research involves developing the adaptive co-management and governance framework for identifying social conditions that enable ecosystem management. Email: per@ctm.su.se

Garry Peterson is an associate professor and Canada Research Chair in the Department of Geography and the School of the Environment at McGill University in Montreal. His research focuses on the dynamics of social-ecological systems for developing both theory and the practical tools for the promotion of sustainable societies. Email: garry.peterson@mcgill.ca

Evelyn Pinkerton is a maritime anthropologist who has integrated common property theory and cultural/political ecology in considering the role communities play in the management of adjacent renewable natural resources. She has played a key role in developing the theory and practice of power-sharing and stewardship through co-management agreements. Beginning with the introduction to her 1989 edited volume, *Cooperative Management of Local Fisheries*, she has been developing co-management theory by generating middle-range theoretical propositions about the conditions under which co-management is likely to arise and to endure. She has published over thirty peer-reviewed articles on fisheries and forestry co-management arrangements, and, in *Fisheries that Work* (1995, co-authored with Martin Weinstein), began to develop a more comprehensive framework for analyzing and comparing co-management arrangements by scope of rights, scale of agreement, level of authority, and degree of formality. This work has since evolved into analysis of the developmental sequence of types of co-management rights and activities, and has focused additionally on the role of senior governments in co-management agreements. Email: epinkert@sfu.ca

Ryan Plummer is Associate Professor in the Department of Tourism and Environment, Brock University, St. Catharines. He is very interested in exploring the concept of adaptive co-management and is the principal investigator of a Social Sciences and Humanities Research Council (SSHRC) Research Development Initiative (RDI) project with that purpose ("Charting the New Territory of Adaptive Co-management: Collaborating, Learning and Adapting through Complexity"). He has published on the subject of co-management in such journals as *Environmental Practice*, *Ecological Economics*, *Journal of Environmental Management*, and *Natural Resources Forum*. His current research pertaining to adaptive co-management focuses on social processes, theoretical development, and evaluation. Email: rplummer@brocku.ca

Robert Pomeroy is Professor in the Department of Agricultural and Resource Economics and Fisheries Extension Specialist with the Connecticut Sea Grant at the University of Connecticut–Avery Point. Dr. Pomeroy works on applications of adaptive co-management to small-scale fisheries and coastal resources in developing countries in Asia, the Caribbean, Latin America, and Africa. He is a co-author of *Fisheries Co-management: A Practical Handbook*. Email: robert.pomeroy@uconn.edu

Index